Mind Cure

Mind Cure

How Meditation Became Medicine

WAKOH SHANNON HICKEY

OXFORD
UNIVERSITY PRESS

OXFORD
UNIVERSITY PRESS

Oxford University Press is a department of the University of Oxford. It furthers
the University's objective of excellence in research, scholarship, and education
by publishing worldwide. Oxford is a registered trade mark of Oxford University
Press in the UK and certain other countries.

Published in the United States of America by Oxford University Press
198 Madison Avenue, New York, NY 10016, United States of America.

Library of Congress Cataloging-in-Publication Data
Names: Hickey, Wakoh Shannon, 1963- author.
Title: Mind cure : how meditation became medicine / Wakoh Shannon Hickey.
Description: New York : Oxford University Press, 2019. |
Includes bibliographical references and index.
Identifiers: LCCN 2018040395 (print) | LCCN 2018055644 (ebook) |
ISBN 9780190864255 (updf) | ISBN 9780190864262 (epub) |
ISBN 9780190864248 (hardcover) | ISBN 9780190864279 (online content)
Subjects: LCSH: Medicine and psychology.
Classification: LCC R726.5 (ebook) |
LCC R726.5 .H53 2019 (print) | DDC 610.1/9—dc23
LC record available at https://lccn.loc.gov/2018040395

9 8 7 6 5 4 3 2 1

Printed by Sheridan Books, Inc., United States of America

For my parents and teachers

We are what we think.
All that we are arises with our thoughts.
With our thoughts we make the world.
—Śakyamuni Buddha, *The Dhammapada* 1:1, trans.
Thomas Byrom

Often we are seriously oblivious of the
ground we stand upon,
the houses we live in, the lenses we see through,
all gifted to us, mostly anonymously, by others.
—Jon Kabat-Zinn, *Coming to Our Senses*

Medicine and sickness heal each other.
All the earth is medicine.
Where do you find yourself?
—Zen Master Yunmen

Contents

Acknowledgments

FIRST THANKS BELONG to librarians! Without their expertise and generous help over two decades of research and writing, this book could not have been produced. I am grateful to have been the beneficiary of dedicated and skillful staff at Duke University's Divinity School Library, Perkins and Bostock Libraries, and Medical Center Library; the University of North Carolina at Chapel Hill libraries; the Graduate Theological Union Library; the Swedenborgian Library and Archives at Pacific School of Religion; the University of California Library system, particularly the Doe Library at Berkeley; the Styberg Library of Garrett-Evangelical Theological Seminary; the Newberry Library; the Unity Village library; the Henry Steel Olcott Memorial Library of the Theosophical Society in America; the Mary Baker Eddy Library; the New York Public Library; Alfred University's Herrick Memorial Library; the Library of Congress; the Loyola-Notre Dame Library; and the Sheridan Libraries of Johns Hopkins University. (Additional thanks to Kathryn Schnurr and Barb Helmuth, who provided access to the Sheridan Libraries.) Particular thanks to Michael Yockey at the Swedenborgian Library and Archives and to Nick Triggs, former Interlibrary Loan wizard extraordinaire for the Loyola–Notre Dame Library, whose help was indispensable. Thanks also to the taxpayers and donors who support all these institutions.

Thanks to my former professors Richard Jaffe, Laurie Maffly-Kipp, Leela Prasad, Julie Byrne, and Tom Tweed, all of whom gave helpful guidance and salutary critiques on the early drafts of the dissertation that became the foundation for this book. Special thanks to Alison Stokes, whose book *Ministry after Freud* enabled me to connect crucial dots in chapters 4 and 5, and to Anne Gordon Perry, who shared her research on Sarah Farmer. Deep gratitude to the late Joan Hildebrant, from whom I learned much of what I know about writing.

Thanks to Cynthia Read, my editor at Oxford University Press, whose responsiveness, encouragement, wit, and feedback I have appreciated throughout the publication process. Thanks to Hannah Campeanu for her administrative alacrity and to Gabriela Torres for indispensable help with indexing and thoughtful suggestions for improving the manuscript. Special thanks to Production Editor Alphonsa James, who shepherded the manuscript through many months of reviews and revisions.

Thanks to the many friends, mentors, and colleagues who sustained me, both academically and personally, through the long process of producing this work. They include Jeanette Stokes, Margarita Suárez, Jeff Wilson, Sid Brown, the Buddhist Community at Duke, members of the Duke Religious Life staff, the worldwide community of InterPlay®, Lynn Rhodes, Kibbie Ruth, John McRae and Jan Nattier, Richard Payne, Brian Nagata, Rita Gross, Judith Simmer-Brown, Miriam Levering, Tom Peterson, Virginia Rasmussen, Corrie Burdick, Denise Yarbrough, Barb Garii, Susie Kossack, Lucinda Mosher, Grace Burford, Sister Sharon Kanis, Rhetta Wiley, Crissa Holder Smith, Hannah Murphy Buc, Joan and Ryan Sattler, Janet Preis, Stacey Peterson, Carol Cook, the Coordinating Team of Faith Communities of Baltimore with Pride, Sisters Mary Roy Weiss and Mary Kerber, Gayle Aube, Pierce Salguero, Ann Gleig, Scott Mitchell, Natalie Quli, Martin Verhoeven, Taigen Dan Leighton, Duane Bidwell, Mary McGee, Marilyn Saxton, Mira Tessman, Ruthie Andrews, Randy Alfred, Linda Jue, Cynthia Winton-Henry, Kevin Blackard, Rumi, Sam, and Inari. Thanks to Deborah Brown for many forms of support during the early years of writing.

This work is a tribute to my mother, Virginia Hickey, who taught me to read and encouraged my love of learning, and to my father, James Hickey, my hero and most loyal fan. Kudos to my sister Kathe Casas for her extraordinary skill in historical research. Thanks to Barb Pahre for countless acts of generosity, kindness, and support since forever.

Thanks to Zen teachers who have prodded and pulled me along the Bodhisattva Path and endured my whingeing over the decades: Sojun Mel Weitsman; Maylie Scott and Zenkei Blanche Hartman, both of blessed memory; Gengo and Yoshie Akiba; Dai-en Bennage; and Shosan Victoria Austin, whose support and inspiration have been immeasurable. Among the countless Dharma mentors, siblings, and friends to whom I owe thanks, Grace Schireson, Hozan Alan Senauke, Kathryn Stark, and Myosho Ann Kyle Brown deserve special mention, as do the Falling Leaf Sangha of Alfred, New York, the Buddhist Students Association at Johns Hopkins University, and the Heart of Zen Meditation Community of Loyola University Maryland. Words cannot adequately express my appreciation, so I offer *kyūhai*: nine bows of gratitude and respect. I could not have completed this project without the help of all of you, plus countless more.

Portions of chapters 1 and 3 were previously published in "Swedenborg: A Modern Buddha?," *Pacific World: Journal of the Institute of Buddhist Studies* 10 (Summer 2008): 101–29. Portions of the Introduction and chapters 5 through 7 were previously published in "Meditation as Medicine: A Critique," *Crosscurrents* 60, no. 2 (Summer 2010): 168–84. Any errors or omissions in this manuscript are my own responsibility. Any merit arising from the work I offer for the benefit of all beings.

Introduction

YOU CAN HARDLY turn around these days without banging into some reference to "mindfulness." Business is booming: tens of thousands of books and articles describing the psychological and physiological benefits of meditation and mindfulness have been published over the past four decades. In 1999 a selective bibliography on the subject listed more than 1,600 books and articles from 1931 to 1996, of which 96 percent had been published since the mid-1970s.[1] In July 2017 a Google search on the term "mindfulness" returned 24.1 million hits. Although that number was a decline from 39.8 million the previous year and 29 million in June 2015, a search of Amazon.com at the same time yielded 151,021 hits, an eight-fold increase over the previous year and nearly forty times more than in June 2015. These included books on mindful eating, mindful childbirth, mindful parenting, mindful work, mindful studying, mindful investing, and mindful sex. (None so far on mindful auto repair.) A review of any major metropolitan newspaper or any national news magazine in the United States, Canada, or Britain will turn up numerous articles on mindfulness. Since April 2013 *Mindful*, a bimonthly magazine devoted entirely to the topic, has pursued its mission to spread a secular gospel of non-judgmental awareness to the "spiritual but not religious." Notably, among the people featured on the magazine's first fifteen covers, three-quarters appeared to be white, and two-thirds were female.

Credit for the wide diffusion of the mindfulness meme belongs chiefly to Jon Kabat-Zinn, a microbiologist with many years of training in Buddhist meditation, who has described mindfulness as "Buddhist meditation (without the Buddhism)." He developed the eight-week Mindfulness-Based Stress Reduction (MBSR) protocol at the University of Massachusetts Medical Center in 1971 and published it in 1991, in the book

Full Catastrophe Living. The program he designed includes weekly, 150-minute class meetings, in which participants learn some basic sitting and walking meditation methods and yoga postures, receive a bit of didactic instruction, and discuss their experiences. Daily homework involves about forty-five minutes of meditation and yoga practices guided by audio recordings. Students keep a journal to log their practices and reflect on their responses to stressful situations.

Kabat-Zinn launched the Center for Mindfulness in Medicine, Healthcare, and Society in 1995; it claims to have trained more than twenty-thousand people. Hundreds of other MBSR programs operate around the world; some are delivered by instructors trained and certified by the Center for Mindfulness, but many are not. A related eight-week protocol, Mindfulness-Based Cognitive Therapy, was developed to treat depression. Other Mindfulness-Based Interventions (MBIs) now include Mindfulness-Based Relapse Prevention for addiction, Mindfulness-Based Childbirth and Parenting, Mindfulness-Based Eating Awareness Training for eating disorders, Mindfulness-Based Elder Care, Mindfulness-Based Art Therapy, Mindfulness-Based Relationship Enhancement, and Mindfulness-Based Mind-Fitness Training, a condensed course designed to make American soldiers more effective and resilient in the high-stress environment of military combat.[2] Congressman Tim Ryan (D-Ohio) is a fan: he leads meditation groups in the nation's capital and wrote *A Mindful Nation: How a Simple Practice Can Help Us Reduce Stress, Improve Performance, and Recapture the American Spirit.*

Ryan and numerous nonprofit organizations promote Mindfulness in education, from primary and secondary schools to colleges and universities, both private and public. The Association for Mindfulness in Education lists nearly four dozen such organizations in the Americas and Europe.[3] The American Mindfulness Research Center (AMRC) publishes a map showing more than four dozen research programs in this field at American universities and medical schools; a half-dozen more at universities in Canada, Mexico, England, and Wales; and other organizations promoting mindfulness in the United States, Scotland, Portugal, Spain, Denmark, Australia, New Zealand, and Greece. Since 2010 AMRC has published the newsletter *Mindfulness Research Monthly.*[4] The Association for Contemplative Mind in Higher Education lists a dozen degree-granting programs in contemplative studies at American colleges and universities, including two bachelor's programs, one academic concentration, eight master's programs, and one PhD.[5]

At Google, Chade-Meng Tan developed an in-house mindfulness-based leadership program called "Search Inside Yourself," which includes two days of in-person training and four weeks of online follow-up. Now administered by the Search Inside Yourself Leadership Institute, a separate organization, the training costs roughly $800 to $1,400 per person and is marketed to individuals and corporations around the globe.[6] A Mindful Leadership Summit held annually in the District of Columbia costs from $500 to $900 to attend, not including travel, lodging, or meals.[7]

More recently Kristin Neff and Chris Gerner have developed Mindful Self-Compassion training, based in the Buddhist practice of cultivating *metta*, or lovingkindness. It involves developing a kind and caring attitude toward one's own suffering, inadequacies, or failings, instead of judging or criticizing oneself for them; relating one's own experiences to those of others and recognizing our common human condition instead of feeling isolated and alienated; and training one's ability to observe negative thoughts and feelings without fueling them, suppressing them, or identifying with them.[8]

In *Mindful America*, Jeff Wilson elegantly details the ways that "mindfulness" has become ubiquitous, through processes he describes as mediation, mystification, medicalization, mainstreaming, marketing, and moralizing.[9] He argues that the manner in which this quasi-Buddhist concept became an American household word is typical of the way Buddhism has moved from culture to culture around the globe, adapting to each new environment it enters. Wilson's scholarship is impeccable and his study highly recommended; I need not recapitulate his survey of the American Mindfulness scene since 1971. I want to tell a story that begins two centuries earlier, about people who set the stage on which Kabat-Zinn became a star.

Meditation as Medicine: The Usual Narrative

Kabat-Zinn has defined mindfulness as "paying attention in a particular way: on purpose, in the present moment, and non-judgmentally."[10] Mindfulness is an English translation of the Pali word *sati* (Sanskrit *smṛti*). In the Pali Canon of Buddhist scriptures, *sati* indicates something like "remembrance" or "calling to mind"—when one is trying to focus on something and attention wanders, remembering to bring the attention back to its object of focus. Described in greater detail in chapter 5, *sati* is not so much a technique or a practice or a goal in itself as a basic mental faculty or quality that enables us to pay attention to anything, and also to distinguish what is wholesome from what is not, what leads to *nirvāṇa* (the cessation of all dissatisfaction and suffering) and what does not. The methods recommended for establishing and strengthening *sati* in the Pali scriptures are not all present-centered or nonjudgmental. They include following the breath, but also contemplating the foulness of the body, the lovely qualities of a Buddha, and corpses in various stages of decay, so as to develop dispassion toward worldly concerns. Buddhist teachings about "mindfulness" and its role in human happiness are embedded in specifically Buddhist ideas about the nature of reality and the workings of the mind.

Kabat-Zinn presents his version of mindfulness in carefully secular terms, so as not to alienate people who might shy away from something Buddhist or Asian or religious—including those who decide which therapies American medical insurance will cover. Although he has described mindfulness as "the heart of Buddhist meditation," he says, "I bent over backward to structure it and find ways to speak about it that avoided as much as possible the risk of it being seen as Buddhist, 'New Age,' 'Eastern Mysticism' or just plain 'flakey.' To my mind this was a constant and serious risk that would have undermined our attempts to present it as commonsensical, evidence-based, and ordinary, and ultimately a legitimate element of mainstream medical care."[11]

Kabat-Zinn, who holds a PhD in molecular biology, has decades of experience training in Buddhist contexts, although he does not describe himself as Buddhist. His motivations for promoting meditation and yoga in medical settings were both personal and social: to "bring my dharma practice together with my work life into one unified whole, as an expression of right livelihood and in the service of something useful that felt very much needed in the world."[12] He wanted to help sick and suffering people become more involved in their own healing processes, in a medical system that can be fragmented and dehumanizing. He hoped to help people who were falling through the cracks of the medical system or for whom conventional treatments weren't working. He pondered

> how to take the heart of something as meaningful, as sacred if you
> will, as Buddha Dharma and bring it into the world in a way that
> doesn't dilute, profane, or distort it, but at the same time is not
> locked into a culturally and tradition-bound framework that would
> make it absolutely impenetrable to the vast majority of people, who
> are nevertheless suffering and who might find it extraordinarily
> useful and liberative.[13]

His pitch varies somewhat according to his audience. When addressing general or medical audiences, he tells them, "I teach Buddhist meditation— then I put in parentheses 'without the Buddhism.' That's for people who don't know anything about Buddhism. For people who know something about Buddhism, I just say I teach Buddhist meditation."[14] The success of his program has been astounding; it has been deployed to help reduce countless people's depression, anxiety, addictions, eating disorders, hypertension, posttraumatic stress, chronic pain, psoriasis, and side effects from cancer treatment—to name a few.

Kabat-Zinn's concerns about resistance within the medical establishment were well founded. Hostility to unorthodox or overtly religious healing methods has a long history in the United States. Since the mid-nineteenth century, mainstream doctors have repeatedly tried (and failed) to quash unorthodox healing systems, first by barring practitioners from medical societies and colleges, then by prohibiting members of the American Medical Association from consulting or cooperating with "irregular" physicians. Beginning in the late 1880s, state legislatures and the courts attempted to establish licensing laws to prohibit people without mainstream medical training from practicing any kind of mental therapeutics. No less a figure than William James testified against such legislation in 1896. At the time, Christian Science and other religiously based mental-healing methods were enjoying a boom similar in many ways to today's mindfulness boom. Professor James urged his colleagues to learn what they could from the "mind-curers," who gained their wide following because they were clearly meeting needs that orthodox medicine seemed unable to address.[15]

Despite efforts to restrict them, alternative healing methods have remained popular, and mainstream medical colleges have gradually absorbed some of them into their curricula. Today, for example, there is little practical difference between a medical doctor (MD) and a doctor of osteopathy (DO), an alternative healing system that developed in the mid-nineteenth century. Contemporary DOs have virtually the same education, licensing, and professional acceptance as MDs, although they receive additional training in holistic and preventive care and in noninvasive techniques of physical manipulation to correct musculoskeletal misalignments. Skeletal manipulation is also part of chiropractic—which, like water-based treatments (hydrotherapies), emerged as an alternative to mainstream medicine during the nineteenth century. Both are commonly used today for orthopedic injuries.[16] Many medical insurance programs cover chiropractic, and some hospitals are even exploring the benefits of *reiki*, a practice originating in Japan, in which the practitioner is said to channel energy into a patient through light touch, thus activating the patient's own healing capacities. Perhaps it should not be surprising that meditation is also employed therapeutically to treat a wide variety of physical and psychological maladies, in both medical and other settings. Yogis have understood the salutary effects of meditation and yoga postures for millennia. During the 1970s young people flocked to high-profile Asian gurus and yogis, as evangelical Christians sounded alarms about "cults," so in order to gain acceptance in the medical establishment, Kabat-Zinn had to present the meditation techniques, muscle stretches, and yoga postures taught in MBSR courses as strictly nonreligious.

Medical research on mindfulness and other types of meditation has helped to support his scientific case. Although the results of clinical trials have been mixed, and in some cases inconclusive, some studies suggest that mindfulness can improve one's immune system, increase the thickness of one's cerebral cortex, and rewire parts of the brain associated with positive mood.[17] The number of such studies has skyrocketed over the past two decades. In 1997 the federal government funded three research projects on meditation, two of which involved Transcendental Meditation (TM), at a total cost of $941,150. In 2017 it funded 161 projects involving various meditative disciplines, for a total just under $55 million. (See Figure I.1.) Since 2004 MBIs have been the most common methods studied, by far.[18]

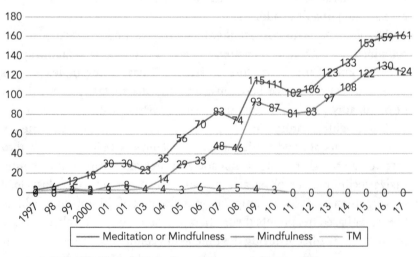

FIG. I.1 Federally funded research projects on meditation, FY 1997–2017.

How We Got Here: Changing the Narrative

But efforts to promote meditation and yoga for psychological and physical health in the United States are hardly new; in fact, as I will show, they are far older in the United States than most people assume. Virtually every source I have seen on the subject traces the history back to the late 1960s and early 1970s. At that time, the Beatles, the Beach Boys, and other celebrities were popularizing TM, a practice developed by the Indian guru Maharishi Mahesh Yogi (1918–2008). Practitioners of TM promoted it as nonreligious and accessible to everyone; they advocated teaching it in public schools and other nonreligious environments. They also encouraged scientific research on the physical and psychological benefits of TM. In 1975 Herbert Benson, a Harvard medical researcher, published a book describing his own research on TM practitioners, who showed measurable decreases in heart rate, respiration, and blood pressure during meditation. Benson called this the "Relaxation Response" and claimed it was good for our health. He went on to found Harvard's Mind/ Body Medical Institute, and later demonstrated that a variety of practices, including repetitive prayer, deep breathing, yoga, T'ai chi, and even jogging and knitting, could evoke the Relaxation Response—the opposite of the fight-or-flight state of arousal experienced under stress.[19]

Jeff Wilson points to the summer of 1974 as another key moment. That is when the Tibetan Buddhist master Chögyam Trungpa launched the Naropa Institute in Boulder, Colorado: as Wilson described it, "a Buddhist summer school for hippies and other alternative spiritual seekers."[20] It has since become Naropa University, a fully accredited institution offering baccalaureate, master's, and doctoral degrees, and a leader in "contemplative education." Joseph Goldstein and Jack Kornfield both taught at Naropa that first summer, and eventually they, together with Sharon Salzberg and Jacqueline Schwartz, cofounded the Insight Meditation Society (IMS) in Barre, Massachusetts. The modern Mindfulness movement relies heavily on the Vipassanā style of meditation they and their students developed and disseminated through IMS and Spirit Rock Meditation Center, a retreat facility in northern California. Now hundreds of Vipassanā meditation groups are scattered around the country and the globe. In 1979 Naropa hosted a groundbreaking conference called "Comparative Approaches to Cognition: Western and Buddhist." Among Trungpa's students were two organizers of that event, the cognitive scientists Eleanor Rosch and Francisco Varela, who later helped to found the Mind and Life Institute, a key player in modern medical research on meditation's effects on the brain.[21]

Wilson says, "Everything prior to the 1970s is merely prelude to the main story of how mindfulness came to America."[22] He is a careful scholar and a cherished colleague and friend, but we differ on this point. I take issue with the phrase "*merely* prelude to the main story." *Far more* was happening before the 1970s than he and other observers of the Mindfulness movement suggest, and I believe that earlier history offers salutary lessons for the present and the future.

Before I explain that, it may be helpful to define some terms. When I refer to the "Mindfulness movement," I mean the broad, diffuse movement that Wilson's book describes as originating in the 1970s. At its core is the MBSR program, which Kabat-Zinn launched in 1979, and it includes all the therapeutic derivatives of MBSR, collectively called MBIs. The Mindfulness movement belongs to three other broad, overlapping groups. The first is the group of individuals and institutions involved in mind-body *healing*. This group seeks to understand the relationship between mental states and physical health in order to help alleviate psychosomatic symptoms. This broad category includes religious and other practitioners who are not generally accepted within the biomedical mainstream: for instance, Christian Scientists, shamans, yoga teachers, and Reiki masters.

A highly influential subset of mind-body healing professionals practices mind-body *medicine*—these practitioners operate within the Western biomedical establishment as physicians, psychologists, clinical researchers, and so on. They typically hold advanced academic or professional degrees (MD, DO, PhD, PsyD, etc.) and are associated with research universities, medical schools, hospitals, and mental health clinics. A second subset of mind-body healing practitioners is specifically interested in therapeutic applications of *meditation*, be it TM, MBSR-style mindfulness, contemplative prayer, or other meditative disciplines to cultivate compassion and lovingkindness. This is the "meditation-as-medicine" group. Many members of the meditation-as-medicine group work in biomedicine, but not all do. Some teach MBSR in medical settings; others teach mindfulness to soldiers or corporate executives and staff; still others are educators trying to help students cope with academic and personal challenges. So, as Figure I.2 indicates, the Mindfulness movement is part of the broad mind-body healing movement; its most visible and influential spokespersons are involved in mind-body medicine; and it specifically advocates the practice of meditation-as-medicine.

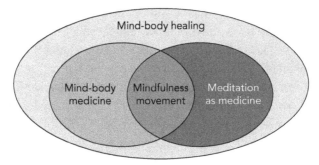

FIG. 1.2 Mind-body healing, mind-body medicine, meditation as medicine.

The Early Mind Cure Movement

The mind-body healing movement, and specific interest in meditation-as-medicine, began well *outside* the medical establishment, more than a century before the Mindfulness movement of the 1970s. It emerged during the late 1860s and 1870s, in two metaphysical religious movements: Christian Science, started by Mary Baker Eddy, and New Thought, a related but more diffuse and eclectic movement. New Thought has religious and medical antecedents dating back to the mid-eighteenth century—and earlier. Although it differs from Christian Science in important ways, when both began to emerge, the boundaries between them were porous and some observers lumped them together into what they called the Mind Cure movement. In the 1890s and early 1900s, a few Asian Buddhist and Hindu missionaries began teaching meditation and yoga to New Thought leaders and congregations. In national lecture tours and classes, they introduced the contemplative disciplines of mindfulness of breathing (*anapana sati*), Zen sitting meditation (Jp. *zazen*), Raja Yoga, Kriya Yoga, and related practices. Meditation of various kinds soon became a central practice in New Thought churches.

New Thought and Christian Science spread rapidly across the country during the late nineteenth and early twentieth centuries. In fact they were so successful at critiquing the medical and religious establishments during their heyday, and exerted so much pressure on them, that in 1906 mainstream doctors and clergy began to fight back. They successfully appropriated some of the Mind Cure movement's key ideas and practices. By channeling mental therapeutics into "scientific" psychology and medicine, which they controlled, they wrested authority away from Mind Cure practitioners, most of whom were women.

The apostles of both New Thought and Christian Science began as disciples of a New England clockmaker-turned-mental-healer named Phineas

Quimby (1802–1866). He was the true American pioneer of what we now call mind-body medicine, though he had little formal education and no academic degrees. Quimby discovered, almost by accident, that our beliefs and mental states affect our physical health, and he ran an enormously successful mind-cure clinic that gave thousands of people relief from all kinds of ailments. His methods were akin to hypnotic suggestion. He was not particularly religious; he called what he did "the Science of Health and Happiness." But his students and their successors went on to spawn a variety of religious organizations.

Eddy, who founded Christian Science in 1879, eventually repudiated her earlier studies with Quimby and her praise for his methods and claimed to have received a unique revelation about the nature of illness, the nature of divine reality, and the hidden meanings of biblical texts. She taught that matter is unreal and that disease is an error of the mind that can be corrected only by divine grace. Eddy exercised tight control over her church during her lifetime and dictated precisely how it should conduct its affairs after her death. She did not tolerate dissent and expelled a number of students for apostasy, several of whom went on to found New Thought churches and denominations.

Where Christian Science is hierarchical and doctrinaire, New Thought is diffuse, egalitarian, and eclectic. It spread primarily through books, periodicals, classes, correspondence courses, and conferences, but some teachers established enduring religious organizations as well. The longest-surviving New Thought churches are Divine Science, founded by Malinda Cramer in 1888; Unity, founded by Charles and Myrtle Fillmore in 1889; and the Church of Religious Science/Center for Spiritual Living, founded by Ernest Holmes in 1926. Seicho-no-Ie, a Japanese group launched by Masaharu Taniguchi in 1930, is probably the largest New Thought denomination in the world today. A more recent one is the Universal Foundation for Better Living, established by Johnnie Colemon, a former Unity minister, in 1974.

New Thought influenced a number of African American religious movements that emerged during the 1920s and the Great Depression. These include Marcus Garvey's Universal Negro Improvement Association (UNIA); the Moorish Science Temple; the Nation of Islam; Father Divine's Peace Mission Movement; Black Hebrew Israelite groups such as the Church of the Living God, the Pillar and Ground of Truth;[23] Rastafarianism; and various forms of the evangelical Christian "Prosperity Gospel."

New Thought is a bricolage, or a confluence of various streams of Protestant, Buddhist, and Hindu *modernism*.[24] Modernist religious movements reinterpret and reform traditional religious doctrines and practices for modern circumstances, adapting them particularly to contemporary scientific understandings of the world. They tend to regard God or the divine as immanent in the world and revealed through nature, rather than occupying a transcendent position outside the created order. They de-emphasize supernatural claims, such as divine interventions or the miraculous powers of adepts. They downplay or eliminate premodern cosmologies, minimize religious ritual, and emphasize the rationality and compatibility of their teachings with modern science. Religious modernists also tend to shift leadership authority away from ordained leaders and toward lay householders, and to present religious teachings, particularly Buddhist and Hindu ones, primarily in psychological, philosophical, and ethical terms.[25] Both the New Thought and Mindfulness movements exhibit many of these modernist characteristics.

A basic premise of New Thought is that if we attune ourselves to the all-pervading presence of the divine and realize our unity with it, then happiness, health, and abundance will naturally result.[26] "Abundance" can mean material prosperity, but the earliest and most influential teachers meant *spiritual* abundance. Because we are inseparable from our divine source, they said, we already have access to all that is necessary for a happy, healthy, satisfying, prosperous life. To cultivate awareness of the divine and experience the healing and empowerment this awareness provides, early New Thought teachers recommended meditating on the breath, a repeated word, or a phrase, or cultivating an open, receptive state called "entering the Silence." They wrote books and trained others in these and other "Mind Cure" methods, drawing language and concepts from Christian, Jewish, Buddhist, and Hindu sources, as well as from Western esoteric traditions.

New Thought authors and leaders were first exposed to Asian religions by European Orientalist scholars, who had begun translating ancient Hindu and Buddhist texts from Pali and Sanskrit into European languages. Some New Thought teachers studied meditation and yoga directly with Asian missionaries, and some of those missionaries established enduring organizations in the United States, such as the Vedanta Society and, later, the Self-Realization Fellowship. Many New Thought leaders also had ties to the Theosophical Society, a metaphysical movement that emerged around the same time, which was a—if not *the*—major purveyor and interpreter of Buddhist and Hindu ideas among Americans and Europeans until the 1950s. (It had quite a few members across Asia as well.)

Early Mind Cure Meant Liberation

Although Mary Baker Eddy regarded Christian Science as distinctly different from New Thought, which she disparagingly called "Mind Cure," for convenience's sake I will sometimes refer to the "early Mind Cure" movement, by which I mean the early phase of *both* Christian Science and New Thought, from the 1870s to World War I and the Spanish Flu pandemic of 1918–1920. These two movements arose together, in dialogue and debate with each other. During their early phase, the majority of Mind Cure leaders and practitioners were women, and many of them were captivated by the idea that if they could change their minds, their unhelpful patterns of thinking, they could also change the oppressive circumstances in which they lived.

At the time, most women could not vote. When they married, they lost control of any property they owned and whatever income they generated during the marriage. Domestic violence, often fueled by alcohol abuse, was common and rarely prosecuted. If a woman left an abusive husband, he got custody of the children. Few women had access to higher education or professional work. The Mind Cure movement enabled women to build careers as counselors, healers, publishers, and public speakers, and to be ordained as ministers. Many of these women were also active in the social reform movements of the Progressive Era: women's suffrage, labor reform, marriage reform, temperance, vegetarianism, hygiene, service to the poor and incarcerated, and the prevention of cruelty to animals.[27]

By 1902 major New Thought centers could be found across the United States, as well as overseas. Seven national organizations were all led by women. More than fifteen journals and thirteen hundred books were in print. By 1910 New Thought was reaching even wider audiences through novels and popular journals, such as *Good Housekeeping* and the *Woman's Home Companion*. The organizations dominated by (white) women began to decline by the end of the first decade of the twentieth century, but during the early years of the Great Migration, when more than six million African Americans moved from the rural South to northern cities (1910–70), several African American religious movements inspired by New Thought began to emerge.

Through the 1920s and the Great Depression, these movements worked to transform the consciousness of black men and women who had internalized the racism of white supremacist society, promoting pride, respectability, and self-esteem. Some were nationalist, such as Garvey's UNIA and the Nation of Islam, which advocated the establishment of black nation-states in Africa and/or separatist communities in the United States. The Peace Mission Movement of Father Divine rejected racial categories altogether and built a nationwide network of *interracial* communities at the height of Jim Crow, as well as hotels, stores, gas stations, and other businesses run largely by women, which served black and white customers alike. Peace Mission members organized politically and lobbied Congress for laws to prohibit lynching. Thus, for many people, particularly women and African American men, New Thought meant *liberation*—not just in a spiritual sense, but in very pragmatic political, economic, and legal terms.

Gradually New Thought diverged into two streams, one centered in religious *communities*, the other concerned primarily with *individual* success, well-being, and prosperity. I refer to the early, reform-minded religious groups—most of which were led by white women or black men—as "community-oriented." Over time, however, the individualist strand of New Thought came to predominate. During the latter half of the twentieth century, the Prosperity Gospel gained strength: it is a blend of individualist New Thought and Evangelical, often Pentecostal, Christianity. Most—though not all—of the most visible spokespeople for the Individualist and Prosperity Gospel streams of New Thought have been white men, many of whom have promoted positive thinking as a pathway to financial wealth. Napoleon Hill said we could *Think and Grow Rich*. Dale Carnegie encouraged us to *Make Friends and Influence People*. Russell Herman Conwell, a Baptist minister and founder of Temple University, exhorted from the pulpit, "I say you ought to get rich, and it is your duty to get rich." In a sermon he delivered thousands of times, titled "Acres of Diamonds," he preached, "Money is power, and you ought to be reasonably ambitious to have it. You ought because you can do more good with it than you could without it. Money printed your Bible, money builds your churches, money sends your missionaries, and money pays your preachers." About poverty he said:

The number of poor who are to be sympathized with is very small. To sympathize with a man whom God has punished for his sins, thus to help him when God would still continue a just punishment, is to do wrong, no doubt about it, and we do that more than we help those who are deserving. While we should sympathize with God's poor—that is, those who cannot help themselves—let us remember there is not a poor person in the United States who was not made poor by his own shortcomings, or by the shortcomings of someone else.[28]

Today Prosperity preachers stress that the more one gives to their ministries, the more one will be "blessed" with good fortune.[29] New Thought ideas also made their way into the New Age movement that emerged during the 1970s. Rhonda Byrne's book and movie *The Secret*, popularized a decade ago with help from Oprah Winfrey, is one example. As New Thought principles became increasingly individualized and commercialized, both the practice of meditation and the social justice agendas of the early community-oriented groups fell by the wayside.

Mind Cure made its way into mainstream medicine as well. Around the turn of the twentieth century, a group of four white, male clergy and medical doctors, who held academic degrees from elite universities, grew alarmed by the popularity of New Thought and Christian Science in their midst. They wanted to stop the proliferation of what they saw as quackery and bad religion. In 1906 they began to wrangle control of mental therapeutics away from the Mind Cure movement and channel it toward Freudian psychoanalysis and pastoral counseling. They founded the Emmanuel Clinic in Boston's largest Episcopal church, a pioneering mental and public health endeavor, and began treating "functional" disorders such as nervous exhaustion, anxiety, melancholy, hypochondria, and phobias, as well as the so-called so-called "moral disorder" of addiction to alcohol or other drugs. Thousands of Bostonians applied for classes in health education and hygiene, participated in rudimentary group psychotherapy, and had individual consultations with clergy and physicians.

Mind Cure Mainstreamed

Through publicity in newspapers and magazines, the Emmanuel Clinic's methods spread rapidly around the United States and internationally. The visibility of what came to be called the Emmanuel Movement soon attracted criticism from physicians who objected to lay counselors offering group psychotherapy without formal medical or psychological credentials. Some clergy thought psychological counseling fell outside their pastoral role. Both clergy and doctors wanted to maintain a sharp distinction between their respective professions.

However, the Emmanuel Movement inspired people and organizations who continued to explore relationships between religion and mental healing throughout the twentieth century, and who melded modern, secular psychotherapy with spiritual "cure of souls." They promoted greater understanding of psychosomatic illness, pioneered Clinical Pastoral Education for chaplains, and developed the psychological subfield of pastoral counseling. Among these pioneers were Norman Vincent Peale, a Protestant minister who teamed with a psychiatrist named Smiley Blanton to create several pastoral-counseling organizations. Peale delivered a blend of Protestant New Thought and psychology to millions through his publications, sermons, and weekly radio show. Gradually Mind Cure was thoroughly medicalized and mainstreamed. This shifted the locus of control for psychoreligious healing toward elite theological and medical schools. That process is what made the contemporary Mindfulness movement, with its advocacy of meditation-as-medicine, possible.

Between 1924 and 1965 laws barring immigration from Asia stemmed but did not stop the flow of Asian missionaries promoting meditation and yoga around the United States. Direct religious instruction by Asian teachers became harder to find, but not impossible: the Vedanta Society, founded in 1894, and the Self Realization Fellowship, founded in 1925, established centers across the United States. These taught meditation, yoga, and Hindu devotional practices to many thousands of people throughout the first half of the twentieth century. A home-grown yogi, Pierre Bernard, a.k.a. "The Great Oom," attracted a celebrity clientele to physical (Hatha) yoga during the Jazz Age.

After World War II the field of psychology expanded rapidly, as doctors and professors fleeing Hitler's Third Reich taught American university courses filled by (mostly white, male) beneficiaries of the GI Bill. During the 1950s and 1960s some of these psychologists got interested in Zen Buddhism, thanks to the efforts of D. T. Suzuki, a Japanese Buddhist reformer who had also taught Buddhism a half-century earlier at New Thought gatherings. When the American ban on Asian immigration ended in 1965, a *second* wave of modernist Asian missionaries toured the country and began building organizations to teach meditation and yoga to eager new audiences. Medical research on meditation and the mind's role in healing began in the 1950s, while Peale preached positive thinking widely through publications and the radio. The counterculture of the 1960s and 1970s fueled further interest in altered states of consciousness and new approaches to psychological and physical health.

This book details the pre-1970 history of meditation-as-medicine and explains how key ideas and practices from a movement that began on the religious margins of American culture ended up in the medical mainstream. It begins in eighteenth-century Europe, with the mystical visions of Emanuel Swedenborg, a Swedish scientist, and the crackpot medical theories of Franz Anton Mesmer, a doctor who practiced in Vienna and Paris. Their ideas and methods converged in the work of Quimby, the American father of psychosomatic or mind-body medicine. Chapter 2 surveys the rise of the religious Mind Cure movements that spread outward from Quimby, including both Christian Science and New Thought. It distinguishes between *community-oriented* and *individualist* New Thought, which had different trajectories, and discusses African American movements inspired by New Thought. Chapter 3 examines the practices of meditation and yoga in New Thought, particularly at the Greenacre Conferences in Eliot, Maine, from 1894 to 1907. It stresses the *transnational* nature of New Thought, which is typically considered to be an American invention.[30] Chapter 4 describes the process by which some of the Mind Cure movement's "suggestive" methods were appropriated by members of the medical and religious establishments in the early twentieth century. It traces the emergence of mind-body medicine over the next half-century.

Chapters 5 and 6 raise a number of critical questions about the contemporary Mindfulness movement: Can it reasonably be considered "religion," despite proponents' claims to the contrary? If so, is it Buddhist? If so, what kind? Does it matter? Is it as clinically effective as proponents claim? Chapter 7 considers the early, community-oriented wing of the New Thought movement and the contemporary Mindfulness movement side-by-side and identifies characteristics they have in common as well as significant differences between them. This analysis reveals some of the problems and limitations inherent in the Mindfulness movement's approach to meditation, from both Buddhist and scientific perspectives.

Piecing together the story told in this book has required not depth in a single field but a broad perspective, which reveals connections that a narrower focus renders invisible. The relationships and lines of influence this book tries to describe are complex. They extend in multiple directions across many fields: religion, medicine, psychology, politics, economics. They cross geographic boundaries in Asia, Europe, and North America, and span all or parts of four centuries. To visualize or map these relationships, I had to develop overlapping timelines and several complicated flowcharts. I have included some of these diagrams in the hope that they will help visually oriented readers understand the historical narrative more easily. Readers interested in a more scholarly discussion of theoretical and methodological issues in the historiography of religions and mind-body medicine should refer to the appendix. Above all, it is important to remember that this is a story about networks and processes, not about a linear progression from Point A to Point B.

Let us turn now to eighteenth-century Europe, where a flamboyant doctor and a scientist-turned-mystic birthed healing movements whose progeny continue to influence religious and medical assumptions to this day.

Mysticism, Mesmerism, Mind Cure

THIS HISTORY OF modern mind-body medicine begins with two figures who have received relatively little attention in histories of religion
in America, despite their far-reaching influences: Emanuel Swedenborg
(1688–1772), a Swedish scientist, mystic, and theologian, and Franz Anton
Mesmer (1734–1815), a physician who practiced in Paris and Vienna.
These two men and their ideological successors profoundly influenced
a number of popular medical, psychological, and religious movements
in the nineteenth-century United States, the effects of which are still discernible in American culture today. This chapter sketches their careers
and their impact on two mental-healing movements that emerged during
the late nineteenth century: Christian Science and New Thought, collectively called the Mind Cure movement. First let us turn to Swedenborg, an
elder contemporary of Mesmer, whose theological writings and mystical
experiences informed many other nineteenth-century American religious
and healing movements.

Emanuel Swedenborg

Swedenborg was the son of a pietist Lutheran bishop and theologian and
a devout Christian. He studied mathematics, physics, chemistry, and engineering throughout Europe, and for most of his career served as chief
assessor for the Swedish Bureau of Mines. His scientific interests were extremely broad: he published some six dozen books, pamphlets, and articles
in the fields just mentioned, as well as anatomy, biology, astronomy, and
mineralogy. He made pioneering discoveries about the nebular formation

of galaxies and the anatomical structures of the human brain. At the age of fifty-six he began to have a series of visionary religious experiences, in which he spoke to angels and other spirit beings, visited heaven and hell, and received revelations about the hidden meanings of Christian scripture. In his visionary excursions to heaven and hell, Swedenborg found those realms populated with spirits who were organized into societies according to their interests and temperaments. From 1745, the year after his visions began, until his death in 1772 at the age of eighty-four, he devoted himself to theology, and his writings in this field were published in thirty thick volumes. Swedenborg believed that these works constituted the Second Coming of Christ.

Among the most popular of his theological works, all written in Latin, were the *Arcana Coelestia* (*Secrets of Heaven*, 1749–56), a multivolume exegesis of Genesis and Exodus; *Revelation Unveiled* (1766), a multivolume exegesis of Revelation;[1] *Heaven and Hell* (1758); *Conjugal Love* (1768), in which the lifelong bachelor discusses the spiritual meanings of gender, sexuality, and marriage;[2] and *True Christianity* (1771), a summary of his ideas composed at the end of his life.[3]

Swedenborg's highly controversial theological treatises from 1749–66 were published anonymously and outside his native Sweden, in London, Amsterdam, Tübingen, and Leipzig. After the publication of *Conjugal Love*, the first to appear under Swedenborg's own name, his exegetical methods and theological challenges to Lutheran orthodoxy became the subjects of a heresy trial. (He was eventually exonerated.) Within two or three decades after his death, all of his theological works had been translated from Latin into English, and by the 1790s the first Swedenborgian churches had formed in England. His ideas also attracted scathing criticism, the most influential example of which was penned by the philosopher Immanuel Kant, who, like other detractors, denounced Swedenborg as a madman.

Gradually Swedenborg fell into obscurity, and today he receives relatively little attention from scholars of American religion—though he fares better among scholars of modern European literature and the history of Western esotericism. The denomination founded upon his teachings, the Church of the New Jerusalem, has always been small, but the direct and indirect influences of his ideas have been far-reaching in American religious thought and alternative medicine (see Figure 1.1).[4]

Swedenborg's most influential ideas have included a correspondence between spiritual and physical realms, divine influx (explained below), the role of sexuality in spiritual development, and the progressive nature of

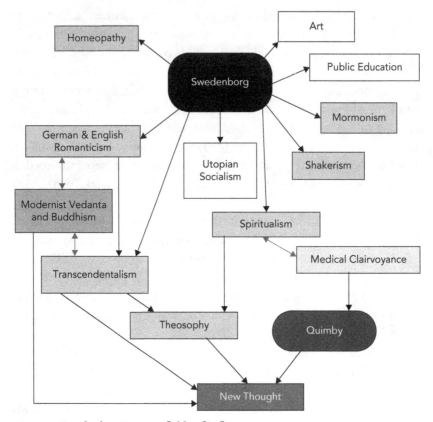

FIG. I.I Swedenborg's many fields of influence.

spiritual awakening through processes of education and self-discipline. He viewed the cosmos as "a single dynamic entity created through successive emanations from a unitary life force."[5] This Neo-Platonic view of divine emanation is a feature of the European Hermetic tradition and Christian Kabbalah. Swedenborg almost certainly studied Jewish Kabbalah when he was a student at the University of Uppsala, and again in midlife.[6] According to his doctrine of influx, "All power to act flows into all of creation from God constantly and unceasingly."[7]

Like Neo-Platonists, and drawing upon the Trinitarian Lutheranism in which he had been raised, Swedenborg saw the cosmos as organized hierarchically in an orderly tripartite structure: the triune God, three realms of existence (celestial, spiritual, and natural), and three aspects of a person (soul, mind, and body). The spiritual and natural realms are related via the correspondence between macrocosm and microcosm. Through his visions and by analyzing scripture in light of his theory of correspondence, Swedenborg believed he had discovered the hidden spiritual implications of the natural world: the purpose of creation, the nature of human life, the presence of the divine in human affairs, and the goal of all existence.

Our purpose is to progress toward union with God, he believed, through a process of study and self-discipline. He rejected the doctrine of Original Sin and asserted that humans are free to choose evil or good. Evil is self-love, turning away from God toward selfishness. Spiritual progress requires gradual relinquishment of self-centeredness. Essential to this process is "use," good works for the benefit of society.[8]

Swedenborg's influences on American religious thought are many and varied and have been relatively understudied in historical surveys of religion in the United States.[9] Catherine Albanese has provided the most extensive treatment by far, in *A Republic of Mind and Spirit*. She traces the Swede's influences on Transcendentalism, Spiritualism, Fourrierist communities, Shakerism, New Thought, and New Age religiosity. Albanese also argues that many Mormon doctrines derive from Swedenborgianism: the progressive deification of human beings (which Joseph Smith introduced in his King Follett Discourse); correspondences between earthly and heavenly realms; the three levels of heaven (telestial, terrestrial, and celestial); eternal marriage; and a divine Heavenly Father and Mother. She notes that Smith had access to books about Swedenborgian theology in the Palmyra library near his childhood home.[10]

Swedenborg's influence on Ralph Waldo Emerson and Transcendentalist thought has been well documented. Emerson owned several books by Swedenborg, read others by the Swedenborgians Sampson Reed and James Garth Wilkinson, and subscribed to a Swedenborgian journal, *The New Jerusalem Magazine*.[11] He introduced the seer's writings to his friends Margaret Fuller, Henry David Thoreau, Bronson Alcott, Theodore Parker, and George Ripley. Emerson's *Representative Men* contains a chapter on Swedenborg, whom the author criticizes but also calls "a colossal soul" whose ethical teachings "entitle him to a place, vacant for some ages, among the lawgivers of mankind."[12] Swedenborg's doctrine of correspondence between spiritual and natural realms is the most obvious contribution to Transcendentalism, but one can also find resonances in Transcendentalist notions of free will, self-reliance, education, and social ethics.

Swedenborg was a major contributor to the Spiritualist teachings of Andrew Jackson Davis (1826–1910) of Poughkeepsie, New York, who claimed to encounter the seer in a vision that changed his life. Davis's "Harmonial Philosophy" drew heavily upon Swedenborg. Séance Spiritualism echoed the Swede's visitations with departed spirits, who conveyed messages to the living. Spiritualism flourished during the second half of the nineteenth century, particularly after the Civil War, and spirit communication became a major feature of Theosophy, in which Helena P. Blavatsky (and others) claimed to be instructed clair-voyantly by a brotherhood of Ascended Masters. With few exceptions, the staid members of the institutional Church of the New Jerusalem, founded upon Swedenborg's teachings, rejected the antics of séance mediums and the surrender of will involved in Mesmerism. Nevertheless Swedenborgianism converged with Mesmerism and flowed into Spiritualism, New Thought, and Theosophy.

Swedenborg's teachings influenced some of the most popular med-ical reform movements of the nineteenth century, including homeopathy and Mind Cure. To understand why these alternatives were so popular, it is important to understand the horrors of nineteenth-century orthodox medicine. In the first decades of the nineteenth century, most doctors relied on so-called heroic measures, popularized in the United States by Benjamin Rush (1745–1813), the best-known physician of his day, as well as a Founding Father of the United States and signer of the Declaration of Independence. Rush believed that all fevers, indeed all illnesses, were caused by nervous excitation and convulsive action in the vascular system, which prompted fluid to accumulate in the body, so his primary method of treatment was to drain off the excess and restore balance by bleeding the patient until she or he passed out. Other methods included blistering, purging the bowels, and vomiting.

> Bleeding was usually the initial treatment. It consisted of venesec-tion (opening up a vein), scarification (using a spring-loaded in-strument to produce a series of small cuts), or cupping (placing a warmed glass cup over a cut which filled with blood as the pressure inside dropped). Blistering involved placing hot plasters onto the skin to raise blisters, which were then drained. The most common purgative was Calomel, a form of mercuric chloride which worked as a laxative in small doses, but usually was prescribed in large doses to purge the system.[13]

Calomel caused "cheeks and gums to bleed and ulcerate and teeth to become loose and fall out. In severe cases, the sufferer's jawbone could be destroyed." Calomel also caused the tongue to protrude and generated "a profuse flow of viscous and foul-smelling saliva"—at the rate of a pint to a quart each day.[14] In addition, Rush administered arsenic and saltpeter, an ingredient of gunpowder. Another common means to draw off fluids was to keep wounds open.[15] It is no surprise that many of his patients died of these methods.

For women, orthodox medicine was even more perilous. Many middle- and upper-class white women were diagnosed with "hysteria," a catch-all term for a variety of physical complaints that had no obvious physical cause. These included anxiety, headache, depression, fatigue, difficulty swallowing, loss of vision or hearing or another one of the senses, paralysis, or seizures. (Note that several of these symptoms are associated with what is today called "stress"—the focus of much contemporary research in mind-body medicine.) The uterus was the presumed source of hysterical symptoms, and gynecological treatments included "leeching, injections, ovariotomies, and/or cauterization of the clitoris. Leeches were placed on the vulva or on the neck of the uterus, and sometimes leeches progressed into the uterus itself, causing acute pain. Cauterization was accomplished by chemicals such as nitrate of silver or hydrate of potassa, or by a white-hot iron, and cauterization treatments were performed several times at intervals of a few days."[16] These methods were employed before the development of chemical anesthesia, so it is no wonder that alternative healing systems emerged, promoting much gentler therapeutics. Other popular alternatives included Thomsonism, a system of botanical remedies that patients were licensed to administer themselves at home; hydropathy, which employed hot and cold baths, wraps in wet sheets, and many drinks of water; various dietary reforms, including vegetarianism and chewing food until it liquefied; and improved personal hygiene.[17]

Among Swedenborgians, one of the most popular forms of unorthodox medicine was homeopathy, developed in Germany by Samuel Hahnemann (1755–1843). Like Spiritualists and the later Mind Curers, Swedenborgian homeopaths regarded disease as a physical manifestation of a problem that was fundamentally spiritual.[18] In a theory that echoed the Swedenborgian doctrine of correspondence between the natural realm and the spiritual realm, Hahnemann asserted the "law of similars": a substance that in large doses causes symptoms of illness, cures those same symptoms when administered in infinitesimal dilutions. For homeopaths, the physical medicine did not cure disease directly; it was a poison that created an artificial disease, which drew the underlying spiritual disease to the surface and effected a cure through the principle that "like cures like." Not surprisingly, the patients of homeopathic doctors fared better than those treated with "heroic" medicine during American cholera epidemics of 1830 and 1849, which gave homeopathy quite a boost in the public mind.

It was brought to the United States by Henry Detweiler, who practiced in Pennsylvania in the 1820s, and Constantine Hering, who opened a major school of homeopathic medicine in Philadelphia in 1848. Hering read Swedenborg avidly; Hans Gram, who introduced homeopathy in New England, belonged to the Swedenborgian church in Boston; Sampson Reed, who introduced Emerson to Swedenborg's writings, was a homeopathic pharmacist; and "the leading homeopath in the South, William Holcombe, was a Newchurchman who spiced his medical treatises with allusions to Swedenborg."[19]

Franz Anton Mesmer

Swedenborg's contemporary, Mesmer, was born near Lake Constance in Swabia (i.e., modern Germany near the Swiss border).[20] He studied theology at Dillingen, a Jesuit seminary in Bavaria, and theology, mathematics, and physics at the University of Ingolstadt, also in Bavaria. In 1766 he earned a medical degree at the University of Vienna; his doctoral thesis argued that human bodies are influenced by the planets and stars by means of gravitation and atmospheric tides.[21] He established a medical practice in Vienna, where he became interested in the work of Maximillian Hell, a Jesuit priest and professor at the University of Vienna who claimed to cure the sick by placing magnets on affected parts of patients' bodies.[22]

Mesmer experimented with magnets in his medical practice and gradually developed his theory of "animal magnetism." According to this theory, spelled out in a 1779 treatise, an extremely subtle fluid with properties "analogous to those of the magnet" pervaded the universe, and imbalances or deficiencies of this "magnetic fluid" were the root cause of all disease.[23] Eventually Mesmer became convinced that it was unnecessary to employ actual magnets for healing; he could manipulate the natural animal magnetism present in his body and those of his patients to effect cures. He induced trances in his patients and brought them to a state of "crisis," during which their symptoms initially increased, but then subsided. This cathartic experience was thought to restore magnetic balance and eliminate illnesses, both "nervous" (what we would call psychosomatic) and organic.[24]

Mesmer moved to Paris in 1778, and his reputation spread. Affluent aristocrats flocked to demonstrations of his cures, and some paid substantial fees to join his Society of Harmony and learn the secrets of animal magnetism. In 1784 the government of Louis XVI established the first of two commissions that tested Mesmer's theory and methods. It was composed of members of the French Academy of Sciences and chaired by Benjamin Franklin, then the American ambassador to the French court. The second, composed of members of the Royal Society of Medicine, examined the work of one of Mesmer's disciples, Charles D'Eslon. The reports of these investigations concluded that no evidence of magnetic fluid could be found and that the convulsions of mesmerized people in crisis were the products of overactive imaginations. On that basis, the commissions dismissed as irrelevant all evidence of cures, including reports from one hundred patients who had undergone mesmeric treatment.[25] Among these,

> all but six had already evidenced marked progress; over one-half claimed complete cure. The ailments included spleen infections, rheumatism, asthma, headaches, skin diseases, as well as various nervous disorders. These documents make it difficult to escape the conclusion that hundreds of persons who had proved incurable by conventional medical practice had found substantial, if not permanent, cure at the hands of Mesmer and his colleagues. . . . Many of the patients protested that the commissioners' reports did disservice to the actual facts.[26]

Although the report discounting Mesmer's theory and methods was widely circulated, popular interest in Mesmerism remained enthusiastic. Robert Fuller has noted that the commissions' dismissal of the powers of "imagination," and its consequent disregard for the cures reported, was itself a failure of imagination: "Unfortunately, no one paused to ponder just what a wondrous faculty the Mesmerists had demonstrated the imagination to be."[27]

Many of the people who developed new systems of healing during the nineteenth and early twentieth centuries began as magnetic healers or were otherwise influenced by Mesmer's ideas. Three major streams of thought emerged among those who studied Mesmer and developed his ideas in new directions. One group believed in the existence of a "mag-netic fluid," imbalances of which produced disease; a second group rejected the fluid theory and regarded the trance state as psychological in origin; the third focused on paranormal or spiritual phenomena such as clairvoyance and communing with the dead.[28] Figure 1.2 illustrates these different trajectories. As with all typologies, the boundaries between these categories are permeable. As long as one bears in mind the untidy realities of ideal types, however, these categories can serve as an illuminating analytical tool.

Theorists drawing on the fluid theory developed different healing sys-tems. According to John Bovee Dods's "electrical psychology," the lungs drew electricity from the air and transferred it to the blood. This elec-tricity then magnetized the iron in the blood and circulated it to the brain. The brain secreted the energy as "nervo-vital fluid," and the will acted upon this fluid to operate the muscles.[29] Andrew Taylor Still (1828–1917), the founder of osteopathy, began his career as a magnetic healer and believed that blockages of the free flow of fluid caused disease. Eventually he decided the fluid in question was blood. Attributing blockages to bone misalignments, particularly in the spinal column, he developed a method of manipulation therapy to restore proper alignment and unimpeded cir-culation. Daniel David Palmer (1845–1913), who developed chiropractic,

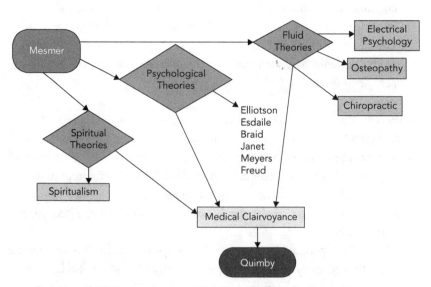

FIG. 1.2 Theories based on Mesmer: fluid, psychological, spiritual.

also began as a magnetic healer and, like Still, decided that skeletal misalignment caused disease—but instead of impeding circulation, he believed, these misalignments impinged on nerves, which affected the proper functioning of internal organs.

Among those who focused on paranormal phenomena were the various founding figures of Theosophy, as well as Andrew Jackson Davis (1826–1910), the most influential philosopher of Spiritualism. Davis was a well-known medical clairvoyant—a person who claimed to be able to see and diagnose illness while in a mesmeric trance—until a visionary experience in 1844 launched his new career. Thenceforward he communed with departed spirits, delivered lectures while entranced, and developed his "Harmonial Philosophy," which informed the Spiritualist movement.[30]

Puységur's Science of the Soul

Important changes to Mesmer's theory, which underlie both nineteenth-century Spiritualism and modern hypnosis, were developed by Mesmer's French student Armand Marie Jacques de Chastenet, the Marquis de Puységur (1751–1825). He eventually abandoned his teacher's ideas about magnetic fluid and concluded that the controlling factor in the remarkable cures was the mesmerizer's will and his rapport with the subject. He also identified an altered state of consciousness in his subjects that he called "magnetic sleep" or "induced somnambulism." Puységur described this state as having five characteristics: it was neither ordinary sleep nor wakefulness but an intermediary condition; the subject had an intimate rapport with the "magnetizer"; the subject was extremely susceptible to suggestion; upon returning to normal waking consciousness the subject did not recall events that occurred during the "magnetic" state; and while "magnetized," the subject could display personality changes and remarkable abilities that were absent during normal wakefulness. Adam Crabtree, a historian of Mesmerism and hypnosis, finds, "These five characteristics of magnetic sleep, along with paranormal phenomena (mental communication and clairvoyance), turn up again and again in the literature of the next hundred years."[31] Although Puységur's approach was more psychological than spiritual, he nevertheless regarded the paranormal phenomena exhibited by "magnetic somnambules" as scientific evidence of the existence of the soul.[32]

Puységur's method was to induce a trance in a "sensitive" person—not everyone was equally susceptible. Contrary to the violent crises involved in Mesmer's cures, Puységur believed the calming effect of the trance effected healing.[33] He also observed that entranced persons seemed to be able to describe in detail places or things they had not seen, to perform acts of telepathy, to predict future events accurately, and to diagnose and prescribe treatments for others who were ill.[34]

Two later reports by the French Royal Academy's Medical Section, one issued in 1825, ten years after Puységur's death, and another in 1831, verified the apparently clairvoyant phenomena and the therapeutic benefits associated with trance.[35] Although contemporary knowledge and applications of hypnotherapy are much more sophisticated than these Royal Academy reports, they did encourage further research, which in turn fostered interest in Spiritualism, Mind Cure, and eventually, psychoanalysis.[36] Yet another Academy report in 1837 denied the mesmeric phenomena. A detailed discussion of subsequent controversies and efforts to verify or debunk the claims of Mesmerists (and later hypnotists) are beyond the scope of this book. The various theories about a pervasive magnetic fluid or universal ether, imagined as the medium by which one body affects another, were laid to rest early in the twentieth century by Einstein's theories of special and general relativity.[37]

Psychological theories deriving from Puységur's work fared much better over time. Today scholarly discussions of Mesmerism and hypnosis are most likely to be found in the literature of psychology, though some can be found in histories of medicine.[38] Alan Gauld's A History of Hypnotism traces theories and experimental observations from the time of Mesmer to 1991. Gauld is appropriately skeptical of most of the phenomena reported, but he also acknowledges that the causes of some continue to defy explanation. He points to a number of problems with theories claiming that hypnosis entails a distinctive "state" of consciousness. For example, the observed phenomena of heightened suggestibility, dissociation, amnesia, and state-dependent memories can be induced by a number of other factors, such as drugs, posttraumatic stress, delirium, meditation, shamanic ritual, and endogenous opioids.[39]

The early literature on Mesmerism documents many interesting medical applications, including numerous independently attested cases in which patients in a "mesmeric coma" received surgery painlessly, without any other form of anesthesia. The British physicians John Elliotson (1791–1868) and James Esdaile (1808–1859) performed many such surgeries on patients before the advent of chloroform and other chemical anesthetics. Many of their patients reportedly recovered more quickly and thoroughly than expected. Esdaile recorded hundreds of surgeries during his years operating a "mesmeric" hospital in the Bengal region of India, where he removed huge tumors and performed other major surgeries employing only "mesmeric coma."[40] Disinterested witnesses verified his results. In one case, he detailed a grisly procedure in which he excised a tumor that had invaded half a man's face, from eye to throat. Three days after the surgery he reported, "The dressings were undone to-day, and the whole extent of the wounds in his face has united completely. . . . He is out of all danger, and can speak plainly: he declares most positively, that he knew nothing that had been done to him till he awoke on the floor, and found me sewing up his cheek."[41] In other cases, Esdaile extracted teeth, amputated limbs, performed a mastectomy, and removed scrotal tumors weighing from eight to eighty pounds.

The Scottish doctor James Braid likewise verified the effects of induced trance, which he dubbed "hypnotic" influence or sleep to dissociate it from the antics of traveling showmen, who were then demonstrating Mesmerism to eager audiences throughout Europe and the United States.[42] Braid first witnessed the phenomenon during an 1841 demonstration by one such Parisian showman, Charles Lafontaine (1803–1888), who performed in Manchester as part of a tour of Britain.[43] Braid is the source of the popular image of a hypnotist dangling a bright object before the eyes of a subject to induce a hypnotic trance; this was his method.

Those who developed psychological explanations for "hysterical" (psychogenic) symptoms included Pierre Janet (1859–1947), who studied hypnotic amnesia and formulated an early theory of dissociation and double consciousness;[44] Frederick W. H. Myers (1843–1901), who cofounded the Society for Psychical Research and argued that a subliminal consciousness is present in both ill and healthy persons and occasionally breaks into ordinary consciousness; William James (1842–1910), who drew on Janet and Meyers in his discussions of the subconscious mind; and Sigmund Freud (1856–1939), who rejected Janet's notion of multiple consciousnesses. Freud argued instead for a hierarchically organized but unitary consciousness in which repression makes some mental processes unavailable to the ordinary waking mind.[45] All of these systems owe intellectual debts of one kind or another to Mesmer.

Mesmerism and Swedenborgianism Converge

In Europe and the United States, Mesmerism and Swedenborgianism converged at several points, and this convergence created fertile cultural soil for New Thought and subsequent mind-body healing movements. Not long after Swedenborg's death, the Exegetic and Philanthropic Society of Stockholm formed to disseminate Swedenborgian teachings and wrote to the Swedish King Gustavus III, urging him to support investigations into Mesmerism. The Swedenborgian society also corresponded with the French mesmeric healing Societié des Amis Réunis, which Puységur had founded.[46] Alfred J. Gabay has traced interactions in Europe (particularly in Strasbourg, Lyon, and Avignon) among Mesmerists, Swedenborgians, and others interested in occult traditions such as Kabbalah, Hermeticism, and Freemasonry. He notes that Puységur studied with Mesmer in Paris alongside a French philosopher interested in Swedenborg, J. C. de Saint-Martin, who "became a sort of metaphysical consultant to the Mesmerists, particularly Puységur." Saint-Martin "directly influenced Puységur's idea that magnetic somnambulism provides a direct link to the spirit world and that these phenomena are tantamount to proof for the spirituality of the soul."[47]

Mesmer's appeal to Swedenborgians, and vice versa, was this: the paranormal phenomena of trance that Puységur identified seemed to validate scientifically the spiritual encounters that Swedenborg described. George Bush (1769–1859), an American Swedenborgian minister and author of the book *Mesmer and Swedenborg*, put it thus: "*If Mesmerism is true, Swedenborg is true*, and if Swedenborg is true, the spiritual world is laid open, and a new and sublime era has dawned upon the earth."[48] In this same volume, Bush included an appendix endorsing Andrew Jackson Davis, who claimed direct inspiration from Swedenborg.[49]

Two of the most important philosophers of New Thought were Swedenborgian ministers: Warren Felt Evans and Horatio Dresser. Evans studied directly with Phineas Parkhurst Quimby (1802–1866), whose mental-healing practice is the basis of New Thought; Evans also wrote the earliest literature of New Thought, as well as a book about Swedenborg. Dresser, whose parents studied with Quimby, was a major leader, writer, and historian of the New Thought movement.[50] William James, one of Dresser's teachers at Harvard, referred favorably to Dresser's writing when describing "the religion of healthy-mindedness" in his 1902 Gifford Lectures, published later as *The Varieties of Religious Experience*.[51] James's father was a Swedenborgian who carried a trunk full of the seer's writings when he traveled.

Phineas Quimby: Father of Mind Cure

In a letter to the Swedenborgian translator, scholar, and cleric John Whitchcad, Quimby's son George remarked, "Father was at one time quite interested in Swedenborg's ideas."[52] The timing of Quimby's interest is unclear; he may have learned about Swedenborg from Evans. But Quimby's connections to Mesmerism are unambiguous. He partook of all three streams of thought deriving from Mesmer: fluidic, spiritual, and psychological, as illustrated in Figure 1.3. He thought of the mind as an ethereal substance or fluid; he employed a kind of clairvoyant trance in his healing practice; and he believed that erroneous ideas caused the mind to condense into diseased tissue.

According to an 1888 biography written by his son George,[53] Phineas Quimby was born on February 16, 1802, in Lebanon, New Hampshire. His family moved to Belfast, Maine, when Phineas was two, and he grew up there with six siblings. Phineas received little formal education but was trained as a clockmaker. Later he also made daguerreotype portraits and patented several (unspecified) inventions. George

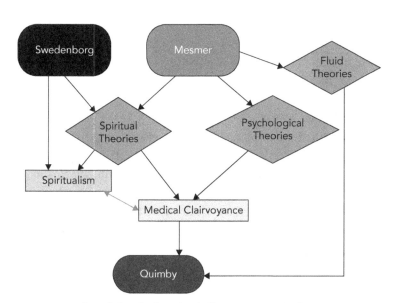

FIG. 1.3 Mesmeric and Swedenborgian influences on Quimby.

characterizes his father as an argumentative fellow interested in mechanics, philosophy, and science, and unwilling to accept ideas that could not be proved by demonstration.

At age twenty-eight Phineas was suffering from what doctors told him were diseased kidneys, lungs, and liver. The calomel (mercuric chloride) they prescribed slowly poisoned him until he was so weak he could barely function. A friend told Quimby he had cured himself of a serious illness by means of a brisk horseback ride. Quimby was too weak for that, but he set out one day in a carriage. The uncooperative horse exhausted Quimby and the carriage stopped, still far from home. With the help of a nearby farmer, Quimby finally got the horse moving again. Exactly what happened next is unclear, but he urged the horse to go as fast as possible, and by the time Quimby reached home he felt well again. Writing about the incident years later, he said he believed his own mental excitement transformed his physical condition.

Less than a decade later, Charles Poyen (d. 1844) and Robert Collyer (n.d.) were demonstrating "magnetic healing" in lecture halls throughout the northeastern United States. Poyen, a Frenchman, was the first to introduce magnetic somnambulism and clairvoyance to American audiences, during an 1838 tour. He had studied Mesmerism in the tradition of Puységur while he was a medical student in Paris.[54] Collyer, an English student of Elliotson, began touring in the United States in 1839, the year Poyen returned to France.[55] Interest in the subject was spurred by publication in the United States of several treatises on magnetism (pro and con).

Demonstrations of magnetic "sleep" and clairvoyant phenomena were popular on the New England lecture circuit, among both the credulous and the skeptical. One such skeptic was Quimby, who attended one of Poyen's lecture-demonstrations. He later wrote that the Frenchman "did not appear to be highly blest with the powers of magnetizing to the satisfaction of his audiences in his public lectures. I had the pleasure of listening to one of his lectures and pronounced it a humbug as a matter of course. . . . [I] considered all stories bordering on the marvelous as delusive."[56] It is not clear whether Quimby actually saw Collyer perform as well, but he wrote that the Englishman "perhaps did more to excite a spirit of enquiry throughout the community than any who have succeeded him. But the community were still incredulous and the general eccentricity of his character no doubt contributed much to prejudice the minds of his audience against his science."[57]

Quimby's own writings make it clear that he read widely about magnetism and was familiar with the theories of both La Roy Sunderland (1802–1885) and John Bovee Dods (1795–1872). Both Sunderland and Dods linked Mesmerism to phrenology, which purported to explain how physiological differences such as cranial bumps corresponded to particular personality traits. Sunderland founded a serial called *The Magnet*, but renamed magnetic sleep "pathetism" to de-emphasize fluidic theories and stress the subject's emotional rapport with the mesmerizer. Dods called it "electrical psychology." Both believed that some mesmeric subjects could commune with the dead and eventually joined the Spiritualist movement, which Quimby also explored but ultimately rejected.

By 1840, two years after Poyen's tour, Quimby was practicing Mesmerism. From 1843 to 1847 he worked with a "sensitive" named Lucius Burkmar. Quimby believed that Burkmar, a medical clairvoyant, had finally cured him of the last vestiges of kidney and liver disease. They toured together throughout Maine and New Brunswick. Burkmar's journal records incidents in which he diagnosed illness and prescribed cures for ailing audience members and demonstrated other clairvoyant and telepathic abilities.[58] Letters of introduction included in Quimby's collected writings affirm that the mesmerized Burkmar could describe "remote places and objects and even the appearances of persons at great distances, which he never before could have heard or thought of."[59] One letter says of roughly a dozen experiments, "In four or five cases he failed entirely. In some others he was partially successful. [Three or four] times he came quite up to the mark, and performed feats where there was no room for deception or mistake."[60]

Regarding his curative abilities, Quimby and others at first believed that Burkmar could discern a patient's internal condition, and thus determine appropriate treatment. Gradually, however, Quimby came to believe that Burkmar was simply reading the beliefs of people present and that his cures worked because people had faith in them.[61] Quimby gave up working with Burkmar and began treating patients directly. He moved to Portland, Maine, in 1859 and saw thousands of patients in his office there until shortly before his death in 1866.

Quimby concluded that illness is real, but that it results from an error of the mind. He opined that doctors were a major cause of illness because they convinced people of the reality of disease. Quimby's writings are unsystematic and tend to ramble, but it is clear that he distinguished between "Wisdom" and "belief" or "opinion." He regarded Wisdom as knowledge of true spiritual reality, in which disease and death are nonexistent. Belief or opinion is our ordinary state of mind, and it creates the reality we perceive most of the time. Quimby's theory of mind, a variant of Mesmer's theory about magnetic fluid, was that mind is an ethereal form of matter, which exists in different stages of development. Mind is related to—but not completely dependent upon—the body, and erroneous beliefs can condense the ethereal substance into diseased tissues, such as tumors. Cure was a matter of correcting wrong beliefs.

Quimby would sit near his patients and take their hands in his. Then he would enter a clairvoyant state in which he retained consciousness of his own body and mind but also could enter the patient's consciousness. He would determine the faulty beliefs causing the patient's symptoms and describe them aloud. He corrected the error by impressing upon the patient Wisdom about his or her true, healthful condition. If the patient affirmed that Quimby's diagnosis was correct, then Quimby's "explanation [was] the cure; and if he succeed[ed] in correcting their error, he change[d] the fluids of the system and establishe[d] the truth, or health."[62]

Quimby likened the "impressions" made on the mind, either by erroneous beliefs or by Wisdom, to the impressions that daguerreotypes made on metal plates. In a dreaming or mesmeric state, he said, the mind "becomes far more susceptible of impressions than before." In retrospect it seems probable that Quimby hypnotized his patients and helped them to experience fewer symptoms through posthypnotic suggestion.

Although he referred in his writings to biblical texts, Quimby was not religious and did not call himself a Christian. He was fiercely critical of clergy and hypocrites. He doubted "that Jesus was the author of the Christian religion or had anything to do with it. . . . I believe it is a stain on the character of the man, Jesus."[63] Quimby believed Jesus was a fully human being who discovered the healing power of Wisdom, which some called "Christ" but which also could be understood as "the Science of health and happiness." According to one of the compilers of his collected writings, Quimby believed "people confused the man Jesus with the science which he taught and called him 'Jesus Christ.' Just as we might associate the man Franklin with his discovery and call him 'Franklin Electricity.' "[64] In a document titled "Questions and Answers," Quimby argued that after the human Jesus was crucified, it was the nonmaterial Christ who appeared to the disciples as resurrected. "Christ was that Wisdom that knew matter was only an idea that could be formed into any shape," so the "resurrected" Christ took the shape

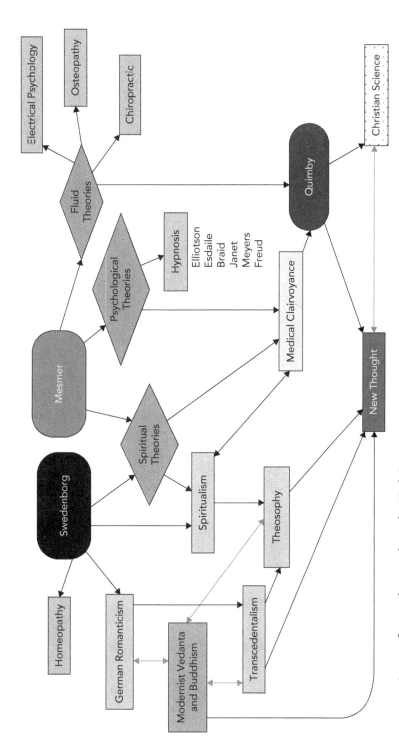

FIG. 1.4 A map of antecedents to the early Mind Cure movement.

of the human Jesus.[65] Theoretically any person could develop Wisdom and heal the sick in the same way that Christ healed through the person of Jesus.

Quimby regarded God as "the name of that essence that flows from wisdom."[66] Like Deists, Quimby believed that God left humans to their own affairs. The deity did not listen to prayers or intervene in people's lives. God probably was the author of the natural laws that governed the workings of both mind and matter, which could be determined scientifically, through experimentation. In these ideas, Quimby was an heir to the scientific assumptions of Isaac Newton and Francis Bacon. In some of his writings, Quimby seemed to equate God, Wisdom, and Science, though his use of terminology was not always consistent or clear. He denied that God punishes people for sin; our own feelings of guilt and the negative consequences of our misdeeds are our punishments. In many of his patients, he believed, destructive and erroneous religious beliefs lay at the heart of their illnesses. He referred to the Bible selectively, insofar as it aided his therapeutic technique.

Quimby was also clearly familiar with Spiritualism, attended séances, and regarded himself as a kind of clairvoyant, but he denied the assertion of Spiritualist mediums that they conferred with the souls of the dead. Although people may have perceived phenomena such as rapping when consulting mediums, he argued, these perceptions were the products of erroneous belief. "I have no belief in regard to religion of any kind, neither have I any belief in another world of any kind. I have no belief in what is called death," he wrote.[67] The "real" world is that of Wisdom, and "matter" consists of more or less dense or refined forms of mind.

None of Quimby's writings was published during his lifetime. His ideas were spread first by his early tours, by word of mouth, by newspaper accounts, and by ephemera such as circulars designed to attract new clients. An edited anthology of Quimby's writings appeared in 1921, but a complete collection was not available until 1988. As Figure 1.4 indicates, Quimby's students were far more successful in spreading his ideas beyond New England.

2

Individualist and Community-Oriented Mind Cure

PHINEAS QUIMBY'S TEACHINGS provided the basis for the two earliest and most significant religious movements to promote mind-body healing in the United States: Christian Science and New Thought. They have common features, but also differ in important ways. Christian Science is much more tightly structured and is centered squarely on the teachings of its founder, Mary Baker Eddy. New Thought has many spokespersons and is quite eclectic, drawing from multiple religious sources, including Christianity, Judaism, Transcendentalism, Western esotericism (particularly Theosophy), Buddhism, and Hindu neo-Vedanta. Although my focus here is primarily on New Thought, for convenience I will sometimes refer to it and Christian Science collectively as the early Mind Cure movement. Mind Cure is an important and vastly underappreciated precursor to the modern Mindfulness boom.

To understand early Mind Cure—as well as contemporary efforts to promote meditation in medicine—it is essential to notice the ways that race and gender shaped the movement and subsequent religious and medical developments. Although the histories of women and African Americans are frequently treated as separate subtopics or subdisciplines within the fields of religious and medical history, they are in fact integral. Inattention to them creates a distorted view of both past and present.

In medicine, women were largely excluded from professional practice until recent decades, and although women physicians have made significant inroads since the 1980s, the field is still overwhelmingly male-dominated. Women have always served informally as caregivers, nurses, midwives, and herbalists. The same is true in religious ministry.

Ann Braude has shown how women, while often excluded from visible positions of leadership, have consistently composed the majority of religious practitioners in the United States. They have filled pews, participated in rituals, funded institutions and schools, and provided religious instruction to children. "Indeed, the numerical dominance of women in all but a few religious groups constitutes one of the most consistent features of American religion, and one of the least explained." This has been true regardless of denomination, geographic region, or race. In short, Braude declares, "Women's history *is* American religious history."[1]

In the Mind Cure movement, women served as ministers, counselors, and healers, founded seminaries, built churches, published books and magazines, and led national and international organizations. In the movement's New Thought wing, women leaders promoted meditation and supported Buddhist and Hindu missionaries who proffered modernist versions of their religions across the United States and Europe. At the turn of the twentieth century, their success prompted white men with elite medical and religious credentials to appropriate the most effective Mind Cure methods and channel them into fields they controlled: "scientific" psychology, mainstream medicine, and mainline Protestant ministry.

Racism too has decisively shaped the histories of medicine and religion in the United States. The rise of specifically African American religious organizations, both Christian and non-Christian, is inseparable from the history of slavery. In American medical history black people, both enslaved and free, were repeatedly subjected to unethical medical research by white, male doctors. For example, J. Marion Simms (1813–1883), the so-called father of modern gynecology, performed multiple surgeries on enslaved women without consent or anesthesia. In the Tuskegee Syphilis Study, conducted by the United States Public Health Service from 1932 to 1972, white doctors observed hundreds of black men as they suffered and died needlessly, without informing patients about their disease or offering penicillin when it was found to be an effective treatment. On average, members of racial minorities continue to have poorer overall health and less access to medical care than white people. These disparities are the long-term results of slavery, segregation, and discriminatory policies that have offered unequal access to education, housing, credit, and other benefits. These are not peripheral or marginal issues in American history; they are front and center. It is imperative that white scholars see and address them as such.

The modern histories of Buddhism and Hinduism are likewise inseparable from the history of colonialism. The academic discipline of the history of religions has been shaped by conquest and the power of conquerors
to define "others."[2] At the same time, oppressed groups also have been
agents in using elements of dominant culture strategically for their own
ends and defining themselves over and against dominant groups.

This chapter focuses on gendered and racial dynamics in the early history of Mind Cure. It begins with brief sketches of the movement's early
leaders, all of whom were white and many of whom were women. From
the New Thought wing of Mind Cure, two streams emerged: one oriented
toward individual success, well-being, and prosperity, and one centered
in religious communities, whose leaders and members were frequently
active in efforts to promote social, political, and legal changes benefiting
women, children, and black men. Several African American religious
movements were inspired by New Thought, including the Peace Mission
Movement of Father Divine and the black nationalist groups Moorish
Science, the Nation of Islam, and Black Hebrew Israelism.

Mary Baker Eddy and Her Critics

Although Mary Baker Eddy (1821–1910) is the most famous of Quimby's
students, she later repudiated him and claimed divine revelation as the
source of her Christian Science teachings. She first consulted Quimby in
1862 in Portland, Maine, for long-standing ailments that rendered her an
invalid. In 1863 and 1864 she also received "absent treatments," in which
she believed Quimby healed her from a distance. She spent many hours
deep in conversation with him and studied copies of his handwritten
manuscripts and the transcriptions of dictation he gave to secretaries.
Eddy attributed her recovery to Quimby and lectured on his methods of
healing for several years. After his death in 1866, she penned a flowery
poem in tribute: "Dr. P. P. Quimby, Who Healed with the Truth that Christ
Taught, in Contradistinction to All Isms."[3]

Three weeks after Quimby's death, Eddy suffered a debilitating fall
and appealed for help to Julius Dresser (1838–1893), another of Quimby's
students. Dresser had consulted Quimby during college in Maine and met
his future wife, Annetta (1843–1935), at Quimby's office. He did not feel
able to take up Quimby's mantle, however, and moved his family west. In
1882, as Eddy's fame and fortune grew, the Dressers returned to Boston
and launched a competing healing practice. Their son Horatio (1866–1964)

studied philosophy at Harvard with William James, who wrote about the Mind Cure movement in *The Varieties of Religious Experience*, calling it "the religion of healthy-mindedness." Horatio earned his PhD in 1907 and went on to produce more than a dozen books, including a handbook of New Thought methods, an anthology of addresses by New Thought leaders, and *The History of the New Thought Movement*, which has shaped most subsequent histories.[4]

After being rebuffed by Julius Dresser, Eddy began a spiritual search and intensive study of the Bible, which led to the divine revelation she claimed as the basis for her religious healing system. The first edition of the primary text for her movement, *Science and Health with Key to the Scriptures*, was published in 1875. In an echo of Swedenborg's *Arcana Coelestia* and *Apocalypse Revealed*, Eddy's "Key to the Scriptures" provides her exegeses of Genesis and Revelation. Eddy had been steeped in Puritan religiosity, though she rejected such Calvinist doctrines as predestination, election, and damnation. She differed from Quimby in that she believed matter is fundamentally unreal. Only the Divine Principle is real, she asserted. To be lifted out of erroneous belief in matter (and thus in disease), one must first undergo a process of repentance and purification, an approach consistent with her Calvinist upbringing.[5] However, healing is not simply a matter of changing one's own beliefs—ultimately it requires intervention and revelation from God, Eddy believed. She also claimed that one could be harmed by others' fears and negative thoughts, a phenomenon she called "Malicious Animal Magnetism."

Eddy "promoted salvific self-denial," and her "theology was in keeping with the social-purity wing of the late-nineteenth-century woman movement," Beryl Satter has argued.[6] Although Eddy was clearly influenced by Quimby and some of her ideas are similar to his, she claimed that divine revelation finally cured her and formed the basis for the distinctive religious movement she developed and led. Later she distanced herself completely from Quimby, calling him an ignorant Mesmerist.

Eddy was the subject of much controversy. The Dressers accused her of plagiarizing Quimby's ideas and fought a long public battle with her through newspapers, books, and the courts.[7] A vicious 1905 article in the *New York Times* repeats their assertions and shows parallels between the text of a Quimby manuscript copied by one of his patients and text in Eddy's *Science and Health*. The *Times* article calls Eddy a "dictator" whose "money-making science" derived from Quimby rather than divine revelation.[8] In

1907 Mark Twain wrote a scathing, sarcastic attack on Eddy's personality and theology.[9]

Because of such controversies, Quimby's son George refused to allow his father's writings to be published during George's lifetime. Eddy offered to publish them herself, provided that she be allowed to examine them first. George declined. In 1921, after George's death, Horatio Dresser published an edited volume of Phineas's writings, called *The Quimby Manuscripts*. It is not always clear, however, when he quotes directly from Quimby and when he has edited or annotated the material.[10] The younger Dresser was also critical of some later varieties of New Thought, which he regarded as shallow and self-serving. Like his mother and like Warren Felt Evans, discussed below, Horatio argued that one should strive toward purity and that happiness could be found "not in self-love and self-glory, but in loving service to others."[11] We will return to him in the following chapter.

New Thought Emerges

Although Eddy was Quimby's most famous and controversial student by far, Warren Felt Evans (1817–1889) was the most important early theorist for what would become the New Thought movement. Evans was a Methodist minister turned Swedenborgian; he first met Quimby in 1863, the year after Eddy's first visit. But he began producing books on Mind Cure several years before Eddy published *Science and Health*. He wrote seven books, six of which deal with the relationship between mental states and health. His first, *The New Age and Its Messenger*, published in 1864, deals primarily with Swedenborg.[12] His second book, *The Mental Cure* (1869), appeared three years after Quimby's death and does not mention him. It was widely read and translated into several languages. *Mental Medicine*, published in 1873, calls Quimby "one of the most successful healers of this or any age." Quimby theorized that disease was caused by wrong belief, Evans wrote, "and by a long succession of most remarkable cures . . . proved the truth of the theory and the efficiency of that mode of treatment."[13]

Evans drew heavily upon Swedenborgian theology and was more explicitly Christian in his theory of mental cure than Quimby, but he also read widely and eclectically, and in some cases he seems close to Hindu monism. After *The Mental Cure* and *Mental Medicine*, he published four more books dealing with Mind Cure: *Soul and Body* (1875), *The Divine Law of Cure* (1881), *The Primitive Mind Cure* (1885), and *Esoteric Christianity and*

Mental Therapeutics (1886). He spent more than twenty years practicing and teaching mental healing in New Hampshire and the Boston area. Evans was the first to advocate the use of "affirmations": positive statements about the results one wants (or expects) to achieve.[14] Ann Taves argues, "Reading Quimby, Eddy, and Evans alongside one another, it is hard not to view Eddy and Evans as sibling rivals descended from the same parent. Where Eddy ultimately rejected the mesmeric tradition as a malicious inversion of Christian Science, Evans viewed the 'influence or action of mind upon mind' as the foundation of religious healing."[15] In this respect, Evans clearly belongs in the lineage of Mesmer's student Puységur, who believed that clairvoyant trance was produced by the mesmerizer's will affecting the mesmerized person, and not attributable to changes in subtle "fluid" or matter.

Over the long term, however, the most influential New Thought figure was Emma Curtis Hopkins (1849–1925), a protégée of Eddy who established her own seminary to teach Mind Cure methods and ordained the women and men who founded the most enduring New Thought churches. From 1884 to 1885 Hopkins edited the *Christian Science Journal* but was fired from that job and expelled from Eddy's church after a disagreement with the founder. Hopkins moved to Chicago and began a spectacularly successful career as a teacher, drawing on ideas from both Evans and Eddy. By the end of 1887, 600 students had taken her classes in Chicago, 250 in San Francisco, and unknown numbers of others in New York and Milwaukee. In 1888 she turned her Chicago school into a seminary, and within five years 350 students had completed the basic course and 111 had completed further training and received ordination as ministers.[16] At least seventeen branches of the Metaphysical Association she founded operated around the country.[17]

> Hopkins became known as the "teacher of teachers," and virtually all early New Thought leaders were Hopkins's students. These include Charles and Myrtle Fillmore (cofounders of Unity); Kate Bingham, the teacher of Nona Brooks (a founder of Divine Science); Malinda Cramer (a founder of Divine Science); Fannie Brooks James (a founder of Divine Science); Annie Rix Militz (founder of Homes of Truth); Frances Lord (who established New Thought in England); H. Emilie Cady (author of *Lessons in Truth*); Ella Wheeler Wilcox (New Thought poet with wide cultural acceptance); and Elizabeth Towne (publisher of the influential periodical *Nautilus* [1898–1954]).

Near the end of her life, Hopkins tutored Ernest S. Holmes, founder of the Church of Religious Science.[18]

One of Hopkins's most prominent disciples was Malinda Cramer (1845–1906). In 1885, after twenty-five years of invalidism from an unspecified disorder, Cramer experienced profound healing from an experience of the omnipresence of the divine during a period of prayer and meditation.[19] She consulted Hopkins to better understand her experience and took a course with her in San Francisco. Cramer was among the first group ordained by Hopkins as a Christian Science minister. In 1888 Cramer cofounded Divine Science with Nona Brooks and her sisters, who lived in Colorado. That year Cramer established the Divine Science Home School in San Francisco and began publishing *Harmony* magazine, one of the earliest and most influential New Thought serials. The school and its library were destroyed in the Great Earthquake of 1906 and subsequent fire in San Francisco; Cramer herself died of injuries sustained in that event.[20]

Nona Brooks (1861–1945) was born in Kentucky and moved with her family to Pueblo, Colorado. She had long suffered a throat ailment deemed incurable. Her elder sister Alethea married Charles Small, who established a real estate firm in Pueblo with Charles Fillmore, who moved to Kansas City, Missouri, in 1884. Fillmore and his wife, Myrtle, studied New Thought there: Myrtle recovered from tuberculosis, and Charles was cured of injuries related to a childhood ice-skating accident in which he had broken a hip. They founded the Society of Silent Unity in 1892.[21] One of Alethea's friends, Kate Bingham, also suffered from an intractable but unspecified illness and sought treatment from specialists in Chicago. Told it would take a year to heal her, she decided instead to take a three-week course with Hopkins and was cured. Bingham subsequently offered courses in Pueblo and taught the Brooks sisters what she had learned. Nona was healed as well.

Fannie Brooks James, another sister, corresponded with Malinda Cramer, who eventually taught a course in Denver that the Brooks sisters attended. Cramer ordained Nona as a minister in 1898, and the First Divine Science Church of Denver was incorporated the following year. Brooks traveled and taught throughout the United States, the United Kingdom, and Australia. Within two decades there were nine Divine Science churches, mostly in the West, and by 1925 there were ten more. Today the Divine Science Federation International lists fourteen churches worldwide.[22]

Hopkins ordained Charles and Myrtle Fillmore in 1906, as well as Ernest Holmes, who founded Religious Science in Los Angeles in 1927. Unity, Divine Science, and Religious Science (now the Centers for Spiritual Living) are among the largest New Thought denominations to have survived in the United States to the present day.

Sarah Farmer and the Greenacre Conferences

Sarah Farmer (1847–1916) hosted many early meetings between New Thought leaders and Asian teachers of meditation and yoga. She was the daughter of the philanthropist Hannah Tobey Shapleigh Farmer (d. 1891) and Moses Farmer (d. 1893), an inventor who developed a number of electrical devices, including an electric trolley, an incandescent lamp, and an electric fire alarm.[23] The Farmers were also staunch abolitionists—their New Hampshire home was a stop on the Underground Railroad—and they had strong Transcendentalist leanings. Sarah was exposed early and often to various systems of religious thought; her father particularly admired the Puritan preacher Jonathan Edwards and Ralph Waldo Emerson. Hannah explored Swedenborgianism, Mesmerism, and Spiritualism. A devoted uncle, the journalist Charles Carleton Coffin, traveled in India, Malaysia, China, and Japan (during the Meiji Restoration) and shared what he had learned of Asian culture during his extended stays at the Farmers' home.[24]

Sarah worked closely with her father and traveled with him to Chicago in 1893 to help prepare a display of his inventions at the Columbian Exposition. Moses, debilitated by a neuromuscular disease, died of pneumonia a few months before the event opened, however, and Sarah, whose health had been frail since childhood, suffered a collapse after his death. Her friend Sarah Bull, who was to become a devotee and major financial supporter of Swami Vivekenanda, founder of the Vedanta Society, persuaded Farmer to accompany her on a trip to Norway to restore her strength. Farmer returned to Chicago just after the close of the World's Parliament of Religions, held alongside the Columbian Exposition. She was inspired by conversations with the Parliament's organizers to arrange a continuation of its work during summers in Eliot, Maine, the site of her family home. Farmer owned a resort hotel in Eliot, Green-Acre-on-the-Piscataqua (later Greenacre), with three other investors. She launched her mini-parliament there during the summer of 1894.

The Greenacre conferences were held annually until 1915, though they were in decline after 1907, when Farmer suffered a serious fall that left her an invalid. The Monsalvat School for the Comparative Study of Religion, which operated alongside the Greenacre conferences from 1896 to 1906, provided more structured and academic opportunities to study religious traditions in greater depth. Among the traditions covered were Swedenborgianism, Quakerism, Judaism, Islam, Zoroastrianism, Jainism, Hinduism, Buddhism, and Bahá'í. Monsalvat teachers also lectured at the regular Greenacre events, which were oriented toward more general audiences.

During the ten-week summer seasons at Greenacre, guests could enjoy lectures on a wide variety of topics. In 1906 Franklin Sanborn described Greenacre as a place where "exponents of Buddhism and Brahmanism . . . come in contact with western thought, with the Concord School of Philosophy, with Christian Science, mind cure, latter day temperance teachings and sociology."[25] Transcendentalism was a consistent theme, with regular lectures on Emerson, occasional talks on Margaret Fuller, Henry David Thoreau, and other writers, and annual reunions for alumni of the Concord School of Philosophy. Other topics included European philosophies, socialism, women's suffrage, diet, hygiene, child-rearing, psychology, education, evolution, ornithology, art, and international peace. Musical performances were a regular part of the programs. Guests stayed at the Greenacre Inn or camped in tents nearby. Lectures and performances took place in a large tent on the hotel grounds and, from 1897 onward, in a lecture hall built for that purpose. In fair weather, many events took place outside under the pine trees.[26]

During the off-seasons, Farmer traveled extensively across the country, seeking speakers and raising funds, which she reportedly did with considerable charm. She wanted Greenacre programs to be offered free of charge—though donations were accepted. (Monsalvat charged a dollar or two to attend its courses.) Speakers received no honoraria, but free room and board, sometimes along with their families, in the Greenacre hotel. They frequently spent weeks, if not the entire season, in Eliot. Although Farmer had several wealthy backers, including Sarah Bull and Phoebe Apperson Hearst, mother of the newspaper magnate William Randolph Hearst, this policy eventually depleted her resources, caused conflicts with her co-investors and more business-minded collaborators, and nearly bankrupted the whole project.

After her debilitating fall in 1907, Farmer became less and less active at Greenacre. Her health had always been frail; she tended to drive herself to exhaustion; and she seems to have suffered occasionally from severe bouts of mania and depression (possibly what is today called Bipolar Disorder).[27] In 1910 she was confined for several months to a sanitarium because of mental illness. Ongoing battles over finances and the direction of the Greenacre conferences exacerbated the difficulty.

Farmer became increasingly devoted to the Bahá'í movement after a 1900 visit to its leader, 'Abdu'l Bahá (1844–1921), in the prison-city of Akká, Palestine (now Acre, Israel), where he was imprisoned by Ottoman and Persian authorities. Farmer saw Bahá'í as the means by which different religious traditions could achieve unity. Hers was not a strictly orthodox view; while Bahá'í explicitly values other religious traditions as sources of truth, it also asserts that the revelation of its founder, Bahá'u'lláh (1817–1892), supersedes earlier traditions. Nevertheless Farmer's increasing emphasis on Bahá'í at Greenacre was still too partisan for those who wanted the conferences to remain eclectic. Franklin Sanborn and Horatio Dresser were among the leaders of this group.[28] Eventually Bahá'í supporters prevailed. After Farmer's death in 1916, the property passed into the hands of the Bahá'í movement, which continues to operate Greenacre as a school.[29] Although Greenacre was a major zone of contact among New Thought, Vedanta, and Buddhism, and meditation was regularly taught and practiced there, scholars have paid almost no attention to these contacts. Chapter 3 discusses them in detail.

New Thought: Community-Oriented, Individualist, and Prosperity

The Mind Cure movement begun by Evans, Eddy, the Dresser family, Farmer, and Hopkins and her successors diverged into multiple streams and flowed in many directions. According to Gary Ward Materra, a historian of early New Thought, Horatio Dresser and Hopkins represent opposite poles of a spectrum. He calls the poles "affective" and "noetic."[30] By "affective," he means the forms of New Thought in which people established local congregations, focused on concerns of family and community, and supported various philanthropic and social-reform programs, such as women's suffrage, temperance, economic justice and labor reform, sexual freedom and marriage reform, and social services for children and impoverished adults. Hopkins, Helen Willmans, Louisa Southworth, and Elizabeth Boynton Harbert were all active suffragists.[31] A number of prominent New Thought leaders, Materra notes, were socialists. The

organizations and publications that Materra groups in the affective category were overwhelmingly led and staffed by women, and they tended to
hold meetings during weekdays, when most men worked.

By "noetic," Materra means the forms of New Thought that stressed
individual mastery, business success, and prosperity. In the early twentieth century, these spread not so much through congregational development as through books, lecture tours, and journals. When group meetings
occurred, they tended to be scheduled at night. This side of the early New
Thought movement appealed primarily to men, though some women did
represent the noetic style, and some men the affective. Most historians of
New Thought have been white, male academics and have tended to focus
on elite, white, male authors as their sources, which has created the impression that New Thought has been, and continues to be, primarily individualist and prosperity-oriented.

Materra's study is a crucial contribution to the history of New Thought,
and extremely sympathetic to the perspectives and concerns of women,
but the terms "affective" and "noetic," as he uses them, tend to reinforce
gendered stereotypes that characterize men as intellectual and women as
emotional. This dichotomy was central to Victorian-era thinking about
gender, so Materra has a valid historical reason for employing these terms.
But such stereotypes have too often been employed to the detriment of
women. The terms "community-oriented" and "individualistic" capture
the distinction without creating this problem, so I use them here.

Yet the categories are slippery. By "community-oriented," I mean primarily the New Thought churches and denominations that emerged
between the mid-1880s and the Stock Market Crash of 1929—a period
when women had much less access to professional careers and public
life than men did—and to certain African American religious movements
that emerged during the 1920s and 1930s. The community-oriented New
Thought churches, denominations, and related organizations founded by
middle-class white women tended to focus on such women's concerns.
They produced numerous publications for women and children, devoted
columns to these groups in magazines designed for general audiences,
and tended to stress love as their primary value. Groups founded by
African American men focused on the needs of black communities, who
endured the indignities of Jim Crow and the terrorism of cross-burnings
and lynching.

Eddy's Christian Science was community-oriented in the sense that it
established local congregations and built spectacular churches for them,

but it was not particularly involved in social reform. Its solution to social problems is to help people realize that we are

> the spiritual idea or reflection of the divine Mind, and not a materially conceived creature representing the fluctuating and uncertain unit of an arbitrarily constituted social system. On this foundation alone can harmonious relations be maintained among men, and an orderly state of society realized, unfettered by the hampering conditions of mortal perversity and short-sightedness.
>
> While, therefore, fully persuaded that mankind can be saved only through the spiritualization of human consciousness, Christian Scientists recognize the desirability, in the present transitional stage of experience, of encouraging, in legitimate and judicious ways, as far as may be compatible with their main endeavor, reformatory movements and measures which make for an improved order of human ideals and conditions; since each step in the progress of mortal consciousness from lower to higher levels, whereby human customs and institutions are made to manifest more of Soul and less of sense, tends to prepare the way for the more definite and general recognition and demonstration of divine Science.[32]

That is hardly a clarion call to activism for social justice.

The community-oriented wing of New Thought is typified by Hopkins and her students. Like Eddy, they founded religious congregations and regarded their work as ministry rather than as a secular "science" of happiness and prosperity. They tended to use Christian language and to engage in Bible study. Unlike Eddy, they "emphasized the unity of all things, with a corresponding involvement in community needs and interest in relational ethics."[33] Community-oriented New Thought leaders talked often and at length about the effects of sin and evil in society.

The individualist wing of New Thought regarded the movement more as a science than as a religion, spoke of practicing "suggestion" rather than "prayer," and seldom discussed issues such as sin, evil, or social reform. "The noetic style emphasized the law of attraction and techniques for attaining prosperity and various kinds of business and personal success. It lent itself to a structure dominated by lectures and self-help books. While healing was a common theme in both styles of New Thought, in the noetic style it was sometimes obscured by emphasis on motivational or other issues."[34] After World War II, a third, hybrid type emerged: the Prosperity Gospel, which blends New Thought with Evangelical or Pentecostal Christianity. Charismatic preachers of the Prosperity Gospel build congregations, megachurches, and networks of churches. These tend to stress individual empowerment and wealth, not social reforms to address political, legal, economic, or medical inequalities related to gender and race. Major white Prosperity preachers include Oral Roberts, Kenneth Copeland, Kenneth Hagin, Benny Hinn, Fred Price, Joel Osteen, and Joyce Meyers. Prominent African American purveyors of the Prosperity Gospel include Sweet Daddy Grace's United House of Prayer for All People, Rev. Johnnie Colemon's Universal Foundation for Better Living, Rev. Ike's United Church and Science of Living Institute, Creflo Dollar Ministries, and T. D. Jakes's Potter's House Church. Although these Prosperity churches are *congregation*-based, theologically they are closer to the style of New Thought that Materra calls "noetic" and I call "individualist." Colemon's church will serve as a brief example. Although it is far from the largest—that distinction likely belongs to Joel and Victoria Osteen's church—it emerged directly from a major New Thought denomination.[35]

Ordained as a Unity minister in 1956, Colemon founded Christ Universal Temple, the first predominantly black Unity congregation in the United States, in Chicago that year. She also served as the first black president of the Association of Unity Churches. Colemon reportedly broke with Unity during the early 1970s because of ongoing racism.[36] In 1974 she founded the Universal Foundation for Better Living, and today its network includes fifteen churches, seven study groups, seven "satellite" organizations, and one discussion group, scattered across the United States, Canada, the Caribbean, and South America.[37]

Christ Universal Temple occupies a hundred-acre campus; the church can seat three thousand people and is served by a team of eighteen ministers. According to its statement of beliefs, "It is God's will that every individual on the face of this earth should live a healthy, happy and prosperous life." The church declares that "such a life is within the reach of each one of us and the way to its attainment begins with the realization that the Kingdom of God is within us, waiting for us to bring it into expression." Jesus is the "Way-Shower" on this journey. "The key to happy and successful living is right thinking followed by right action," and "the basis for right thinking is LOVE—love of God and all that is good in ourselves and others." The church offers fellowship groups for different constituencies within the congregation, Toastmasters clubs, and a group devoted to

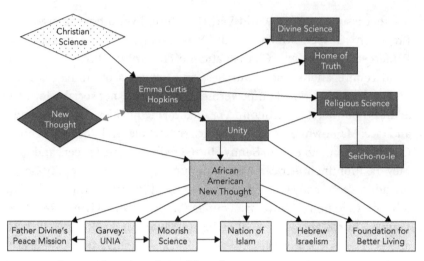

FIG. 2.1 Community-oriented New Thought.

meditation. Its ministries focus primarily on the needs of the church and its members, though one group provides literature, flowers, cards, and gifts to residents of local nursing and group homes. The church website betrays no interest in social-justice issues or advocacy. Among Colemon's achievements, it lists the construction of "a luxury banquet hall and restaurant in service to a community that, previously, had little access to a high end dining experience."[38] Its statement of beliefs says, "Rather than devoting our primary efforts to providing for the needy of the world, the time has come to make available to all people everywhere a teaching that will enable them to provide for themselves by learning to release the divine potential within them."[39] That is the church's mission.

More detailed consideration of the Prosperity Gospel is beyond the scope of this study; for a history of that movement, see *Blessed* by Kate Bowler.[40] When I refer to early, community-oriented New Thought, I mean predominantly black and white groups that were or are both centered in congregations and socially engaged. Figure 2.1 shows the variety of groups included in this category.

Gender and New Thought

The basic New Thought message that one can develop mastery over one's circumstances by changing one's mental habits sounded very different to women than to men, Materra observes. Women at the time could not vote; they had relatively few legal rights; and their social standing was based on their roles as wives and mothers. Middle-class white women were largely confined to the "domestic sphere." So "for the businessman, New Thought was like a cosmic pep talk; for the housewife, especially one who was regularly ill, it was potentially life-changing."[41] The Mind Cure movement gave women opportunities to exercise leadership, to work as healers, and to serve as clergy, at a time when medical schools would not admit them and other churches would not ordain them. To white men,

> New Thought meant something more philosophical than existential, since by and large, they did not find themselves in need of liberation beyond the level of the interior self. For them, to eliminate barriers to success meant to expand personal awareness of inherent possibilities. This dovetailed nicely with the general social support for [white] male leadership. For women, the same awareness of inherent possibilities was not a bolstering of cultural messages. Rather it became the leveraging tool to crack open entire ideological structures for themselves and others whose sense of personal limitation was bound up with a broader pattern of social restriction.[42]

During Jim Crow, similar patterns of restriction based on race made community-oriented New Thought appealing to some male African American leaders.

By 1905, however, several community-oriented groups began to decline. That year, the Hopkins Christian Science Association—the first nationwide New Thought organization and one of the most significant—ceased publishing its journal. Over the next fifteen years, the number of women-oriented, women-edited journals gradually decreased, while the number of books authored by male New Thought teachers increased. Some important women New Thought leaders died or became less active in their ministries because of advancing age.

In addition, the political activism and social-reform efforts that peaked among women during the Progressive Era diminished in the more nationalistic, politically repressive climate that accompanied World War I. Socialism declined during the first Red Scare of the early 1920s, as government agencies actively persecuted and suppressed radical political groups. The Eighteenth Amendment to the U.S. Constitution, passed in 1920, prohibited the production, sale, and transport of most forms of alcohol—a key concern of many women social reformers. That same year, the Nineteenth Amendment established women's right to vote.

The individualist style of New Thought expanded, particularly among white people, because it

> adapted itself to support the turn-of-the-century industrial explosion and the beginnings of the modern consumer society. . . . [It] cast people as individual consumers of God as All-Supply. The more they consumed, that is, claimed the abundance that was rightfully theirs, the more they were promised the cure for whatever ailed them. Business-oriented people were attracted to noetic New Thought because it did not question capitalist structures but instead told a universal Horatio Alger story.[43]

With few exceptions, historians have focused on the individualist and Prosperity-oriented strands of New Thought. The precedent for this tendency was set by Horatio Dresser, whose 1919 *History of the New Thought Movement* was the first such survey. Dresser's credibility as a spokesman was underscored by his parentage and his PhD in philosophy from Harvard. He noted in passing the prominence of women but focused his attention on Quimby, Evans, New Thought conventions, and the International New Thought Alliance. Geographically, he concentrated on activities in the Boston area. Dresser did note that the Boston Metaphysical Club, though founded mostly by men, had become "essentially a woman's club," adding, "After 1890, there were probably more leaders among women than among men."[44] His lists of the leaders of New Thought organizations and events bears this out. Nevertheless Dresser downplayed the significance of gender in New Thought and glossed over or ignored the large, women-led organizations in the American Midwest and West. These biases strongly influenced subsequent histories of the movement.[45]

In *The Positive Thinkers*, Donald Meyer points out the movement's large female majority and recognizes that its popularity was related to women's social, political, and economic status. Yet he argues that New Thought encouraged passivity and inwardness, and thus did not help women in any practical way. He characterizes New Thought as a retreat from practical reality, a denial of evil and suffering. His assessment: "It was the genius of mind-cure to discover how the weak might feel strong while remaining weak."[46] Such a characterization does not apply to the reform-minded women described by Materra. Charles Braden and J. Stillson Judah mention Hopkins's role and those of other women leaders only in passing. Just one book-length study has focused on Hopkins.[47] John S. Haller, Jr., provides a much more comprehensive picture of the movement in his 2012 book, *The History of New Thought*, but he too focuses most of his attention on white, male authors and says little of early New Thought women's roles in promoting social reform. Gender analysis will help to illuminate the histories of some African American religious movements influenced by New Thought, as well.

African American New Thought

Histories of the movement are remarkable for the scant attention they devote to African American groups influenced by New Thought. From the 1920s to the 1940s, New Thought spread into the interracial Peace Mission led by Father Divine, the UNIA led by Marcus Garvey, the Moorish Science Temple founded by Noble Drew Ali, and Black Hebrew Israelite groups, including Rabbi Wentworth Arthur Matthew's Commandment Keepers. Moorish Science and UNIA, in turn, influenced the Nation of Islam, developed by Wallace Fard and Elijah Muhammad. These movements sought to repair the self-esteem of black people oppressed by white supremacy and Jim Crow. Father Divine, as we will see, rejected racial categories altogether; black nationalist groups promoted a positive black identity, and in some cases racial separatism and/or the establishment of black nation-states in Africa or North America.

Charles Braden's *Spirits in Rebellion*, a fairly comprehensive history of New Thought published in 1963, mentions Unity branches in Africa but does not mention African American leaders or groups influenced by New Thought. This omission is particularly surprising because fourteen years earlier, Braden had published *These Also Believe*, a survey of several new religious movements in the United States, which included a fine and lengthy scholarly assessment of the Peace Mission Movement, whose New Thought theology he described.[48] J. Stillson Judah's *History and Philosophy of the Metaphysical Movements in America* does not mention Divine either. John Haller's more recent and thorough account of New Thought is completely silent about the movement's impact on black people; he discusses mostly white leaders and authors. Given the Peace Mission's size and level of integration during Jim Crow, these absences are curious. Discussions of Father Divine tend to be found instead in the literature of African

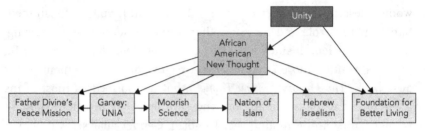

FIG. 2.2 African American movements influenced by New Thought.

American religious history, particularly in discussions of predominantly black "cults" or urban new religious movements.

Albanese's *A Republic of Mind and Spirit* devotes fifteen pages to African American Spiritualists, whom she dubs "subalterns in the Spiritland." She also discusses the Mexican healing tradition called *curanderismo* and briefly describes Father Divine. She mentions neither the UNIA nor the Moorish Science Temple, both of which were important black nationalist movements influenced by New Thought and other metaphysical traditions.[49] Albanese's discussion of New Age religion includes a lengthy section titled "Ethnic Scripts and Subscribers," referring to ethnic minorities. It is important to reconsider this way of employing the term "ethnic," however, because whiteness is an "ethnic" characteristic in the United States, and subgroups of whites have particular ethnicities as well. Figure 2.2 shows the range of African American religious movements influenced by New Thought.

Father Divine's Peace Mission

At the height of American racial segregation, Father Divine's Peace Mission Movement built an enormous, interracial organization whose members regarded their dark-skinned leader as God incarnate. Scholarly estimates of Father Divine's following range from thirty thousand to fifty thousand at its peak during the late 1930s and early 1940s, depending upon how strictly membership is calculated.[50] According to Braden's 1949 study, seventy-two Peace Mission centers and groups existed in 1934; the number reached 178 in 1941. This figure had declined to 154 by 1944, a trend that has continued to the present. At the movement's zenith, however, groups could be found in twenty-six U.S. states, the District of Columbia, Canada, the British West Indies, Panama, Switzerland, England, Australia, and Hawai'i, which became a U.S. state in 1959.[51] About 10 percent of the total were in New York State. While approximately 70 percent of Peace Mission followers in the northeastern United States were black, in California, which was home to the largest concentration of followers west of the Mississippi, about 70 percent were white.[52] Robert Weisbrot observed in 1983 that many of the white followers were well educated and affluent. The smallest number of groups was found in the South, where promoting racial integration could be fatal—particularly to black people.

Father Divine was clearly influenced by New Thought and Theosophy. Jill Watts has argued that he was most strongly influenced by the Unity teaching of Charles Fillmore; Weisbrot points to the strong influence of the New Thought author Robert Collier. Divine distributed various New Thought publications early in his career. He also studied the teachings of Jiddu Krishnamurti (1895–1986) and read Baird T. Spalding's *Life and Teachings of the Masters of the Far East*, a New Thought–Theosophical work that claimed to reflect the teachings of "Great Masters of the Himalayas."[53] The New Thought writer and teacher Eugene DelMar wrote a glowing endorsement of Divine after spending a month in his community at Sayville, New York.[54] Many of Divine's followers, particularly those who were white, had been involved previously in New Thought and Christian Science congregations.

Divine stressed positive thinking, affirmative speech, and abundance in this life. His followers did not greet one another with the word "hello" because it contains the word "hell." The standard greeting was "Peace!" and conversations were liberally sprinkled with the phrase "It is wonderful."[55] Divine prohibited smoking, intoxication, and profanity, and required strict celibacy among his followers. Residential communities were gender-segregated. Beryl Satter writes, "The existence of large-scale, racially mixed communal living that was *not* celibate would likely have triggered white hysteria and even violence."[56] As Braden puts it, celibacy forestalled the "major objection" of whites by preventing interracial marriage and thus "intermingling of the two blood streams."[57]

Satter has argued that New Thought emerged out of a gendered conflict about the nature of desire and WASP anxieties about racial purity. For middle-class (white) Victorian women, she says, desire was extremely problematic. They were economically dependent on men and confined to the domestic sphere, and their erotic needs were denied. This was a major factor in the "nervous complaints" that beset middle-class and elite white women during the Victorian period. For men, desire was positive: ambition and competitiveness were the means to success. New Thought thus divided into "pro-desire" and "anti-desire" factions. During the nineteenth century, a debate raged about which approach would most contribute to the advancement of the "race"—not just the human race, but the white race, which seemed threatened by massive influxes of poor, darker-skinned European immigrants to urban slums.

According to Satter, Eddy epitomized the anti-desire faction: she denied the reality of the material world and therefore any attachment to it. Women drawn to this form sought an escape from compulsory heterosexuality and the freedom to think and act for themselves. (To achieve this, however, they needed money, and there was plenty to be made teaching Mind Cure!) Evans represented the pro-desire faction; Hopkins integrated them both. In *Mind Cure in New England*, Gail Thain Parker sees New Thought as a way that people *integrated* conflicting desires for both spiritual life and material prosperity.[58] As a focus on health gave way to a focus on wealth during the rise of consumer capitalism, she argues, New Thought justified people's desire for success and material riches.

The Peace Mission Movement is a significant exception to Satter's pro- and anti-desire theory: it was a racially integrated, community-oriented New Thought group that had both pro- and anti-desire characteristics. Father Divine affirmed the goodness of the body, liked the women around him to be plump, and served enormous banquets as the central ritual of his movement. He and his followers stressed that he was God embodied. At the same time, he required celibacy of his disciples and claimed that his two marriages were completely spiritual. In addition to gender-segregated quarters for his followers, he emphasized modest dress and a strong work ethic. He and his followers eschewed debt and government entitlement programs and promoted economic self-sufficiency.

The Peace Mission Movement attracted black and white people of all economic classes, including some affluent supporters who contributed lavishly to the movement. Divine claimed to own nothing himself, but wealthy supporters made cars, houses, land, and other resources available for him to use. In the early years and throughout the Great Depression, however, a major factor in Father Divine's appeal was that the Peace Mission provided food, clothing, housing, and jobs. His signature events were daily banquets that fed hundreds or thousands of guests at racially integrated tables. Weisbrot asserts that he attracted many urban African Americans who were alienated by black churches that failed to address hardships caused by the economic collapse.[59] Citing a study during the 1930s of more than six hundred urban black congregations, he notes that only 3 percent provided food for the unemployed, and only two helped them find work. "Divine's ministry to the needy therefore helped fill a crucial void in clerical activity, and in so doing, he rapidly became one of the ghetto's most influential figures."[60] He promoted education and voter registration. His followers lived communally and practiced cooperative economics, and the Peace Mission's numerous businesses thrived.

Divine and his followers integrated the white suburb of Sayville, New York, when Divine and his first wife lived there from 1919 to 1932. By 1930 the community included some white members. The Peace Mission relocated its headquarters to Harlem in 1932, and by 1935 began establishing the first racially integrated households in Ulster County, about a hundred miles north of New York City, along the Hudson River. Beginning in New Paltz, they eventually acquired properties and established businesses in a dozen Ulster County communities, including five farms and two resorts, as well as boarding houses, hotels, gas stations, and restaurants. In the hamlet of High Falls, members of the movement ran a grocery, department store, shoe shop, dress shop, barber shop, garage, and bakery.[61] Divine's Krum Elbow estate, acquired in 1938, lay across the Hudson River from President Franklin Delano Roosevelt's Hyde Park home. In 1936 the movement issued a "Righteous Government Platform" and lobbied for fair wages and an end to segregation, lynching, and capital punishment.

Although critics dismissed Divine as a fraud and a predator, other factors account for his wide appeal: "The Peace Mission possessed a vital communal life, a spiritual commitment, and a strong social vision—it was never merely a passive haven for the weak."[62] Thus its appeal was similar to that of other community-oriented New Thought groups, such as the Hopkins Metaphysical Association, the Divine Science of Malinda Cramer and Nona Brooks, and Annie Rix Militz's Homes of Truth.

Divine and Gender

Gender equity drew many women to the Peace Mission. Satter learned that 75 to 90 percent of Divine's followers were female, and many of these women had shifted to his movement after the collapse of Garvey's UNIA in 1927. Garvey sought to promote a pan-African identity among people of the African diaspora, encourage black business enterprises, and establish a homeland in Liberia. He asserted that God, Jesus, and the Madonna are black, and encouraged his followers to think positively about themselves, their capacities, and their collective identity. Satter notes, "He used New Thought ideas about the power of influence to shore up his calls for a renewed black art, literature, and history."[63] By 1918 the circulation of Garvey's *Negro World* newspaper was 50,000.[64] In 1925 he was imprisoned for mail fraud because of efforts to sell worthless stock in the defunct Black Star shipping line. He was pardoned in 1927 by Calvin Coolidge, but then deported to Jamaica, his native country.

Like many white men during the Victorian era, Garvey stressed racial purity and valorized women primarily for their roles as wives and mothers and relegated them to the private sphere under male protection and control. In contrast, the Peace Mission provided many opportunities for women to function as leaders and to operate businesses and farms. Celibacy freed them from traditional gender roles, isolated housekeeping, and childrearing. Many black women in the movement had worked as domestics, but in the Peace Mission they believed that God Himself served them at elegant banquets. Divine "spoke the language of the black working class," validated black women's experience, encouraged a testimonial style of religious expression, and infused prayers with political content.[65]

Eventually, however, Divine's stress on celibacy shifted to a stress on virginity, and during the 1950s his movement increasingly adopted the gender norms of the white middle class. His race neutrality gave way to American nationalism, and since "the purity claimed for the nation is too easily symbolized by the female virgin body," argues Satter, this too can lead to the same "strict policing of women's bodies" that Garvey's calls for racial purity had produced.

Scholars have differed somewhat on Divine's approach to race. It is generally acknowledged that he regarded race as a social construct and refused to acknowledge its validity. Watts is quite critical, arguing that Divine rejected black identity, "accepted many of the unflattering characteristics ascribed to black Americans by whites and believed that African Americans who defined themselves as black internalized and manifested negative qualities." In some ways, she argues, he blamed blacks for white racism and their own oppression, because they had bought into the notion of color in the first place. Divine never mentioned Africa, had Victorian tastes, and during the early years of his movement surrounded himself with white secretaries, Watts observes.[66] After the death of his first wife, who was black, Divine married a young white woman in 1946, and by the

1950s photographic images of him were being manipulated to downplay his dark skin.[67]

Satter and Weisbrot offer more sympathetic accounts of Divine's attitudes about race. Satter claims that Divine initially offered a millenarian perspective in which "both the concept of race purity and the very existence of racial division had been transcended."[68] Weisbrot says that Divine regarded "all racial designations as unwarranted and invidious." In particular, Divine believed the label "Negro" was employed to stereotype and restrict people. "If Father Divine opposed racial pride, he also assailed any sign of racial shame. This was not to be taken for granted in an age when ghetto residents commonly employed hair straighteners and skin whiteners so as to resemble more closely the Nordic look of the dominant social stratum."[69] Divine promoted the self-esteem of black people, particularly unskilled laborers and domestics, who had been wounded by the constant, corrosive effects of white supremacy. The "Righteous Government Platform" adopted by the Peace Mission was a passionate and detailed call for antilynching laws and the abolition of every form of segregation and racial discrimination.[70] Although Satter agrees with Watts that Divine adopted a rhetoric of racial self-blame, she points out that it was a later development, during World War II, when the movement's membership declined dramatically and Divine shifted to a more conservative, nationalistic, anti-Communist stance.[71]

Other than Satter's article, the only published work providing an extended discussion of Father Divine in the context of New Thought history is R. Marie Griffith's *Born Again Bodies: Flesh and Spirit in American Christianity*. She devotes fifteen pages to a discussion of Peace Mission dietary practices and Divine's theology of the body.[72]

Black Nationalist Islam and Hebrew Israelism

In addition to the Peace Mission and the UNIA, New Thought also influenced the Moorish Science Temple and the Nation of Islam, as well as Black Hebrew Israelite groups. Noble Drew Ali, founder of Moorish Science, asserted that black Americans were actually Moors, by which he meant an "Asiatic" people descended from the Moabites of Canaan, whose homeland was Morocco. (Some Europeans applied the term "Moors" generically to Muslims, including those in India and other Southeast Asian cultures.) Ali founded his first temple in Newark, New Jersey, in 1913, established a headquarters in Chicago in 1925, and by 1928 had eighteen temples in fifteen states.

In 1927 he published *The Holy Koran*, a text specific to Moorish Science that differs from the Arabic Qur'an. It draws heavily upon Levi Dowling's 1908 *Aquarian Gospel of Jesus the Christ*, a text strongly influenced by Theosophy and Spiritualism, which claims to recount Jesus's "lost years" in India. *The Holy Koran* also draws upon *Infinite Wisdom*, a 1923 book purportedly derived from Tibetan manuscripts.[73] Other influences on the movement include Rosicrucianism and Freemasonry. Like followers of Father Divine's movement, converts to Moorish Science adopted new names as well as distinctive dress. Their stress on affirming a positive religious and ethnic identity in the face of racism indicates continuities with Community-Oriented New Thought.[74] Both Wallace Fard and Elijah Muhammad, the founders of the Nation of Islam, were members of the Moorish Science movement before Ali's death in 1929, and Fard had studied Theosophy.[75]

Black Hebrew Israelite groups teach that the ancient Israelites were black; observe Jewish holidays, including a Saturday Sabbath; believe Jesus was the Messiah; and practice glossolalia, or "speaking in tongues." Jacob S. Dorman describes Hebrew Israelite groups as "polycultural bricolages" of elements from Judaism, Western esotericism, and Pentecostal Christianity. The earliest congregation was founded by Mother Mary L. Tate in Tennessee in 1903, according to Dorman. One of her students, Bishop John Hickerson, launched his own version in Harlem in 1914, and five years later Rabbi Wentworth Arthur Matthew founded the Commandment Keepers Church of the Living God, the Pillar and Ground of Truth, also in Harlem. Dorman traces New Thought influences on the latter two leaders and other black nationalist religious groups, particularly the popular writings of Lauron William deLaurence.[76] Figure 2.3 combines previous illustrations to show the complexity of early New Thought.

It is clear that a thorough understanding of the Mind Cure movement and its influences in American culture requires attention to issues of race and gender. The African American groups described here do not seem to have emphasized meditation to the extent that the earlier, predominantly white New Thought denominations did, although new research is just beginning to trace the history of black interest in yoga and meditation.[77] Yet the African American religious movements influenced by New Thought did share a communal orientation and critiques of structural inequality that individualist New Thought lacks. The following chapter offers a detailed discussion of meditation in early New Thought. As Mind

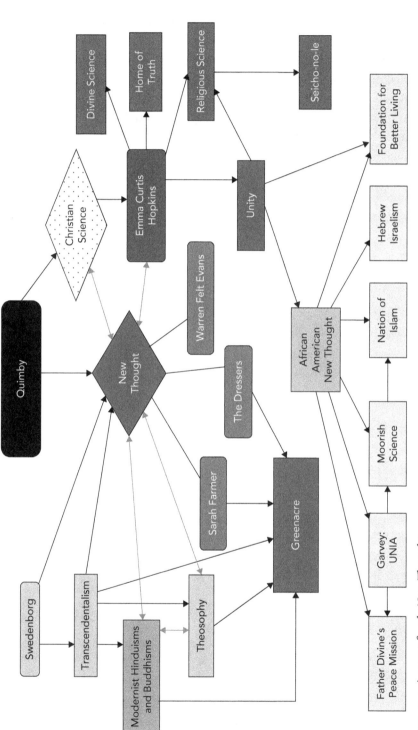

FIG. 2.3 A map of early New Thought.

Cure ideas and methods spread, their popularity began to exert pressure on mainstream American religion and medicine. Chapter 4 describes the process by which Mind Cure and meditation became mainstreamed and medicalized. Because that process was controlled largely by white men, the social-justice concerns of early New Thought women and African Americans fell off the radar. In Chapter 7 I will return to such concerns and explore the limitations they reveal in the contemporary Mindfulness movement.

3

Mind Cure and Meditation at Greenacre and Beyond

MORE THAN A century before mindfulness appeared on the American medical scene, New Thought teachers and communities were promoting meditation for physical, mental, and spiritual healing. While meditation on religious themes has long been a Christian practice, particularly in Christian monastic traditions, it is generally *not* a feature of Protestantism, the dominant type of Christianity in the United States. Protestants rejected monasticism during the Reformation, so in the West, contemplative practices largely have been confined to the contemplative, monastic orders of the Roman Catholic, Anglican, and Orthodox communions and to the mystical traditions of Judaism and Sufi Islam. Among Protestants, Quakers practice silent worship, sitting together quietly unless and until a participant feels moved to speak a brief message to the congregation. But that certainly was not typical of mainstream, nineteenth-century American religiosity. As the historian Leigh Schmidt describes it, "By one account after another, the culture's religious trademark was not devotional quietude and serene meditation, but evangelical fervor and anxiety-ridden conversion. The hoopla of the Methodist camp meeting seemed to mirror perfectly the commotion of the American marketplace and the rough-and-tumble of American politics."[1] New Thought teachers, however, regularly recommended daily meditation, a fact largely overlooked by historians of the movement.[2] They suggested two styles: focused concentration on a single object, such as the breath, a phrase, or an image; and relaxed openness, with no particular object of attention. Where did they learn or how did they develop these methods? What were their sources?

Both styles are consistent with meditation methods found in Buddhism and Raja yoga. *Śamatha*, or "calming" practices, involve focusing attention fully on a single object, to the exclusion of all else, to still the mind and produce states of deep absorption or trance, called *samādhi*. In Buddhism, *Vipaśanā* ("insight" practices) involve a state of relaxed, open awareness, observing thoughts and sensations as they come and go, so that the practitioner can apprehend directly what Buddhism teaches about the nature of reality: that everything is impermanent (*anitya*); that every phenomenon arises from myriad causes and conditions (*pratītya-samutpāda*), so none has any independent, enduring essence or "self" (*anātman*); and that ignorance about these realities lies at the root of much of our mental distress (*duḥkha*). Buddhist tradition recommends practicing both types of meditation together: a certain amount of focus and calm is necessary as a foundation for developing the religious insights that liberate one from suffering and enable the practitioner to cultivate qualities such as equanimity, wisdom, compassion, virtue, and beneficence.

Careful study of New Thought material reveals that the movement's leaders learned Buddhist and Hindu teachings and practices from several sources, including directly from Asian missionaries. This chapter explores some of the written sources, particularly the works of Orientalist scholars and members of the Theosophical Society, as well as contact zones in which New Thought leaders interacted directly with Buddhist and Hindu teachers. The most important contact zones were the 1893 World's Parliament of Religions, part of the Columbian Exposition in Chicago; the Greenacre conferences and Monsalvat School of Comparative Religion, held jointly in Eliot, Maine, particularly from 1894 to 1907; and lecture tours by Asian missionaries around Europe and the United States. Two of the first and most important missionaries were Swami Vivekenanda, a monk of India's Ramakrishna Order who launched the Vedanta Society in the United States,[3] and Anagarika Dharmapāla, a Ceylonese Buddhist layman and Theosophist. Both men wowed audiences at the World's Parliament of Religions, taught New Thought leaders directly during subsequent summers at Greenacre, and delivered public talks in New Thought venues around the United States.

New Thought teachers widely promoted the meditation methods they learned, sometimes Christianizing them in the process. For example, Annie Rix Militz, founder of the Homes of Truth, taught what she called "Christian Yoga."[4] In the Gifford Lectures on Mysticism that William James delivered at the University of Edinburgh (1901–2), he described *samādhi* as practiced in Raja yoga, according to the famed Vedanta missionary Swami Vivekenanda, as well as Buddhist *dhyāna* (meditative absorption, trance) and Sufi mysticism, then remarked, "It has been left to our mind-curers to reintroduce methodical meditation into our religious life."[5] He quoted best-selling authors Horatio Dresser (a student of James's at Harvard) and Ralph Waldo Trine on the importance of regularly setting aside time in a quiet place for "entering the Silence."[6]

The earliest sources of information that most Americans had about Hinduism and Buddhism were translations of Asian scriptures into European languages by Orientalist scholars. (Immigrants from China, some of whom were Buddhist, began arriving on the West Coast beginning in the mid-nineteenth century, followed by Japanese in the 1880s, but they faced considerable hostility from white settlers.) Sir Charles Wilkins's English translation of the *Bhagavad Gita* was published in 1785 and inspired both Emerson and Thoreau. Eugène Burnouf (1801–1852) produced his *Introduction à l'histoire du Buddhisme indien* in 1844, and F. Max Müller (1823–1900) and others translated a number of Buddhist and Vedic texts from Sanskrit and Pali in the following decades.[7] Müller edited *The Sacred Books of the East*, a fifty-volume series of translations published by Oxford University Press, forty-nine of which were produced between 1879 and 1894. Among the texts included were the *Upanishads*, the *Bhagavad Gita*, the *Dhammapada* (Sayings of Buddha) the *Sutta Nipāta* (a collection of Buddha's teachings), the *Mahā-Paranibbāna Sutta* (the Buddha's final teaching before his death), the *Vinaya* (Buddhist monastic regulations), a legendary biography of the Buddha, the *Questions of King Milinda*, and the Māhāyana texts the *Lotus Sutra*, the *Pure Land Sutras*, the *Diamond Sutra* and other *Perfection of Wisdom* texts, as well as a variety of other Hindu, Zoroastrian, Islamic, Taoist, and Confucian works.[8] Sir Edwin Arnold's 1879 poem *The Light of Asia*, a biography of the Buddha written in blank verse, sold between half a million and a million copies in the United States alone.[9] Arnold also published a translation of the *Bhagavad Gita*, called *The Song Celestial*, in 1885. Some information about Chinese, Tibetan, and Japanese Buddhism was also available in English and other European languages.

Writers associated with the Theosophical Society, founded in 1875, drew heavily upon such materials and for decades were the major interpreters of Buddhist and Hindu thought and practice in the West. (Theosophy was also an important influence in some parts of Asia.) Warren Felt Evans, the first philosopher of New Thought, definitely had access to Theosophical literature and likely had access to translations of Pali and Sanskrit texts; he drew upon some of this material in developing his approach to mental therapeutics and in recommending meditation as a key practice for well-being.

Warren Felt Evans and Hindu and Buddhist Thought

Evans wrote six books on mental therapeutics from 1869 to 1886, during a healing career that spanned more than twenty years. In the first three of these books, he drew upon a variety of European and American philosophers, particularly the theology of Emanuel Swedenborg. His fourth book, *The Divine Law of Cure* (1881), indicates that he had begun to explore Buddhist and Hindu ideas as well, as he made passing reference to the Orientalist F. Max Müller and to James Freeman Clarke, a Unitarian minister who authored an early book of comparative religion and became an important Western interpreter of Asian religions. In this book Evans also articulated two themes that would become key features of New Thought: that all religious traditions were valuable for their various efforts to heal maladies of the human soul, and that sectarian creeds and fixed liturgies were unnecessary to spiritual healing. His next book, *The Primitive Mind Cure* (1884), made numerous favorable references to Buddhism and Vedanta and shows that Evans had read two important Theosophical texts—H. P. Blavatsky's *Isis Unveiled* (1877) and A. P. Sinnett's *Esoteric Buddhism* (1883)—as well as *Oriental Christ* (1869) by Protap Chunder Mozoomdar (or Protap Chandra Majumdar), a leader of the Hindu reform movement Brahmo Samaj and later a speaker at the World's Parliament of Religions.[10]

Evans's sixth book, *Esoteric Christianity and Mental Therapeutics* (1886), draws repeatedly upon Hindu and Buddhist ideas. Carl T. Jackson characterizes it as reflecting "almost a conversion to the Theosophical viewpoint, or better yet, a 'Christian Theosophy,' since the Christian element remained quite central."[11] Evans, who was first a Methodist minister and then a Swedenborgian, did share some of the prejudices about these traditions common among Protestant clergy and Orientalists of his day: he saw Christianity as the culmination of all religious thought and believed that the pure essences of Asian religious traditions were to be found in their scriptures rather than in rituals expressing devotion or performed to generate merit: that is, positive karmic causes. For example, he said Buddhism "was once a truly spiritual religion before it became degraded into an external mechanism of rites and ceremonies."[12] (This prejudice is characteristic of what scholars call "modernist Buddhism," or "Buddhist modernism," as well as of the contemporary Mindfulness movement.)

However, Evans did find value in Hindu and Buddhist teachings and practices; he just interpreted them in Christian terms. In describing the practice of mental healing, he mentioned

> a method of instruction practiced by the Hindu adepts in teaching the neophyte the principles of their occult philosophy. The *chela*, or scholar, is subjected to the psychological influence of the *guru*, or teacher, who aims to impart to him knowledge through the Universal Mind. The disciple waits upon the master in *a spirit of emptiness*, and the intellectual sphere of the teacher's mind fills the vacuum. This is a method of education and of acquiring spiritual knowledge entirely unrecognized in our Western systems of instruction, but has long been known in the Orient, and was practiced by Jesus, and belongs to Christianity.[13]

Given that Helena P. Blavatsky and other authors of the Theosophical Society referred repeatedly to "adepts," "chelas," and occult philosophy, it seems likely that the Buddhist and Hindu concepts and practices to which Evans was exposed had already been refracted through the interpretive lens of Theosophy, which drew upon both Swedenborgian and mesmeric ideas.

Theosophy and Mental Healing

A detailed history of Theosophy is well beyond the scope of this book, but as the previous chapter explained, both New Thought and Theosophy have common ancestors in the experiments of Anton Mesmer and his successors on hypnotism, clairvoyance, and other psychic phenomena, and in the teachings of Emanuel Swedenborg on spirit realms and correspondences. Just as Evans's New Thought philosophy—like that of many later New Thought authors—drew upon Theosophical ideas, Theosophists were interested in altered states of consciousness, clairvoyance, psychic phenomena, and mental healing. At its founding in 1875, the Theosophical Society's stated objectives included "investigation . . . of the psychical powers latent in man [*sic*]."[14]

A. P. Sinnett, a British Theosophist, produced a 163-page book on Mesmerism in 1892, including a discussion of the surgeries performed by Elliotson and Esdaile on hypnotized patients, discussed in chapter 2.[15] Both Henry Steel Olcott, a cofounder of the Theosophical Society, and his protégé Anagarika Dharmapāla engaged in "mesmeric healing." As a young man, Olcott mesmerized a patient for surgery and healed others, and he performed several healings in Ceylon beginning in 1882. [16] According to his biographer Stephen Prothero, "Olcott publicly attributed his healings to the Buddha, but privately he credited the Austrian [sic] physician Franz Mesmer."[17] Dharmapāla's diary records at least one mesmeric treatment he performed during his 1897 tour of the San Francisco Bay Area, on "the little girl Mabel Vander Zweip, who had her foot sprained."[18]

Blavatsky and Annie Besant believed in mental healing as well. In her opus *Isis Unveiled*, Blavatsky wrote, "Healing, to deserve the name, requires either faith in the patient, or robust health united with a strong will, in the operator. With expectency supplemented by faith, one can cure himself of almost any morbific condition. . . . It is a question of temperament, imagination, self-cure."[19] Besant wrote at least two lengthy articles on hypnosis in healing, in 1889 and 1990, and lectured on "Clairvoyance and Mental Healing" in Chicago.[20] In her lecture, she attempted to harmonize apparently competing or contradictory schools of mental healing by saying that each offered a partial understanding of the relevant spiritual and physical laws, and Theosophy provided a comprehensive view. "It is true that the mind can cure disease. It is true that the action of the mind can either kill or cure and can either wound or heal."[21] Science had proved this, she said, through experiments in France and elsewhere involving hypnosis.

Several important New Thought teachers and writers in addition to Evans studied Theosophy: Charles Fillmore and Ernest Holmes, among others. Ursula Gestefeld was active in the Theosophical Society in Chicago.[22] Sarah Farmer, in a 1903 description of Greenacre, quoted the Theosophist leader C. W. Leadbeater's description of Buddhist *nirvāṇa*: "When the last shred of the personality is gone, all that can thus suffer has passed away, and in the perfected adept there is unruffled peace and everlasting joy. He sees the end toward which all is working and rejoices in that end, knowing that earth's sorrow is but a passing phase in human evolution."[23] Annie Besant lectured on Theosophy at Farmer's Greenacre resort in 1897, when many New Thought leaders were present, and C. Jinarajadasa (president of the Theosophical Society from 1946 to 1953) did so from 1905 to 1908.[24]

In his 1916 book, *Theosophy and New Thought*, Henry C. Sheldon claims that although New Thought writers did not often comment directly on Theosophy, some borrowed ideas about such things as astral bodies and reincarnation.[25] Charles Fillmore, whose publishing company sold numerous Theosophical titles, is perhaps the most prominent example. Horatio Dresser opined that Theosophists were correct in asserting the doctrine of karma, which "harmonizes with the New Thought," but he believed that cause and effect operates in one's present lifetime, not that it continues into future lifetimes.[26] He described Theosophy as a "kindred movement" to New Thought: "A theosophist might assimilate the New Thought and practise mental healing in the same way as the healers. The writings of Annie Besant and others make clear the power of thought. The theosophists have much to say about 'planes' and 'auras,' and other subjects of interest to devotees of the New Thought."[27] Meditation too was regularly promoted by Theosophists; it was central to Besant's teaching.[28] Blavatsky stressed the importance of concentration in *The Voice of the Silence* (1889) and Besant in *Thought Power: Its Control and Culture* and *An Introduction to Yoga* (both 1908).[29] Olcott stressed it in his *Buddhist Catechism*.[30]

Buddhism in Christian Terms

Evans appears to have read Olcott's *Buddhist Catechism* and quoted it in explaining mental healing. Arguing that the root cause of disease is ignorance, Evans cited the legendary story of the Buddha's enlightenment:

> It is said of Gautama, who did for the East what Jesus, six hundred years later, did more fully for the West, that he sought long and earnestly, and with extreme ascetic mortifications, which proved of no avail, for the *cause* of all human misery. At last the light from the supreme heavens broke in upon him, and his mind became entirely opened, "like the full-blown lotus-flower," and he saw by an intuitive flash of the supreme knowledge, that the secret of all the miseries of mankind was *ignorance*; and the sovereign remedy for it was to dispel ignorance and to become wise. If this is not the key that unlocks our dungeon, it shows where the lock is to be found.[31]

Although Evans did not identify the source for his quotation, "like the full-blown lotus-flower" is the exact phrase that Olcott used to describe the

Buddha's awakening in the *Buddhist Catechism*, first published in 1881, five years before Evans's *Esoteric Christianity*.[32]

Like his Mind Cure teacher Phineas Quimby, Evans believed that disease results from erroneous thinking and that the cure is Wisdom about the true nature of reality. As a Christian, he read the story of Buddha's enlightenment in terms of religious ideas more familiar to him. "The teaching of the Buddha is here identical with the principles of esoteric Christianity," Evans explained. Jesus taught that the root of suffering is sin, which is "an error of the understanding, which may lead to wickedness in the life."[33] That, in turn, leads to dis-ease of various kinds.

Evans explained other Buddhist concepts in terms of Christian doctrine:

> The birth into the spiritual life is called *Moksha* and *Nirvana*, and is that of which Jesus speaks, as entering into the kingdom of the heavens, or the kingdom of God, a condition of spiritual development, or education, that is attainable on earth, and not to be taught, as is usually done, as belonging exclusively to a future state. . . .
> Even Nirvana is attainable on earth. The Buddha is represented as teaching that "those who are free from all worldly desires enter Nirvana."[34]

His reference to "spiritual development" as "education" probably reflects a Swedenborgian belief in spiritual progression through processes of self-discipline and scholarship.

Evans also attributed to Swedenborg teachings that sound remarkably like Buddhist doctrines about *dukkha*, usually translated as "suffering" or, more accurately, as "unsatisfactoriness." In discussing pain, Evans wrote that we have three types of responses to our experiences: indifference to neutral sensations, desire for pleasurable sensations, and aversion to unpleasant sensations. Pain arises from desire and aversion. In Buddhist thought, pleasant, unpleasant, and neutral sensations are called *vedanā*, "feeling," and constitute one of the five *skandhas*, or constituents of a human being.[35] The examples Evans gives for desire are thirst and hunger. According to the second of the Four Noble Truths, one of the most basic Buddhist doctrines, the root cause of *dukkha* is *taṇhā* (Skt. *tṛṣṇā*), translated as "thirst" or "craving." The "three poisons" of craving, aversion, and ignorance are what keep us trapped in *saṃsāra*, the cycle of birth, death, rebirth, redeath.

In this section of his book, however, Evans did not refer directly to Buddhist teachings but to Swedenborg. After his discussion of the roots of pain in craving and aversion, he wrote, "Swedenborg defines pain to be a feeling of repugnance arising from *interior falses*."[36] The prescription: "If we can bring ourselves to feel that pain is not an *evil*, but a good, and that all good is desirable and delightful, and remove from our minds repugnance to it, and replace it by a state of perfect patience and tranquil endurance, the pain will subside and finally cease."[37] While Buddhist doctrine regards pleasant sensations as equally a source of dissatisfaction because we become attached to them, it does regard equanimity as one of the seven factors of enlightenment.[38] This passage does not provide direct evidence that Evans's discussion was informed by actual Buddhist sources, but the similarities are at least intriguing.

In the midst of a discussion about healing by the power of the Holy Spirit, Evans wrote, "In the earlier [than Christianity] and purer philosophy of Buddhism it was taught that the Akasa contained a permanent record of all that was ever thought, felt, said, or done. These are all preserved in that universal principle as in 'a book of life,' or living book. All our states of thought and emotion exist in it, and can never have existence outside of it."[39] *Ākāśa*, a term employed by Theosophists such as Blavatsky and Sinnett, refers in Hindu philosophy to a subtle element pervading the cosmos ("space"). In Buddhist thought, "space" is sometimes used as a simile for "emptiness" (*śūnyatā*), which refers to a Mahāyāna manner of speaking about *anātman*, a key Buddhist doctrine that says the putative self and all apparent phenomena lack any substantive, independent, unchanging, eternal essence.[40] Evans's reference to the "book of life," in which experiences are stored, is reminiscent of the *ālaya vijñāna*, "storehouse consciousness," which contains the "seeds" of past experience and is the source of all present and future experience, according to Buddhist Yogācāra philosophy.

The *Dhammapada* is the only Buddhist text Evans cites directly in *Esoteric Christianity*, so it is impossible to determine exactly how much he knew about Buddhist thought. It is unlikely that he had direct access to Yogācāra or other Mahāyāna literature, although the *Sacred Books of the East* series had made a few texts available by 1886, when *Esoteric Christianity* was published. Most of the Buddhist scriptures translated into European languages during the late nineteenth century were originally in Pali, the Pali Text Society having been founded in 1881. Given Evans's references to Blavatsky and Sinnett (and probably to Olcott) and his interests in

Mesmerism, psychic phenomena, Swedenborgianism, Kabbalah, and other forms of esotericism, the Theosophical Society is his most likely source. The Society drew rather indiscriminately from both Mahāyāna and Theravāda doctrines. In addition to Theosophical books on Buddhism, the journal *The Theosophist* regularly published articles on Buddhist topics— and in 1887 it published a review of Evans's book, quoting the passage about Buddha's enlightenment that I included above.[41]

However, several other sources available by the time Evans wrote *Esoteric Christianity* make it at least conceivable that he had more direct access to Buddhist literature. If he read French or German, he could have had access to scholarly translations by European Orientalists. He was clearly well read and had studied at Middlebury College and Dartmouth University.[42]

In addition, some information about Tantric Buddhism was available during Evans's time. Italian Jesuit missionaries had lived in Tibet and studied Tibetan Tantric Buddhism as early as the eighteenth century, and various other scholars had studied the Tantric Buddhism present in Mongolia and among the Kalmyks in Russia during the eighteenth and early nineteenth centuries. Finally, Evans was a Swedenborgian minister, and at least two Swedenborgian scholars have argued that Swedenborg was probably exposed to Tantric Buddhism.

Swedenborgian Tantra?

Anders Hallengren suggests that Swedenborg learned about esoteric Buddhism from Swedish soldiers who had been prisoners of war in the Siberian and Tartar areas of Russia and returned to Sweden in the 1720s. Among these were Swedenborg's cousin Peter Schöenström, an avid collector of manuscripts along the Silk Route, particularly Mongolian religious texts. Other sources were the explorer Philip Strahlenberg, whose travel journals Swedenborg mentions in his *Spiritual Diary*, and a Russian historian and geographer whom Swedenborg met in Stockholm. Marsha Keith Schuchard argues that Swedenborg also could have learned about Tantric yoga from Moravian missionaries who traveled to India, China, Tibet, Tartary, and central Russia, and from Moravian converts in the Malabar region of India who traveled to London and Holland. Although some Swedenborgian scholars reject this argument, at least two contemporary scholars of Buddhism have seen similarities between Swedenborgian thought and Buddhist Tantra.[43]

In two books, Swedenborg said he had spoken with spirits from "Great Tartary," a region that in his time was understood to encompass the entire East Asian continent.[44] These spirits, Swedenborg said, carefully preserved and guarded ancient scriptures and religious practices predating the Hebrew Bible. This "Ancient Word" provided the basis for later Judaism and Christianity.[45] In London, Swedenborg and his Moravian associates studied Kabbalist forms of meditation, visualization, breath control, and sexual yoga that were similar to Left-Hand Tantric practices.[46] Blavatsky had said in at least one book and two articles published between 1877 and 1882 that Swedenborg's revelation about Great Tartary referred to the esoteric Buddhist and Hindu teachings of Ascended Masters in the Himalayas.[47]

Two Forms of Meditation

Whatever Evans's sources of information about Buddhism and Hinduism, "his works undoubtedly encouraged New Thought readers to a more serious interest in the Eastern message."[48] Evans strongly recommended two meditative practices—contemplation of the breath and one-pointed concentration—at least seven years before the first Buddhist and Vedanta missionaries began teaching them to white Americans in the wake of the 1893 World's Parliament of Religions.[49] "Right *thinking* and right *breathing* are the two things most essential to happiness and health," he wrote.[50] The rhythmic motion of inhaling and exhaling reflects the "forward and backward movement of the pendulum, the ebb and flow of the tides, the succession of day and night, the systolic and diastolic action of the heart. . . . When we breathe in harmony with this movement, we are well, and our individual life marches forward in exact step with the tranquil life of nature; when our respiration is discordant with it, our life-force is out of tune."[51] In addition:

A very essential qualification for the practice of the mental-cure system, is . . . the ability to fix our thought upon one thing and to banish all other things from the mind. This state of mental concentration was called in the Hindu metaphysics *Ekāgrāta*, that is, one-pointedness. The attainment of that power was considered as an indispensable condition of all philosophical speculation and religious development. In order to obtain this abstraction from external things, and concentration of thought, they repeated the holy syllable *Om*. . . . The ability to concentrate the mind upon one thing is a natural endowment, but can be cultivated by practice.[52]

A more relaxed form of meditation that Evans also recommended is called "entering the Silence": "We must lay aside the toiling oar and float in the current of the infinite Life."[53] Both of these practices would be recommended by numerous subsequent New Thought teachers and authors; Horatio Dresser's first book was titled *The Power of Silence*.

The World's Parliament of Religions

The first personal contacts that New Thought leaders had with actual Buddhists or Hindus in the United States occurred at the 1893 World's Parliament of Religions in Chicago. Other scholars have discussed the Parliament at length, so my consideration of it will be brief.[54] The celebrity of Swami Vivekenanda and Anagarika Dharmapāla at the Parliament, and their roles in introducing large numbers of white Americans to Vedanta and Buddhism, respectively, have been well documented. As an adjunct to the Parliament, a number of denominational congresses met, and among these were gatherings of Swedenborgians, Christian Scientists, Theosophists, and Buddhists, which members of other denominations and religious traditions attended.[55] These congresses, which have received far less attention than the primary Parliament proceedings, provided additional opportunities for followers of different traditions to meet, mingle, and learn about one another's beliefs and practices.

Although the Christian Science congress was organized by the National Christian Scientists' Association, led by Mary Baker Eddy and presided over by Mrs. Eddy's adopted son, E. J. Foster Eddy, at the time the term "Christian Science" did not refer exclusively to Mrs. Eddy's organization. Rather a variety of mental-healing teachers and groups used the name. More than four thousand people from all over the country attended the Christian Science congress, and others were turned away for lack of space.[56] Judge J. S. Hanna, editor of the *Christian Science Journal*, read a paper composed of approved excerpts from Eddy's writings, and another ten men and women delivered addresses.[57] No records of congress attendees appear to have been kept, but it is highly probable that a number of heterodox Mind Curers attended this event.

Two major New Thought teachers who had been expelled from Eddy's church were headquartered in Chicago at the time: Emma Curtis Hopkins and Ursula Gestefeld. Hopkins's Christian Science Association was the largest network of heterodox Christian Science groups in the country. The Emma Curtis Hopkins College of Christian Science, in downtown Chicago, had trained 350 mind-curers by the end of 1893 and had ordained 111 clergy. Gestefeld, like Hopkins, was an apostate from Eddy's movement; she called her approach to mental healing the Science of Being. She wrote numerous books, tracts, and novels with feminist and New Thought themes, and her congregation in Chicago regularly attracted five hundred to eight hundred people.[58]

Hopkins was heavily involved in organizing a major gathering of heterodox Christian Scientists in Chicago during the World's Fair: the Columbian Congress of Christian Scientists, which met on August 28–30, 1893, less than two weeks before the Parliament. It was headquartered at the fair in the Queen Isabella building, along with the Queen Isabella Association, a group formed to facilitate networking among women. All but six of the speakers on the program for this gathering of Christian Scientists were women.[59] While standard histories of the Parliament do not mention this meeting, it is clear that followers of what came to be called New Thought attended the fair shortly before the Parliament. Given this national gathering at the fair, the substantial, ongoing presence of heterodox Christian Scientists in Chicago, their religious eclecticism, and the recorded audience of more than four thousand at the Parliament's Christian Science Congress, it seems probable that at least some New Thought practitioners attended the Parliament, where they would have encountered Buddhism, Vedanta, and Theosophy.

Modernist Buddhism and Hinduism at the Parliament

Even more important for the later development of mental therapeutics were the ways that a few key Asian missionaries at the Parliament— Swami Vivekenanda, Anagarika Dharmapāla, and the Japanese Rinzai Zen master Sōen Shaku—shaped American perceptions of their respective religious traditions. Unlike the Brahmo Samaj leader Majumdar, who received less attention, Vivekenanda equated Hinduism with Vedanta philosophy, and specifically with the modernist version associated with his Ramakrishna Order. His talks at the Parliament led to a four-year speaking tour across the United States. He spent six months lecturing to New Thought audiences in California in 1899 and 1900. Later these groups also hosted Paramahansa Yogananda, who founded the Self-Realization

Fellowship in southern California in 1925.[60] In 1905 Shaku spent nine months teaching in San Francisco.[61]

Dharmapāla and Shaku both presented modernized, reformist versions of Buddhism: one Theravāda, one Zen. They and Vivekananda portrayed their traditions as universally relevant, philosophical rather than "religious" (by which they meant devotional, ritualistic, or concerned with the supernatural), and compatible with modern science. These characterizations profoundly influenced subsequent perceptions of Buddhism and Hinduism in North America, down to the present day.

Scholars such as James Ketelaar, Judith Snodgrass, Robert Sharf, Donald Lopez, Richard Jaffe, Carl T. Jackson, and David McMahan have all shown that these missionaries had significant contact with Christianity and Western philosophies, and that they were motivated by specific religious, political, and economic concerns.[62] Vivekananda's India and Dharmapāla's Ceylon were both under British colonial rule; Shaku's Japan was simultaneously enthralled by Western technology, afraid of American imperialist expansion, and suffering a fierce persecution of Buddhism under the Meiji regime. Robert Sharf observes, "Government propagandists, who sought to turn Shinto into a tool of state ideology, condemned Buddhism as a corrupt, decadent, anti-social, parasitic, and superstitious creed inimical to Japan's need for scientific and technological advancement. Buddhist reformers responded by acknowledging the corruption and self-interest . . . but they insisted that [it] merely indicated the degree to which Buddhism had fallen from its spiritual roots."[63] A number of Japanese Buddhist reformers traveled overseas, studied Western philosophy and Christian theology and practice, and used the knowledge they gained to revitalize their religious traditions at home and to present them abroad as equal or superior to Christianity.

> They noted the organization and reach of the various Christian missionary societies . . . the active translation of the [B]ible, and the use of Christian doctrine in public education. They took careful note of Christianity's conflict with the emerging scientification of knowledge and the various theological arguments in defense of the religious life. They noted Christian involvement in social concerns such as temperance, monogamy, individual rights, suffrage, the education of women. . . . Many of these practices were in fact incorporated into the Meiji-era restructuring of Buddhist institutional interaction with society.[64]

In their efforts to modernize, Japanese Buddhist reformers were "drawn to the European critique of institutional religion—the legacy of the anti-clericism and anti-ritualism of the Reformation, the rationalism and empiricism of the Enlightenment, the romanticism of figures such as Schleiermacher and Dilthey, and the existentialism of Nietzsche."[65] Snodgrass has shown that the Japanese delegation to the Parliament had the additional aims of portraying the Mahāyāna as authentic Buddhist teaching, to counter Orientalist prejudices that saw Theravāda as earlier and therefore purer; to critique Christian aggression; and to persuade the United States to revise unequal treaties that put Japan at a disadvantage.[66]

In Southeast Asia, reform-minded Theravāda Buddhists had similar concerns and adopted similar strategies.

> The Sri Lankan and Burmese elites responded to their colonial situation [by] reasserting their traditional cultural and spiritual heritage under the banner of Theravāda Buddhism. Buddhism thus became the vehicle through which they affirmed their national identities, their cultural values, and their self-esteem. But the Buddhism of the new urban middle-class was far from the traditional Buddhism of the village. Like Meiji New Buddhism, Theravāda was refashioned in the image of post-Enlightenment Christianity.[67]

Buddhism has blended with indigenous religious traditions—and political systems—everywhere it has spread. That is a central argument in Jeff Wilson's study of the modern Mindfulness movement in *Mindful America*. In many cultures, Buddhist specialists engage in divination, shamanism, folk medicine, the production and sale of amulets, and other activities that modern, scientifically minded people would call "magic": instrumental rituals invoking suprahuman forces to achieve specific practical benefits. Buddhist sacred literature frequently describes supernatural powers and events as well, usually among Buddhist adepts, as a way of validating the truth of their religious insights and teachings.[68]

Modernist Buddhists like Anagarika Dharmapāla, Sōen Shaku, and D. T. Suzuki downplayed these aspects of their traditions. They dispensed with premodern cosmology, monasticism, devotional rituals, and traditional symbols, or reinterpreted them in psychological terms. They emphasized the tradition's philosophical and ethical dimensions and proclaimed Buddhism's superiority to Christianity while criticizing the colonialism that went hand in hand with Christian missionizing in Asia.

They presented a Buddha who was a scientist, who anticipated modern discoveries, and who taught a rational doctrine compatible with a scientific worldview.[69] They also made good use of evangelical methods and media they had gained from Christians: hymnals, catechisms, and anthologies of Buddhist texts called "Bibles." Their modernist versions of Buddhism differ not only from the early Indian monastic Buddhism described in the Theravāda and Māhāyana scriptures but from the ways Buddhism is and has been practiced on the ground in most contexts around the globe. All religious traditions change over time, but Donald Lopez asserts that this philosophical, textually based version of Buddhism was possible to construct only because the Orientalist scholars who first translated Buddhist texts into European languages did so in India, where Buddhism had been dead for centuries.[70]

Vivekenanda, Dharmapāla, and Shaku promoted their agendas, domestically and abroad, in part by appropriating Western authority for their own purposes, a process Ketelaar has called "strategic Occidentalism," which I discuss in chapter 7. These missionaries deployed Western interest in their religions to show that their traditions were modern, relevant, universal, and superior to Christianity. They were heavily aided in these efforts by white Theosophists, particularly Olcott, who was a key figure in the Buddhist revivals of Ceylon and Japan.[71]

Paramahansa Yogananda, who founded the Self-Realization Fellowship in the United States in 1920, was more devotional than Vivekananda and other neo-Hindu reformers. His own guru, Sri Yuketswar, had attended a Christian school and studied the Bible, which he interpreted in terms of yogic ideas. He sent Yogananda to the United States with a mission to reconcile Hinduism and Christianity. Yogananda spoke about the Bible in his own teaching; modeled weekly religious services on Christian services, with hymns, prayers, and sermons; and revered both Jesus and Krishna as avatars. Images of both, flanked by pictures of Yogananda and his lineage of gurus, adorn Self-Realization Fellowship altars. He lectured widely to New Thought audiences and wrote a book called *Scientific Healing Affirmations*. These include:

> *I am submerged in eternal light. It permeates every particle of my being.*
> *I am living in that light. The Divine Spirit fills me within and without.*
> *Perfect Father, Thy light is flowing through Christ, through the saints*
>   *of all religions, through the masters of India, and through me. This*
>   *divine light is present in all my body parts. I am well.*

I know that God's power is limitless; and as I am made in His image, I,
  too, have the strength to overcome all obstacles.
I relax and cast aside all mental burdens, allowing God to express
  through me His perfect love, peace, and wisdom.[72]

Thus the religious perspectives presented by neo-Vedanta and Buddhist missionaries were the products of complex cultural, religious, economic, and political interactions with the West. American audiences, unaware that these versions of Buddhism and Hinduism were modern, reformist, and designed to appeal to Western sensibilities, perceived them as authentic. (I do not mean to suggest that they were actually inauthentic; my point concerns the naiveté of the audiences.) The missionaries themselves appealed to Americans because they seemed both exotic and familiar at the same time. They were particularly successful among practitioners of New Thought, which in turn appropriated Buddhist and Vedanta ideas and practices into their own teachings.

Carl T. Jackson has written at some length on New Thought interest in neo-Vedanta and Raja yoga, particularly during the first decade of the twentieth century. Philip Goldberg and Lola Williamson mention it in their histories of American neo-Vedanta, *American Veda* and *Transcendent in America*, respectively. Although I devote some space to this topic in what follows, I focus on a subject that has received far less attention: contacts between New Thought teachers and Buddhists, and New Thought teachers' roles in popularizing meditation. A key site for these contacts was the Greenacre conferences in Maine.

Greenacre: A Crucial Contact Zone

Greenacre hosted numerous, well-known New Thought leaders from 1894 to 1899 and from 1906 to 1911 (except 1908).[73] Horatio Dresser was deeply involved in the conferences; he taught there from at least 1896 to 1897 and again from 1906–11; one historian indicates that he also taught in 1898 and from 1901 to 1905.[74] Other New Thought luminaries at Greenacre were Abby Morton Diaz, a social reformer, feminist, former resident of the Transcendentalist community Brook Farm, and cofounder of the Boston Metaphysical Club launched by Dresser;[75] Ursula Gestefeld, a novelist who became a major teacher in Chicago;[76] Fanny Harley, an author;[77] Orison Swett Marden, a prolific writer and founder of *Success Magazine*;[78] Charles Brodie Patterson, who wrote several books and edited the magazine *Mind*;[79] Ralph Waldo Trine, one of the best-selling New Thought writers in history;[80] Helen Van-Anderson, founder of Church of the Higher Life;[81] and Henry Wood, a prominent New Thought writer, publicist, and philanthropist, who recommended autosuggestion, or "mental photography."[82] Dresser credits Sarah Farmer with inspiring Wood and Trine to explore New Thought; they went on to become two of its best-known writers.

> In his 1915 history of the New Thought movement, Dresser said Sarah Farmer was deeply interested in the New Thought and was known as a leader of the movement. Greenacre naturally became the centre in the summer for those who were active in the New-Thought gatherings in Boston and New York during the winter. Many of the mental-healing leaders from different parts of the country were heard at Greenacre, and Miss Farmer's conferences set the example for New-Thought meetings held elsewhere. . . . At least a week was devoted to the New Thought each year at Greenacre, and in addition to the regular lectures smaller meetings or Sunday afternoon sessions in the large tent were led by New-Thought speakers.[83]

James Douglas Martin, Farmer's biographer, also calls her one of the most influential figures in the New Thought movement during its early decades and writes that "her diary, and later her Greenacre programs, are both studded with the names of the principal figures" in the movement.[84] In addition to providing an East Coast headquarters during the summer months, she was a close friend of many of the movement's female clergy, and in 1899 she was elected to the executive committee of the first national New Thought association, formed that year.[85]

Franklin Sanborn reported in 1897 that "what was termed 'metaphysics' was greatly in evidence" during Greenacre's early seasons. "By [metaphysics] was meant a peculiar form of mental healing, and much stress was laid on the warding off of disease, and even of death and old age. . . . A more systematic teaching of the spiritual truth which underlies sound living and preserves from the worst bodily ills, is now pursued by those who take up this subject."[86] This "more systematic teaching" was provided by the School of Applied Metaphysics, which operated for several years beginning in 1897, in conjunction with the regular Greenacre conferences and the Monsalvat School for Comparative Religion.

A fire in 1905 destroyed Farmer's home and many Greenacre records, but a few accounts of its early days survive. Martin's 1967 master's thesis is the most detailed biography of Farmer and history of Greenacre available. It draws heavily on Farmer's correspondence and other materials held in Bahá'í archives. The journalist Sanborn, who became a close friend of Farmer's and a Greenacre regular, wrote more than one hundred newspaper and magazine articles about Greenacre activities; in 1980 Kenneth Walter Cameron compiled these, as well as prospectuses and programs from the conferences. [87] Anna Josephine Ingersoll, who also attended Greenacre events, produced a short history in 1900.[88] Charles Mason Remey, an ardent Bahá'í, wrote an unsystematic memoir of his Greenacre experiences from about 1906 through World War II.[89] The Bahá'í Publishing Trust also produced a history of Greenacre in 1991, which it revised in 2005 to celebrate the centennial of the Portsmouth Treaty ending the Russo-Japanese War.[90] (Farmer was the only woman allowed to attend the treaty signing, and the Japanese delegates visited Greenacre afterward.) In addition, the diaries of Vivekenanda and Dharmapāla describe some of their Greenacre experiences.

Buddhism and Neo-Vedanta at Greenacre

Both neo-Vedanta and Buddhism had very strong presences at the Greenacre conferences for most of their history. At one point, Farmer hoped that Dharmapāla and a Vedanta Society swami could be in permanent residence at Greenacre.[91] Even before she launched the summer gatherings, she indicated an acquaintance with Buddhism and Hinduism. In an 1889 speech to the first convention of the International Metaphysical League, she quoted both the Vedas and *The Light of Asia*, Sir Edward Arnold's biography of the Buddha.[92] At Greenacre, Vedanta was taught in at least eleven of the years from 1894 to 1913, and Buddhism in at least a dozen of those years.[93] Of the Vedantists, Swami Vivekananda taught in 1894; Swami Saradananda in 1896 and 1897; Swami Abhedananda in 1898 and 1899 (he helped to run the Monsalvat School of Comparative Religion at Greenacre for at least the first of those two years); Swami Rama in 1904; Swami Parananda in 1906, 1910, 1911, and 1913; Sakharam Ganesh Pandit in 1907; and Swami Bodhananda in 1910 and 1911.[94]

Sarah Bull, Vivekananda's chief financial backer in the United States and one of Farmer's closest friends, was also very much involved in the annual summer programs. She purchased a cottage next to the

Greenacre Inn and established it as a study center for the Vedanta Society, which she had helped to found. Vivekenanda, Abhedenanda, and Sister Nivedita, Vivekenanda's closest Western disciple, stayed in that house during their visits to Eliot.[95] In fact Farmer apparently received some complaints that Greenacre was weighted too heavily in favor of Hinduism.[96]

Among the Buddhist teachers at Greenacre were K. Nakamura in 1895;[97] Anagarika Dharmapāla in 1897; Sister Sanghamitta, a.k.a. Marie deSouza Canavarro, who lectured for eleven days in 1901 and helped her companion Myron Phelps run Monsalvat in 1904; D. T. Suzuki (1907); B. S. Kimura (1902 and 1903); and Kentoku Hori (1906).[98] Paul Carus, a Buddhist sympathizer, lectured in 1897.[99] Ernest Fenollosa, an influential collector and curator of Buddhist art, who had spent several years in Japan and been initiated into Tendai Buddhism, lectured on religion and art during Greenacre's opening season, assisted by Arthur Dow of the Boston Museum of Art.[100] Solon Lauer spoke of "Christianity's debt to Buddhism" the following year, quoting the Orientalist T. W. Rhys Davids, noting parallels between Christian and Buddhist ethics, and asserting that Catholic practices such as celibate clergy, the use of incense and candles during liturgies, ecclesiastical hierarchies, rosaries, and chanting, all had Buddhist antecedents.[101] Rev. F. Huberty James, a Baptist minister and Orientalist who lived for many years in China and was murdered during the Boxer Rebellion, lectured on Buddhism and other Asian traditions from 1895 to 1897.

In addition, Professors David Saville Muzzey of Harvard and Jean de Buy of Yale lectured on Buddhism in 1901; the Theosophist and Sanskrit scholar Charles Johnston, MRAS, did so in 1901–3; and Nathaniel Schmidt of Columbia University in 1908.[102] Rev. Kakuryo Nishijima of the Buddhist Mission of San Francisco (Jōdo Shinshū) served on the Greenacre Advisory Board in 1901.[103]

Dr. Lewis Janes, who served as president of the Free Religious Association and was a noted sympathizer of both Buddhism and Vedanta, directed the Monsalvat School from 1896 to 1899. Myron Phelps, another Buddhist sympathizer, ran Monsalvat for its first four years.[104] Also represented in the summer programs were several Theosophists whose teaching drew upon both Hindu and Buddhist literature and practices. These included Annie Besant (1897), C. Jinarajadasa (1905, 1906, and 1908, possibly also 1907), Charles Johnston, and Sister Sanghamitta, mentioned earlier.[105]

Vivekananda and Raja Yoga at Greenacre

The Hindu and Buddhist lecturers did not just talk about their respective religions in the abstract; they taught their practices. Although I have not located specific descriptions of Vedanta meditation instruction at Greenacre, the circumstantial evidence strongly suggests that it was regularly provided. One 1903 newspaper article reported, "You will find Hindoo priests sitting cross-legged under the pines in deep meditation."[106] In the Raja yoga taught by Vivekenanda and his fellow Vedanta missionaries, meditation was a central practice, and numerous exhortations to meditate can be found in Vivekenanda's collected writings.[107] Daily meditation was required in the American Vedanta communities that Vivekenanda and others founded.[108] It was virtually certain to be included in the "morning devotions" that various Vedanta swamis led at Greenacre.[109]

Martin finds that Vivekenanda made a powerful impression on Lewis Janes, who was "deeply attracted to Hinduism," and so Vedanta followers were "given a freedom at Monsalvat which no other faith enjoyed."[110] There was a "sharp difference between the lectures on Hinduism and those on all the other faiths," because they were "part of a systematic program of instruction in the Hindu faith beginning from an implicit acceptance of its truth and completeness." Lectures on other traditions, in contrast, were "academic in nature, reflecting an overriding awareness of standards of historical and scientific evidence" and containing "sociological and cultural material." The Vedanta lectures were "unvaryingly didactic . . . [and] supplemented by instruction in Yogic exercises in breathing, posture and meditation, all of which involved the student deeply in Vedantist assumptions about the nature of reality."[111]

Sanborn's detailed account of an 1897 lecture by Swami Saradananda supports this characterization. It is full of references to the Vedas and Upanishads and lengthy poetic quotations—whether of texts or Saradananda's commentary is not clear. For example, "The universe is the expression of God, the ocean of absolute love." God, who is infinite Being, is "formless, yet in all form; changeless, yet in all change[;] knowing that Self, the Lord, the great enlightened man never grieves again!"[112]

Vivekenanda apparently made as strong an impression on Greenacre audiences as he had on Janes and on audiences at the Chicago World's Parliament of Religions; he was said to be the main attraction during Greenacre's opening season in 1894. That year he conducted a specialized course in Vedanta alongside the regular programs.[113] In an article devoted to the swami, Sanborn described him as "attired in his flowing red robes and yellow turban, sitting cross-legged under the ground under a wide-spreading pine, and surrounded by a group of eager listeners, men and women, to whom he pours out freely his treasures of knowledge and experience."[114] The pine under which he and his fellow Vedanta missionaries taught came to be known as the "Swami Pine." Vivekenanda recalled, "A while back several hundred intellectual men and women were gathered in a place called Greenacre, and I was there for nearly two months. Every day I would sit in our Hindu fashion under a tree, and my followers and disciples would sit on the grass all around me. Every morning I would instruct them, and how earnest they were!"[115] Note that he refers to all of his listeners as "followers and disciples," although surely not every person who attended Vedanta sessions was an adherent. Greenacre attracted hundreds of guests each season, filling local accommodations to overflowing. Sanborn reported in 1898 and Ingersoll in 1900 that thousands of guests had attended the conferences, and thousands more had been turned away for lack of facilities.[116] According to Martin, from 1894 to 1897 "record crowds attended the lectures and concerts, filled all of the available accommodation on the Maine side of the Piscataqua, and compelled between one and two thousand visitors to seek rooms in Portsmouth, at the height of the season."[117] In 1931 *The Open Court* reported that some Greenacre lectures had attracted more than eight hundred people.[118]

The more formal Monsalvat courses, which began after Vivekenanda's stay, drew smaller numbers, but Monsalvat instructors likewise lectured to the larger Greenacre crowds. (A few surviving records of the early Monsalvat years show that approximately one hundred students enrolled in its courses during 1897 and 1898, and 122 enrolled in 1899.)[119] Although most of the people who attended Vedanta lectures probably were not devotees in any formal sense, the swamis did reach many Greenacre visitors, to whom they taught both Vedanta theory and practice, according to the Ramakrishna Order they represented.

The fact that at least one and sometimes two swamis taught at Greenacre and Monsalvat for much of its history, particularly during its early years, indicates that they saw Eliot as an important site for missionary activity in the West. Martin writes that the most

aggressive and influential missionaries at Monsalvat were . . . the apostles of the new Hinduism, whom the Vedanta Society was dispatching to what it regarded as key centres across America. Vivekenanda's reception at Greenacre in 1894 had convinced them that few places in the United States held so great an opportunity as the school which had been founded at Eliot around the initial work done by their leader. Accordingly, Vivekenanda's immediate associates, Saradananda and Abhedananda themselves served as the representatives of the Hindu faith from the time of the school's founding [from 1896 to 1900].[120]

These missionaries clearly had a major impact on New Thought. A photograph taken around 1900 from the Greenacre archives shows Swami Abhedananda standing beside the popular New Thought authors Trine and Patterson.[121] Farmer and Vedanta swamis addressed New Thought gatherings during the winters, and this continuation of Greenacre-style encounters led to the formation of two early and important New Thought institutions in Boston: the short-lived Procopeia and the more enduring Metaphysical Club.[122] According to Dresser, Farmer-inspired encounters with the swamis in these various venues were "the beginning of a common interest which endured for a number of years."[123] Examples of this common interest—ways that Raja yoga (as well as Buddhist) meditation practices were incorporated and promoted by New Thought groups, books, and journals—are discussed below.

Dharmapāla and Mindfulness of Breathing

Less information is available about the Buddhist teachers at Greenacre, but at least one of them, the Ceylonese lay devotee Anagarika Dharmapāla, clearly practiced and taught Buddhist meditation during the peak 1897 season, when a host of New Thought leaders were also in residence. Excerpts from his diary that year, published sixty years later in the journal he founded, *Maha Bodhi*, record Dharmapāla's stay at Greenacre, as well as numerous contacts elsewhere with important Greenacre supporters such as Sarah Bull, Myron Phelps, and Lewis Janes.[124] Dharmapāla initially lodged at the Greenacre Inn, but after discerning "a bad atmosphere unsuited for the spiritual student where the women are," he moved to solitary quarters in a tent at "Sunrise Camp," on the bank of the Piscataqua River.[125] Nearby was the dwelling of Trine, who wrote his New Thought blockbuster *In Tune with the Infinite* at Sunrise Camp, "in a willow-woven hut by the side of the Mystic Rock."[126] At one point Dharmapāla recorded giving Trine "hints on 'Buddhist Nirvana.'"[127] Many other New Thought disciples tented for the season at the Sunrise Camp as well.

One account of Dharmapāla's activities is worth quoting at length because it indicates that he did not simply lecture on philosophy:

> One night the Buddhist monk [sic], Dharmapāla, who had astonished the natives of Eliot by going about clad in bright orange colored robes and equally gaudy yellow shoes, organized a pilgrimage to the Pines in which all Greenacre took part, to celebrate the festival of the Full Moon. The Greenacreites gathered at nightfall, arrayed in white, each person carrying a bunch of flowers and a lighted candle-lantern. Headed by Dharmapāla, who chanted in sing-song tones as he walked, the picturesque procession wended its way to the Pines where the posies were used to build an altar of flowers under a magnificent tree which had been named The Bodhi Pine in memory of the Tree of Wisdom under which tradition says the Gautama Buddha sat. By its side Dharmapāla seated himself on the ground, crosslegged, in Buddha posture, while the Greenacreites, kept en rapport by a circlet of yellow cord which each held by one hand, grouped themselves around him, endeavoring to adjust themselves to the same uncomfortable position. For several hours each gazed at his own candle on which he concentrated all his thoughts, and some of the pilgrims who had taken the matter so seriously as to follow Dharmapāla's injunction to prepare for the occasion to fast beginning at daybreak, and had let nothing but a few drops of water pass their lips all that day, were rewarded by imagining they saw the ghostly forms which they had been told might be made manifest to them.[128]

According to Dharmapāla's diary, he performed the rite on August 27, 1897.[129] A Bahá'í practitioner also recorded that on "some evenings" Dharmapāla, similarly clad, led such processions about a half-mile to the pines, where he "would sit cross-legged meditating and talking on the Eight-Fold Path of Buddha." She pointed out that "a good 'Greenacreite'" would not hesitate to take part in the ceremonies of an alien Faith."[130]

Another of Dharmapāla's journal entries, dated two weeks earlier, on August 14, 1897, recorded that he spent the morning reading instructions for meditating on the breath in a classic Pali meditation manual. ("Read the *Visuddhi Magga* chapter *Anapana Sati* and its details.") The

Visuddhimagga, composed by Buddhaghosa in the fifth century CE, is
the most influential commentary on Buddhist doctrine and practice in
Theravāda Buddhism. It includes detailed instructions for a number of
meditation practices. *Ānāpāna-sati* (mindfulness of breathing) is one of
the oldest and most basic practices of meditative concentration. It entails
focusing on the physical sensation of inhalation and exhalation, sometimes
accompanied by counting breaths from one to ten, then returning to one.
This practice is foundational for other forms of mindfulness and is probably
the most common form of Buddhist meditation practiced in the United
States today. Dharmapāla recorded spending an hour and a half meditating
under a tree near his tent, then instructing Greenacre guests in the practice.
He also asked them to observe the Eight Precepts for Buddhist laypeople the
following day.[131] On August 15 he "got up at 4:30. Sat in *ānāpāna* concentration. Began counting 1 to 10 at each breath and it was successful."[132]

He taught meditation elsewhere on his American tour as well. In
March 1897, during travels around the San Francisco Bay Area, he
"explained the Ānāpāna concentration" to a Young Ladies Club, probably
in San Francisco.[133] Shortly before his arrival at Greenacre, Dharmapāla
had taught mindfulness of breathing and cross-legged meditation at Lily
Dale, a Spiritualist resort town in western New York State: "I gave the boys
a lesson on *ānāpāna* and *baddha pariyanka*."[134] (The latter term refers to
the seated posture for meditation.)

Dharmapāla's diaries make clear that yogic breathing practices were
also popular among the people he visited. While he appreciated the Vedanta
swamis he encountered, particularly Saradananda, he also competed
with them, believing Buddhist teachings and practices to be superior to
Vedanta versions. During his March 1897 tour of the San Francisco Bay
Area, he wrote, "Went to a reception at Mrs. Willcox [*sic*]. She is practicing
breathing. American writers on health have copied the breathing process
as given in Hatha Yoga. I told Mrs. Willcox to practice the Ānāpāna." At
Greenacre, he said, his students "are all mixed up. Vedantin and Jain rules
of breathing are popular, but not Buddha's." He then reaffirmed his commitment to answering their questions, no matter how wearisome.[135]

Other Buddhist Teachers at Greenacre

Greenacre was known to Buddhists halfway around the globe. A 1903
newspaper article stated, in typically florid language, "In the Buddhist
monasteries in the far, mysterious fastnesses of India and China the

priests and scholars know of and watch with intense interest the movement started by Miss Farmer."[136] According to Anne Gordon Perry, a
historian of Greenacre, a book about the famous conference center
had been published in Japan in the summer of 1897.[137] Ten years later,
Buddhism was not so visible at Greenacre, although D. T. Suzuki
lectured there in 1907. During the previous year, Sanborn had observed,
"Those ornamental and meditative Asiatics, who have formerly been
so noticeable and so numerous here, are not so much in evidence this
year yet; although a Japanese Buddhist, Kentok Hori, has been here
for a week or two, and yesterday expounded the Japanese idea of an altruistic Nirvana, so much more practical and less contemplative than
the Ceylonese Buddhists describe."[138] The Rev. Kentoku Hori was the
director of the Buddhist Mission of North America, the San Francisco
headquarters for the Jōdo Shinshū (True Pure Land) tradition, from
March 1902 to September 1905. From late 1905 to May 1907 he was the
Mission's director for East Coast Propagation, and based in Boston.[139]
Jōdo Shinshū is a devotional rather than a contemplative tradition. Its
central practice is *nenbutsu*, recitation of the phrase "Namu Amida
Butsu" (Homage to Amida Buddha), an expression of gratitude and
faith in the power of a particular Buddha, Amida, to ensure a favorable
rebirth in the Pure Land over which he presides.

Hori's entry in Farmer's autograph book, in both English and Kanji,
reads, "To cease from wrong doing, to promote goodness, and to cleanse
one's own heart, this is the teaching of all the Buddhas."[140] This phrase,
known in Japanese as the *Shichibutsu tsūkaige* (Admonition of the Seven
Buddhas), was promoted as a pan-Asian expression of Buddhist unity
by late nineteenth- and early twentieth-century Buddhist reformers, particularly Japanese.[141] It is said to encapsulate the entirety of Buddhist
teachings. Despite the decline of "ornamental and meditative Asiatics" at
Greenacre that Sanborn had mentioned, by the time Hori left his mark on
Farmer's guest book, Buddhists—Asian and Euro-American, meditative
and devotional—had left their mark on New Thought.

New Thought, Neo-Vedanta, and Buddhism Converge

The year 1897 seems to have been an especially important period of contact
among New Thought teachers, Buddhist missionaries and sympathizers,
and Vedanta swamis, although contacts occurred in other years as well.
The Greenacre conference program that summer included New Thought

teachers Horatio Dresser, Ellen M. Dyer, Van-Anderson, Trine, Gestefeld, Patterson, and Marden, as well as Swami Saradananda, Dharmapāla, Paul Carus, and Annie Besant of the Theosophical Society.[142]

In addition, Dharmapāla visited several New Thought groups around the country that year, including the Home College of Divine Science in San Francisco, founded by Malinda Cramer.[143] He also spoke to a "meeting of ladies" in Alameda, a locus of the Home of Truth founded by Annie Rix Militz, on the way to which he met "Mr. Cramer, a Science Healer."[144] He "addressed the Christian Scientists at Miss Fulton's residence," although he does not identify the Bay Area locale; at that time, "Christian Science" referred broadly to various forms of mental healing, and Eddy's exclusivist organization probably would not have hosted a Buddhist guest.[145] In Iowa City he lectured at "Miss Gordon's Church"—most likely a New Thought congregation. Although a handful of American women, mostly Unitarians and Universalists, had been ordained by then, the only organizations regularly ordaining women clergy in those days were Hopkins's seminary in Chicago and Malinda Cramer's Home College in San Francisco.[146] In New York Dharmapāla attended a reception hosted by "Miss Walton" for "Mrs. Gesterfield"—probably Ursula Gestefeld, who had six books published in New York (four by the Gestefeld Publishing Company) between 1892 and 1897.[147] According to Stephen Gottschalk, Eddy had ejected her from Eddy's organization in part because Gestefeld's teaching of Christian Science drew conspicuously upon Buddhism and Theosophy.[148] In Boston, Dharmapāla was hosted by Sarah Bull and escorted around town by Janes and Swami Saradananda and spoke to the Free Religious Association and at the Procopeia.[149]

New Thought journals such as the *Metaphysical Magazine, Mind, New Thought, Nautilus,* and the *Journal of Practical Metaphysics* devoted considerable space to Vedanta and other Asian religious traditions. Swamis Abhedenanda, Saradananda, and Paramananda lectured frequently to New Thought audiences around the country and drew many New Thought adherents into Vedanta. A number of prominent New Thought writers practiced yoga. One important author, William Walker Atkinson, published dozens of New Thought books, including thirteen on yoga and Hindu philosophy under the pseudonym Yogi Ramacharaka. These books in turn influenced the work of Indra Devi, a Russian émigrée who studied with Krishnamurti and various teachers in India, established a yoga studio in southern California, and promoted the revival of American interest in yoga from the 1950s onward.[150]

Meditation in New Thought

In an 1889 address to the International Metaphysical League, Farmer had closed with a quotation from a poem titled "Peace; Be Still!": "Only in meditation the Mystery speaks to us."[151] By the summer of 1897, meditation was a regular feature of the New Thought offerings at Greenacre. As Sanborn reported, in the School for Applied Metaphysics led by Dresser and the Philadelphia New Thought leader Ellen Dyer,[152] the latter taught that "management of the ordinary day . . . must begin and end with a period of rest and mental re-collection, in which the soul submits itself to the influence of the infinite soul, and but for the terminology . . . it might have been [the advice of a Quaker or the Renaissance monk Thomas à Kempis, or] of a pious Brahmin or Buddhist to his co-religionists."[153] In 1904, a year that Monsalvat was run by Myron Phelps and Marie Canavarro, Sanborn reflected on Greenacre's first ten years and commented on the prominence during that time of "forms of religious meditation which have taken the general name Christian Science, without being identified with Mrs. Eddy," and "a strong Asiatic or oriental influence, which was conspicuous at Chicago, and which appeared also in . . . the books of Emerson, Alcott and Thoreau."[154]

Meditation also became a central practice elsewhere in the world of New Thought. Given that meditation on the breath, intensive concentration, and "entering the Silence" were not typical Protestant practices but *were* typical of Raja yoga and Buddhism, and given the references to these practices in Asian missionaries' writings, New Thought literature, and journalistic accounts, it seems clear that Buddhist and Hindu teachers and texts were important sources for meditation in New Thought. Although New Thought teachers typically described meditation in Christian terms, Christian meditation, such as the currently popular "Centering Prayer," was not otherwise common among Protestants until after the 1960s, except perhaps among Quakers. In the late twentieth century, Christian meditation was advocated by Catholic monks such as Thomas Merton and Bede Griffiths—who also had important encounters with Asian Buddhists and Hindus.

Dresser called the New Thought meditation meetings at Greenacre "among the best that have ever been held and gave the impetus to establish similar work elsewhere." They "had direct influence upon the religious development of the mental-healing movement in later years."[155] His own first book was *The Power of Silence*, and even in his later years, after he had ceased to be active in New Thought organizations, Dresser led an hour of meditation on Friday afternoons at the Church of Our Savior in Brooklyn Heights, a Unitarian Congregational church to which he belonged.[156] Under the auspices of the Metaphysical Club of Boston, an important organization that Dresser cofounded and that led to the formation of the International New Thought Alliance, Henry Wood established a "silence room" where one could practice meditation and affirmations.[157] Wood recommended "a daily practice of meditation and concentration, performed in solitude and silence in a seated and restful posture." He also recommended visualizing the actual words of short affirmations, which he called "mental photography."[158]

Meditation was practiced daily or weekly in a number of New Thought congregations. Nona Brooks, regarded as a cofounder of Divine Science along with Malinda Cramer, led meditation services with her sisters on weekday mornings at the Colorado College of Divine Science, a branch of Cramer's college in San Francisco. Gary Materra quotes an article Brooks wrote for a New Thought magazine in which she urged readers to make time for an hour of meditation each morning.[159] Militz's Homes of Truth offered daily meetings for meditation and prayer. Her organization was a national network of about thirty branches (primarily on the West Coast and in the Midwest), which made it the second-largest New Thought organization after Hopkins's Metaphysical Association.[160] Elizabeth Towne, whose *Nautilus* magazine grew from one thousand subscribers in 1900 to twenty-two thousand in 1904, also advised a daily practice of entering the silence, as well as breathing exercises and vegetarianism.[161] Beryl Satter has shown how novels written by women leaders of New Thought, particularly Van-Anderson and Gestefeld, characterize stillness, meditation, or "entering the Silence" as a form of female resistance to male abuses and as a source of empowerment.[162]

Harriett Luella McCollum, a teacher of practical psychology, likewise encouraged both meditative concentration and relaxation. She suggested that students begin with fifteen minutes per day for three months, then thirty minutes per day for another three months, then an hour a day for six months, and thereafter to proceed as one felt best. This practice would "clean out the under-brush and debris of personality," provide "an abundance of energy," and enable one to attain whatever one desires and overcome chronic disease, which she said resulted primarily from "fear, an acute sense of injustice, grief, and regret."[163]

One of the most widely read New Thought books of all time, Trine's *In Tune with the Infinite*, recommended taking oneself

> for a few moments each day into the quiet, into the silence, where you will not be agitated by the disturbances that enter in through the avenues of the senses. There in the quiet alone with God, put yourself into the receptive attitude. . . . Then in the degree that you open yourself to it you will feel a quiet, peaceful, illuminating power that will harmonize body, soul, and mind, and that will then harmonize these with all the world.[164]

Eventually, he wrote, "the time will come when in the busy office or on the noisy street you can enter into the silence by simply drawing the mantle of your own thoughts about you and realizing that there and everywhere the Spirit of Infinite Life, Love, Wisdom, Peace, Power, and Plenty is guiding, keeping, protecting, leading you. This is the spirit of continual prayer."[165] Trine drew upon the Swedenborgian doctrine of the correspondence between natural and spiritual realms, the Buddhist teaching expressed in the first verse of the *Dhammapada* that thoughts shape experience, and the Upanishadic notion of the individual soul's identity with God. An open, receptive attitude was essential for one to be able to experience divine influx and spiritual illumination. He also wrote about the "Law of Attraction"—that we draw pleasant or unpleasant things to ourselves by thinking positively or negatively—a theme still popular today, as evidenced by the success of the movie and book *The Secret*, which reiterate this theme. By the end of the 1950s, more than two million copies of *In Tune with the Infinite* had been sold, and the book had been translated into more than twenty languages, including Japanese, Braille, and Esperanto.[166] It continues to be heavily promoted on New Thought websites.

Emmet Fox (1886–1951), ordained by Nona Brooks as a minister of Divine Science, led a period of silent, healing meditation at the services he led in New York City. He drew crowds large enough to fill hotel ballrooms, then the 5,300-seat Hippodrome Theater, and later Carnegie Hall, where overflow crowds seated in auxiliary rooms listened to Fox's services over the public-address system. According to New Thought historian Charles Braden, these gatherings constituted "the largest congregation in New York City, and probably the greatest in all America," and Fox's meditation sessions "seemed to be the most effective part of the service."[167]

Science of Mind, the central textbook for Religious Science, founded in 1927 by Ernest Holmes, promotes daily meditation using affirmations and visualization of the circumstances that one wants to manifest (physical healing, prosperity, etc.). These are basically concentration practices. Holmes instructed students to return again and again to the phrase or image selected as the focus for meditation. "At first you may find that the thought wavers; do not oppose this, but mentally brush the wrong thought aside, much as you would brush a fly from the face with a hand. Be sure that you make no great mental effort, feel at ease and at peace, gently bringing the thought back to the point of attention."[168] These instructions are similar to those provided today in MBSR courses for meditation on the breath.

The overall text contains a series of six lessons in Holmes's theology, which is monistic but also incorporates Swedenborgian ideas such as correspondence, a tripartite cosmos (Spirit, Soul, and Body) that functions according to discernible laws, and the necessity of education to understand the spiritual truth underlying apparent reality. Healing, Holmes taught, occurs when a practitioner fully realizes the fundamental unity and perfection of all things. Religious Science practitioners could thereby bring about healing for themselves or for others.

Although he did not use the Sanskrit term, Holmes expressed an idea very similar to the Hindu concept of *lila* (play)—that all phenomena are manifestations of the creative playfulness of Brahman, a term that refers to the inconceivable Ground of Being or ultimate reality. In his words, "All seeming change is really only the play of Life upon itself; and all that happens must happen by and through It."[169] Holmes did explicitly employ the terms *maya* (illusion), which refers in both Hindu and Buddhist thought to ignorance about the true nature of reality, and *karma*, or volitional action and its consequences.

Science of Mind includes fifty-five pages of short affirmations that can be contemplated as foci for daily meditation, in a process similar to Christian *Lectio divina*. One example, which provides a good summation of Religious Science theology and practice, is this:

HERE AND NOW
Perfection is already accomplished.
I do not have to wait for the Perfect Life.
I am that Perfect Life here and now.
To-day I express the Limitless Life of the All Good.
To-day I manifest my Completion in every part of me.

To-day I am saved.
Here and now I am healed.[170]

Holmes wrote that affirmations, "followed by a silent meditation, have been most effective in the healing work" of Religious Science. This text did not, however, provide detailed instructions for silent meditation.[171]

Holmes's brother Fenwicke taught that any form of meditation was as good as any other: "Whatever leads the mind to recognize the truth that the soul is not bound, and therefore the body is not bound, is as 'good' as some other 'method' if it changes the state of consciousness from disease to health."[172] But he did recommend meditative concentration. Like his brother, Fenwicke also taught the law of karma: "What we have done in this life or in other lives—if such there were—may for a time linger in the stream of consciousness, but we can pour into that stream new hopes, thoughts, desires and purposes and change the current of the stream so powerfully that we turn the channel in a different direction."[173] Ancient Vedic religion associated the term "karma" primarily with ritual action; Buddhist thought gave it a moral inflection; that is, actions motivated by greed, aversion, or ignorance produce unwholesome effects; actions motivated by generosity, friendliness, and wisdom produce beneficial effects. Karma is not "fate" or destiny; it can be changed.

Seichō-no-Ie

The Holmes brothers were influential in the development of Seichō-no-Ie (Truth of Life), a Japanese religious organization that is one of the largest New Thought organizations in the world. Today its website lists twenty centers or groups in the United States, two in Canada, five in Brazil, fifteen in Western Europe, one each in Hong Kong, Taiwan, and Korea, and unspecified numbers in Thailand, Indonesia, and Australia.[174] Its central practice is a form of meditation called *shinsokan*. Masaharu Taniguchi, who founded Seichō-no-Ie, was deeply impressed by Religious Science, particularly by Fenwicke Holmes's book *Law of Mind in Action* (1919). In 1927 Fenwicke collaborated with Taniguchi in writing *The Science of Faith*, for which Ernest Holmes wrote the foreword.[175] In 1962 Taniguchi toured the United States, Canada, South America, and Europe and lectured at Unity and Divine Science churches in the United States, hosted in part by Dr. William Hornaday, then the minister at the Founder's Church of Religious Science in Los Angeles. Taniguchi also contributed to the magazine *Science of Mind* and other New Thought publications.[176] Describing his tour, Taniguchi wrote, "The purposes of Seichō-no-Ie and the Church of Religious Science are very much in accord."[177]

Taniguchi drew on both Buddhist and Christian ideas in formulating his doctrine. According to a sympathetic biographer, he believed that "man creates disease, poverty, adversity, favorable conditions, happiness or unhappiness according to what goes on in his mind on a conscious or unconscious level." This seemed "compatible with the Buddhistic thought that all things have their beginning in mind."[178] In the first volume of his forty-volume opus, *Truth of Life*, Taniguchi wrote, "Christ and Amida [Buddha] are two manifestations of that same Savior, Son of God, sent by the Great Life, Father, for our perfect freedom from the sufferings of existence."[179] He equated karma with Original Sin and defined *nirvāṇa* as the potential to exercise the infinite freedom and power of God or Buddha.[180]

> The real self is the Son of God; it is Buddha Nature; it is truth; and it is the only reality. The false self, the self that is subject to disease, the self of bad character, however real it may appear, is a delusion that one builds by himself in his mind and has no more real existence than a mirage in the air. To enter the life of the Son of God, the child of Buddha, the ideal self that is free from both disease and faults, we need to throw away the old and false self little by little every day. This . . . is called penitence in Buddhism, repentance in Christianity, and purification in Shintoism. They all mean the same thing. . . . Your enlightenment will be reflected in your health and environment and you will find your everyday life much easier.[181]

The "Holy Sutra" of Seichō-no-Ie, a central scripture, includes teachings attributed to an angel, about God, spirit, matter, reality, wisdom, errors, sin, and humanity. It ends with a dedication of merit very similar to those typically offered after Buddhist sūtras are recited: "May the merits of this Holy Sutra extend to all beings, and may we, together with all living beings, awaken to and fulfill our True Image."[182]

Shinsokan, the Seichō-no-Ie form of meditation, is practiced in the kneeling posture called *seiza*, with palms pressed together in the Buddhist gesture called *gasshō*. It is typically done for thirty minutes at a time. Taniguchi equated it with *prajña paramitā*, the "perfection of wisdom," a Mahāyāna virtue.[183] It includes regulated breathing, affirmations, and expressions of gratitude.[184] Practicing this meditation and reciting the Holy Sutra is said to be able to cure virtually any illness. Taniguchi's *Recovery from All Diseases* reports seventy-four cases in which followers experienced seemingly miraculous cures, and in which failures to recover from physical or psychological ailments are characterized as reflections of incorrect beliefs, mental disharmony, bad attitudes, and the like.[185]

By 1963, Charles Braden wrote, Seichō-no-Ie had attracted more than a million followers.[186] In 1966 Taniguchi's biographer said the organization claimed 300,000 tithing members, including 60,000 in South America. (Brazil has a large Japanese population.) It had "well over 2,000 centers in Japan alone," including study groups that met in people's homes. Furthermore, Taniguchi lectured to audiences as large as twenty thousand; the organization's Tokyo headquarters could accommodate two thousand; its shrine in Kyoto could seat five thousand in its main hall; and its Tobitakyu training school could seat six thousand. Its Prayer for Divine Healing Department received 67,638 requests for intercession in 1957–60.[187] By the early 1980s Seichō-no-Ie claimed 4 million members. This number declined sharply after Taniguchi's 1985 death, however, to about 800,000. In 1995 the membership still numbered "in the high six figures."[188]

Unity

Perhaps the most vivid example of meditation in an American New Thought group is Silent Unity, the central practice of the Unity School of Christianity, founded in 1889 by Charles and Myrtle Fillmore, in Kansas City, Missouri. The Fillmores studied with Hopkins and attended the Christian Science congress at the World's Parliament of Religions.[189] In 1890 they began the Society of Silent Help, now called Silent Unity, which is dedicated to silent meditation and affirmative prayer on behalf of anyone who requests it. Initially the Society met nightly in the Fillmores' home; today it operates twenty-four hours per day, seven days a week, at Unity Village, the organization's Missouri headquarters. Silent Unity now responds individually to more than two million prayer requests annually.

According to a 1925 Unity pamphlet titled *Silence*, "The first step in prayer is to direct the attention; the second is to shut the door of your inner chamber. To aid in this, close your eyes and ears to everything in the outer, that your attention may not be drawn to the without, but centered within." It goes on to say, "The best thing about stillness is that it gives God a chance to work."[190] In *Unity* magazine, Charles Fillmore wrote, "prayer with Unity is purely meditation and affirmation. It is distinctly different from the Christian prayer of supplication to an objective God."[191]

H. Emilie Cady's *Lessons in Truth*, an important text for Unity and in New Thought generally, admonishes:

> Every man must take time daily for quiet and meditation. In daily meditation lies the secret of power. No one can grow in either spiritual knowledge or power without it. Practice the presence of God just as you would practice music. No one would ever dream of becoming a master in music except by spending some time daily alone with music. Daily meditation alone with God focuses the divine presence within us and brings it to our consciousness.[192]

In addition, Charles Fillmore studied Buddhism, Vedanta, and Theosophy and incorporated the doctrine of reincarnation into his teachings. The inaugural issue of the Fillmores' magazine *Modern Thought* recommended a pamphlet summarizing Theosophical teachings, "including Reincarnation, Karma, Adeptship &c," and provided copies for twelve cents.[193] The second issue included an article suggesting that it is "probable that our Bible is partially of Oriental origin"; the third recommended and offered copies of a book titled *Illuminated Buddhism Or, The True Nirvana*.[194] The fifth included an article bylined "Roman," which said that while Christianity is better suited to American culture than Buddhism, the latter's practice of contemplation "can recall us when we carry our faulty ideals too far in fierce action."[195] In February 1890 a front-page article by Hopkins said that the teachings of Buddha and Jesus were believed because of the miraculous works they both performed, and that people have the power to perform similar feats today.[196]

The Fillmores' Modern Thought Publishing Company sold copies of Sir Edwin Arnold's poetic biography of Buddha, *The Light of Asia*, Henry Steel Olcott's *Buddhist Catechism*, A. P. Sinnett's *Esoteric Buddhism*, Spence Hardy's *Legends and Theories of Buddhists*, the *Bhagavad Gita, The Yoga Philosophy* (no author given), and a number of other books by Blavatsky and other Theosophists.[197] In 1891 the group changed its name to Unity, and in 1896 Unity Books made available copies of several lectures by Vivekenanda.[198]

Today Unity's reach is considerable. It produces several serial publications, including the *Daily Word*, a monthly booklet of affirmations that is sent to regular subscribers and distributed without charge to hospitals and prisons. It is published in six languages and twenty countries. In 1963 Braden cited a *Daily Word* circulation of 800,000; in July 2008 the figure was 913,358, with a "total reach" of more than 1.8 million.[199] Today it is also available in a digital edition and a smartphone app. Unity published *Wee Wisdom* continuously from 1893 to 1991, making it the longest-running children's magazine in the United States.[200] Unity also operated a radio station from 1924 to 1934, and produced television programs from 1953 to 1992. It now hosts a substantial website and operates a retreat and conference center and a motel at Unity Village, which covers more than fourteen hundred acres. Unity claims nine hundred affiliated churches and study groups in the Association of Unity Churches International.[201]

Just as Unity promoted interest in Buddhism and Vedanta, early American converts to Buddhism promoted interest in Theosophy and New Thought. Herman Carl Vetterling, a.k.a. Philangi Dàsa, was a Swedenborgian, Theosophist, and Buddhist who published *The Buddhist Ray*, the first Buddhist magazine in North America; he also read New Thought publications. His serial, distributed to Buddhists and Buddhist sympathizers in the United States, Southeast Asia, and Japan, promoted the mental-healing journals *Woman's World*, *The Messenger of Truth*, and *New Thought*, and periodically commented upon articles about Buddhism in *New Thought*.[202] He also published numerous articles on Theosophy and by Theosophists, including one by William Quan Judge on mental concentration.[203]

Leigh Schmidt has summarized well the relationships among New Thought, Vedanta, Buddhism, and Theosophy. These traditions, along with Unitarianism and liberal Judaism,

> crisscrossed one another in an intensive series of encounters and innovations. However distinct the metaphysical starting points of the various traditions were, they all shared an absorbing concern with the concentrated mind—a curiosity that flowed from overlapping impulses, desires, and anxieties. These exchanges were global in reach, but the larger dynamic that held them together—or, at minimum, made possible productive alliances—was religious liberalism's imagining of an essential, universal, and practical spirituality in which meditation would serve as a technique held in common.[204]

While several community-oriented New Thought groups died out after 1905, some have built enduring institutions, including Divine Science, Religious Science (now the Centers for Spiritual Living), Unity, the Foundation for Better Living, and Seichō-no-Ie. In the following chapter, we will see how the popularity of Mind Cure, promoted primarily by women-led New Thought groups, began to exert pressure on more conventional American churches and medical institutions. Gradually Christian clergy and orthodox medical doctors with elite academic credentials began to appropriate Mind Cure methods, such as affirmations and relaxation exercises, and channel them into Freudian psychology and mainstream medicine. As this process proceeded, the social concerns of many early women Mind Curers gradually faded away. But Individualist New Thought continued to spread through books, lectures, and workshops. As we will see in chapter 7, the modern Mindfulness movement most closely resembles Individualist New Thought (and vice versa).

4

Mind Cure Medicalized: The Emmanuel Movement and Its Heirs

BOTH NEW THOUGHT and Christian Science bloomed spectacularly around the turn of the twentieth century. Immediately after its publication in 1897, Ralph Waldo Trine's classic book *In Tune with the Infinite* became a best-seller: more than two million copies were sold, in more than twenty languages, including Braille. It is still in print, in both paper and electronic versions.[1] By 1902 major New Thought centers could be found in Boston, Hartford, New York, Florida, Chicago, St. Louis, Kansas City, Denver, Los Angeles, San Francisco, and Seattle. One magazine estimated that year that the movement had a million adherents.[2] By 1905 seven national New Thought organizations had been launched, all led by women.[3] The National New Thought Alliance (NNTA) formed in 1908. In 1914 representatives from Britain, France, South Africa, and Australia attended the NNTA's congress in New York, and the organization renamed itself the International New Thought Alliance (INTA). In 1915, August 28 was declared "New Thought Day" in San Francisco, launching a week-long convention of the INTA, in conjunction with the Panama-Pacific International Exposition.[4] Today the INTA claims seventeen New Thought seminaries and schools and 110 member groups across thirty-one states in the United States, plus eleven more in Canada, Australia, France, the Philippines, Jamaica, and Trinidad and Tobago.[5]

New Thought ideas also spread rapidly through publications. More than 700 New Thought books and 117 weekly and monthly serials were in print by 1905—more than 40 percent of them authored or edited by women.[6] Although several journals and organizations ceased operations by 1905, from 1906 to 1918 another forty-one journals appeared, as did 600 more books, roughly a third of which were written by women. Sixty or more serials continued to circulate throughout the first decades of the twentieth century. At least one, *Unity*, is still in print.[7] New Thought ideas also reached audiences through popular magazines such as *Good Housekeeping* and the *Woman's Home Companion*, novels, and cartoons such as *Buster Brown*.[8] Horatio Dresser's history of the movement was published in 1919.

Christian Science flourished in the early years of the twentieth century as well. In 1900, two decades after Eddy founded her church in Boston, the denomination included 470 congregations around the country, 940 ministers, and almost 49,000 members. A decade later it boasted more than twice as many churches and ministers—1,100 and 2,200, respectively—and more than 85,000 members.[9] The original Mother Church in Boston, completed in 1894, seated about nine hundred and immediately filled to capacity. An extension completed in 1906 seats more than three thousand. (Although the Mother Church is a spectacular edifice, a tour guide told me in 2015 that services held there today are quite small.)

The dramatic growth of New Thought and Christian Science early in the twentieth century led the philosopher and psychologist William James to remark, "The mind-cure principles are beginning so to pervade the air that one catches their spirit at second-hand."[10] He added, "The medical and clerical professions in the United States are beginning, though with much recalcitrancy and protesting, to open their eyes."[11]

This chapter traces the process by which the medical and clerical professions gradually began to do so. It describes the Emmanuel Movement, a collaboration between elite, psychologically trained clergy and orthodox physicians that began to shift control of mental therapeutics away from predominantly female mind-curers and toward Freudian psychology and mainstream medicine. Eventually people associated with the Emmanuel Movement went on to pioneer the fields of psychosomatic medicine, hospital chaplaincy, and pastoral counseling. In the latter half of the twentieth century, Norman Vincent Peale, D. T. Suzuki, and neo-Vedanta swamis generated interest in meditation among a new generation of neo-Freudian and humanistic psychologists. Medical research on the placebo response and on practitioners of Transcendental Meditation began at this time as well. These developments paved the way for Jon Kabat-Zinn and the contemporary Mindfulness boom. But in the process, as meditation became increasingly medicalized, individualized, and commodified, the social concerns of the early New Thought and Emmanuel Movement churches fell by the wayside.

Why the Mind Cure Movement Succeeded

As we saw in chapter 1, in James's day mainstream medicine relied on methods such as bloodletting, leeches, blistering, purging, and medications containing mercury, strychnine, and arsenic.[12] Medical education was largely unregulated, and many doctors' credentials were issued by diploma mills. So when outbreaks of cholera, influenza, typhoid, and tuberculosis swept through impoverished, industrial-era slums, Mind Curers and other practitioners of unorthodox therapies such as homeopathy and osteopathy were likely to do less damage to their patients than "regular" physicians; hence the popularity of these alternative forms of treatment.[13]

When it came to mental illness, orthodox medicine was staunchly materialist. American neurologists who treated such disorders assumed that psychological symptoms invariably resulted from some underlying physical lesion: "Wounded minds were products of wounded bodies. Diseases fell into two categories: structural and functional. The former implied a known cause; the latter an unknown cause. . . . The overwhelming majority of American physicians, regardless of their school or specialty, had ceased even to consider the possibility that psychological factors might play a role in exciting, maintaining, or treating mental and nervous disorders."[14] The widespread popularity of suggestive therapeutics did not enhance their plausibility in neurologists' minds. In order to maintain "a sense of scientific and professional credibility," most doctors avoided "at all costs anything that even remotely resembled the practices of their nonmedical rivals."[15]

The medical establishment tried repeatedly, from the mid-nineteenth century onward, to quash unorthodox healing systems. Practitioners of "irregular" medicine were excluded from medical colleges and societies, and members of the American Medical Association were prohibited from consulting or cooperating with them. In the late 1880s, state legislatures and the courts began enacting laws barring unlicensed providers, including Mind Curers, from practicing their healing arts. James, the most eminent psychologist of his day, testified against such legislation in 1896 and urged his medical colleagues to learn what they could from mental healers, who clearly were meeting a need that they were not.[16]

Mainstream churches were also failing to meet many needs. During the late Victorian period, traditional Christian understandings of the world were eroded by Darwin's discovery of evolution by random mutation and natural selection, new discoveries about the earth's age from the fields of geology and paleontology, growing awareness of religious and cultural diversity outside Europe and North America, and "higher criticism" of the Bible, in which scholars applied the same historical and literary methods of analysis to scriptures that they applied to other ancient texts.[17] At the same time, American cities were confronted with the social and economic upheavals caused by rapid industrialization and urbanization and the arrival of millions of immigrants: on the West Coast from China and other parts of Asia, and on the East Coast from Central, Eastern, and Southern Europe. During post–Civil War Reconstruction, millions of African Americans fled the Jim Crow South and moved to northern cities in search of greater freedom and economic opportunity. Many northern churches were unprepared to deal with the changes wrought by this Great Migration and wave after wave of immigration from abroad.

It was a time of extreme income inequality, unmatched by any era in American history except our own. During the Gilded Age, from the 1870s to the turn of the twentieth century, fabulous wealth concentrated in the hands of a few robber-baron industrialists: Andrew Carnegie, J. P. Morgan, Andrew Mellon, John D. Rockefeller, Henry Ford, John Jacob Astor, Leland Sanford, James B. Duke, and Charles Schwab. Although some of these men were generous philanthropists, the disparity between rich and poor was extreme, and the social safety net was nonexistent. The Socialist and Labor movements emerged in response to low pay and brutal working conditions, and competition for jobs and conflicts over wages and working conditions often turned violent.[18]

The progressive journalist Ray Stannard Baker, writing in 1908, described a sense of malaise in the religious mainstream, which largely failed to respond to these upheavals:

> With expensive equipment, large funds, an educated clergy, often costly music and other attractions, the church, taken as a whole, no longer leads or even deeply stirs the American people. Able young men do not go into the ministry as they once did; last year

there were seven hundred fewer students in fifty-eight Protestant theological seminaries than there were twelve years ago. Ministers generally are underpaid and often disheartened with the prevailing apathy and neglect. Thousands of churches, especially in the East, stand empty and deserted. . . . There is not less of moral enthusiasm or spiritual activity in America, rather far more of it, but the church somehow has ceased to lead or inspire it as it did in former times.[19]

Elwood Worcester Fights Back

In Boston, however, the Rev. Dr. Elwood Worcester was eager to address the city's pressing social needs—and to curb the growth of Christian Science, whose Mother Church was about ten blocks away from his Episcopal parish in the fashionable Back Bay. Worcester was trained as a psychologist. In 1889 he completed a PhD at the University of Leipzig, where he had studied with two of the leading experimental psychologists of the day, Wilhelm Wundt and Gustav Theodor Fechner.[20] After completing his studies in Europe, he lectured in philosophy and psychology at Lehigh University for six years, then served as rector of St. Stephen's Episcopal Church in Philadelphia from 1896 to 1904.[21] One of his parishioners and close friends there was the neurologist S. Weir Mitchell, who developed a highly restrictive "rest cure" for neurasthenia and hysteria, as many psychosomatic symptoms were then classified. In 1904 Worcester moved to Emmanuel Church, Boston's largest Episcopal congregation, where he served as rector for twenty-five years. His associate rector, the Rev. Dr. Samuel McComb, held a doctorate from Oxford, where he too had studied psychology. Both men were well read in contemporary scientific literature about the subconscious mind, dissociative states, and hypnosis, and both were critical of the materialist assumptions of mainstream medical science. They were convinced that emotional states and habits of mind could affect physical health.

"We believe with Professor [William] James that the subconscious powers of the mind really exist and that the recognition of them forms the most important advance which psychology has made since the days of Fechner and [Ernst Heinrich] Weber," Worcester wrote.[22] He assumed the reason that homeopathic and some patent remedies seemed effective was that patients had faith in them because they had been recommended by a trusted physician or the patient had been persuaded by advertisements and testimonials about their curative powers. Decades earlier, Phineas Quimby had ended his collaboration with the "medical clairvoyant" Lucius Burkmar after reaching a similar conclusion. Several decades after Worcester, this phenomenon would be dubbed "the placebo effect."

As religious liberals, Worcester and McComb accepted higher criticism of the Bible. As psychologists, they believed that many of the miraculous healings attributed to Jesus in the Gospels were really psychosomatic symptoms that Jesus cured through the power of suggestion. Although "God has the power to cure all disease," Worcester wrote, "we do not believe God cures all disease by the same means."[23] Modern, scientific psychology was one of the means by which God could effect "the cure of souls." But psychology should be practiced only by those who were scientifically trained: Worcester and McComb were appalled by the proliferation of what they regarded as quackery in the Mind Cure movement, particularly by Christian Science. Worcester fulminated:

> The doctrines of Christian Science . . . have been denounced, ridiculed, exploited times without number, apparently with as much effect as throwing pebbles at the sea checks the rising of the tide. Preachers, physicians, editors of powerful journals, philosophers, humorists, unite in pouring contempt upon this despicable superstition . . . but in spite of them it lives. While most other religious bodies are declining or barely holding their own, it grows by leaps and bounds. All over this country solid and enduring temples are reared by grateful hands and consecrated to the ideal and name of Mrs. Eddy. And this strange phenomenon has occurred in the full light of day, at the end of the 19th and at the beginning of the 20th century, and these extraordinary doctrines have propagated themselves not in obscure corners of the earth, among an illiterate and a fanatical populace, but in the chief centers of American civilization.[24]

Worcester felt more charitably toward New Thought, which he called the "Metaphysical School." He remarked favorably on the works of Henry Wood, Charles Brodie Patterson, Ralph Waldo Trine, Annie Payson Call, "Horatio Dunn"—presumably Horatio Dresser—and other New Thought writers.[25] He regarded Christian Science as "vulgar and repulsive" and deplored Eddy's rejection of material reality and conventional medical treatment. Yet he also understood the appeal her movement held for many: it met real needs that many churches of his day did not.[26] He conceded, "It does unquestionably bestow certain great benefits on believers: it makes men happy, it improves tempers, it frequently weans men from evil habits, it can reduce or remove pain, it cures certain types of disease and it gives courage to endure these which it cannot heal. It concerns itself with the present and its effects are direct, practical, immediate. Therein lies its great superiority to preaching that is vague and impractical and which deals largely with a distant future."[27] Proponents of evangelical faith healing, like the evangelist John Alexander Dowie, were popular for similar reasons: they got results, even if the cures turned out to be short-lived. Worcester believed the mainstream Church should actively continue Jesus's healing ministry by using the best scientific, medical, and psychological means available. So he began to wrest control of mental therapeutics away from the Mind Curers and shift it into the hands of doctors and clergy with elite, orthodox, academic credentials.

The Emmanuel Church that he led already offered an extensive menu of classes, camps, athletic and music programs, a library, volunteer services, and even a sort of settlement house in a poor Boston neighborhood.[28] Tuberculosis and venereal disease were rampant in the slums. In 1905 the church teamed with Dr. Joseph H. Pratt, an internist at Massachusetts General Hospital, to host weekly Tuberculosis Classes for people who were ill but too poor to afford sanitarium treatment. The weekly health and hygiene classes offered at Emmanuel taught people to care for themselves at home and included consultations with the doctor and a social worker. Women social workers surveyed patients' home environments, diet, economic situation, family circumstances, and so on, and helped patients create conditions more conducive to their overall health and well-being.

The Emmanuel Movement

In 1906, the same year the Mother Church of Christian Science completed its three-thousand-seat extension, Worcester, McComb, and two eminent physicians launched a lecture series on religion and health. After the last public talk, Worcester announced that he and McComb would be available the following morning for consultations. Nearly two hundred people, suffering from all manner of problems, showed up at the parish house the next day. The clergy and doctors did their best to triage the needs, and thus the Emmanuel Clinic was born.

The key medical partners in this endeavor were James Jackson Putnam, head of the Department of Neurology at Harvard Medical School, who would later become the first Freudian psychoanalyst in the United States; Richard C. Cabot, a Harvard-educated internist who opened the first medical social work clinic at Massachusetts General Hospital; and Isador Coriat, a psychiatrist and neurologist trained at Tufts University, who later founded the Boston Psychoanalytic Society. Figure 4.1 illustrates the currents of thought influencing the Emmanuel project.

Workers at the Emmanuel Clinic focused on treating only "functional nervous disorders"—what today are called "mental health conditions." Gradually a system developed for screening the thousands of people who applied for treatment, but demand always far exceeded available resources. In 1908 Worcester wrote, "Although our staff numbers eight men, we are unable to see one person in four who wishes to come to us, even for a single conversation."[29] The clinic provided individual consultations with doctors, the opportunity to meet individually with clergy for counseling, health education, rudimentary group counseling led by laypeople trained by McComb and Worcester, and a Wednesday night "health class" and prayer service that regularly drew eight hundred to a thousand participants. It began with singing and readings from the Bible, then a recitation of requests for prayer. After prayers were offered, one of the clergy gave "a short practical address, applying the teachings of Christ to human ills." A social hour followed.[30] Worcester observed that Catholics, Jews, and non-Episcopal Protestants regularly attended these events.

The doctors who examined each patient took a medical history and performed a physical exam. Organic diseases such as appendicitis, tumors, tuberculosis, diphtheria, and smallpox were referred elsewhere for medical treatment. People requiring psychological or religious counseling were referred to Worcester and McComb. Worcester said the clinic used the same recordkeeping methods as Massachusetts General Hospital,

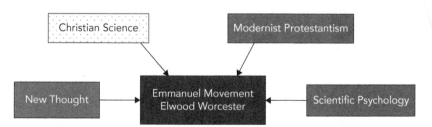

FIG. 4.1 Influences on the Emmanuel Movement.

"supplemented by notes on the moral and spiritual advice given and on the effect of this advice."[31] Cabot later complained that records were unsystematic and disorganized, making follow-up difficult in some cases.[32]

To help publicize their methods, Worcester, McComb, and Coriat cowrote *Religion and Medicine: The Moral Control of Nervous Disorders*. It described the clinic, the nature and causes of "functional neuroses," the workings of the nervous system, hypnosis and its applications, general principles of psychotherapy, and the salutary effects of faith, prayer, and a supportive religious community. In 1908, the year it was first published, the book went through nine printings: nearly 200,000 copies sold. It "was reviewed in virtually every major newspaper and medical and religious periodical and soon became the single most important text of so-called scientific psychotherapy in the United States."[33] Worcester took pains to assure readers that everything at the Emmanuel Clinic was done under the supervision of physicians: "We have done nothing without their co-operation and advice. Had this assistance been withheld, we should not have proceeded further."[34]

Functional Nervous Disorders

The ailments treated at the clinic would be described today as insomnia, anxiety, depression, posttraumatic stress, obsessive-compulsive disorders, bipolar disorder, dementia, and so on. But those classifications had not been invented yet; psychiatry and psychology were in their infancies. The *Diagnostic and Statistical Manual of Mental Disorders*, now in its fifth edition, would not be published until after World War II. In Worcester's day, common terms for such conditions included neurasthenia, hysteria, psychasthenia, nervousness, melancholy, and mania.

People suffering from neurasthenia, for example, exhibited irritability, excitability, and exhaustion: "They are apt to suffer from depression and from pains in the back and limbs, from headache and insomnia. Their enfeebled condition exposes them to other maladies such as digestive disturbances, vertigo and palpitation of the heart, weakness of vision, and in severe cases it may amount to absolute prostration."[35] Today such symptoms are frequently identified as "stress-related." In Worcester's time, observers believed that some nervous disorders seemed to be hereditary, but others resulted from the challenges of modern civilization: urban noise, overcrowding, overwork, traffic, bad weather, environmental toxins, and intoxication. "Unless we find some better means than we possess at present to calm and simplify our lives, the end of our civilization is in sight," Worcester warned, "for we cannot continue to use up our forces faster than those forces are generated."[36]

Rampant poverty was a factor in nervous disorders, Worcester found. Today it is well understood that poverty is associated with higher stress, poorer diets, and a wide variety of medical and psychological problems, from hypertension and diabetes to depression. People living in poor neighborhoods face much higher rates of morbidity and mortality than residents of more affluent neighborhoods.[37] As the leader of a wealthy congregation, Worcester mildly observed, "Without an uncharitable thought we may admit that the same system which has made one portion of society rich has made a large portion poor." Extreme income inequality affected everyone negatively, he said—not merely those who couldn't reach the bottom rung of the economic ladder. "We are slowly learning that it is impossible for anyone to be happy in this world so long as he is obliged to lower his eyes in the presence of the misery of his fellow men. . . . After awhile we shall learn that it is better to leave our children pure examples and high ideals than abnormal fortunes."[38] Worcester believed that a partnership between the church and the medical establishment was the best approach to treating nervous conditions, "because this branch of medicine is least developed in America and adequate treatment is difficult to obtain, especially by the poor."[39]

As a psychologist, he regarded all nervous disorders as "diseases of the subconscious mind," which were "produced by morbid auto-suggestion over which normal consciousness has little control." If unwholesome habits of mind could be changed and mental equipoise established, he said, symptoms would typically disappear.[40] Because these symptoms were produced by suggestion, they could be eliminated by similar methods: suggestions offered by a trusted source of authority, those made to oneself, and, in the most intensive form, hypnosis. As a pastor, he was confident that relief would "come in the discovery and use of those inexhaustible subconscious powers which have their roots in the Infinite."[41] Humanity "will learn the great lesson of 'hitching its wagon to a star,' and then it will no longer faint and stagger on its way as it does now while it childishly insists on carrying its burden on the weak shoulders of flesh."[42] In this Worcester struck chords very like those heard among authors of the New Thought movement.

Moral Disorders

Worcester and others of his day believed that the root causes of some nervous disorders were essentially moral. These included alcoholism, cocaine and opioid addiction, and sexual problems, all of which were regarded primarily as failures of will: "The most constant moral symptoms presented by the various functional neuroses are weakness of will, i.e., inability to make a decision, lack of concentration, i.e., inability to fix the mind on one subject, weakness of memory, lack of self control, irritability, rapid exhaustion, apathy, despondency, and fear. It is these moral sufferings and this sense of abject weakness which make the conditions we have described so terrible."[43] Alcoholism topped Worcester's list of devastating moral disorders. "Among all the predisposing causes of nervousness, the first place must be assigned to drunkenness," he wrote.[44] After describing the negative effects of alcohol use on individuals and their families, he concluded, "As the flood of alcohol rises the prevalence of neurotic weakness rises with it."[45]

The second most common cause of nervous ailments "is venereal disease and the moral and physical consequences of illicit sexual relations,"[46] Worcester believed. Young people were waiting longer to get married, divorce was more common, and many were losing religious faith and relaxing ethical standards. "The result of this is a constant increase of sexual vice." Men also used prostitutes, then infected their wives with venereal diseases, particularly syphilis, at alarming rates. "Prostitution is the cancer of our civilization," Worcester said, but

> it is the penalty to be paid for our ideal of monogamy, which in the present state of humanity can never be perfectly realized. The result is the existence of a large class of sad and degenerate beings which polygamous countries hardly know, a class branded by every infamy, preyed upon by every brutal passion and by the foulest disease. The women of this class suffer from every form of nervous, mental, and moral disease; that their lives are short and that they are frequently shortened by suicide, goes without saying. No human being suffers so disproportionately for human frailty as the fallen woman.[47]

This Victorian view of sexual and gender relations—that men cannot control themselves, that sexual trafficking is inevitable, and that unmarried, sexually active women are either degenerates or victims—is cause for eye-rolling, if not outrage, among contemporary readers with feminist and womanist sensibilities. Worcester's friendly nod toward polygamous societies, which he suggested arrange for all unattached or socially marginal women to be married, is worthy of raised eyebrows at least. Clearly he was a creature of his time, place, and social position.

Worst of all, in his view, was the fact that women were entering the workforce in greater numbers: "Girls and young women who were formerly brought up in the privacy of the home and under parental control are now found in large stores and factories, and in offices where, freed from all moral restraint, they work side-by-side with men, often for wages which barely suffice for subsistence. The result is an immense increase in irregular or temporary sexual connections."[48] Such connections caused remorse, guilt, secrecy, and fear of discovery. These pressures and the "horror which attends the discovery of pregnancy all react powerfully upon the nervous system and they may lead to insanity."[49] Unmarried pregnant women were generally shamed and shunned. Not surprisingly, Worcester does not identify sexual shaming, moralizing, violence, or lack of access to effective methods of birth control as factors contributing to these problems.

Menstruation and physical labor, however, *were* causes of nervous illness, he opined. "Domestic servants over the age of forty are quite frequently slightly demented"—not just because of the drudgery and economic insecurity they endured but because they were obliged to perform manual labor during their periods. Intellectual stimulation was another risk factor for women: the "nervousness frequently discoverable among students in women's colleges is also due . . . to the overtaxing of the brain and nervous system during the menstrual period."[50]

Herein lies a key difference between Worcester and the female ministers of the Mind Cure movement. For all his scientific rhetoric, Worcester's attitudes about gender were traditionally patriarchal and paternalistic—very different from those of women New Thought leaders who wanted to improve the rights, status, and powers of women. Given Worcester's views, it is unfortunate that the most frequent users of Emmanuel Clinic services were "unmarried women teachers and married women, mostly mothers, of moderate or restricted means." Female teachers, who were generally expected to be single, complained of monotony, loneliness, sadness, the difficulty of their work, and fears of growing old and helpless.[51] At the same time, many wives suffered from "marital incompatibility . . . the intemperance or bad conduct of their husbands . . . shock, or . . . some painful moral experience."

One wonders to what extent Worcester was referring to rape, incest, or other forms of interpersonal violence. One also wonders how the counsel offered to such women by clergy and doctors like those at the Emmanuel Clinic compared to that offered by women Mind Curers, particularly those working to secure women's right to vote and hold public office and to reform laws governing marriage, marital property, and working conditions. Unfortunately Worcester burned the Emmanuel Clinic records when he retired in 1929, so we may never know.[52]

Regarding sexual behavior other than married heterosexuality, Worcester primly remarks, "Of sexual perversions I shall not speak except to say that they are recognized forms of mental and nervous disease which can frequently be removed by suggestion"[53]—a belief that subsequent medical and psychological research has disproved. His more direct colleague Coriat claimed that hypnosis works well for "various sexual aberrations," including masturbation, low or high libido ("sexual neurasthenia, sexual hyperexcitability"), sadism and masochism, fetishes, and homosexuality.[54] It is also good for insomnia, alcoholism, constipation, bed-wetting, and irregular menstruation, he said, but less effective for cocaine and morphine addiction, which require medically supervised withdrawal in an institutional setting.[55] Interestingly, Coriat regarded alcoholism as a disease—a hypothesis that subsequently gained widespread acceptance and that has only recently begun to be critiqued.[56] Coriat identified its main predisposing factors as heredity and environment. He also offered an early discussion of what today is called neuroplasticity: the brain's ability to form new neural connections in response to experience, learning, or injury.[57]

Suggestive Therapeutics

The primary therapeutic methods employed at the Emmanuel Clinic were rest or work, depending on the patient's particular needs, and various forms of suggestion. The latter included waking suggestions, offered to patients in a simple relaxed state; training in autosuggestion, which patients could later perform at home; and hypnosis, for more extreme cases. Worcester described waking suggestions, the mildest form of therapy, in detail. First, he instructed,

> make the patient calm and quiet. This in itself is a decided advantage, especially if one explains to the patient how to obtain

this condition at home. If a very nervous person who is suffering from acute moral or physical agitation can become profoundly still for an hour, the benefit is frequently noticeable. . . . I place the patient in a comfortable reclining chair, instruct him how to relax his arms, his legs, his neck and body, so that there shall be no nervous tension or muscular effort. Then standing behind him I gently stroke his forehead and temples, which has a soothing and a distracting effect. Without attempting to induce sleep I inform him that his body is resting and that his mind too will rest, that he will not let his thoughts run on unchecked, but that it will lazily follow my words, and that when I make a useful suggestion to him he will repeat it to himself. I then tell him that all nervousness is passing from him, that everything is still within him, that his heart is beating quietly and regularly and that he is breathing gently and slowly. I suggest to him that he is entering into peace . . . and his thoughts are becoming vague and indistinct. As soon as I see these suggestions are effective I pass to the curative suggestions. If the patient is suffering pain I assure him that the pain is diminishing and that in a little while it will be gone. If I am treating a patient for insomnia, I tell him he will sleep soundly to-night, that he will feel drowsy and fall asleep soon after he goes to bed and that if he awakens at all in the night he will make a few suggestions to himself and immediately fall asleep again. In short I make the suggestions as positively and simply as possible and under these conditions I usually find it advisable to repeat them more than once.[58]

It is not clear whether Worcester used this method with female clients. Treatment usually lasted fifteen minutes to an hour, and some patients took a short nap. He also encouraged mothers and other trusted persons to make "good suggestions to . . . children while they are in a state of natural sleep." By employing this method, he claimed to have helped children overcome various fears, masturbation, bed-wetting, nail-biting, sleepwalking, nocturnal emissions, nervous twitches, anger, violence, lying, and stammering.[59]

Although Worcester found waking suggestions effective for "ordinary neuroses," as an Episcopal priest he did not believe that mere human agency—his or the patient's—ultimately produced a cure. "When our minds are in a state of peace and our hearts open and receptive to all good influence," he wrote, "I believe that the Spirit of God enters into us and a power not our own takes possession of us." That is what catalyzed the transformation when people who had struggled with addiction or "sexual vice" felt suddenly freed after years of struggle. "[Although] we may call this suggestion, I can hardly believe that the mere assurance of a human being can effect moral changes so stupendous and to the unaided victim so impossible."[60]

Worcester also recommended contemplative prayer. Unlike many forms of American Protestantism, the Episcopal Church had not entirely rejected the contemplative traditions of its Roman Catholic parent. Such prayer

> consists not in offering some definite request to God, but in sinking the soul in Him, in the union of the finite self with the infinite. This practice is as old as religion itself, is found in all higher contemplative religions as well as among the Quietists and Mystics. It has formed a prominent part of the devotions of the earlier Friends. Passive prayer is only possible when the body is still, placed in such a posture that it is perfectly relaxed and so not able to distract or tax the mind. Then the soul is absorbed in the form of God, His presence, His power, His peace, so that for the time being all other feelings are obliterated.[61]

Meditation calms and refreshes "like a healing bath."[62] Again, it is difficult to discern a major difference between Worcester's advice in these areas and those of New Thought writers.

Hypnosis and Autosuggestion

McComb contributed a chapter to *Religion and Medicine* on autosuggestion, which he defined as "a self-imposed narrowing of the field of consciousness to one idea, by holding a given thought in mental focus, to the exclusion of all other thoughts."[63] (Buddhists call this method *śamatha*, a calming form of meditative concentration.) The best time for this, McComb believed, is during the "hypnagogic state" immediately before falling asleep or just as one is waking up. "Lying in bed or in a comfortable arm chair, with the eyes closed and the limbs relaxed, formulate and repeat mentally the thought that contradicts the unhealthy state of consciousness or that expresses the virtue or quality you desire to possess.

The auto-suggestion must be made over and over again, not with a sense of stress or strain, but calmly and with quiet assurance."[64] The affirmative formula he recommended that meditators recite to themselves in this state is worthy of an automaton: "I am organically sound: the nervous system is intact; the bodily organs are discharging their proper functions, therefore I ought to have a mind clear and alert, able to grasp ideas and to relate to them logically: therefore, such a mind can be mine. Henceforth I will think easily and correctly; study will be a delight and work a joy."[65]

McComb ascribed to autosuggestion a wide range of religious phenomena: the powers attributed to amulets; dreams or hallucinations in which divinities offered guidance; a yogi's union with Brahman in Hindu Vedanta;[66] speaking in tongues among early Christians (and the American Pentecostals who began to emerge during McComb's career at Emmanuel); stigmata and the religious visions of medieval Christian mystics; and Swedenborg's visits to heaven and hell. In keeping with the Christian triumphalist and Orientalist views of his day, McComb assumed that religions ranged from "primitive superstition" (e.g., belief in amulets) at the lowest level, to Christian faith at the pinnacle. But hypochondriacs, hysterics, faddists, and fanatics of all kinds suffered from dissociation and pathological forms of autosuggestion, he believed. Such people simply needed to see the world more like he did, tempering Christian doctrine with a scientific worldview.[67]

When it came to bad habits, he argued, one must simply will oneself to change: "The power to will comes by willing just as the power to think comes by thinking."[68] This is "the secret of that new sense of power which has come into so many lives to-day through the medium of Christian Science, Faith-healing, Metaphysical Healing, the Raja Yoga of Indian theosophy, and other forms of mental gymnastics. These systems are so many aids to the training of the will by auto-suggestion so that the reserves of mental and moral energy within us may be made available for physical and spiritual health."[69] McComb ended with this disclaimer: "The success attending auto-suggestion varies with the mental constitution and the degree of suggestibility of the subject and the nature of the trouble to cure which the suggestion is made."[70] While there is no doubt truth to this, one could as easily claim that failures of faith healing result from insufficient faith on the part of the patient.

The neurologist Isador Coriat insisted in his contribution to *Religion and Medicine* that hypnosis is "one of the most important methods of treatment and investigation possessed by medical science." Although its "use by traveling charlatans and mountebanks for public exhibition purposes has made it the subject of wide-spread misconception, fear, and even ridicule,"[71] it is nevertheless "one of the triumphs of modern science . . . far removed from the occult." Many functional disorders "have been greatly ameliorated and in many cases absolutely cured by hypnotic suggestion," he wrote. In addition, "experimental hypnosis has enabled us to penetrate deeply into the workings of consciousness, especially the baffling states of double personality and subconscious phenomena."[72]

Coriat defined hypnosis as "an intense form of artificial abstraction (absent-mindedness) brought on by suggestion," which "either narrows or dissociates the consciousness."[73] It is marked by amnesia and suggestibility.[74] Although hypnosis cannot be used to force unwilling people to act against their moral convictions, he insisted, it should only be performed by physicians for medical treatment "or for the analysis of certain abnormal mental states."[75]

Communal and Character Development

Such individual therapies were not the only treatments for nervous disorders at the Emmanuel Clinic. The church's Wednesday evening service for healing prayers was extremely popular, as was the social hour that followed. Although Worcester was a psychologist, he was primarily a priest and pastor. Thorough and careful assessment of a patient required not just physical diagnosis but a spiritual assessment: attention to an individual's character, habits, theology, and motivations—which varied from person to person. There was no one-size-fits-all treatment.

Qualities such as selfishness, entitlement, worry, resentment, poor impulse control, and compulsions could all produce "neurasthenia and allied troubles," Worcester wrote. Negative theologies, such as obsessive concern with a punitive God, unresolved guilt, or religious delusions could also cause intense psychological distress.

> The sense of some moral fault unpurged by penitence creates a dissociation of consciousness which in turn may lead to hysteria, and hysteria, as we know, can stimulate almost any disease and turn life into a prolonged wretchedness. Or again, wrong conceptions of God and of His relations to his creatures depress the soul, sink it into melancholy delusions and thereby set up all sorts of functional nervous disturbances. . . . If then the representatives of Christ to-day

are to speak that healing and reconciling word, they must first understand more of the relations between abnormal states of mind or soul and the reflections of these states in the physical organism.[76]

He cautioned that this kind of psychologically and spiritually astute discernment "is not a task which every shepherd is qualified to perform."[77]

Although Worcester believed that religious faith played a key role in healing, and on rare occasions could produce "sudden and spectacular cures," these were exceptional and "seldom permanent." Clearly positioned on the liberal, modernist end of the Protestant spectrum, he explained, "Although we try to awaken faith on the part of our patients, we do not desire blind or fanatical faith." Clinic workers claimed no personal power, tried to explain carefully the rationale behind the therapeutic methods they employed, noted their limitations, and maintained "a good library of standard works which we freely lend" so patients could educate themselves about current developments in psychology and theology.[78]

Worcester, unlike the women leaders of New Thought churches, had access to university training in theology and psychology. But like New Thought women, Worcester and his church *were* oriented toward ethical and spiritual development and service to the wider community. He and his colleagues believed that spiritual, psychological, and physical well-being involved not just concern about one's own problems and personal character development but religious discipline, social support, and attention to the needs of others. In many cases, Worcester argued,

before the patient can be restored to health it is necessary to eradicate powerful habits, to supply new motives, to supplant the most intense egotism by new and real interest in others, to hew out new pathways in the brain, sometimes to create or re-create a will. This requires an effort on the part of the physician greater than is involved in writing a prescription. It demands moral qualities of the highest order, intuition, sympathy, kindness of heart, and an absolutely inexhaustible patience. Character can be imparted only by those who possess it.[79]

Healing had to be holistic. "We desire not merely to give [patients] temporary relief, but to do them permanent good, to open to them the possibility of a new life, not merely to restore them to health but to give them motives for living."[80] Although people who used clinic services were not pressured to join the church or to convert to Christianity, they were invited to participate in social activities the church offered and to get involved in helping others. Group therapy provided opportunities for lonely, despairing people to share their troubles, receive an empathetic hearing, and build supportive relationships.

> In the congregation one member sustains another. Worship breaks in upon the daily drudgery with days of rest and meeting, and orders the life of the individual and of the community by the establishment of fixed customs. The more religion descends into life, the more it remains at man's side early and late, the more it affects our daily life, the more powerful its consoling influence. In proportion as it disappears out of the human life, and as the individual and the nation become irreligious, the more comfortless and irritating life becomes.[81]

The journalist Ray Stannard Baker illustrated the clinic's wraparound approach to care. He described the case of an alcoholic man treated at Emmanuel, who received follow-up care from social workers, both paid and volunteer. The church provided a loan to help him support his family until he could begin making a living again, and the family received social support. The patient recovered and paid back the loan. Because of this holistic approach, Baker said, "the lives of many men and women have been utterly transformed: from weak, hopeless, complaining, suffering beings, they have changed [into] hopeful, happy, courageous beings."[82] The Emmanuel Clinic likewise benefited the church and enlivened its ministry, Worcester declared.

> Instead of sustaining merely conventional relations with people, our relations have been sacred and delightful. For we have been called upon to help and permitted to help in the real and serious business of life. We have passed through the deep waters with hundreds upon hundreds of men and women. We have stood between them and temptation, between them and despair, between them and death. We have had the supreme satisfaction of using constantly our highest faculties and of exerting our utmost power in behalf of our people in their hour of need.[83]

McComb's approach was more moralistic than Worcester's. Reading the chapters he contributed to *Religion and Medicine*, one gets the sense that his advice to many of the patients who consulted him was "Get ahold of yourself." In a chapter on suicide and its prevention, he described suicide as "a sign of moral weakness." His comments evoke the spirit of "muscular Christianity," a cultural backlash against the perceived "feminization" of Christianity during the mid-nineteenth-century Victorian era.[84] In a chapter on fear and worry, he advised anxious readers:

> Cultivate that condition of mind which, conscious of God's fatherly regard, feels safe in His hands, and is willing to meet good or evil as He wills it. In a word, reeducate yourself, morally and spiritually. Summon the forces of your nature against this debasing fear, and through prayer, through obedience to law moral and law physiological, through concentration on some enterprise that carries you beyond your petty interests, win back the gift of self-control which is the secret of every life worth living.[85]

The ethical formation of children was key: "It is within the power of the humblest to train their children in habits of poise, of industry, of duty, of unselfish service, of temperance in eating and drinking, of total abstinence so far as stimulants are concerned. And this is done by example even more than by precept."[86]

It is important to notice that although the Emmanuel Movement stressed "scientific" medicine and psychology, it was fundamentally oriented toward *community*, both the church congregation and the needs of Boston's poor. It stressed spiritual and practical support, ethical and spiritual development, and service to others. Courtenay Baylor, one of the clinic's lay counselors, focused on helping those who abused alcohol. Eventually he developed a method of peer counseling among recovering alcoholics called the Jacoby Movement. While no direct relationship has been documented between Baylor's group and Alcoholics Anonymous, both emerged around the same time and used similar methods.

Publicity: Positive and Negative

Through publicity in popular magazines, the Emmanuel Movement spread rapidly around the United States and internationally.[87] Beginning in 1907 Worcester and McComb published a series of articles in *Good*

Housekeeping that described the movement and its founders and responded to letters from (mostly female) readers, offering advice on various topics, including childrearing. From 1907 to 1910 the *Reader's Guide to Periodical Literature* indexed thirty-nine articles about the movement—including seven by McComb, six by Worcester, and one by Cabot—in outlets such as *American Magazine, Arena, Century, Current Literature, Everybody's Magazine*, the *Hibbert Journal*, the *Independent, Ladies' Home Journal, Living Age*, the *North American Review, Outlook, Popular Science Monthly, Putnam's Magazine*, the *Review of Reviews, Science, Survey*, and *World's Work*. Worcester published a series of four articles in the *Ladies' Home Journal* from November 1908 to February 1909 called "The Results of the Emmanuel Movement," describing how the clinic had helped people with problems ranging from alcoholism to insomnia, repetitive strain injury, fear of surgery, stage fright, and marital distress.[88] He and McComb also produced a series of pamphlets describing their work and lectured in several American and European cities, where local press covered their visits. In June 1908, at the invitation of the Archbishop of Canterbury, McComb described the movement to the decennial Lambeth Conference of bishops from around the worldwide Anglican Communion. According to a *New York Times* account the following November, when McComb's allotted thirty minutes ended, the audience insisted that he continue for another hour and a half.[89] During the summer of 1908, Worcester, McComb, Coriat, and others offered a three-week course on psychoreligious therapeutics that drew more than 140 participants.

Baker's December 1908 article on the Emmanuel Movement in the *American Magazine* stated that forty Protestant churches around the country were then running clinics or providing other health services. Among the best known were headed by Bishop Samuel Fallows of St. Paul's Reformed Episcopal Church in Chicago; by the Rev. Lyman Powell of St. John's Episcopal Church in Northampton, Massachusetts; and by the Rev. Loring Batten of St. Mark's Healing Mission in New York City.[90] In San Francisco, Episcopal authorities established a Department of Psychotherapy at St. Luke's Hospital, as well as a training program for clergy, nurses, and physicians. By 1909 clinics were operating in Brooklyn, Buffalo, Detroit, Philadelphia, Baltimore, and Seattle, under the auspices of Baptists, Presbyterians, Congregationalists, Unitarians, and Universalists.[91]

At the same time, Baker noted, "doctors, health departments and hospitals are extending their work into wholly new fields, social, psychic, philanthropic, which were formerly more or less within the province of the church."[92] In January 1909 he published another lengthy article in *American Magazine* describing the Social Service Department of the Outpatient Clinic at Massachusetts General, founded by Cabot, which tried to address the environmental, economic, and social conditions fueling disease among many poor Bostonians.[93]

Eventually the national visibility the Emmanuel Clinic received attracted sensational stories claiming that Worcester had resurrected someone from the dead and made the lame walk—claims Worcester vigorously denied.[94] Widespread publicity drew blistering criticism from physicians who objected to lay counselors offering psychotherapy without academic credentials, and from clergy who thought psychology was outside their purview. Both groups wanted to maintain a sharp distinction between clergy and medical doctors.

In response to these critiques, two of the doctors who helped to found the Emmanuel Clinic eventually withdrew their support. James Jackson Putnam told Baker he thought the movement "has gone too far and too fast, that it will escape from the hands of its well-grounded originators and be used by unwise and careless imitators." Cabot withdrew as well, "not because he thought the movement not worth while, but because . . . [he] was regarded as a 'scab' (strike breaker) by most of his colleagues, and was losing professional prestige and chances of promotion in the medical faculty of which he was a member."[95] Putnam and other critics worried that clergy and lay counselors without sufficient training would give psychological treatment to people who actually needed skilled medical care. If clergy wanted to engage in therapeutic work, they should "form a new *institution* analogous to that of the medical profession devoted wholly to the work."[96] These were prophetic words, foreshadowing the development of professional chaplaincy and the psychological subfield of pastoral counseling—but the time was not yet ripe. Emmanuel Movement leaders conceded that some therapists might go overboard. But because their clinics and churches provided ongoing relationships, education, and support for patients, the movement was "better fitted through its many avenues of personal influence and social work to influence the patient and change his life than is the busy, privately paid doctor."[97]

Some doctors believed "that both clergymen and physicians should strengthen each other's position and influence," Baker wrote. But efforts to provide social work services through medical facilities rather than through churches indicated a growing rift between religious and medical

approaches to mental therapeutics. "Though there is a union of ministers and doctors in the work of the Emmanuel movement, yet back of it
all lies a real struggle of the two professions to attain a greater influence
over the lives of men."[98] As the medical establishment asserted more control over mental therapeutics, its approach to them became increasingly
individualized. The holistic approach to treatment and the social reform
efforts promoted by religious communities faded away.

Sigmund Freud formally introduced Americans to his staunchly
atheist brand of psychoanalysis in 1909, in a series of lectures at Clark
University in Worcester, Massachusetts.[99] His work began in the French
hypnotic tradition; he employed hypnosis in his early practice, and his
theory of personality is in part a response to Pierre Janet's work on
hypnotic amnesia and dissociation. Eric Caplan argues that the positive reception Freud received was a direct result of widespread interest
in New Thought, Christian Science, and similar lay forms of mental
healing. The Emmanuel Movement was the linchpin in the process of
persuading the medical establishment that mental therapeutics were
worth investigating.

> The fundamentally positive reception of psychoanalysis in the
> United States during the second decade of the twentieth century
> can be attributed to a host of factors that had little to do with the
> substance of Freud's theories. The allure of psychoanalysis derived
> in large measure from the unprecedented combination of popular
> and professional enthusiasm for mental therapeutics that existed
> at the time of its introduction to the United States. . . . When
> Freud first set foot on American soil, psychotherapy was already
> integrally woven into the fabric of American culture and American
> medicine.[100]

Before 1910, Caplan notes, the *Reader's Guide to Periodical Literature* listed
not a single article on psychoanalysis or Freud, but thirty-one articles on
the Emmanuel Movement. "In contrast to both Christian Science and New
Thought, each of which had been painted in relatively unflattering colors,
the Emmanuel program's fusion of 'science' and established religion
was initially depicted in highly favorable terms."[101] The appeal to mainstream medical science by white, male spokespersons with Establishment
credentials is also a factor in the success of the contemporary Mindfulness
movement's efforts to promote meditation as medicine.

Emmanuel's Heirs

Because of the controversy created by sensational press and vocal critics, Worcester stopped giving interviews and publishing articles. Press reports declined sharply in 1910 and had ceased altogether by 1911. But the work continued quietly for the next two decades. A small group of doctors and clergy continued to explore relationships between religion and health and eventually developed the fields of chaplaincy and pastoral counseling. Figure 4.2 illustrates the process by which Mind Cure methods were medicalized.

One of the people Worcester counseled was Anton Boisen (1876–1965), a Presbyterian minister who later pioneered Clinical Pastoral Education (CPE). This program trains prospective clergy to work as chaplains in hospitals and other nonchurch institutions during their seminary education, ministering to people of any faith or none. Some Christian denominations require at least one four-hundred-hour unit of CPE training as a prerequisite for ordination. Professional chaplains wishing

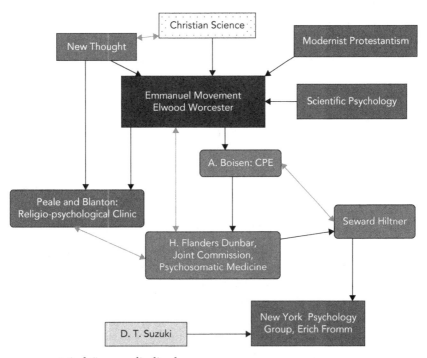

FIG. 4.2 Mind Cure medicalized.

to be Board Certified by the Association of Professional Chaplains must complete at least four units of CPE, among other requirements.

Clinical Pastoral Education for Chaplains

During their clinical training, chaplains learn to integrate theology and psychology, assessing and addressing patients' spiritual needs as members of interdisciplinary treatment teams. Boisen studied theology and the psychology of religious experience with Dr. George Albert Coe at Union Theological Seminary. Boisen himself suffered from bouts of mental illness, including five major psychotic events. Two of these episodes were severe enough to require hospitalization. The first occurred in October 1920, when Boisen was forty-six, and was precipitated by a personal crisis: the religious organization for which he worked dissolved, and the love of his life refused to marry him. Boisen was escorted by police to the Boston Psychopathic Hospital, then spent fifteen months in the Westboro State Hospital. Toward the end of this time, in November 1921, Elwood Worcester began counseling him and continued to do so for several months after Boisen's release in January 1922. They corresponded for the rest of Worcester's life.[102]

Boisen took up residence at the Episcopal Theological School in Cambridge, Massachusetts, and spent the next couple of years studying behavioral sciences and theology in seminars at Harvard and Andover in an effort to understand his own experiences. He studied social ethics and learned to prepare case records with Richard Cabot, who had helped to found the Emmanuel Clinic and the Social Service Department at Massachusetts General Hospital. Case studies later became a standard teaching method in CPE. Boisen differed with Cabot on a key point: he believed that mental illness could have emotional or psychological causes, such as guilt or shame; Cabot was a staunch materialist who believed mental illness had only physical, chemical causes. In 1924 Boisen become the chaplain at Worcester State Hospital, which housed some 2,200 patients. The following year, four theological students joined him for a summer session of clinical training and work. The seminarians met with patients during the day and attended seminars in psychology and religion in the evening. That September, Cabot published "A Plea for a Clinical Year in the Course of Theological Study," arguing that seminarians should learn "applied theology" by tending to hospital patients' emotional and spiritual needs, while physicians worked to heal patients' bodies. Over the next four years, the number of students participating in Boisen's summer program nearly quadrupled.

One of Boisen's first students was Helen Flanders Dunbar, who went on to complete a Bachelor of Divinity degree at Union, a PhD in comparative literature at Columbia, and an MD at Yale. She also collaborated with Worcester when he traveled weekly to New York to do his healing ministry at Grace Church on Broadway. The rector there, Rev. Dr. Russell Bowie, was Dunbar's pastor. In 1930 the Council for Clinical Training of Theology Students (CCTTS) was incorporated, with Cabot's home address listed as the headquarters. Dunbar became its first medical director after completing her medical degree. That same year the death of Boisen's mother precipitated another psychotic episode, and he was hospitalized for three weeks. At that point Cabot terminated his support of Boisen's program and shifted it to a program at Massachusetts General: a medical rather than a mental hospital. In 1932 Boisen moved to Elgin, Illinois, near Chicago, to become chaplain at Elgin State Hospital. He established the Chicago Council for Clinical Training there. After a final episode of acute mental illness in 1935, when the woman he loved died of cancer, he remained symptom-free until his death in 1965.[103]

Gradually CPE began requiring chaplain trainees to do their own personal psychological work during the training program, to surface emotional issues that could compromise pastoral care. It is now a standard feature of seminary training in mainstream theological schools, and chaplains are employed in thousands of hospitals, hospices, correctional facilities, schools, and other institutional settings around the country.

The New York Psychology Group and Psychosomatic Medicine

Under Flanders Dunbar's leadership the CCTTS moved to New York City, and from 1931 to 1936 she was also director of the Joint Committee on Religion and Medicine, a collaboration between the Federal Council of Churches and the New York Academy of Medicine, which promoted understanding of psychosomatic illness.[104] In 1935 she published *Emotions and Bodily Changes*, a groundbreaking bibliography of research on the somatic effects of emotional states. In 1943 she published *Psychosomatic Diagnosis*; a popularized version of this work came out in 1947 as *Mind and Body: Psychosomatic Medicine*, which became a best-seller. She proposed a theory not so different from that of unorthodox healers who preceded her: that psychological energy manifests as physical symptoms when it cannot find an outlet. She identified self-harming behavior as an expression of emotional distress. In 1936 the Joint Committee dissolved. The New York Academy of Medicine developed the Committee on Emotions and Health, and the Federal Council of Churches (later the National Council of Churches) established the Commission on Religion and Health. Charter members of the Commission included people whose significance will be outlined below: the Rev. Norman Vincent Peale, Dr. Smiley Blanton, and the Rev. Dr. Seward Hiltner, a theologian at the Princeton Theological Seminary who became a major leader in the developing field of pastoral counseling. He was the Commission's secretary for more than a decade.

Hiltner was the executive secretary of the CCTTS under Flanders Dunbar from 1935 to 1938, when he became executive secretary of the Federal Council of Churches Commission on Religion and Health, a post he held until 1950. He also helped to launch a regular but informal gathering called the New York Psychology Group, which assembled faculty and graduate students from Columbia University and Union Theological Seminary to discuss religion and health from 1942 to 1945.[105] He and the psychoanalyst Erich Fromm launched the group after meeting at a conference. Other members were the anthropologist Ruth Benedict, who studied Japanese culture and Zen, and the psychologists Rollo May and Carl Rogers. The group's unofficial leaders were Fromm and the theologian Paul Tillich. Although information on the group is scarce, Allison Stokes provides an enormously helpful reconstruction in *Ministry after Freud,* based on archival sources and material she received directly from Hiltner. She found that by 1973, half of the top ten books assigned in seminary courses on pastoral care and counseling were authored by members of the New York Psychology Group. They produced nearly a quarter of the eighty-one seminary texts she identified.[106]

Positive Thinking, Pastoral Counseling, and the Placebo Effect

Not far from Columbia University, modern psychology and New Thought were also converging in the ministry of Norman Vincent Peale, who pastored New York's Marble Collegiate Church from 1932 to 1984. In 1937 he and the psychiatrist Smiley Blanton launched a mental health clinic in the church basement, and over the next several decades they founded a series of organizations that offered pastoral counseling and trained other clergy and psychologists to do so.[107] Peale credited the Religious Science teachings of Ernest Holmes with making him a positive thinker.[108] His 1952 book, *The Power of Positive Thinking*, spent three and a half years on *The New York Times* best-seller list. His blend of Protestant positive thinking, Western psychology, nationalism, and libertarianism reached many millions. He preached to four thousand people a week at Marble Collegiate, reached millions through a radio show broadcast for fifty-four years, and had 4.5 million subscribers to his magazine, *Guideposts*.[109]

Among the techniques he recommended for achieving a happy, satisfying life was one called "Relax for Easy Power." In addition to physical relaxation, even for a moment or two during traffic jams, he encouraged fifteen minutes of meditation per day. "I know a number of men and women who practice this . . . for reducing tension. It is becoming a quite general and popular procedure nowadays," he wrote.[110] In 1955 *The Power of Positive Thinking* sold more copies than any book but the Bible. Three years later, in 1958, Peale's book and Trine's *In Tune with the Infinite* continued to be the top two best-selling inspirational books in the United States, and New Thought themes were conspicuous in many of the other top fifty.[111]

That same year the placebo effect began to generate significant attention in American medicine.[112] The term refers to a phenomenon in medical research, in which some clinical study participants report reductions in their symptoms even after receiving placebos, substances (e.g., pills or injections) that are physiologically inert, or after undergoing sham surgical procedures. In some cases these responses are even greater than those attributable to pharmaceuticals.[113] Henry K. Beecher, an anesthesiologist at Harvard Medical School, published a paper in the *Journal of the American Medical Association* arguing for the necessity of administering placebos to control groups in medical research. This sparked further interest in the mind's role in physical healing.

Zen and Psychotherapy: D. T. Suzuki at Columbia

Interest in Buddhist meditation enjoyed a renaissance during the 1950s, thanks to D. T. Suzuki (1870–1966), the single most influential modernist Buddhist in the West for most of the twentieth century. As a lay student at Engakuji, a Rinzai Zen temple in Kamakura, Japan, he translated Zen master Sōen Shaku's lecture for the 1893 World's Parliament of Religions, as well as Shaku's subsequent book, *Zen for Americans*. From 1897 to 1907 he worked with Paul Carus at Open Court Publishing in LaSalle, Illinois, translating ancient Chinese and Sanskrit texts and working on other projects. Both Suzuki and Carus taught at Greenacre. Carus, who believed that Buddhism was particularly compatible with science, edited the journals *The Open Court* and *The Monist* and wrote *The Gospel of Buddha*, an introduction to Buddhism that Suzuki translated into Japanese. Suzuki's own collected writings fill more than thirty volumes: he translated Māhāyana scriptures, wrote extensively on Zen and Shin Buddhism, and translated the work of Swedenborg, whom he dubbed "the Buddha of the North." He married Beatrice Lane, an American Theosophist, in Japan in 1911. In 1921 they launched *The Eastern Buddhist*, a quarterly journal designed for Western audiences, which continues to circulate today. Lane died in 1939, and Suzuki remained in Japan throughout World War II and the postwar occupation by the United States.

In 1949 Suzuki taught at the University of Hawaiʻi; in 1950 he moved to Claremont University in California; and from 1952 to 1957 he lectured at Columbia University in New York, where he instructed many influential writers, artists, and psychologists. The pioneering American Zen teacher Philip Kapleau attended Suzuki's lectures, as did the composer John Cage. (Jon Kabat-Zinn credits Kapleau, author of *The Three Pillars of Zen*, for introducing him to Zen.) For many Americans, Suzuki himself epitomized Zen, which enjoyed a surge in popularity, particularly among writers and artists of the Beat Generation.[114] Articles about him appeared in *Time, Newsweek, The New Yorker*, and the *Saturday Review*. The psychoanalysts Erich Fromm and Karen Horney sat in on Suzuki's classes as well, and Fromm, a leader of the earlier New York Psychology Group, developed a strong interest in Zen.

> As presented by Suzuki, Zen was a radically antiauthoritarian practice and philosophy that was concerned, not with textual authority and scholastic training, not with ritual, dogma, or even ethics, but with the transformative effects of experiencing the world as it really was. It was not a religion, he insisted, so much as it was the spirit behind all religions. It was not an ethic, but rather a way of gaining direct and spontaneous access to the world as given, in ways that help one to move beyond all preconceived notions of right and wrong.[115]

Suzuki's portrayal of Zen seems idiosyncratic to anyone who has spent time in Zen training monasteries, in Japan or elsewhere. Contrary to the freewheeling image Suzuki painted of Zen spontaneity and iconoclasm,

Zen is extremely formal, a highly ritualized, liturgical tradition. A training monk's day is carefully structured and minutely scheduled. Every gesture is prescribed: how to walk; which foot one uses to pass through the meditation-hall door; the route one travels through the meditation hall to one's seat; how to fold one's hands, bow, sit, stand, and adjust voluminous, multilayered robes; how to handle a cleaning rag; how to cook rice. The daily meals are elaborate rituals as well, using special bowls, cloths, and utensils. The precise ballet of the Japanese Tea Ceremony is related to the Zen meal ritual (*oryōki*). The monastic day is punctuated by several chanted liturgies, accompanied by various bells and drums. Instead of describing this regimented, rigorous, ritualized life, Suzuki emphasized *satori*: a momentary, intuitive, ineffable insight into the self-less nature of reality.

He had studied Western philosophy and psychology for many years, including the work of William James and Carl Gustav Jung. In 1939 Jung had written a foreword for *Introduction to Zen Buddhism*, Suzuki's first book on Zen for a general audience, initially published in German. Like other Buddhist modernizers, Suzuki "did not hesitate to showcase aspects of the Eastern tradition that he felt would best resonate with his Western readers. Nor did he hesitate to use the explanatory approaches from Western philosophy and psychology that would support his claim for seeing Zen, not as a Japanese tradition but as a universal form of spirituality that could be potentially brought into secular spaces like psychotherapy offices."[116] He described Zen in terms of spontaneity, authenticity, and freedom:

> Zen in its essence is the art of seeing into the nature of one's own being, and it points the way from bondage to freedom. By making us drink right from the fountain of life, it liberates us from all yokes under which finite beings are usually suffering in this world. We can say that Zen liberates all the energies properly and naturally stored in each of us, which are in ordinary circumstances cramped and distorted so they can find no adequate channel for activity. . . . This is what I mean by freedom, giving free play to all the creative and benevolent impulses inherently lying in our hearts.[117]

Such descriptions appealed especially to Horney, Fromm, and other psychologists during the 1950s, when the Cold War, McCarthyism, and the rise of suburban culture were exerting strong conformist pressures on middle-class Americans. Humanistic and existentialist psychologists believed that "patients in the 1950s . . . were uniquely burdened by the drive to conform, produce, and consume at all costs, even as they were haunted by the specter of atomic devastation."[118] Horney and Fromm, who had also been influenced by Jung, sought ways to help people break free of these pressures so that they could "become more authentically themselves." Fromm became "convinced that Zen Buddhism offered a worldview more consistent with true freedom than any other religion he knew."[119]

In 1957 Fromm organized a week-long conference on Zen and psychoanalysis in Cuernavaca, Mexico, attended by about fifty psychologists. Suzuki was the featured speaker. The book *Zen Buddhism and Psychoanalysis*, coauthored by Fromm, Suzuki, and Richard DeMartino, was a product of that event, published in 1960.[120] The following year, Alan Watts, a major popularizer of Taoism and Buddhism during the 1960s and 1970s, published *Psychotherapy East and West*, which describes Zen as a sort of Eastern psychotherapy.

American Vedanta, Yoga, and Meditation

Interest in Vedanta philosophy, meditation, and yoga also continued in pockets around the country. At the Vedanta Society in Los Angeles, Christopher Isherwood, Aldous Huxley, and Gerald Heard trained for decades with Swami Prabhavananda. In New York, Vedanta Swami Nikhilananda trained Joseph Campbell, and in St. Louis, Huston Smith studied for a decade under Swami Satprakashananda. Huxley, Campbell, and Smith all helped to popularize Perennialism, the idea that the mystical traditions of all religions point to the same ineffable truth.

The Indian guru Paramahansa Yogananda arrived in in Boston in 1920 to speak at the International Conference of Religious Liberals. He launched the Self-Realization Fellowship (SRF) that year, lectured widely to large audiences on the East Coast, and in 1924 settled permanently in California. In 1925 he packed the Los Angeles Philharmonic Auditorium with an audience of three thousand, and thousands more were turned away. His teachings spread through a twelve-month series of biweekly lessons that arrived in the mail, which his followers still read as a prerequisite to formal initiation into the Kriya Yoga he taught. The SRF incorporated in 1935, and when Yogananda's *Autobiography of a Yogi* was published in 1946, it quickly became a best-seller. It is considered by some to be a classic in spiritual literature. By 2010, Lola Williamson reports, nearly five hundred SRF centers could be found in fifty-four countries around the globe, including more than 150 in the United States.[121]

The silent mystic Meher Baba toured the United States in the 1930s. Jiddu Krishnamurti, initially hailed as a "World Teacher" by the Theosophical Society, renounced that role in 1929 but remained an influential spiritual teacher until his death in 1986. Books by Sri Aurobindo (1872–1950) and by the British author Paul Brunton about Ramana Maharshi (1879–1950) nourished interest in meditation and other yogic practices among American audiences through the 1930s, 1940s, and 1950s. Ramana Maharshi was profiled in a twelve-page feature article in *Life* magazine in 1949. Philip Goldberg notes Ramana's influences on Georg Fuerstein, Ken Wilbur, Andrew Harvey, Eckhart Tolle, Thomas Merton, Bede Griffiths, Dom Henri Le Saux (a.k.a. Swami Abhishiktananda), and Francis X. Clooney.[122] Kabat-Zinn cites him as one of the religious thinkers who has influenced him.[123] Swami Satchidanada Saraswati, the developer of Integral Yoga®, spoke at Woodstock in 1969.

These Indian gurus developed what Lola Williamson calls "neo-Hinduism," or "Hindu-inspired meditation movements" (HIMMs), which can also be described as neo-Vedanta or modernist Hinduism. Members of groups like the Self-Realization Fellowship do not regard themselves as Hindu, however; they stress that their textual sources are *Vedic* rather than Hindu. They emphasize the philosophical *Upanishads* rather than the mythical *Puranas*, which include stories about the activities and incarnations of Hindu deities, or the great epics of the *Ramayana* and the *Mahabharata*, which includes the *Bhagavad Gita*.[124]

Like modernist Protestantism and Buddhism, neo-Vedanta is presented as primarily philosophical and ethical, experiential, universal, and compatible with a modern, Western, scientific worldview. This emphasis on rationality and science "begins with Enlightenment ideas in Europe and America, travels to India through the British, becomes part of the Hindu Renaissance, and then returns to America in the nineteenth and twentieth centuries with the teachings of Hindu gurus."[125] Adapting elements of Protestant Christianity, HIMMs minimize ritual, and thus the need for priests, and encourage laypeople to read scriptures for themselves.[126] They stress practices that are relatively rare among ordinary laypeople in India: meditation, hatha yoga (physical postures), guru yoga (devotion to a teacher as an embodiment of the divine), mantra yoga (chanting), and *laya* yoga (focused on the movement of kundalini energy through particular *chakras,* or spiritual nodes of the "subtle body" within the material body). In contrast, in India the most common form of yoga is *bhakti* yoga, or devotional practices oriented toward particular deities, including *puja* (making offerings), *bhajans* (devotional songs), stories, and plays. HIMMs promote meditation as a primary practice, suitable for anyone, and not requiring lengthy preparation. They actively seek converts and spread through schools, conferences, and congregational gatherings modeled after Protestant church services. Instead of tithing, members pay fees for instruction. Neo-Vedanta also relies on English-language words and concepts rather than Sanskrit or vernacular Indian languages.[127]

Transcendental Meditation

In 1959 the neo-Vedanta teacher Maharishi Mahesh Yogi (c. 1917–2008) visited the United States and introduced his signature practice, Transcendental Meditation. He toured widely, and in 1968 the Beatles made a highly publicized visit to his ashram in Rishikesh, along with the folk singer Donovan, Mike Love of the Beach Boys, and the actress Mia Farrow. Other rock stars soon tried TM: members of the Doors, the Grateful Dead, the Rolling Stones, and the Jefferson Airplane, as well as celebrities such as Clint Eastwood, Mary Tyler Moore, and the tobacco heiress Doris Duke. The Maharishi was interviewed by David Frost, Johnny Carson, and Merv Griffin, "whose daily program was the *Oprah* of its day."[128] In 1973 the guru founded a university in Fairfield, Iowa, now called the Maharishi University of Management (MUM), and on October 13, 1975, he was featured on the cover of *Time* magazine. More recently, TM's benefits have been touted publicly by the comedians Jerry Seinfeld and Ellen DeGeneres; George Stephanopoulos, a political correspondent and anchor for *ABC News* and formerly the White House director of com-munications under President Bill Clinton; and Deepak Chopra, a physician and advocate of alternative medicine. David Lynch, a film director, screen writer, actor, and musician, established a foundation to support medical research on TM and training for middle- and high-school students. The Maharishi's obituary in the *New York Times* said the TM organization claimed to have trained more than forty thousand teachers and taught the method to more than 5 million people.[129]

TM advocates emphasize that the practice is compatible with any re-ligion or none, and that its physiological and psychological benefits have been verified by modern science. Until the turn of the twenty-first century, the majority of medical research in this area focused on Transcendental

Meditation. A graduate student at the University of California–Los Angeles, M. Robert Keith Wallace, did the first experiments on TM practitioners. But one of the first and most influential studies of the method published in the United States was conducted by a Harvard researcher, Herbert Benson, who documented physiological changes among people practicing TM, such as lowered blood pressure and heart rate. He dubbed this phenomenon "the Relaxation Response."[130] When Benson began studying TM practitioners at Harvard, Wallace moved there to assist. Benson later showed that many kinds of simple, repetitive practices can evoke the Relaxation Response; it is not limited to formal meditation. Benson saw it as a useful self-care technique that healthcare practitioners could offer to all patients, regardless of their religious beliefs, to empower them rather than subjecting them to the authority of medical professionals or religious gurus. Anne Harrington argues that this marked "an explicit and deliberate break with both the counterculture and specific religious traditions."[131]

Since then, hundreds of clinical studies have examined TM, many of them conducted at MUM.[132] The sheer range of conditions for which MUM-affiliated researchers have proclaimed TM beneficial invites skepticism. In a 1982 MUM bibliography listing 454 published and unpublished studies of TM, the citations that include summary annotations are overwhelmingly positive. They say TM improves physical functioning, perceptual acuity, cognitive processing, memory, academic performance, mood, social behavior, pain tolerance, self-image, creativity, mental health, sleep, job and marital satisfaction, altruism, and open-mindedness, and that it decreases criminal recidivism and addiction. Groups of TM practitioners engaging in concentrated meditation are also said to have averted typhoons headed toward the Philippines; lowered rates of crime, fires, and auto accidents in various cities; and improved the weather, in a phenomenon dubbed the "Maharishi Effect" and attributed to a shift in "transcendental consciousness."[133]

Some independent articles reviewing TM research have reported moderately positive results in people experiencing depression, hypertension, or anxiety. Although TM advocates—like Mindfulness advocates—are quick to distinguish it from simple relaxation, these results are consistent with studies of other relaxation techniques.[134] Critical reviewers have found that very few TM studies have involved randomized clinical trials with adequate controls; that various methodological problems are present; and that results may be influenced by the expectations of both researchers and participants favorably predisposed toward TM.[135] The more modest claims, more rigorous study designs, and more prestigious institutional affiliations of recent research on MBSR, Cognitive-Behavioral Therapy, and Dialectical-Behavioral Therapy may account for the warmer reception these methods have received in the scientific community.

Esalen

In 1965, when the Immigration and Naturalization Act lifted the ban on immigration from Asia imposed in 1924, a second wave of modernist Hindu and Buddhist missionaries entered the United States and began training new generations of students in various forms of meditation and yoga. Meditation as a therapeutic method attracted the attention of Michael Murphy and Richard Price, founders of the Esalen Institute at Big Sur, California. Murphy, a student of Sri Aurobindo who also practiced Zen at temples affiliated with the San Francisco Zen Center, compiled an early and important bibliography of medical research on meditation, altered states of consciousness, and health.[136] Esalen became a locus for interest in that topic and for other forms of "East-West encounter." These strongly influenced the psychological theories of the Human Potential Movement, whose chief theorists included Fritz Perls; Carl Rogers, previously a member of the New York Psychology Group at Columbia; and Abraham Maslow, who studied "peak experiences," developed the theory of "self-actualization," and recommended meditation. Their theories were promoted at Esalen and tested in "encounter groups."

Esalen became an important contact zone for Western psychologists and popular Buddhist and Hindu teachers promoting meditation and yoga among American youth. These contacts further fueled interest in meditation as a means for cultivating greater physical and psychological well-being.[137] In his history of Esalen, Jeffrey Kripal writes, "There is a rather clear line of historical development from the European Mesmerists and Swedenborgians, through the Spiritualists of the 1850s and '60s (who were also religious rationalists and wanted to understand their experiences in terms of the science of the day), to the early psychology of religion and, a bit later, the American alternative religious scene of the 1960s and '70s."[138] Adam Crabtree is even more blunt: "All modern psychological systems that accept the notion of dynamic unconscious mental activity must trace their roots, not to Freud, but to those animal-magnetic practitioners who preceded him by a century."[139] Here enters Jon

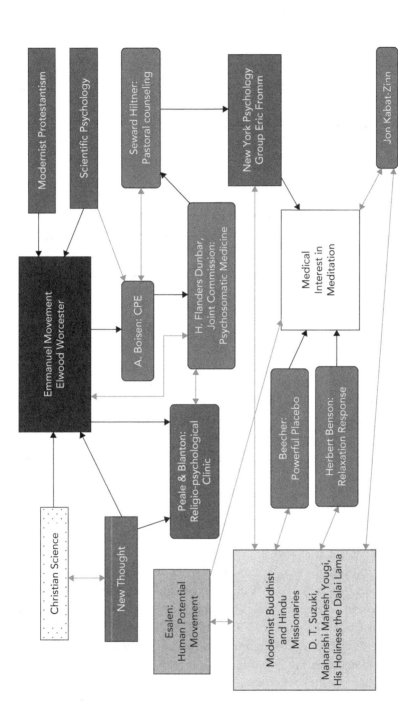

FIG. 4.3 From Mind Cure to Mindfulness.

Kabat-Zinn, Mindfulness-Based Stress Reduction, and the contemporary Mindfulness movement.

Figure 4.3 shows the complex processes by which the early Mind Cure movement prepared the soil of American culture for medicalized Mindfulness-Based Interventions. So far I have traced various currents in Euro-American and Asian religious history and seen how they have converged with and diverged from one another, as well as with and from Western science, psychology, and medicine. Swedenborgianism and Mesmerism converged in the Mind Cure methods of Phineas Quimby, and diverged from Quimby into Christian Science and New Thought. The latter was fed by currents from Transcendentalism and Theosophy, which had connections of various sorts to Swedenborgianism, spiritualism, and the theories deriving from Mesmer. Transcendentalism and Theosophy were informed by and contributed to modernist reinterpretations of Buddhism and Hindu Vedanta.[140] Early New Thought leaders drew from all these streams and exhibited some of the reformist tendencies of modernist Protestantism as well.

The Emmanuel Movement, informed primarily by modernist Protestantism, European experimental psychology, and American neurology, channeled some of the Mind Curers' methods of suggestive therapeutics toward scientific psychology and Freudian psychoanalysis. Freud's own early career had involved studying theories derived from Mesmer's work and Swedenborg's theology regarding trances, the unconscious, dissociation, the psychologist's rapport with patients, and paranormal or clairvoyant phenomena. Some of Freud's successors, including Jung, Horney, Fromm, Maslow, and Perls, became interested in Hindu and Buddhist philosophy, cosmology, and practice—thanks to the efforts of Buddhist and Vedanta modernizers like Vivekananda, Dharmapala, Suzuki, Yogananda, and Sri Aurobindo. All of that set the stage for Kabat-Zinn and Mindfulness to enter the scene during the 1980s and 1990s.

It is important to note, however, that as suggestive therapeutics and meditation penetrated further into mainstream medicine and psychology, they became more individualized, and more removed from the social concerns of the Emmanuel Church and the community-oriented New Thought–inspired groups led primarily by women and African Americans. Chapter 7 explores the implications of this shift. Chapters 5 and 6 raise a series of critical questions about the contemporary Mindfulness movement: Is Mindfulness something we could reasonably call "religion"? Is it Buddhist? Does it matter? And is it as effective as advocates claim?

5

Is Mindfulness Religion?

WHEN JON KABAT-ZINN started the Stress-Reduction Program at the University of Massachusetts Medical School in 1979, he faced the same two challenges the Emmanuel Movement and Transcendental Meditation had faced earlier: providing a scientific rationale for the therapeutic services offered by his clinic and distancing his methods from religious doctrines or practices that key stakeholders might find unpalatable, even disreputable. For Elwood Worcester at the Emmanuel Church, that meant drawing a very sharp line between what the church clinic was doing and what Christian Scientists and other Mind Curers were doing. The clinic offered what he called "sound religion and medical skill"[1] at the hands of white, male clergy and doctors with elite, academic credentials. Likewise, TM proponents had to distinguish their technique from devotional Hinduism and assuage fears that it was a foreign "cult" seeking to recruit vulnerable youth. They did so by encouraging medical research on TM and stressing the universal applicability of their method. In developing the eight-week Mindfulness-Based Stress Reduction protocol (MBSR), Kabat-Zinn's bugaboos were Buddhism, neo-Vedanta, and American metaphysical religion.

> From the beginning of MBSR, I bent over backward to structure it and find ways to speak about it that avoided as much as possible the risk of it being seen as Buddhist, "New Age," "Eastern Mysticism" or just plain "flakey." To my mind this was a constant and serious risk that would have undermined our attempts to present it as commonsensical, evidence-based, and ordinary, and ultimately a legitimate element of mainstream medical care.[2]

Prior research by theologically trained doctors such as Helen Flanders Dunbar, a pioneer in psychosomatic medicine, and more recent research by Richard Davidson at the University of Wisconsin and other scientists helped Mindfulness advocates overcome their first challenge: providing a scientific rationale for the meditation and yoga methods taught in MBSR.

Kabat-Zinn overcame the second challenge, distancing these practices from their religious contexts, by carefully describing his methods and underlying philosophy in secular terms, separating MBSR rhetorically from Buddhist religiosity or explicitly Hindu understandings of yoga as pathways to union with God. Although he is much more open today than he was forty years ago about his own Buddhist background and the Buddhist roots of MBSR,[3] during a 2006 lecture promoting his book *Coming to Our Senses*, he said repeatedly that "mindfulness is the heart of Buddhist practice, but it has nothing to do with Buddhism."[4]

Kabat-Zinn's rhetorical strategy is driven by pragmatic concerns. In 1997 he told an audience composed largely of Buddhists, "If you want to be able to integrate into medicine . . . you've got to be able to charge the insurance companies for this."[5] The unfamiliar worldview underlying Buddhist philosophy and practice makes MBSR "very hard to talk about, to put it into words," he said. "But we try. And to put it into words that don't depend on some 2,500-year-old tradition whose vocabulary is not appropriate in the setting that you're working in."[6] He explained how to reach his intended audiences effectively: "The language that we use . . . is how to take better care of yourself; how to live more skillfully and more fully; how to move toward greater levels of health and well-being." He also argues that core teachings of Buddhism are transhistorical, transcultural, and universal, and can be extracted from their Asian "cultural trappings."

I have no doubt that his motivations are sincere. "From the very beginning," he has written, "there was for me one primary and compelling reason for attempting to bring mindfulness into the mainstream of society. That was to relieve suffering and catalyse greater compassion and wisdom in our lives and culture."[7] Having benefited himself from years of Buddhist training and study, he wanted "to make meditation so commonsensical that anyone would be drawn to it."[8] This meant removing overtly religious and "cultural aspects" that might be impediments for some people. His efforts to promote meditation in a manner that does not scare people off by associating it with unfamiliar religious practices and technical terms is similar to efforts by New Thought writers to describe meditation and yoga in either nonsectarian or Christian language.

But let us consider more closely these rhetorical bifurcations between science and religion, and specifically between Mindfulness and Buddhism. Despite Kabat-Zinn's and other advocates' claims to the contrary, is the Mindfulness movement, like early New Thought, something we could reasonably call religion? Is it Buddhist? If so, what kind of Buddhism is it? Does it matter? Should we care, and if so, why? What is at stake, and for whom? This chapter will consider these questions from various angles, through various lenses.

First I will apply several other scholars' theories about what counts as religion to the Mindfulness movement and its rhetoric. Then I want to look at it through different sorts of Buddhist lenses: Theravāda, Māhāyana, and modernist. I will argue that Mindfulness is, in fact, a blend of American metaphysical religion and Buddhist modernism. In the next chapter, I will consider questions about its clinical effectiveness. In the final chapter, I examine the Mindfulness movement through the lens of early New Thought, particularly the community-oriented forms led by women and African Americans. If we turn the questions I raise this way and that, shining various kinds of light on them, certain features that might otherwise be obscured become more apparent, and these suggest some concerns or problems that I think deserve further attention. I anticipate critiques and refinements of my analysis. Religions, Buddhisms, sciences, and historical scholarship are all ongoing conversations and arguments, centuries and millennia old, spanning the globe. I hope this analysis will advance the discussion in fruitful directions.

There is no neutral "view from nowhere" from which to answer questions about cultural phenomena such as religions with complete objectivity. All observers' perspectives are conditioned by particular circumstances and contexts, and therefore limited. As my former professor Thomas Tweed pointed out, all theories of religion are merely positioned sightings from particular sites. We view them through particular frames of reference, with particular perceptual equipment. Nor, Tweed added, is there any such thing as religion in the abstract—no religion "in general"; scholars of religion "are only situated observers encountering particular practices performed by particular people, in particular contexts."[9] The thirteenth-century Japanese Zen master Dōgen put it more poetically: all perspectives, even fully enlightened ones, are "like gazing at a corner of the sky through a bamboo tube."[10] The big picture is always bigger than we can see from our present vantage point. Nevertheless, considering the Mindfulness movement—particularly its flagship program,

MBSR—through the lens of some theories about religion can help to illuminate features that might not otherwise be readily visible.

Religion: Some Definitions

Attempts to define what is and isn't religion abound; Tweed surveyed and categorized many of them in *Crossing and Dwelling: A Theory of Religion.* Each definition reflects the theorist's particular social and historical position and concerns, revealing some features of this complex human phenomenon and obscuring others. Here I will apply five approaches: recent observations offered by my colleague Jeff Wilson; a formal definition proposed by Tweed; a descriptive approach suggested by Ninian Smart, which I have found helpful in teaching courses in comparative religion; and two frameworks offered by Catherine Albanese, one describing general features of religions, and one specifically about American metaphysical religions.

Wilson: Vision, Values, Rituals, Boundaries

In the fall 2016 issue of *Tricycle* magazine, Wilson argued that the Mindfulness movement can usefully be understood as a form of religion:

> From a religious studies standpoint, what I see before me is a movement of people who share common values and visions about human beings, life, society, and reality, who place great faith in a particular set of practices and engage in a ritual [meditation] meant to bring about self-transformation and liberation from suffering, who are convinced of its worth for themselves and promoting it to others, who react defensively to critiques and police the boundaries of who properly and improperly speaks for and about their movement, and who engage in an ongoing discussion about religion. Maybe that doesn't meet your definition of a religion, but it sure seems pretty close to being religious to me.[11]

This description has resonances with one proposed some years ago by Albanese, who argued that religions have four elements: *creeds*, meaning doctrines and worldviews; *codes*, legal or ethical guidelines; *cultus*, meaning ritual practices; and *community*, organizational and institutional structures. The "common values and visions" Wilson mentions could be likened to "creeds" as Albanese uses this term; the "policing of boundaries" helps to define the "community" of Mindfulness teachers and practitioners; and the "cultus" or ritual is meditation and yoga *asanas* (poses). What is missing from his relatively informal analysis is "codes," a topic to which we will return below.

In *Mindful America*, Wilson argues that the Mindfulness movement is simply one more example of how Buddhism has historically moved from one culture to another: by drawing upon and adapting to elements of each host culture, and by changing that culture in the process. This has happened repeatedly over two and a half millennia. As Buddhism moved southeast from northern India into what is now Sri Lanka, Myanmar, Thailand, Laos, and Cambodia, it developed into present-day varieties of Theravāda. As it spread eastward into China, Vietnam, Korea, and Japan, many streams of Māhāyana Buddhism emerged, including Zen (Ch'an, Thien, Son), Pure Land, and Nichiren or Lotus. As Indian Buddhism flowed northward into Nepal, Bhutan, Tibet, and Mongolia, Tantric or Vajrayana variants flourished. As it flowed west to Afghanistan, Buddhism encountered Greek culture, and Gandharan artists began representing the Buddha in human form rather than by his absence (a footprint, an empty chair, a Dharma Wheel). In each place, Buddhism mingled with indigenous traditions and took on distinctive new flavors, practices, and garb. In the United States, these various forms of Buddhism have mingled with Protestantism, Romanticism, Roman Catholicism, Judaism, modern biomedicine, and consumer capitalism. In addition, Wilson points out that for as far back as we have records, people in all Buddhist traditions have engaged in various practices to gain practical benefits, such as health, longevity, and prosperity.[12] But let us now consider Mindfulness through the lens of a more detailed theory offered by Thomas Tweed.

Tweed: Confluences and Flows

Tweed offers the following formal definition of religions (note the plural), which will require a little unpacking: "Religions are confluences of organic-cultural flows that intensify joy and confront suffering by drawing upon human and suprahuman forces to make homes and cross boundaries."[13] In other words, religions are fluid; they don't have fixed boundaries; they move and change through time and across landscapes. They converge with other streams of tradition and culture and diverge. They are embodied phenomena, having to do with how we developed as human organisms, with brains and limbs and senses that work in particular ways. They include physical disciplines such as prayer and meditation; they prescribe how people should dress, eat, fast, have sex or not, modify their flesh or not, and so on. They are also social and cultural. They address our emotional lives—occasions that bring sorrow, such as illness, hunger, violence, and death—as well as moments of celebration: births, marriages, and holidays. They call upon the powers we have as human beings and powers believed to transcend the human condition, be they God or gods or the Dao, angels, Buddhas and bodhisattvas, or Brahman, or the nameless Ground of Being. Religions help to orient people, like watches, compasses, maps, and itineraries: they tell us *who* we are and *where* and *when* we are in space, time, and the cosmos; *to whom we belong* and where "home" is. They indicate where we are headed, in this life and hereafter, and how best to get there. Certainly Tweed's definition is broad enough to encompass the modern Mindfulness movement—at least its more "spiritual" and Buddhism-inflected wings, even if we have to shoehorn it a little here and there.

Mindfulness is clearly an organic and cultural flow, a physical practice fed by a number of religious and philosophical streams, some older and some newer. It is embodied in meditative postures, in attention to the breath and one's responses to stimuli, in yoga *asanas*. It is promoted as a way to reduce suffering and enhance one's joy in living. It is humanistic, claiming to cultivate capacities innate to human organisms: abilities to pay attention in nonjudgmental ways, to be kind, to grow in compassion. Yet as we will see, its proponents claim it reflects a universal dharma, truths that transcend history, culture, and even religion. They say Mindfulness orients us in the here and now and helps us meet the challenges and crossroads of life more wakefully and wisely. (*And* it's backed by scientific research!)

Smart: Seven Dimensions

Ninian Smart helpfully suggested that religions can be understood has having seven dimensions: (1) *ritual*: public or private ceremonies; (2) *narrative and mythic*: stories and myths, including cosmogonies and cosmologies; (3) *experiential and emotional*: grief, guilt, joy, dread, awe, peace, ecstasy, and so on; (4) *social and institutional*: shared beliefs, identity, membership, and institutions; (5) *ethical and legal*: values and rules governing behavior; (6) *doctrinal and philosophical*: systematic belief structures and intellectual frameworks; and (7) *material*: things and places representing or manifesting the sacred.[14] We can discern all these more or less clearly in the Mindfulness movement.

Its *rituals* include meditation and yoga, classes with group discussions, and longer, silent retreats. The *narrative and mythic* dimensions will depend on the instructor but may include references to religious stories, symbols, or poetry, and the Mindfulness movement also draws on scientific explanations of the universe and its origins. These are all culturally and historically conditioned. MBIs certainly aim to improve people's *emotional* lives by turning them inward toward their moment-by-moment experience. The *social and institutional* dimensions of Mindfulness include networks of organizations, retreat centers, research labs, professional conferences, and credentialing programs. Its *ethical and legal dimensions* could include the Hippocratic Oath ("First, do no harm"), the Golden Rule, and the various laws, regulations, and professional standards governing medical research involving human subjects and therapeutic relationships between health professionals and their patients. As for *doctrine*, I have already traced strands of metaphysical religion and modernist forms of Protestantism, neo-Vedanta, and Buddhism. The Perennialism and eclecticism of the Mind Cure movement also turn up in Mindfulness discourse and praxis. (Those parallels are discussed in chapter 7.) The Mindfulness movement partakes of scientific materialism, as well: the idea that what is "really real" is that which can be measured scientifically, and that the world is "out there," separate from us, consisting of objects to investigate experimentally. As for the *material*: in any issue of *Mindful, Tricycle, Lion's Roar*, or *Buddhadharma* you will find an endless panoply of meditation and yoga gear, clothing, books, audio recordings, and DVDs, not to mention ancillary services: retreats, classes, matchmaking, financial advice, psychotherapy, and more.

The Four Marks of Metaphysical Religion

The foregoing theories or descriptions suggest that Mindfulness might not be as secular as proponents claim, but the approach I have found most illuminating was offered by Albanese in *A Republic of Mind and Spirit: A Cultural History of American Metaphysical Religion*. She argues that the tendency to think about American religious history primarily in terms of institutions and denominations prevents us from recognizing metaphysical religions as normal and pervasive in American religious life. This tendency also prevents us from recognizing that, by Albanese's definition, MBSR is not merely an interesting trend in complementary medicine or biomedical research; it is actually another species of American metaphysical religion. In defining the category "metaphysical religion," Albanese identifies four characteristics: (1) a preoccupation with the mind and its powers; (2) a predisposition toward the ancient cosmological theory of correspondence between natural and spiritual worlds; (3) a tendency to describe these two in terms of movement and energy; and (4) a yearning for salvation understood as solace, comfort, therapy, and healing.[15] The modern Mindfulness movement displays all four.

The Mind and Its Powers

MBSR and other MBIs are certainly concerned with the powers of the mind, in particular, the capacity to focus nonjudgmental attention on one's own experience, moment by moment. Advocates assert that this capacity is transformative and promotes psychological and emotional well-being, regardless of whether one's physical problems can be cured, and they are working to substantiate this claim through scientific research. At a public talk by Kabat-Zinn that I attended, he showed the audience a slide image of a Buddha statue and remarked, "In some fundamental way, this statue, or other artistic representations of a similar kind, [doesn't] actually represent the deity, although in some traditions [images are] spoken of that way. But the fundamental representation here is of a state of mind, and that state of mind is best characterized by this word: *awake*."[16] From a perspective less inclined to universalize, one might argue that this is like saying a crucifix represents not a deity, but a virtue such as love or obedience, or a perhaps a concept such as redemption—which statements would be incoherent without reference to Christian theology. Likewise Kabat-Zinn's characterization of the Buddha image is incoherent without reference to Buddhist doctrines about the Buddha, whose title means "the Awakened One."

MBSR's interpretation of Buddhism is thoroughly psychological: its goal is essentially a psychological transformation that produces better mental—and possibly physical—health. ("Salvation" is a problematic term because it is fundamentally a Christian concept.) The traditional goal of Buddhist practice is *nirvāṇa*: a state of *moral* and spiritual transformation: the elimination of greed, aversion, and delusion, particularly through monastic training, as well as eventual liberation from the cycle of death and rebirth.[17] In MBSR, Kabat-Zinn wrote,

> when we use the word *healing* to describe the experiences of people in the stress clinic, what we mean above all is that they are undergoing a profound transformation of view. This transformation is brought about by the encounter with one's own wholeness, catalyzed by the meditation practice. . . . It is a perceptual shift away from fragmentation and isolation toward wholeness and connectedness. With this change of perspective comes a shift from feeling out of control and beyond help (helpless and pessimistic) to a sense of the possible, a sense of acceptance and inner peace and control. Healing always involves an attitudinal and emotional transformation. Sometimes, but not always, it is also accompanied by a major reduction in physical symptoms and by improvement in a person's physical condition.[18]

Optimism, a sense of personal control, emotional and psychological well-being, and improved health are likewise benefits promised to practitioners of Christian Science and New Thought.

Theories of Correspondence

MBSR also stresses a version of the metaphysical theory of correspondence: that one's own body reflects the macrocosm. This is probably related to the neo-Vedanta and Mahāyāna Buddhist influences on Kabat-Zinn. As he has explained it, each body includes numerous interrelated systems—physiological and psychological—and each person is fundamentally "whole," regardless of whether or not one recognizes this wholeness and whether or not one has health problems. "While we are whole ourselves as individual beings, we are also part of a larger whole, interconnected through our family and our friends and acquaintances to the larger society and ultimately to the whole of humanity and life on the planet."[19] The impermanence and interdependence reflected in our own bodies also corresponds to the impermanence and interdependence of all phenomena in the cosmos, a basic Buddhist idea. Such theories of correspondence also harken back to Swedenborg and the Western esoteric traditions that influenced him.

Energy and Flux

Albanese's third criterion for metaphysical religion is an emphasis on theories of energy and flux. Chapter 18 of Kabat-Zinn's first book on MBSR, *Full Catastrophe Living*, is titled "Change: One Thing You Can Be Sure Of." He writes, "The meditation practice itself brings us face-to-face with the undeniable experience of continual change within our own minds and bodies as we watch our constantly changing thoughts, feelings, perceptions, and impulses. This alone should be enough to demonstrate to us that we live immersed in a sea of change, that whatever we choose to focus on changes from one moment to the next, it comes and it goes."[20] Buddhism teaches that everything is characterized by impermanence (*anitya*).

On the last page of an MBSR workbook is a quotation from Nisargaddata Maharaj (1897–1981), a guru of nondual (*Advaita*) Vedanta from Bombay. A volume of Nisargaddata's transcribed talks, *I Am That*, became a best-seller after it was published in 1973. In an essay reflecting on MBSR forty years after he first developed it, Kabat-Zinn ends with the same quotation:

> By watching yourself in your daily life with alert interest with the intention to understand rather than to judge, in full acceptance of whatever may emerge, because it is here, you encourage the deep to come to the surface and enrich your life and consciousness with its captive energies. This is the great work of awareness; it removes obstacles and releases energies by understanding the nature of life and mind. Intelligence is the door to freedom and alert attention is the mother of intelligence.[21]

In other words, everything is in a state of flux, and Mindfulness releases captive energies and illuminates the mind.

Religion as Therapy

Albanese's fourth characteristic is what marks MBSR most clearly as a form of American metaphysical religion, despite its claim to be nonreligious: it understands "salvation" in terms of therapy and healing. Metaphysical religions, including those of the Mind Cure movement, tend to regard evil fundamentally as a problem of ignorance. For example, the Metaphysical Club of Boston issued a statement of New Thought philosophy asserting that "sin and moral evil are largely an ignorant selfishness."[22] Kabat-Zinn, in a series of short essays on mindfulness and politics, characterized evil in similar terms. Among the examples he included were attachment to one's own opinions, the tendency to stereotype or dehumanize those with whom one disagrees, self-centeredness, and the inability or unwillingness to see things "as they really are," that is, as "one body, one seamless whole, one organism really."[23] Because the problem of human suffering is seen as rooted in incorrect or inadequate perceptions of the world, both New Thought and MBSR tend to treat religious practice as essentially psychological and therapeutic. Additional similarities—as well as some important differences—between Mind Cure and Mindfulness will be explored in the final chapter.

Others are welcome to debate whether I have applied these theories appropriately or accurately. My point is simply to show that while many of its proponents argue that it is secular and scientific, it is possible to construct an argument that the Mindfulness movement is a religious phenomenon: a modernist, globalized, metaphysical one, which draws upon scientific discourse to validate its healing claims. If that is so, then critics have a point when they protest that teaching mindfulness in public schools, prisons, and hospitals may violate the Constitutional separation of church and state. We will return to that issue below.

Is Mindfulness Buddhism?

As to whether mindfulness is *Buddhism*: Kabat-Zinn and his compatriots are emphatic that the answer is no. They have been quick to distinguish between "mindfulness" and Buddhist tradition. Kabat-Zinn said:

> It's not like we're trying to disguise Buddhism and sneak it in. We're not talking about Buddhism, we're talking about mindfulness. It happens to be that mindfulness was most finely developed and refined on this planet, in this era, in the Buddhist tradition.[24]
>
> [But what] I'm most interested in is the use of Buddhist meditative practices, as opposed to spreading Buddhism, if you will. There was a time that I considered myself to be a Buddhist, but I actually don't consider myself to be one now, and although I teach Buddhist meditation, it's not with the aim of people becoming Buddhists. It's with the aim of them realizing they're buddhas. There's a huge

distinction, and so I prefer to think in terms of Dharma as opposed to [thinking in] terms of Buddhism per se.[25]

It is not clear, though, how people can "realize they're buddhas" without any reference to Buddhism.

In response to a questioner's expressing concern that MBSR practitioners might be misappropriating Buddhist traditions without fully understanding them, Kabat-Zinn once said, "I really don't care about Buddhism. It's an interesting religion but it's not what I most care about. What I value in Buddhism is that it brought me to the Dharma."[26] He could make this rather striking remark because he defines the key term as transcultural and transhistoric: "The word *Dharma*, to me, is pointing to something that really is universal. The cultural and ideological overlays, and the historical elements of [Buddhism], beautiful and honorable and wonderful as they are, are not necessarily the heart of the Dharma, which transcends them."[27] But this claim, that meditation and the Dharma can be extracted from the rest of Buddhism because they are universal, is a product of very particular historical circumstances.

From a perspective situated in academic Buddhist studies, the answer to the question of whether Mindfulness is Buddhism depends on what kind of Buddhism we're talking about. Rupert Gethin observes that from some traditional or conservative Buddhist perspectives, abstracting mindfulness from its broader Buddhist context "might seem like an appropriation and distortion of traditional Buddhism that loses sight of the Buddhist goal of rooting out greed, hatred, and delusion." From another Buddhist perspective, it could be seen as *upāya-kauśalya*, or skillful means, an accessible way to introduce Buddhadharma to help people take their first steps on the path toward freedom from suffering. From a modernist Buddhist perspective, it could be seen as a way of stripping away "unnecessary historical and cultural baggage, focusing on what is essential and useful." A non-Buddhist might see it as "revealing the useful essence that had hitherto been obscured by the Buddhist religion." Perhaps combining "practices derived from Buddhism with the methods of modern western cognitive science" might be "a true advance that supersedes and renders redundant the traditional Buddhist practices." Or perhaps it is part of a cultural shift away from religion "to heal our souls," toward science and medicine.[28] All of these positions have been argued in recent years, in a flurry of conference papers, articles, and books. See, for example, *Mindfulness: Diverse*

Perspectives on Its Meaning, Origins, and Applications, a reprint edition of the May 2011 volume of the journal *Contemporary Buddhism*,[29] and *Mindfulness: What's Wrong with It [and What Isn't]* (Wisdom, 2016). Let's look at a few of these arguments in closer detail.

Early Indian and Theravāda Buddhism

Specialists in early Indian and Theravāda Buddhism have pointed to important ways that mindfulness as defined by Kabat-Zinn—nonjudgmental awareness of present-moment experience—differs from the understanding of mindfulness reflected in the Pali Buddhist scriptures and commentaries. Rupert Gethin, Donald Lopez, Gil Fronsdal, and the American Theravāda monk and translator Bhikkhu Bodhi have all pointed out that the word *sati*, translated into English as "mindfulness," does not refer to a type of meditation practice or to a goal of meditation practice. It is said to be one of five basic mental faculties that are foundational for *developing skill in practices* that lead to the goal of *nibbāna* (Sanskrit *nirvāṇa*), the complete extinguishment of suffering and total release from the cycle of birth, death, and rebirth. The other four mental faculties are faith, energy, concentration, and wisdom. The Buddha did not instruct followers to engage in mindfulness, Fronsdal notes, but to engage in activities that strengthen it, which can include "frequent and ardent attentional exercises, actively letting go of thoughts that obscure present moment awareness, and choosing helpful areas of life to focus attention." Such practices require "having put away covetousness and grief for the world."[30]

Sati, or "Mindfulness," in the Pali Canon

The British scholar T. W. Rhys Davids seems to have been the first to translate the Buddhist term *sati* into English as "mindfulness" in 1881.[31] *Sati* is the Pali equivalent of the Sanskrit word *smṛti*, which means "memory" or "remembrance." In a careful analysis of Pali scriptures in which the word *sati* occurs, Bhikkhu Bodhi argues that it has "two primary canonical meanings: as memory and as lucid awareness of present happenings. Sati makes [an] apprehended object stand forth vividly and distinctly before the mind." When the object of attention is a past event, it is remembered clearly. When the object is a current event or activity, such as breathing or walking, or having a thought or feeling, it is held in lucid awareness in the present. One *establishes sati* or mindfulness by adopting "a stance of watchfulness towards one's present experience."[32]

As the practitioner strengthens the faculty of mindfulness by bringing the wandering attention back to an object of focus and holding it there, "clear comprehension supervenes and adds the cognitive element."[33] In other words, the meditator must then *apply* Buddhist teachings to *analyze* and *interpret* the experience of meditation in *Buddhist terms*, to see that thoughts, emotions, inner monologues, pain, and *all* phenomena are characterized by impermanence (*anitya*) and the absence of any independent, enduring, unchanging essence or "self" (*anātman*). Everything, without exception, is process, *all the way down*; there are no essences at the "cores" of things. Thus the basic premise of mind-body dualism underlying the entire Western, scientific enterprise is explicitly rejected: there is no self "in here" perceiving objects in the world "out there." Perception itself is a process of *interactions* among sense organs, the consciousness that animates them, and the objects of perception, all of which are in a perpetual state of flux. Buddhism teaches that attachment to the idea of a "self" is what keeps us trapped in suffering and the cycle of rebirth.

The faculty of *sati* can be strengthened by a number of practices, for example, by observing the breath and other bodily sensations, thoughts, and feelings as they arise and pass away. The *Satipaṭṭhāna Sutta*, the Buddha's "Discourse on Establishing Mindfulness," offers a number of other methods, which are not included in modern Mindfulness training: contemplating basic Buddhist teachings such as the Four Noble Truths and the Seven Factors of Enlightenment (*sati*, keen investigation of *dhamma*, energy, happiness, calm, concentration, and equanimity); contemplating one's own body as a skin bag of repulsive substances; and observing corpses being devoured by animals or in various stages of decay, to cultivate detachment toward the body. More pleasant methods are to recall the qualities of the Buddha and to cultivate lovingkindness toward oneself and others, which requires one to hold an image of oneself or another person clearly in mind. It is *these* practices, not mindfulness itself, that lead to liberation from attachment to the "self" and release from suffering. The *Satipaṭṭhāna Sutta* clearly identifies the *goal* of these practices to be *nibbāna*, the elimination of suffering, and the Theravāda tradition maintains that this can be achieved only by devoting one's life to rigorous monastic training and renunciation, a life in which hundreds of rules govern every aspect of daily life and deportment.

The Four Noble Truths of Buddhism are, first, that sentient existence is fundamentally unsatisfactory because nothing is permanent. Second, the root cause of suffering is attachment to things that are impermanent: objects, pleasant feelings, other beings, our very "selves." Third, when this cause of suffering is rooted out, its effect will cease. Fourth, the way to uproot it is the Eightfold Path of Buddhist practice. *Sati* is listed as one of the elements of the Eightfold Path, which all work together. They begin with Right View: an understanding of the workings of karma and the Four Noble Truths (suffering, its origin, its cessation, and the path leading to cessation); Right Intention: to cultivate renunciation, benevolence, and harmlessness; Right Speech: avoiding lying, gossip, idle chatter, and harsh or divisive words; Right Conduct: not killing, stealing, misusing sexuality, or using intoxicants; Right Livelihood: one based on Right Speech and Conduct; Right Effort: to overcome unwholesome and cultivate wholesome behavior and states of mind; Right Mindfulness: paying attention to what one is doing, thinking, feeling, and saying; and Right Concentration: sustained, single-pointed attention to an object. Concentration produces calm. Mindfulness, the ability to hold things vividly in awareness as they arise and pass away, leads to *insight* into impermanence and no-self. Right Effort includes seeing and renouncing one's own greed, aversion, and ignorance and engaging in practices that actively cultivate alternative states, such as the four "Divine Abodes" (*brahmavihara*): lovingkindness, compassion, altruistic joy (in the good fortune of others), and equanimity or even-mindedness, regardless of circumstances.

The eight elements of the Eightfold Path are grouped into three broad categories, called the "Three Legs of Training," a metaphor evoking the stability of a three-legged stool. These are moral conduct (*śila*), meditation (*samādhi*), and wisdom (*prajña*). Moral conduct (Right Speech, Conduct, and Livelihood) is a *foundation* for meditation (Right Effort, Mindfulness and Concentration), which leads to Wisdom (Right View and Intention), because moral behavior fosters mental stability and serenity. Wisdom, understood as complete realization of the impermanent, interdependently co-arising, self-less nature of all things, is what ultimately liberates a person from suffering. These are not the "universal" teachings that Kabat-Zinn and his compatriots would have us believe; they are specifically *Buddhist* teachings, preserved and developed over two and a half millennia by avowed Buddhists, both monastic and lay.

Sati in the Eightfold Path

One modern Buddhist monk, Bhikkhu Bodhi, observes:

> There are certainly occasions when the cultivation of mindfulness
> requires the practitioner to suspend discrimination, evaluation,
> and judgment, and to adopt instead a stance of simple observation.
> However, to fulfill its role as an *integral* member of the eightfold
> path mindfulness has to work in unison with right view and right
> effort . . . to distinguish wholesome qualities from unwholesome
> ones, good deeds from bad deeds, beneficial states of mind from
> harmful states.[34]

Thus *sati* "has an ethical function, being part and parcel of the attempt to
eliminate the unwholesome and establish the wholesome."[35] It has the
effect of reminding practitioners that they are followers of the Buddha's
teachings, cultivating Buddhist values and worldviews.

Gethin adds that mindfulness is "always presented as one among several qualities that need to be equally balanced." These include abandoning
the Five Hindrances (sensuous desire, hatred, sloth, anxiety, and vacillating
doubt) and developing the Seven Factors of Enlightenment. Investigating
dhamma means analyzing one's experience of body and mind in terms of
Buddhist teachings, such as the Four Noble Truths. Awakening is "a function of the seven constituents of awakening working in balance rather than
as issuing from just the practice of mindfulness" or some other quality.[36]
To define mindfulness as nonjudgmental awareness of present experience
is an extremely simplified view, which obscures *sati's* ethical function and
its role in helping Buddhists to remember whole systems of thought and
practice to which serious adherents commit themselves.

Monastic Renunciation

Donald Lopez points out that, far from wanting to *alleviate* stress in his
monastic followers, the Buddha wanted to *induce* it, by emphasizing the
fundamental unsatisfactoriness of life, the pain and suffering that accompany the endless round of birth, death, and rebirth in *saṃsāra*. He did this
in order to motivate his disciples to renounce the world and devote themselves entirely to seeking *nibbāna*. That meant purifying the consciousness of attachments, as well as other mental states that produce suffering;
eradicating all past and future karma; and allowing the body and mind
to disintegrate utterly at death, never to be reborn. *Nibbana* is described

as *cessation, extinction*: it is a fundamentally anti-evolutionary and world-denying goal, Lopez observes.

Robert Sharf concurs:

> Early Buddhist sutras in general, and Theravada teachings in particular, hold that (1) to live is to suffer, (2) the only genuine remedy to suffering is escape from samsara (the phenomenal world) altogether, and (3) escape requires, among other things, abandoning hope that happiness in this world is possible. . . . It is necessary to . . . confront the unmitigated horror of sentient existence—so as to acquire the resolve necessary to abandon the last vestiges of attachment to things of this world. . . . Yet today . . . rather than cultivating a desire to abandon the world, Buddhism is seen as a science of happiness—a way of easing the pain of existence. Buddhist practice is reduced to meditation, and meditation, in turn, is reduced to mindfulness, which is touted as a therapeutic practice that leads to an emotionally fulfilling and rewarding life.[37]

Traditional Buddhist doctrines and practices are rooted in a premodern cosmology, as well. From a modern scientific perspective, we know, for example, that the early Indian Buddhist map of the world is factually incorrect: scientifically speaking, it is *not* an enormous mountain surrounded by four continents, with gods dwelling on the slopes above us and hell-beings lurking below our feet. The universe is *not* "incalculable eons" old; our best available current evidence indicates that it is about 14.2 billion years old. Our planet belongs to a spiral galaxy containing billions of stars, one of hundreds of billions of galaxies whirling in a space-time continuum expanding rapidly in all directions. As a historian, Lopez wants to preserve the strangeness of early Buddhism, its incompatibility with science—the ways it teaches the *opposite* of fundamental assumptions underlying the modern, scientific worldview. These differences, he says, offer helpful challenges to our usual ways of seeing and thinking about reality, our basic assumptions about "how things are." He points out that meditation was not seen—and until quite recently had never been seen—as a practice everyone could and should do; it had always been the province of specialist monks and nuns, a minority among the more numerous scholars of Buddhist doctrine.

Much of the activity occurring in Buddhist temples and homes throughout the tradition's history has been ritual and devotional: making offerings to Buddhas, bodhisattvas, monastics, loved ones, and/or ancestors; bowing before shrines; chanting scriptures; dedicating karmic merit to various beings and purposes. Since ancient times, Buddhist communities have built and maintained stupas (reliquaries) and pilgrimage sites; temples have raised funds by selling medicines and amulets; and monastics have performed rituals for the benefit of lay supporters and governments.[38] Orientalist scholars of Buddhism, focused on the doctrines expressed in Buddhist texts, have tended to regard these ritual, devotional, and pragmatic dimensions of Buddhist practice as "corruptions" of Buddhist doctrine. Asian modernists like Jiddu Krishnamurti, D. T. Suzuki, and Maharishi Mahesh Yogi have tended to support such interpretations.

Mahāyāna Buddhism

Mahāyāna Buddhism offers more world-affirming perspectives and philosophical resources for the versions of Buddhism found among leaders of the modern Mindfulness movement. Certain Mahāyāna scriptures, such as the *Vimalakīrti Nirdeśa Sūtra*, the *Śrimālādevī Siṃhanāda Sūtra*, and the *Platform Sūtra* of Huineng, the Sixth Patriarch of Chinese Ch'an (Zen), feature protagonists who realized enlightenment as laypeople. Vimalakirti was a businessman who moved unperturbed among markets, brothels, and gambling halls, and bested the Buddha's wisest disciples in Dharma debate; Śrimālādevī was a queen; and Huineng was an impoverished, illiterate gatherer of firewood and later a millworker. The *Lotus Sūtra* attributes supreme wisdom to an eight-year-old girl who isn't even human, but a *naga*, a water-dwelling serpent. Mahāyāna philosophies offer understandings of key terms such as "Buddha," "*nirvāṇa*," and the "Path" that differ significantly from Theravāda understandings of these terms.

Specialists in Buddhist philosophy will note that I am oversimplifying complex philosophical and historical developments here. Nevertheless it is safe to say that in various Mahāyāna scriptures and treatises, the Buddha is described not merely as an awakened man, called Shakyamuni (Sage of the Shakya Clan), who wandered around northern India during the Iron Age, taught his followers, and died, never to be reborn. Instead, in Mahāyāna discourse, the Buddha has three bodies. The *Nirmānakāya* is the human, historical body just mentioned. The *Sambhogakāya* or "bliss body" is an idealized, celestial figure, represented in art and iconography and visualized in meditative practices, particularly in Tantric Buddhism.

In the *Lotus Sūtra*, such Buddhas well up out of the ground; they appear any- and everywhere. The Buddha's ultimate body, the *dharmakāya*, is coextensive with the cosmos. *Nirvāṇa* is not a permanent escape from *samsāra*, but a perceptual shift, explained further below. The Path of awakening is the *bodhisattva path*, which emphasizes not so much purifying one's mind of defilements as cultivating the virtues or perfections (*paramitā*) of a Buddha: generosity, morality, patience, zeal in practice, meditation, and wisdom.[39] The development of these virtues requires long cultivation, many lifetimes worth.

The Madhyamika philosophy developed by Nāgārjuna during the second century C.E. includes a critique of early Indian scholasticism and of the idea that *nirvāṇa* is an ontological escape from *samsāra*, a final cessation or extinguishment of consciousness and the other constituents (*skandhas*) of what we imagine to constitute the "self." It is, instead, an epistemological escape, a different way of seeing and understanding the phenomenal world. If all phenomena lack any essence whatsoever, then the categories *samsāra* and *nirvāṇa* do as well; they are meaningless except in relation to each other. They co-arise in mutual dependence upon each other; they are "empty of self-nature" (*śūnyatā*). Thus *nirvāṇa* and *samsāra* are, in fact, the same reality, perceived differently. It is like perceiving the face of the Man in the Moon (or the Rabbit in the Moon) for the first time, or gazing at a picture containing optical illusions, which reveals different things when viewed from different angles or focal points. Emptiness—the endless interplay of processes without any essences—manifests as phenomenal reality. Only by investigating phenomenal reality in Buddhist terms—using our provisional, impermanent bodies and minds—can we come to see the self-less, essence-less nature of reality, including ourselves and "others." In the words of the *Heart of Perfect Wisdom Sūtra*, "Form itself is emptiness, emptiness itself form." To recognize this emptiness *is* to "escape" from *samsāra*. A person on a Mahāyāna path thus vows to remain "in *samsāra*" in order to become a Buddha (or to realize Buddhahood) and to help other suffering, deluded beings toward this liberating insight, which can happen in an instant but must be cultivated for a lifetime.

If we compare the Mindfulness movement to various streams of Mahāyāna Buddhism, including Ch'an (Zen), Pure Land, and the Tantric or Vajrayana traditions, which include guru and deity yogas, we can see that Mindfulness is a very different animal indeed. It does *not* require vows of loyalty and faithfulness between teacher and student. It does not require monastic renunciation. It may not even include the five basic moral precepts required of all Buddhists, lay or ordained: not to kill, steal, lie, misuse sexuality, or use intoxicants. It certainly does not require the lengthy preliminary practices (*ngöndro*) of some forms of Vajrayana Buddhism: 100,000 prostrations, 100,000 offerings, 100,000 recitations of a mantra, and so on, before more advanced instruction can begin.

While Mindfulness advocates are analytical in a Western scientific sense, their analysis may be missing something fundamental from a Buddhist philosophical point of view. At the end of a 2005 Mind and Life Institute conference, the Dalai Lama, who had been regaled for days with the latest research on clinical applications of meditation, remarked, "For me, analytical meditation is more useful." He explained, through his translator, that it is important to analyze the *source* of one's pain. Often it is rooted in an effort to grasp at impermanence, or in self-centeredness, or in an unrealistic view of one's situation. Each of these problems requires a different kind of approach, he said. His parting shot produced peals of laughter, but was also telling: "In order to use your intelligence more effectively, I prefer sound sleep better than meditation."[40]

Zen Critiques

A number of American Zen teachers, ordained and lay, reflect on the Mindfulness movement in a recent anthology, *What's Wrong with Mindfulness (and What Isn't)*. They describe both creative engagements with Mindfulness—in higher education, in art, etc.—and also express a number of "critical concerns." Psychiatrist and lay Zen teacher Barry Magid and one of his students, Mark Poirier, describe three troubling trends in the modernization of Buddhism and the rise of the Mindfulness movement: deracination, secularization, and instrumentalism. Deracination literally means "to pull up by the roots"; in this context it means to remove meditation practices from their original religious contexts. Secularization means to downplay the specifically religious dimensions of Buddhism and meditation. Instrumentalization is to locate "the value of an activity, not in the activity itself, but exclusively in its outcomes or commodified products."[41]

Buddhist awakening, they point out, "entails a radical deconstruction of the very notion of self; it's not a formula for that self to gain increasing mastery over its environment or gain a sense of control or autonomy, let alone achieve calmness or relaxation."[42] They acknowledge that "materialistic, for-gain Buddhism may well be an unavoidable part of Buddhism's transmission to the West as it adapts to, and is translated into, the deep-rooted individualist, materialist, and secular structures in Western culture—including the culture of science itself as a technique for achieving control and thus better satisfying needs." Zen Buddhism can and does address greed, anger, and confusion, they say, "but from a totally different angle—by seeing through them, not by eliminating them."[43] And while Mindfulness can be an instrumental technique, Zen is a religious practice.

ZEN IS NOT INSTRUMENTAL

In Zen, meditation is not goal-oriented. "Zazen is the very expression of enlightenment, not a step along the path to enlightenment, not a means to bring about a change or state of consciousness. Zazen is in and of itself the alternative to our usual state of grasping, clinging, and goal-oriented life in general. By sitting down, we have arrived."[44] This reflects an "innate-ist" view of enlightenment, as opposed to a "constructivist" view. In the Theravāda, one must actively eliminate habits of mind and dispositions that produce suffering, and cultivate the qualities of Buddhahood. This eliminates past karma and stops the production of future karma, so that at death one will be freed from the round of rebirths. An innate-ist approach says, in contrast, that we already inherently possess Buddha-nature; we simply must drop the delusions that obscure our ability to see it. In some Mahāyana sources, Buddha-nature is equated with emptiness (*śūnyatā*), and is therefore the fundamental nature of all phenomena.[45]

Dōgen, the thirteenth-century Japanese monk who established Sōtō Zen in Japan, seems to have used the term "Buddha" in this way, to refer to the process of impermanence and interdependent co-arising, that is, to "emptiness" itself. Because everything arises from and dissolves back into this process, everything expresses the truth, everything is Buddha, everything "preaches" or teaches the Dharma. Thus Zen meditation (zazen) is not a means to the end of awakening; zazen is a ritualized instantiation of the fundamental nature of reality: *anitya, pratitya-sammutpāda, anātman*: impermanence, interdependent co-arising, no-self. "Zen monasticism was and continues to be a highly ritualized tradition that emphasizes public performance and physical deportment at least as much as 'inner experience.' Enlightenment is not so much a 'state of mind' as a form of knowledge and mode of activity, acquired through a long and arduous course of physical discipline and study."[46] The performance of zazen, and all the other ritualized behaviors of Zen Buddhism—sitting, walking, standing, lying down, toileting, bathing, cooking, cleaning, sewing, etc.—are expressions of the absolute: Buddha, the fundamental truth, manifest in every prosaic detail of daily life. Ritualizing every act in Zen training frames ordinary experience in such a way that the practitioner can see and relate to the "ordinary" as "sacred": categories that are also "empty."

ZEN IS RELIGIOUS

For Dōgen, wholehearted engagement, with all of one's body and mind, in the activities of daily life *is* an expression of awakened reality, of Buddhahood: practice *is* awakening.[47] This is a profound and subtle teaching that can be understood and digested only after years or decades of experience with the ritual behaviors of Zen. Monastic training in Zen is an embodied pedagogy, a physical discipline. It includes wearing robes; making bows, prostrations, and offerings; chanting scriptures in a carefully choreographed ritual ballet, accompanied by various bells, drums, and clappers; eating meals in a complicated ritual involving special bowls, cloths, and utensils that must be handled in particular ways. These are the methods of Zen training, the matrix of awakening. They function as a mirror, revealing to practitioners the workings of their minds and the places they get stuck in grasping, aversion, and the delusion of separateness. To dispense with such disciplines, without first deeply inhabiting and understanding them "from the inside," is to cast the baby out with the bathwater, critics of Mindfulness say. As a scholar and long-term practitioner of Zen, trained and ordained by teachers trained both in Japan and the United States, I agree. Zazen, or meditation, is not a means to an end; it is an expression of fundamental Buddhist truth-claims about the nature of reality.

Although seated meditation is crucial, Zen training involves far more than that. "A zendo, whether in a temple or lay center, is a locus of reverence, ritual, and the marvelous expression of Buddha nature in each moment of our practice. It is not a place where we simply engage in spiritual exercises to cultivate this or that state of consciousness. It is not the spiritual equivalent of the gym or health club."[48] In a zendo, one enters through the left side of the doorway, on the left foot. One places one's palms together in a particular way, fingers touching rather than spread, fingertips at the level of the nose, the hands a fist's width away from the nose. One bows from the waist toward the altar. Folding one's hands at the solar plexus, one then walks a prescribed path to one's seat, taking care not to cross in front of the altar unless one is officiating. Arriving at one's seat, one bows toward it in the same manner, with palms joined, then turns 180 degrees clockwise and bows to the room and to the community of fellow practitioners, then carefully sits down and arranges one's body in the meditation posture, which prescribes the precise positions of the legs, hands, spine, head, tongue, and eyes. Bells, drums, and offerings at the altar punctuate the meditation practice.

Enacting reverence in these ways helps one to cultivate that quality, to become a more reverent person, and to relate to other beings and objects as Buddha. Ideally, the dispositions cultivated physically in the training hall carry beyond it. Although the philosophy and methods of Theravāda differ somewhat, the monk Bodhi would likely agree about how this sort of monastic formation works. In the Mindfulness movement, which dispenses with overt religiousness, "there is a real danger that the contemplative challenge might be reduced to a matter of gaining skill in certain techniques, dispensing with such qualities as faith, aspiration, devotion, and self-surrender, all integral to the act of 'going for refuge' " to Buddha, Dharma, and Sangha.[49]

Buddhist and Neo-Vedanta Influences on Kabat-Zinn

Kabat-Zinn was first exposed to Zen during college, at a lecture at MIT by the late American Zen teacher Philip Kapleau, and began meditating in 1966. Eventually he began Zen training with the Korean Zen master Seung Sahn, at the Cambridge Zen Center.[50] Seung Sahn's Kwan Um School of Zen now has centers in the United States, Mexico, Israel, Korea, Malaysia, Singapore, and more than a dozen European nations.[51] For a time, Kabat-Zinn served as director of the Cambridge Zen Center, where he says he was "a Dharma teacher in training."[52]

In *Full Catastrophe Living*, Kabat-Zinn's book on MBSR, he acknowledges a number of Vipassanā teachers, including the movement's three best known American founders, Jack Kornfield, Joseph Goldstein, and Sharon Salzberg. Also acknowledged are Philip Kapleau, founder of the Rochester Zen Center; Seung Sahn; Vietnamese Zen Master Thich Nhat Hanh, who wrote the book's preface; Shunryu Suzuki, the Japanese founder of the San Francisco Zen Center; and Chögyam Trungpa, the Tibetan master who founded Naropa in Boulder, Colorado, and the organization Shambhala International. Other teachers Kabat-Zinn names include the neo-Vedanta gurus Swami Chinmayananda, the American Ram

Dass (neé Richard Alpert), Nisargadatta Maharaj, and Ramana Maharshi.[53] He lauds the uncompromising individualism and anti-institutionalism of Jiddu Krishnamurti.[54] Elsewhere he mentions the German Theravāda monk Nyanaponika Thera and the Indian social activist and spiritual teacher Vimala Thakar.[55] All of these teachers, Asian and American, have something in common: they are exemplars of religious modernism.

When describing MBSR publicly, Kabat-Zinn has repeatedly employed Buddhist terms and concepts. For example, at a conference on Buddhist meditative practices in the West, he referred to *dukkha* (unsatisfactoriness); *Dharma* (Buddha's teachings); *Sangha* (Buddhist community); *kōan* (a Zen teaching story); the Four Foundations of Mindfulness (attention to breath, physical sensations, feelings, and mental formations, described in the *Satipaṭṭhāna Sūtra*);[56] Indra's Net (a metaphoric description of the cosmos from the Māhāyana *Avataṃsaka Sūtra*); nonstriving (a Zen approach to meditation); the hell realm (an aspect of traditional Buddhist cosmology); the Sixth Patriarch (a mythic Chinese Zen hero); Dharma combat (a Zen ritual); Buddha-nature (multiple meanings, but in this context a capacity for enlightenment); Buddha-field (an environment generated by a Buddha's enlightenment); Vipassanā (both a specific Buddhist meditation method and an American Buddhist movement); and greed, hatred, and ignorance: the three root causes of suffering, according to Buddhist doctrine.

Furthermore, Kabat-Zinn describes the organizational structure of the Center for Mindfulness he founded as "a take-off on the *kalachakra mandala*," a Tibetan Buddhist representation of the cosmos. The MBSR course design was inspired by Vipassanā retreats, also called "courses," and an important part of the eight-week curriculum is an all-day meditation retreat. The interviews that Kabat-Zinn conducts with MBSR students before and after his courses, and the process of "inquiry" between students and teacher during courses, are modeled on Zen interviews between teacher and student.[57] He calls the community of researchers in Mindfulness a "a distributive global sangha of overlapping, if not entirely commonly shared perspectives, concerns, and purposes."[58]

Vipassanā and Zen in MBSR

The style of MBSR courses resembles most closely the style of retreats in the Vipassanā movement, a stream of American Buddhism derived from the reformist Theravāda Buddhism of the Burmese monks Mahasi Sayadaw and Sayagi U Ba Khin and the Thai Forest monks Achan Chah and Achan Sumedho. (I will return to them below.) MBSR participants learn Vipassanā approaches to sitting and walking meditation, as well as *metta* practice, a Buddhist method for cultivating lovingkindness as an antidote to the "poison" of anger and ill will. MBSR participants practice mindful eating in a manner derived from Zen and popularized by the Vietnamese Zen master Thich Nhat Hanh. MBSR courses employ "Council Process," a method of discussion attributed to Pueblo Indians, popularized in Buddhist circles by the American Zen teacher Joan Halifax.[59] Mindfulness itself is characterized as "choiceless awareness," a practice recommended by Nanaponika Thera, Jiddu Krishnamurti,[60] and Vipassanā teachers such as Christopher Titmuss.[61] Kabat-Zinn expresses strong affinities with Zen and its "innate-ist" understanding of awakening:

> There was from the very beginning of MBSR an emphasis on non-duality and the non-instrumental dimension of practice, and thus, on non-doing, non-striving, not-knowing, non-attachment to outcomes, even to positive health outcomes, and on investigating beneath name and form and the world of appearances, as per the teachings of the *Heart Sutra*, which highlight the intrinsically empty nature of even the Four Noble Truths and the Eightfold Path, and liberation itself and yet are neither nihilistic nor positivistic, but a middle way. The emphasis in Ch'an on direct transmission outside the sutras or orthodox teachings also reinforced the sense that what is involved in mindfulness practice is ultimately not merely a matter of the intellect or cognition or scholarship, but of direct authentic full-spectrum first-person experience, nurtured, catalyzed, reinforced and guided by the second-person perspective of a well-trained and highly experienced and empathic teacher. Therefore, MBSR was grounded in a non-authoritarian, non-hierarchical perspective that allowed for clarity, understanding, and wisdom, what we might call essential Dharma, to emerge in the interchanges between instructor and participants, and within the meditation practice of the participant as guided by the instructor.[62]

Thus it is clear that Kabat-Zinn's philosophy and methods are thoroughly shaped by Buddhism (and neo-Vedanta), and his claims to the contrary seem disingenuous. He seems to want to have it both ways: to convey modernist Buddhist and neo-Vedanta worldviews and practices to people who might not otherwise explore them, and to have them accepted as nonreligious.

Kabat-Zinn's Dharma: Universal or Particular?

Kabat-Zinn and Saki Santorelli, the current director of the Center for Mindfulness, are clearly steeped in specifically *Buddhist* methods and teachings. But they use non-Buddhist words to describe them and claim they are "universal." For example, Buddhist contemplative methods "are concerned with embodied awareness and the cultivation of clarity, emotional balance (equanimity) and compassion," rather than with, say, *nirvāṇa*. And because "these capacities can be refined and developed via the honing and intentional deployment of attention, the roots of Buddhist meditation practices are *de facto* universal."[63]

Because MBSR's approach to meditation is universal, Kabat-Zinn has argued, "it can be learned and practiced, as we do in the stress clinic, without appealing to Oriental culture or Buddhist authority to enrich it or authenticate it."[64] Mindfulness may be "the heart of Buddhist meditation, Kabat-Zinn says, but in reality it "has little or nothing to do with Buddhism per se, and everything to do with wakefulness, compassion, and wisdom. These are universal qualities of being human, precisely what the word *dharma* is pointing to. The word has many meetings, but can be understood primarily as signifying both the teachings of the Buddha and the lawfulness of things in relationship to suffering and the nature of the mind."[65] Yet Kabat-Zinn goes on to say that MBSR reflects and teaches a "universal dharma that is *co-extensive, if not identical, with the teachings of the Buddha, the Buddhadharma* [emphasis added]."[66] His descriptions of MBSR training, and the ways it teaches Buddhist wisdom without using overtly Buddhist language, are worth quoting at length:

> Over time, with ongoing practice, dialogue, and instruction, [it] is not unusual for even novice practitioners to see, either spontaneously for themselves or when it is pointed out, that the mind indeed does have a life of its own, and that when we cultivate and stabilize attention in the body, even a little bit, it often results in apprehending the constantly changing nature of sensations, even highly unpleasant ones, and thus, their impermanence. It also gives rise to the direct experience that "the pain is not me," and thus the option of non-identification not only with the sensations, but

also with any attendant inflammatory emotions and thoughts that might be arising within the attending and the judging of the experience. Thus we become intimate with the nature of thoughts and emotions, and mental states such as diversion, frustration, restlessness, greed, doubt, sloth and torpor, and boredom, to name a few, which constitutes the territory of the third foundation of mindfulness, without ever having to mention the classical map of the four foundations of mindfulness, nor the five hindrances or the seven factors of enlightenment.[67]

The law of impermanence reveals itself without any need to reference a Buddhist framework or lens for seeing it. The same is true for all four noble truths—perhaps better spoken of as the four realities. The same is true for *anatta*, although this one is trickier and scarier, and needs to be held very gently and skillfully, letting it emerge out of the participants' own reports of their experience rather than stated as a fact. Often it begins with the realization, not insignificant, that "I am not my pain," "I am not my anxiety," "I am not my cancer," etc. We can easily ask the question, well then, who am I? This is the core practice of Chinese Ch'an, Korean Zen, Japanese Zen, and also of Ramana Maharshi.[68]

Kabat-Zinn calls his approach in MBSR part of "the emergence of what we might call American Dharma," which, in the long run, probably will not "be Buddhist, in the small-minded idea of Buddhism."[69] It is not entirely clear what he means by "small-minded" here, but one possibility is that it means identifying with any specific Buddhist lineage. Clearly, Kabat-Zinn draws on many Buddhist lineages. What he seems to mean by "universal American Dharma" is actually his own eclectic, modernist style. However, it too is a culturally and historically situated approach.[70] In an introduction to a survey of sixty-five years of scientific research on meditation, the psychologist Eugene Taylor remarks, "The attempt to abstract out the primary characteristics of meditation from a grab bag of traditions in order to come to some purified essence or generic definition is a uniquely Western and relatively recent phenomenon. This tendency should be considered, however powerful and convincing its claim as an objective, universal, and value-free method, to be an artifact of one culture attempting to comprehend another that is completely different."[71]

Buddhist Modernism

Far from being universal, transcultural, and transhistoric, the Dharma Kabat-Zin preaches is modernist, metaphysical Buddhism, a product of very particular historical and religious circumstances. Richard Payne explains that Buddhist modernism is a version of the religion

> created during the latter part of the nineteenth and first part of the twentieth centuries in response to the assault on Buddhism by liberal Protestant missionaries. In an attempt to assert the value of Buddhism, Buddhist apologists—both Euro-American and Asian— created a representation of Buddhism that itself reflected the religious ideas and values of liberal Protestantism. . . . Three of these religious ideas seem to have been particularly formative for the modernist reinterpretation of Buddhism. . . . First, that religion should be a rational system of personal self-development—which has as its corollary an opposition to superstition and ritualism. Second, that the religions important in the modern world all have an historical founder whose self-appointed task was the purification of a decadent religious system. Third, in keeping with the social gospel of nineteenth century liberal Protestantism, Buddhist modernism also emphasized social reform as a more general expression of its purification of a decadent religious system. This reformist program included emphasizing the role of the laity in decision-making, extending practices and standards previously only undertaken by monks, such as meditation, to the laity, and asserting a congruence between Buddhism properly understood and modern science.[72]

Modernist Vipassanā

The specific methods that came to dominate what is now known as the Vipassanā movement, as well as various Mindfulness-Based Interventions, derive from a small number of Burmese teachers in the lineages of Ledi Sayadaw (1846/1847–1923), Mingun Sayadaw (1869–1955) and Mingun's disciple Mahasi Sayadaw (1904–1982). Mahasi made the radical claim that one did not need advanced skill in meditative concentration. Instead he emphasized "moment-to-moment, lucid, nonreactive, nonjudgmental awareness of whatever appears to consciousness." One of his most influential students was Nyanaponika Thera, a German-born monk who described this as "bare attention." It is important to remember that this practice was designed for laypeople and did not require an understanding of Buddhist philosophy, literature, or liturgy. Nor did it require renunciation or long periods of monastic training.[73]

Modernizers like Mahasi and D. T. Suzuki reconceived meditation. It was no longer

> the ritual instantiation of Buddhahood, nor . . . a means to accumulate merit, but rather [a] "mental discipline" designed to engender a particular transformative experience. The rationalization of meditation, coupled with the Westernized values of the middle-class patrons of urban meditation centers, led naturally to a de-emphasis on the traditional soteriological goal—bringing an end to rebirth. Instead, we find an increasing emphasis on the worldly benefits of meditation: *vipassanā* was said to increase physical and psychological health, to alleviate stress, to help one deal more effectively with family and business relationships, and so on.[74]

In Buddhist Asia, this approach to meditation, now adopted by the Mindfulness movement, "was a minority position that was met with considerable criticism from traditional quarters," Robert Sharf says.[75] The concerns that more traditional observers raised deserve attention. Critics objected to "(1) Mahasi's devaluation of concentration techniques leading to [meditative] absorption (Pali: *jhana*); (2) claims that practitioners . . . are able to attain advanced stages of the path, including the four stages of enlightenment (Pali: *arya-magga*), in remarkably short periods of time; and (3) the ethics of rendering *sati* as bare attention, which would seem to devalue or neglect the importance of ethical judgment."[76] Certain early Zen teachers in China also rejected traditional practices such as repentance and meditating on corpses and the body's impurities, Sharf notes, and instead directed students "to simply set aside all distinctions and conceptualizations, and allow the mind to come to rest in the flow of the here-and-now."[77] These teachers had sizable lay followings, as well. "The early Zen reformers, like the Burmese reformers in the twentieth century, were popularizers: they touted a method that was simple, promised quick results, and could be cultivated by anyone in a short period of time." Similar tendencies can also be found in Tibetan Dzogchen. All such reformers

> were interested in developing a method simple enough to be accessible to those who are unschooled in Buddhist doctrine and Scripture,

who are not necessarily wedded to classical Indian cosmology, who may not have had the time or inclination for extended monastic practice, and who were interested in immediate results as opposed to incremental advancement over countless lifetimes. It is thus not surprising that [these] teachers found themselves . . . castigated for dumbing down the tradition, for devaluing ethical training, for misconstruing or devaluing the role of wisdom, and for their crassly "instrumental" approach to practice.[78]

From more traditional Buddhist perspectives, the gradual spiritual trans-formation of a person requires study of Buddhist doctrine and engage-ment in Buddhist ways of life. Without those things, the meditator runs the risk of "paralyzing self-absorption"[79] Various Buddhist masters used the expression "meditation sickness" to criticize techniques focusing on "noncritical or non-analytical presentness," in which "the practitioner loses touch with the socially, culturally, and historically constructed world in which he or she lives. The practitioner becomes estranged from the web of social relations that are the touchstone of our humanity as well as our sanity. The key to avoiding this is to learn to see both sides at once."[80]

The Sanbō-Kyōdan

A Japanese movement called the Sanbō-Kyōdan (Three Treasures Association) is another stream of modernist Buddhism promoting a universalized, transcultural vision; it has clearly influenced Kabat-Zinn, as well as Marsha Linehan, the developer of Dialectical-Behavioral Therapy, and others active in the movement to promote Mindfulness in medicine.

Sanbō-Kyōdan was founded in 1954 by Hakuun Yasutani (1885–1973), who trained as a priest of Japanese Sōtō Zen but severed his ties to it in order to focus on the new organization. The influence of Sanbō-Kyōdan in the United States has been enormous, greatly disproportionate to its small numbers and marginal status in Japan. A number of important teachers of Zen in America studied directly with Yasutani, although they later de-veloped separate organizations of their own. These include Philip Kapleau (1912–2004), founder of the Rochester Zen Center; Robert Aitken (1917–2010), founder of the Hawai'i-based Diamond Sangha; Eido Tai Shimano (1932–2018), founder and disgraced former leader of the Dai Bosatsu Zendo in New York; and Taizan Maezumi (1931–1995), former abbot of the Zen Center of Los Angeles. These teachers in turn trained a large number of other American Zen teachers. Toni Packer (1927–2013), who eliminated overtly Zen elements from the training she offered, studied with Kapleau. Charlotte Joko Beck (1917–2011), a student of Maezumi's, took a similar, iconoclastic approach. John Daido Loori (1931–2009), founder of the Mountains and Rivers Order, and Bernie Glassman (b. 1939), head of the White Plum Asangha and founder of the Zen Peacemaker Order, trained with Maezumi. Aitken was the teacher of John Tarant (b. 1949), who was the teacher of James Ford (b. 1948), also ordained as a Unitarian Universalist minister. Ford is the teacher of Melissa Myozen Blacker (b. 1954), who directed professional training programs for the Center for Mindfulness in Medicine, Healthcare, and Society, but left to focus on teaching formal Zen practice in Ford's Mindful Way lineage.

Yasutani's successor, Kōun Yamada (1907–1989), was a lay businessman who attracted a number of Roman Catholic priests and religious to the Sanbō-Kyōdan style of Zen training. One of these was Willigis Jäger, OSB (b. 1925), a German Benedictine who was authorized as a Zen Master in the Sanbō-Kyōdan until his departure from that organization in 2009. He was a teacher of Marsha Linehan (b. 1943). According to scholar Sharf, the movement's leaders

> consider the elaborate ceremonial and literary culture of a Zen monastery to be, at best, a mere "means" to an end, at worse [*sic*], a dangerous diversion. The Sanbō-Kyōdan insists that "true Zen" is no more and no less than . . . a personal and profound realization of the essential nonduality of all phenomenal existence. As such, Sanbō-Kyōdan teachers claim that Zen is not a "religion" in the common sense of the word, since it is not bound to any particular cultural form, nor is it dependent on scripture or faith. One need not be a Buddhist, not to mention an ordained priest or monk, to practice Zen, and thus the robes, liturgies, devotional rites, scriptures, and so on may be set aside. . . . Years of [formal monastic] training have been replaced by participation in frequent short retreats lasting a week or less. . . . Even the study of basic Buddhist doctrine is deemed incidental to the goal of Zen training and thus not required. This reconfiguration of Zen clearly serves the interests of a lay congregation that has neither the time nor the inclination to embark on a more formal course of monastic education.[81]

Sanbō-Kyōdan has some features in common with a number of other modern religious movements in Japan, including Seichō-no-Ie, other forms of New Thought, and MBSR. These include emphasis on a transformation of consciousness; belief that both the means to and the goal of this transformation is to deepen one's personal intercourse with a spiritual reality that pervades all existence; belief that individuals' enlightenment contributes to a collective spiritual transformation of humanity; faith in individuals' ability to achieve enlightenment independent of rituals or external powers; and an assumption that there is no opposition between science and religion.[82] It is important to recognize how much this particular strand of modernist Buddhism has shaped American assumptions about meditation and other Buddhist practices in the United States.

A New Way Forward?

There is no escaping "the fact that traditional Buddhism and modernity have jarring contradictions," observed Linda Heuman in the Buddhist magazine *Tricycle*. "But if our solution then is just to lift from the tradition the teachings that make sense to us, while remaining unaware of both the context in which the teachings were given and our own blind spots in appropriating them, we risk getting the message wrong. We might even reinforce the very things that are problematic about ourselves and our society that the teachings are meant to subvert."[83] She gives an example originally offered by the sociologist of religion Robert Bellah, who observed in *Tricycle* that Japanese monastic Zen began at a time and in a culture shaped by Confucian social values, in which one's family of origin and social relationships strongly determined (and constrained) one's life chances. To ordain as a monk or nun was to "leave home" and join the Sangha—a radical act. (It was particularly appealing to those who, for various reasons, could not or did not want to risk the dangers of childbirth or the demands of parenting.) Today, in an American society characterized by weak family bonds and social institutions, to emphasize meditation as an individual practice is simply to reinforce our pathologically individualistic culture, not to critique its excesses.

In order to understand an unfamiliar Buddhist worldview, it is natural at first to translate it into more familiar terms, but over time we must come to "understand Buddhist traditions on their own terms." To do that, we must become "aware of a whole slew of tacit assumptions that could be biasing our interpretation," Heuman says.[84] We need to be reflexive about our social, historical, and cultural position and the ways it shapes whatever assumptions and attitudes we bring to the study of something unfamiliar. Our subconscious background of assumptions and values is "hard to identify because we are embedded in it, but it lights up when it hits against difference."[85]

Navigating different points of view "is not a matter of objective study, but a matter of interpreting meaning," Heuman says. For example, in an argument with her partner, each of them might assume initially that the other's perspective is "wrong." But

> when she shows me how she arrived at her standpoint, I may see how it makes sense, given her background. To get to that under-standing, I need to reflect on my own assumptions. What was I taking for granted that made her position a problem? The mo-ment I see the nature and source of our difference, the tension dissipates. Her point of view opens a new possibility for me. My world gets bigger.[86]

Dialogue between ancient traditions and our present circumstances requires conversation skills, she says. And that

> calls for showing up in our entirety and inviting our dialogue partner to do the same—which means putting background assumptions on the table. It calls for learning how to listen, which means allowing Buddhist tradition to speak from its own ground while we bracket our preconceptions, pay attention respectfully, and confirm that we understood accurately. Then it calls for knowing how to reflect on how what we've just heard jibes with our own sense of things. In this way, encountering the tradition can show us that what we are taking for granted may be very different. When those background differences light up, they become—in this context—not obstacles to understanding but the conditions of possibility for it; it is precisely because the modern Western and traditional Buddhist worldviews have very different background assumptions that they can illumi-nate each other. And once an assumption is illuminated as such, when we can see it as one way—rather than *the* way—for things to be, then we are up to something new: relinquishing certainties rather than confirming them.[87]

Rather than being universal, transcultural, and transhistoric, Kabat-Zinn's "Dharma" is actually a particularly modern, American blend of Buddhism, neo-Vedanta, and American metaphysical religion, whose priests and evangelists are frequently clinical scientists. Not incidentally, many of them are also white men with credentials from major research universities.

6

Is Mindfulness Effective?

CLINICAL RESEARCH SUGGESTS that MBSR training in meditation and hatha yoga postures—sometimes *in conjunction with* medication and other supportive therapies—can be beneficial in a number of ways. It seems particularly helpful for people who have difficulty regulating their emotions, such as those suffering from posttraumatic stress, addiction, eating disorders, depression, anxiety, and other mood disorders. It seems to help practitioners to become more aware of their emotional states as they arise and to remain focused on present experience rather than on painful memories or anxious ruminations about the future.

The transformative power of mindfulness practice, advocates say, lies in its ability to help people notice their subconscious internal narratives more clearly—their running commentaries about themselves and the world—without reacting to them according to habitual patterns. Jeff Brantley, a psychiatrist and MBSR instructor at Duke University, explains that much human distress arises from unconscious habits of avoiding what is unpleasant and clinging to what is pleasant. This is a key dynamic of addiction, for example. (It is also the Second Noble Truth of Buddhism.) Even when one cannot eliminate an illness, unhappiness, or pain, Brantley says, one can shift one's attitude toward it, to "recognize our own habits of inner reactivity to the point that they no longer rule us."[1]

Kabat-Zinn is emphatic that mindfulness is "a way of being and not a technique"; it is not merely to be employed solely for instrumental purposes under stressful conditions.[2] He defines healing *as a coming to terms with things as they are* in full awareness. We often see that healing takes place on its own over time as we align ourselves with what is deepest and best in ourselves and rest in awareness moment by moment without an attachment to outcome."[3] Many patients

> become motivated to live a life of greater awareness that extends far beyond the eight weeks they are in the program. That greater awareness includes, of course, our intrinsic interconnectedness as beings, and [extends] to the possibility of greater spontaneous compassion toward others and toward oneself. For many, it also includes formal meditation becoming an ongoing feature of one's daily life, often for years and decades after the initial experience of MBSR.[4]

Kabat-Zinn acknowledges that directing people's attention inward, toward their pain, developing intimacy with it and with other members of an MBSR cohort, is a radical act, and that people need a lot of encouragement and guidance to stay with it, which is why they do it in a group setting over an eight-week course. It is necessary to deepen stability and commitment over time in a supportive context.[5]

In Dialectical-Behavioral Therapy (DBT), a protocol employed in treatments for a variety of mental illnesses, the psychologist Marsha Linehan encourages her clients to cultivate what she calls their "wise mind." DBT is one of the best available treatments for Borderline Personality Disorder, sufferers of which have difficulty regulating their emotions and tend to view the world in very black-and-white terms. Linehan's text *Cognitive-Behavioral Treatment of Borderline Personality Disorder* refers repeatedly to Zen in describing the regimen and the qualities required of a therapist. She characterizes Zen as intuitive, present-focused, spontaneous, at times irreverent and paradoxical, flexible, nonjudgmental. The overall treatment regimen, however, is characterized as empirical, practical, effective, and scientific.[6]

Clearly, mindfulness practice can be very helpful to people, and I do not mean to suggest otherwise. As a person who has engaged intensively in meditation practices over more than three decades, and who teaches meditation, I can attest that learning to recognize and detach from one's habits of mind can be transformative. Such training also can be beneficial without being overtly Buddhist. Learning to attend to one's own physical or psychological pain with compassion is a truly worthwhile practice. Furthermore, various Buddhist traditions acknowledge personal happiness as a legitimate purpose for practice. The Dalai Lama has argued that recognizing that all beings wish to be happy can be the basis for an ethical system that is broadly applicable and independent of any particular religious framework.[7]

A therapeutic approach to practice has other warrants in Buddhist tradition. The Buddha is sometimes described as a great physician, and the Four Noble Truths are explained by a medical analogy: the presenting symptom (*dukkha*, dissatisfaction or suffering); the diagnosis of its etiology or cause (craving, or the "three poisons" of greed, aversion, and delusion); the prognosis (the possibility of liberation); and the prescription (the Eightfold Path, subdivided into three categories of training: moral conduct, meditation, and wisdom). It is certainly worthwhile to cultivate personal well-being, and meditation may well enhance well-being. In both Hindu and Buddhist traditions, however, ethical conduct is the necessary foundation for meditative practice. It is not necessarily part of MBIs, a point that will be explored in chapter 7.

The Neuroscience of Mindfulness

The Mind and Life Institute was founded in 1987 to promote dialogue among Buddhist leaders, scholars in the humanities and social sciences, and researchers studying the brain, consciousness, and meditation. One of its major efforts has been to validate scientifically the psychological and physiological benefits of meditation and to communicate research results to both scientists and general audiences. A 2005 conference in Washington, DC, devoted three days to the topic "The Science and Clinical Applications of Meditation." It featured lectures on current scientific research in the field and panel discussions that included Buddhist teachers.

One particularly visible affiliate of the Institute is Daniel Goleman, a writer with a PhD in psychology from Harvard and the author of the best-selling books *Emotional Intelligence* as well as *Social Intelligence: The New Science of Social Relationships*; *The Meditative Mind*; *Destructive Emotions: A Scientific Dialogue with the Dalai Lama*; and *Healing Emotions: Conversations with the Dalai Lama on Mindfulness, Emotions, and Health*. One of Goleman's discussions of brain research on a meditating monk, a chapter in *Destructive Emotions* titled "The Lama in the Lab," illustrates some of the problems associated with the science of research on meditation.

Goleman describes functional MRI (fMRI) studies of "Lama Öser," a pseudonym for a European monk of Tibetan Buddhism, most likely Matthieu Ricard, another affiliate of the Mind and Life Institute who holds a PhD in genetics. Richard Davidson, a Harvard-trained psychologist and author of multiple studies on meditation, was the researcher in this case. The studies showed that while generating emotions such as compassion, Öser's brain showed a dramatic—and highly unusual—increase in activity of the left frontal cortex, an area of the brain associated with positive mood. One implication of the finding, Goleman and others have argued, is that mental training—for example, Buddhist practices to generate compassion—can improve certain kinds of brain function because of *neuroplasticity*: the brain's ability to modify and develop new neural networks. If Öser's decades of monastic training can effect such dramatic changes, proponents say, then even modest training can be beneficial.

Without denying this possibility, it must be noted that Goleman elided some important methodological issues in this kind of brain research. For example, he wrote, "The fMRI could give Davidson a crystal-clear set of images of Öser's brain. . . . These images could then be analyzed in any dimension to track precisely what happens during a mental act, tracing paths of activity through the brain."[8] This suggests that fMRI technology provides a standardized, perfectly reliable image of brain activity. The reality is much messier. Goleman glossed over the messiness, noting in passing that technicians had to sort out "various glitches" during the study, and that the data on Öser's brain activity had to be converted "to a 'standard space,' a mythic uniform brain that allows one person's brain to be compared with others."[9] He also noted that the protocol was difficult to modify, because "once the computers have been programmed . . . the technology drives the procedure." Finally, the "project ran on a crash deadline, compressing seven days of data analysis into half a day" so that preliminary results could be reported to the Dalai Lama the following morning.

Peering into the Procedural "Black Box"

All of these passing remarks, in an otherwise glowing assessment of the study, refer to significant issues in brain-imaging research. Brain activity can vary according to factors such as time of day and whether the subject has recently ingested substances such as caffeine or nicotine. Because the technology is expensive, the numbers of participants in studies are typically small, which affects the degree to which particular results can be generalized. Extraordinary results depend upon comparison to a theoretical "normal" result, but "normal" is very difficult to define. In studies of brain activity using PET scans (positron-emission tomography, which creates three-dimensional images of the brain by tracing movements of radioactive isotopes), "normal" has typically meant a right-handed white male. This means that variations in race, gender, handedness, and possibly age could produce different results. Scans of research subjects' brains are compared to the hypothetical "average" brain—a mathematical model that can vary from laboratory to laboratory. That may change, however. In 2016 researchers at Washington University in St. Louis developed the most detailed digital map of the human cortex ever produced: 180 distinct regions, of which 97 had been previously unknown. They did so by comparing MRIs from 210 healthy adults—who, remarkably, included more women than men. This detailed picture could provide a new standard for the "average" brain in neuroscientific research.[10]

Data from scans are translated into colored images, an interpretive process that has not necessarily been consistent from study to study and that inevitably highlights some differences and downplays others. A focus on activity in a particular area of the brain also tends to obscure the ways that brain functions may be distributed across several areas simultaneously. The "resting" state between activities under study may be defined inconsistently from study to study as well, which affects how results are compared. Even "meditation" is inconsistently defined in clinical research. The interpretation of images requires cooperation across multiple scientific disciplines, among researchers who have different types and degrees of expertise, and possibly competing agendas when it comes to issues like publication credit, research funding, and career advancement. So while the images produced may appear to be very clear and compelling, at every stage they are interpretive productions serving rhetorical purposes, generated in a "black box" of assumptions, technical procedures, and human factors hidden from view.[11] Worse, in 2016 a paper published by the National Academy of Sciences reported that "the most common software packages for fMRI analysis (SPM, FSL, AFNI) can result in false-positive rates of up to 70 percent," showing brain activity where there is none. This finding calls into question the reproducibility of results in some forty thousand published papers over the past two decades or more.[12]

Robert Meikyo Rosenbaum, a skeptic trained as a psychoneurologist and psychotherapist, remarked, "Meditation (of any sort) does change the brain. But *everything* we do changes the brain." Any activity one repeats over and over, from playing the violin to laying bricks, affects the wiring of one's brain. "I suspect if you were to spend eight hours a day in front of the TV doing nothing but watching reruns of *Star Trek*, we'd see some interesting changes in the white matter of your brain." Working now as a lay teacher of Zen and Quigong, Rosenbaum asks, "Instead of relying on magnetic imaging and radioactive isotopes to tell us meditation is 'working' for a person, wouldn't it be better to assess the effects of meditation on individuals by finding out if they treat the people and objects around them with more kindness and compassion?"[13]

Willoughby Britton, a psychologist at Brown University, has pointed out that some neuroscientists don't understand various types of contemplative practice well, or the qualitative differences between them, so they tend to default to defining contemplative "expertise" simply in terms of the number of hours spent meditating, without attending to the nature or quality of research subjects' contemplative practices. Studies inconsistently define mindfulness as a mental *state*, a personal *trait*, a *method* of practice, and the *goal* of practice.[14] In addition, observed Marc Poirier (1952–2015), a law professor and lay Zen teacher, "brain science does not describe the experience of meditation or mindfulness in a way that can be used to help guide the practitioner's explorations. . . . In a fundamental sense, the science is disconnected from meditative experience and practice and teaching, even as it seeks to investigate it."[15] These problems make the veridicality of brain research on meditation much more problematic than it might at first seem. Nevertheless such research appears to be extremely persuasive rhetorically, particularly among audiences untrained in neuroscience.[16] Britton has called this the "Blobology Effect": "When people see colorful blobs on a brain scan, they can be convinced of anything . . . even if what you're saying makes no sense, or if it's absolutely preposterous."[17]

Other Methodological Issues in Mindfulness Research

Clinical research on mindfulness is beset by a number of other problems. One of the most basic is that researchers who are not trained in Buddhist understandings of mindfulness set out to measure it and believe their results accurately reflect Buddhist understandings. Neither do most neuroscientists understand the stages of contemplative development as canonical texts and expert practitioners in different Buddhist traditions would describe them. One 2015 meta-analysis of mindfulness research begins, for example, "Meditation can be defined as a form of mental training that aims to improve an individual's core psychological capacities, such as attentional and emotional self-regulation."[18] This seems to be a perfectly secular goal. But as we have seen, Buddhist understandings of meditation are concerned with more than "attentional and emotional self-regulation."

> Buddhists differentiate between Right Mindfulness (*samma sati*) and Wrong Mindfulness (*miccha sati*). . . . Clearly, the mindful attention and single-minded concentration of a terrorist, sniper assassin, or white-collar criminal is not the same quality of mindfulness that the Dalai Lama and other Buddhist adepts have developed. Right Mindfulness is guided by intentions and motivations based on self-restraint, wholesome mental states, and ethical behaviors—goals that include but supersede stress reduction and improvements in concentration.[19]

This meta-analysis and others identify a number of additional methodological issues in mindfulness research: small sample sizes, few longitudinal studies, the risk that researchers will be biased in favor of mindfulness and that this will color how they interpret results, and the difficulty of designing studies with adequate experimental controls. In short-term, cross-sectional studies that compare nonmeditators to meditators, when differences are detected between groups, it is difficult to determine a clear causal relationship between meditation and the difference measured because there may be "pre-existing differences in the brains of meditators, which might be linked to their interest in meditation, personality or temperament. . . . Correlation still cannot prove that meditation practice has caused the changes because it is possible that individuals with these particular brain characteristics may be drawn to longer meditation practice" in the first place.[20]

Researchers also define mindfulness in different ways and have developed a number of different instruments to measure it, which typically rely on study participants' self-reports. These instruments include the Freiberg Mindfulness Inventory, the Mindful Attention Awareness Scale, the Kentucky Inventory of Mindfulness Skills, the Cognitive and Affective Mindfulness Scale–Revised, the Southampton Mindfulness Questionnaire, the Philadelphia Mindfulness Scale, and the Toronto Mindfulness Scale. These questionnaires ask people to rate themselves on qualities such as "judgmental attitudes, openness to experience, attention to the present moment, and personal identification with present experience."[21] Rosenbaum argues that self-report questionnaires are highly problematic and results may not match data obtained by more objective means.[22] Paul Grossman and Nicholas Van Dam point out that people with meditation experience may understand the meanings of terms on these questionnaires differently than nonmeditators do, and that long-term meditators may understand them differently than short-term meditators. Britton has pointed out that both canonical Buddhist texts and living experts in Buddhist contemplative practices indicate that progress in meditation is not linear, and therefore any mindfulness scale based on an assumption that it is so is flawed.[23]

Ruth Baer, an advocate of self-report questionnaires and designer of the Five Facet Mindfulness Questionnaire, a composite of questions from other surveys, acknowledges that no objective test of mindfulness has been developed, but she argues that mindfulness questionnaires do provide useful data.[24] In an essay on the subject, she provides sample questions from the surveys listed in the previous paragraph; I found many of them difficult to interpret. For example, the Freiburg Mindfulness Inventory, designed for use with long-term meditators, asks respondents to rate how strongly they agree with statements like the following:

  I am open to the experience of the present moment.
  I sense my body, whether eating, cooking, cleaning, or talking.
  When I notice an absence of mind I gently return to the experience of
    the here and now.

As an experienced (I would not say expert) meditator, I immediately wonder: When? Now? Or in general? How can I possibly rate myself on such qualities *in general*, when I know from meditation experience that my state of mind varies from moment to moment, day to day, circumstance to circumstance? Sometimes I am preoccupied, and sometimes I am not. I can concentrate and focus my attention well enough to research and write this book, and I am usually pretty good at identifying and describing my emotional states and internal physical sensations. But awareness of my body also varies, as does my openness to whatever experience I happen to be having at any particular moment.

"In general," Rosenbaum says, "questionnaires that assess transient *states* are less valid the more time there is between performing the activity and the administration of the questionnaire. On the other hand, if mind-fulness is conceived as a *trait* rather than an activity, how do stable traits fit in with a practice that emphasizes continuous shifts of transient inner experiences?"[25]

He discusses a meta-analysis of Mindfulness-Based Interventions that began with 727 studies and found only 39 of them suitable for further examination because of various methodological flaws. When Mindfulness-Based Interventions were compared to other treatments, the measurably beneficial effect was quite small. In another review of research, Rosenbaum found that

> the mindfulness intervention is actually superior to the comparison intervention in only about two thirds of the studies: the majority of instances, to be sure, but hardly an overwhelming finding, given the probable effects of experimenter bias (since neither participants nor instructors were blind to what was being studied), and the fact that the mindfulness meditations were always mixed in with other interventions (group therapy, dialectical behavioral therapy, psychoeducation, etc.). One cannot be sure how much mindfulness meditation itself was at the root of the improvements. In short the research is encouraging but not definitive.[26]

Rosenbaum does not deny that mindfulness is effective and beneficial for many people, but he remains "somewhat skeptical that mindfulness is remarkably *more* effective than other meditations or, in clinical settings, other treatment options."[27]

Psychological research has found that clinical outcomes depend a great deal on the client's motivation, general psychological health, and socio-economic status, as well as the relationship between the client and the therapist, Rosenbaum observes. "Research on mindfulness tends to direct our attention to the technique rather than to the person, to the method rather than the practice journey, to the manualized curriculum rather than the relationship between the student and the teacher."[28] He adds that we have far less control over our minds and behavior than we might wish to believe. "A huge amount of our behavior is automatic. We are subject to the limitations of attention, to the frailties of our cognitive biases, of our habits, and of emotional currents we are not even usually aware of."[29] So "the idea that meditation will make me into an 'I' who, completely 'mindful,' is self-sufficient, happily in charge of the world within and the world around me, is a fantasy."[30] Ultimately, he says, "the test of the wide realm of Buddhist practice is how you face your life and face your death. And the former is difficult to quantify, and it's very difficult to do a self-report outcome assessment of the latter."[31]

The Teacher's Role

Kabat-Zinn, like many of the other authors in the volume *What's Wrong with Mindfulness (and What Isn't)*, says that "the quality of MBSR as an intervention is only as good as the MBSR instructor and his or her understanding of what is required to deliver a truly mindfulness-based programme."[32] Early teachers were typically people committed to and trained in religious traditions that emphasize meditation: Buddhism, neo-Vedanta, Sufism, the yogas, Taoism. Although that is no longer necessarily the case, Kabat-Zinn insists that mindfulness "can only be understood from the inside out. It is not one more cognitive-behavioral technique to be deployed in a behavior change paradigm, but a way of being and a way of seeing that has profound implications for understanding the nature of our own minds and bodies, and for living life as if it really mattered."[33] In fact, he says, it is *"virtually essential and indispensable* for teachers of MBSR and other mindfulness-based interventions" to have "a strong personal grounding in the Buddhadharma and its teachings [emphasis added]."[34] By "Buddhadharma," as we have seen, he means his own eclectic, iconoclastic, modernist, "universal" version—but he regards extended meditation retreats of at least seven to ten days, "and occasionally much longer," to be "an absolute necessity" for mindfulness teachers.[35] I am inclined to agree with him. And such training is generally available at ashrams and Buddhist and yoga retreat centers—which, I cannot help but notice, are run mostly by middle-class white, converted, meditation-oriented Buddhists and yogis, and cater mostly to white, affluent consumers who have sufficient money and social capital to afford extended retreats.

Kabat-Zinn's wise recommendations are based on his own long and deep meditation experience. Nevertheless some mental and medical health providers, even well-meaning ones, may want mostly to acquire techniques for their clinical toolkits, to beef up their résumés, or to offer new billable services, rather than to endure the rigors of extended, intensive meditation training. And students may expect a quick fix from an eight-week course. Psychologists have strong incentives to think in terms of short-term interventions rather than long-term practice over many years, in part because medical insurance programs favor short-term, goal-oriented interventions with measurable results. Psychologists may also have little or no training in extended exploration of their own subjective experience; they may not even have undergone psychotherapy themselves, as it is not necessarily a requirement for licensure as a mental health professional (or mindfulness instructor). If a teacher understands and articulates the value of meditation only in terms of short-term gain, students will be less likely to discover its depths.

As anyone who has done extended meditation retreats in a monastic or semimonastic setting can attest, such training is at times grueling and tedious, and insights gleaned from it develop slowly, over years. Such long-term approaches do not have strong consumer appeal in our quick-fix, there's-an-app-and-a-pill-for-that culture.

> The very difficulty of staying the course is a crucial part of a spiritual practice—and its own reward, no matter the path. Like staying with a relationship through times of boredom and fear, staying with a religion through time is the only way to confront certain truths about one's self and what we call the divine. . . . Nothing much is learned by sampling. If the world's wisdom traditions have anything to teach, if there is a truth that seems to cross methodology, it is this: stick to one thing. Say *yes* to something in particular—which means you mostly say *no* to everything else. Every wisdom tradition I know promises the opposite of an easy road: that discomfort and fulfillment lie side by side, entwined with scary and sometimes lonely inner work. Like art, religion is as much as anything about the long haul.[36]

The Center for Mindfulness that Kabat-Zinn founded has developed a certification program that requires a serious, long-term—and quite expensive—commitment to meditation practice. But there is nothing to stop psychotherapists, addiction counselors, and other mental health professionals from reading books or attending workshops and hanging out shingles as teachers of mindfulness. I once watched an addictions counselor try to teach mindfulness to a group of recovering addicts. She asked them to lie down on the floor and close their eyes, then read additional instructions from a sheet of paper that she carried while pacing the room. It was clear she had no depth of experience in contemplative practice. On another occasion, I observed a counselor play recorded instructions from the *Headspace* app on her cell phone for a psychotherapy group's guided mindfulness practice because, she said, she did not feel competent to provide instructions on her own.

Another risk of poorly trained teachers is that students may experience insights or psychological turmoil that an inexperienced instructor is unable to recognize or address. Meditation, particularly intensive meditation, can surface traumatic memories, strong emotions, or a distressing sense of depersonalization, as if one were watching oneself in a movie. In Britain, *The Guardian* reported growing interest in Mindfulness-Based Cognitive Therapy courses, and cases in which instructors with only an introductory course under their belts offered courses themselves through the National Health Service. These inexperienced teachers did not know how to guide students adequately through disturbing experiences because they had not deeply internalized a long-term meditation practice.[37]

In mindfulness research, negative experiences are seldom assessed, largely because investigators do not ask about them and participants are unlikely to report them voluntarily.[38] For that reason, researchers at Brown University undertook a study focusing specifically on experiences that practitioners found "challenging, difficult, distressing, or functionally impairing." They identified fifty-nine types of these experiences across seven domains: physical, emotional, cognitive, perceptual, motivational, social, and related to the practitioners' sense of self. They also identified twenty-six influencing factors "that can impact the nature, duration, and trajectory" of these experiences.[39] Such factors were related to the practitioners themselves (e.g., their histories, identities, motivations, and worldviews); the amount, intensity, or consistency of practices they undertook; their relationships with others; and their health behaviors.

Challenges were experienced both by new and long-term meditators in Zen, Theravāda, and Tibetan Buddhist lineages. For forty-three of the sixty men and women studied, such experiences occurred during or immediately after a retreat.[40] While some of the reported experiences were interpreted as positive (e.g., euphoria, increased energy, empathy), others were not. The latter included fear, paranoia, hallucinations, delusions, depression, suicidality, irritability, anger, and social or occupational impairments. Seventy-three percent of participants reported moderate to severe impairments in at least one domain, lasting from a few days to more than a decade, with a median duration of one to three years. Seventeen percent required hospitalization.[41] Negative experiences were not limited to people with prior histories of trauma or mental illness, or to those on long-term retreats, or who were insufficiently prepared or supervised.[42]

While the study did not specifically explore challenging experiences in Mindfulness-Based Interventions, it noted that some of the experiences reported did occur under conditions similar to those of MBIs: an hour or less of meditation per day, undertaken primarily for health, well-being, or stress relief. It also noted that while participants of MBIs are frequently encouraged to participate in longer retreats after the eight-week program ends, researchers seldom follow research subjects for longer than a year, so little is known about the long-term trajectories of their meditation practice.[43]

Buddhist traditions offer a variety of ways of explaining challenging experiences related to meditation. Whether a particular type of meditation-related experience is interpreted as pathological or as a sign of progress along the spiritual path, however,

> may differ across traditions, lineages, or even teachers. Furthermore, these models may only be immediately available to practitioners working closely with a teacher or Buddhist community. . . . Even when traditional frameworks are available, these models may be inadequate for Western meditators who seek meditation for therapeutic reasons and who are embedded in a scientifically-oriented culture, where biomedical and psychological frameworks have a pervasive influence. . . . It may be the case that *some* of the "adverse" responses to meditation experiences can be attributed to a lack of fit between practitioner goals and expectations and the normative frameworks of self-transformation found within the tradition. Thus, Western Buddhist practitioners not only have to navigate multiple interpretative frameworks, but also different opinions about which frameworks have authority.[44]

Mark Poirier argues that from his perspective as a Zen teacher, a goal-oriented approach to practice can do nothing but reinforce what Buddhists claim are the root causes of suffering. "What is at stake," he writes, "deeply at stake, is unexamined greed and aversion. 'Do X and you may well get Y' as a premise for meditation and mindfulness leaves the particular kind of pain caused by greed and aversion unexplored."[45]

Conclusions

I have examined the Mindfulness movement through several interpretive lenses and asked a number of questions about it. I considered whether or not it qualifies as religion; I argued that it has all four marks of American metaphysical religion, according to Albanese's definition. I asked whether it is an American *Buddhist* metaphysical religion, and if so, what kind of Buddhism does it reflect? I argued that insofar as it is a "way of life" and intended to help people "discover they are Buddhas," as Kabat-Zinn described his purpose in developing MBSR—rather than simply, say, to help people develop attention and regulate their emotions—then MBSR *is* Buddhist, albeit a modernized, Westernized, simplified, and commodified version. If its purpose is to help people liberate themselves from suffering by internalizing an understanding that all phenomena are impermanent, including both suffering and pleasure, and that all things exist in relation to one another, including oneself, that is a *Buddhist* purpose. If teachers of Mindfulness should, in Kabat-Zinn's view, have deep and long-term training in Buddhist thought and practice, although they avoid using Buddhist terminology when teaching MBSR, then critics have a fair point when they call it "stealth Buddhism."

Candy Gunther Brown has argued that if people are teaching "stealth Buddhism" in institutional settings like federally funded hospitals, prisons, or public schools, this violates the Constitutional separation of church and state. At a minimum, "Mindfulness instructors have an affirmative ethical obligation to supply full and accurate information needed for participants to give truly informed consent."[46] They cannot simply declare Mindfulness "secular" without defining what they mean by "religious" or "secular": "Alleging that mindfulness is a 'nonsectarian,' 'universal' human capacity—to simply 'wake up' and 'see things as they really are'—justifies upholding one culturally particular worldview as superior to others. This not only smacks of cultural arrogance; it is precisely a *religious* attitude—a claim to special insight into the cause and solution for the ultimate problems that plague humanity."[47] The fact that clinical studies suggest that mindfulness may improve physical and mental health and promote learning does not make it secular, she says. Some clinical studies of prayer report similar benefits, but we would not incorporate it into public school curricula.[48]

It certainly is possible to describe the goals of mindfulness training in non-Buddhist terms: improving attention and emotion regulation, for example. But that makes it an instrumental technique, not a way of life. This medicalized approach to meditation training makes a potentially helpful practice accessible to a broader range of people than those likely to be drawn to overtly Buddhist meditation groups, and generally speaking, I think that is fine, even if it is limited in scope and value. But I am an ordained Buddhist, in a tradition that emphasizes meditation, and I think such an approach also leaves most of what is valuable and helpful about Buddhist thought and practice on the cutting-room floor.

At a private, Catholic university where I taught religious studies, I began class meetings with a minute or two of silent sitting, encouraging students to follow their breath and relax into their chairs, to notice how they are at that particular moment, without any specific goal. I didn't use any overtly religious terminology. We began and ended with two or three deep breaths, sighing audibly as we exhale, and shaking out our limbs afterward. Sometimes we stretched a little, or walked down a hallway with no purpose other than walking, so students could see how seldom they did this in the rest of their lives. These practices helped them transition from the world outside the classroom to the world inside it, so they could focus on our work. No one was forced to participate in this activity, however; I explicitly offered an "out" to those who wished to skip it. And while I am open about my personal religious affiliation, I am careful not to say or do anything—or allow my students to say or do anything—that smacks of proselytizing for any particular religious path. In fact, I also explicitly state my bias toward pluralism: my belief that religious diversity is a good and valuable thing, worth exploring, whether one is personally religious or not.

I have also taught courses in Buddhist and Christian contemplative practice and a course titled Caregiving at the End of Life, which asked students to engage in and write about a variety of contemplative practices. Students reported that these methods gave them new insights into themselves and enabled them to bring themselves more fully to encounters with other people and to listen more deeply to others, as well as attend more compassionately to their own inner lives. These students represented a variety of religious and nonreligious affiliations, which remained unchanged by the end of the course, but most found the contemplative practices valuable, and some even described them as life-changing. That seems to me a good thing.

I agree with the Theravāda monk Bhikkhu Bodhi, who does not object to people taking elements of Dharma that they find useful and employing them for secular purposes. If health care providers can use mindfulness to help people feel less anxious or depressed, or to cope better with pain and illness; if social activists find lovingkindness practices helpful in doing their work more peacefully; if Zen-style meditation makes businesspeople more considerate of their clients, all of that is good and to be commended, he says.

If such practices benefit those who do not accept the full framework of Buddhist teaching, I see no reason to grudge them the right to take what they need. . . . As long as they act with prudence and a compassionate intent, let them make use of the Dhamma in any way they can to help others. At the same time, I believe it is also our responsibility, as heirs of the Dhamma, to remind such experimenters that they have entered a sanctuary deemed sacred by Buddhists. Thus, respectful toward their sources, they should pursue their investigations with humility and gratitude. . . . They should recognize . . . they are drawing from an ancient well of sacred wisdom that has nourished countless spirits through the centuries and whose waters still retain their potency for those who drink from them today.[49]

7

From Mind Cure to Mindfulness: What Got Lost

IN CHAPTER 5, I ARGUED that the Mindfulness movement as described by Jon Kabat-Zinn, like the Mind Cure movement before him, has all the characteristics of American metaphysical religion identified by Catherine Albanese: it is concerned primarily with the powers of the mind; it draws upon theories of correspondence between spiritual and natural realms; it speaks in terms of energy, flow, and flux; and it sees "salvation" from suffering primarily in terms of therapy and healing. Like the Individualist wing of Mind Cure and some other metaphysical traditions, the Mindfulness movement consists of networks of people and ideas, circulating internationally through books, periodicals, digital media, conferences, and workshops, rather than being organized like a traditional church or denomination. This chapter explores several additional similarities, or—to borrow a term from Swedenborg—"correspondences" between Mind Cure and Mindfulness.[1] I also consider some important differences between Mindfulness and the early, community-oriented wing of Mind Cure, and the implications of those differences. In the journey from Mind Cure to Mindfulness, as meditation became medicalized, individualized, and commodified, at least three important things got lost along the way: the ethical frameworks in which the disciplines of meditation and yoga historically have been embedded, the benefits and challenges of long-term spiritual community, and systemic analysis of suffering.

Correspondences

First, the correspondences. As we have seen, both New Thought and the Mindfulness movement stress the value of a disciplined mind and the therapeutic value of meditation. Both also share a Perennialist assumption that different religious traditions have an essential unity that is transcultural and transhistoric, and that this universal truth is to be found through contemplative practice and spiritual or mystical experience.[2] Perennialism has roots in Transcendentalism, which has roots in German and American Romanticism. Because of their Perennialist orientation, all of the traditions considered here—New Thought, Theosophy, the Mindfulness movement, modernist Buddhism and neo-Vedanta—draw eclectically from multiple traditions and thereby obscure their religious sources. They share modernist values: egalitarianism, democratic decision-making, and an orientation toward lay householder life rather than toward monastic renunciation. Thus they also all have a liberal religious ethos, like that of Unitarian Universalism, another child of Transcendentalism. All stress individual practice as a key to well-being.

The Mind Cure and Mindfulness movements both offer critiques of scientism (the belief that science will ultimately answer all questions about reality), scientific materialism (the assumption that only what can be measured scientifically is real), and medical orthodoxy, yet both also present themselves as compatible with modern science and appeal to scientific authority to validate their healing claims. Both separate spiritual disciplines such as meditation and yoga from their Asian religious contexts and repackage them for Western consumption, yet they valorize the East as holding sacred wisdom that Western culture lacks. These similarities are discussed below.

Therapeutic Applications of Meditation

Because most historians of New Thought have not distinguished between its Community-oriented and Individualist streams and have paid so little attention to meditation in the Mind Cure movement, New Thought's role in promoting meditation and yoga a century earlier than the Mindfulness movement has largely gone unnoticed. Chapter 3 is one preliminary effort to correct that; further research is warranted. A more thorough investigation would require extensive review of early New Thought materials for discussions of meditation and yoga. Good collections of such materials, particularly serials, are scattered among a small number of archives across the United States, which makes the research challenging and expensive to pursue.[3]

The Mindfulness movement generally, and MBSR in particular, resembles the Individualist wing of New Thought more closely than the Community-oriented wing. Participants in MBSR and other Mindfulness-Based Interventions (MBIs) are offered classes, books, retreats, and videos to buy. These are mostly accessible to people who have enough disposable income to purchase such items and can devote about eight hours a week to such programs for a couple of months. MBI instructors may or may not encourage participants to build communities outside their classes, and if they do so, these groups generally are not like religious congregations; they are more like networks or clubs for people with a common interest. MBIs function like what sociologists Stark and Bainbridge called "client cults": they provide instruction on a fee-for-service model.[4] Class participants develop relationships with instructors, but unless those instructors work actively to promote horizontal relationships among student peers, inside class and beyond, ongoing spiritual community is not part of the program. As with the early Mind Cure movement, some MBSR teachers are well trained and some are not; no licensing laws prohibit anyone from hanging out a "Mindfulness" shingle. Nowadays one can even take an MBSR course at home, alone, online or using video guides on DVD. Thus both Individualist New Thought and the Mindfulness movement have adapted themselves well to American consumer capitalism, a point to which I will return.

Perennialism

Philosophically, both New Thought and Mindfulness advocates like Kabat-Zinn share an assumption that religions have an underlying unitary core that is transcultural and transhistorical. Called Perennialism, it was promoted by Leibniz in the seventeenth century and popularized in the twentieth century by Aldous Huxley and Huston Smith. Perennialism is

> the metaphysic that recognized a divine Reality substantial to the world of things and lives and minds; the psychology that finds in the soul something similar to, or even identical with, divine Reality; the ethic that places man's final end in the knowledge of the immanent and transcendent Ground of all being—the thing is immemorial and universal. Rudiments of the Perennial Philosophy may

be found among the traditionary lore of primitive peoples in every region of the world, and in its fully developed form it has a place in every one of the higher religions.[5]

A corollary to faith in a unitary core of religions is the assumption that historical and cultural differences both within and among religions are "merely" accretions, which can be discarded, leaving the core intact. Thus Sarah Farmer envisioned Greenacre as a place where the fundamental unity of different religious traditions could be explored—and ultimately subsumed in Bahá'í.

The assumption that religious differences are incidental allows Perennialists to cherry-pick ideas and practices from different, even incommensurable traditions, and combine them at will. Theosophists drew from disparate Hindu, Buddhist, and Western esoteric and Spiritualist sources, for example. Neo-Vedic groups such as the Vedanta Society and the Self-Realization Fellowship revere Jesus as an avatar. The modernist Hindu group Brahmo Samaj has ties to Unitarianism. Kabat-Zinn speaks of a universal Dharma that is expressed in both Buddhism and Hinduism but is ultimately independent of both.

A glossy magazine sold recently at the checkout counter of my local Whole Foods Market, the *Power of Mindfulness*, offered a particularly crass example. Short articles served up "100+ Easy Tips to Achieve Balance." Among advice for decluttering your house, doing chair stretches at your desk, improving your relationships, eating more slowly, sleeping better, and exercising more, one article suggested that to "feel more centered" one could try any of the following practices derived from major religious traditions: meditation (from Buddhism), prayer and volunteerism (Christianity), recitation of a personal mantra (Hinduism), or carving out a weekly Sabbath (Judaism). These disciplines can be appropriated at will, the article suggested, without any substantive commitment to their underlying religious worldviews, meanings, or goals. If such disciplines seem too onerous, they can simply be reinterpreted in terms that are less demanding. For example, instead of saying set prayers five times a day or fasting from sunrise to sunset during Ramadan, as devout Muslims do, it's enough to live more mindfully and take inspiration from Islam by setting an intention for each day in the morning, reflecting on it again before bed, and thinking of one thing for which one feels grateful.[6] Various types of meditation are elsewhere described in one sentence each: zazen, vipassana, lovingkindness, contemplative prayer, mantra recitation, TM, and several yogic practices involving the chakras, kundalini, or tantric vis-ualization.[7] Among "14 Ways to Find More Zen" are recommendations to chew gum, wear red garments to instill self-confidence, and buy flowers.[8] Thus religious disciplines, developed and maintained by devotees for millennia, are reduced to stress-busting techniques.

Over the past several decades, many scholars have challenged the Perennialist erasure of differences within and among religious traditions, as well as changes over time and from culture to culture. Perennialists seem blind to the ways that they project specifically Protestant and Western assumptions and categories onto other religions and presume that these assumptions apply universally. Deployed by white people, Perennialism becomes hegemonic because it obliterates differences that are meaningful and important to other cultural groups. Asian religious reformers and missionaries also deployed Perennialism for their own strategic purposes, but their efforts were a *response* to white, Protestant hegemony, that is, to European and American colonialism and imperialism: political, eco-nomic, religious, and cultural. Given that most of the spokespersons— and apparently most of the consumers—of Mindfulness-related products are white, the hegemonic character of Perennialist assumptions under-lying the Mindfulness movement deserve attention and critical analysis.

Critiques of Medical Orthodoxy

The most obvious similarity between Mind Cure and the Mindfulness movement is that both offer critiques of prevailing medical orthodoxies. They do so in different ways, however, because orthodox medicine has changed dramatically since the late nineteenth century. The most ex-treme Mind-Curers, particularly Christian Scientists, denied the reality of matter altogether, and thus rejected any need for orthodox medicine. The Mindfulness movement accepts Western biomedicine but presents itself as complementary.

As we saw in chapter 1, nineteenth-century physicians relied on blood-letting, leeches, blistering, and highly toxic emetics and purgatives. Treatments for "hysteria" in women were even more horrifying. The germ theory of disease did not begin to gain acceptance until the end of the nineteenth century, and antibiotics were not widely used until World War II. So it is no surprise that many people were receptive to critiques of mainstream medicine and that Mind Cure was an attractive option. Like other unorthodox healing systems, such as homeopathy, hydrotherapy, and osteopathy, it was far less painful and dangerous than mainstream medicine, particularly for women. It was certainly *less* likely to kill patients than so-called heroic measures, and people flocked to it as an alternative.

Advocates of Mindfulness, on the other hand, say their methods fill in certain gaps in orthodox medicine. Although medical science has made enormous advances since the nineteenth century, Kabat-Zinn observes, "no matter how remarkable our technological medicine, it has gross limitations that make complete cures a rarity, treatment often merely a rear-guard action to maintain the status quo, if there is any effective treatment at all, and even diagnosis of what is wrong an inexact and too often woefully inadequate science."[9] MBIs add a more human dimension to modern biomedicine, proponents say; it is not a substitute. Like patients at the early twentieth-century Emmanuel Clinic, MBI patients are frequently referred to a program by doctors, and one of Kabat-Zinn's explicit reasons for using nonreligious language was to make MBSR acceptable to medical professionals, health insurers, and anyone else who might feel spooked by Asian religious disciplines. The first group of MBSR students at the University of Massachusetts Medical Center included "medical patients who could be said to be falling through the cracks of the health care system, people who were not being completely helped by the medical treatments available to them. That turned out to be a lot of people. It also included a great many people who had not improved with medical treatment or were suffering from intractable conditions for which medicine has few options and no cures."[10] As with Mind Cure, some patients do not resort to meditation until after other options have failed. Both require sustained commitment and skillful guidance.

Rhetorical Uses of Scientific Authority

Despite their critiques of mainstream medicine, both MBIs and Mind Curers have deployed the authority of science to validate their claims about the efficacy of the contemplative disciplines they promote. They do this in slightly different ways, because the meaning of "science" has changed since the mid-nineteenth century. Early Mind-Curers claimed that their methods were scientific: Phineas Quimby called his method "the Science of Health and Happiness." Mary Baker Eddy called her teachings "Christian Science," as did some of her students, who later founded their own groups under the banner of New Thought. These included "Divine Science" and "Religious Science," also known as "Science of Mind." (Which is not to be confused with the Scientology founded by L. Ron Hubbard.) By "science," they did not mean modern controlled, clinical trials; they simply meant that their claims were demonstrably true: ill people reported cures, and others reported observing them.

In fact, the term "demonstration" is central to Eddy's Christian Science. She wrote, "Late in the nineteenth century I demonstrated the divine rules of Christian Science. They were submitted to the broadest practical test, and everywhere, when honestly applied under circumstances where demonstration was humanly possible, this Science showed that Truth had lost none of its divine and healing efficacy, even though centuries had passed away since Jesus practised these rules on the hills of Judaea and in the valleys of Galilee."[11] Stephen Gottschalk, a historian of Christian Science, explained, "That which is demonstrated is always the allness of God and the spiritual perfection of man. The full demonstration of these realities constitutes salvation as defined in Christian Science. And salvation in this sense is the only thing that Mrs. Eddy ultimately claimed to offer. Healing is considered indispensable in Christian Science, for in no other way can spiritual fact be demonstrated."[12]

Ernest Holmes, the founder of Religious Science, also used the term "demonstration." Like Eddy, he believed that the healing powers of mind were not miraculous, in the sense of divine intervention; they were manifestations of natural law: "We hold no argument with any one over the possibility of demonstrating the Law. There is such a thing as Universal Law and Mind, and we can use It if we comply with Its nature and work as It works. We do not argue, ask, deny, nor affirm; WE KNOW. Thousands are to-day proving this Law, and in time, all will come to realize the Truth."[13]

It is clear that Christian Science and New Thought were popular because many people benefited from their teachings. Although Christian Science has declined dramatically since its heyday, New Thought ideas continue to captivate audiences. "The Law of Attraction," popularized by Ralph Waldo Trine's 1897 best seller, *In Tune with the Infinite*, is "The Secret" that Rhonda Byrne's twenty-first-century film and best-selling book claim to reveal.

Of course, there is no way to validate—or invalidate—any past claim about the efficacy of mental healing, by contemporary scientific methods. Nineteenth-century medical diagnosis was far less sophisticated than it is today, and it is impossible to determine physiological causes of the symptoms for which people reported cures. Available historical records are insufficient to determine whether the cures lasted or whether people suffered relapses. Nevertheless, the claim that cures were demonstrable, and therefore empirical or "scientific," was certainly effective rhetorically, especially at a time when science was beginning to offer serious challenges to Christian orthodoxy.

In the present day, for a hypothesis to be valid scientifically it must be testable, and therefore it must be falsifiable: it must be at least theoretically possible to show that the hypothesis is incorrect. For the results of scientific experimentation to be considered valid, they must be replicable in experiments using control groups, and the experimental methods and data must be subject to peer review. These conditions are impossible to satisfy in case of cures attributed to Christian Science and New Thought practitioners. Controlled clinical trials did not become the standard in scientific research until the late twentieth century, thanks in part to Henry Beecher's analysis of the placebo response.

Likewise, proponents of MBIs rely on medical and scientific authority to validate claims about the physical and psychological benefits of meditation. Kabat-Zinn wrote, "The medical and scientific model . . . is based on years of scientific research and the careful attempt to move away from voodoo and witchcraft and spiritualism and all sorts of things that have no basis in the scientific framework."[14] He even asserted, like the modernist Buddhist reformers from Asia before him, that "the Buddha was a great scientist" because his teachings were based on empirical observation of his own psychophysical processes.[15]

But as chapter 6 indicated, modern clinical trials are far from infallible. In addition to the difficulty of designing studies that account for multiple variables and provide adequate control groups, negative results may not be fully reported in medical journals, which compromises the integrity of the peer review process; research may be funded by organizations (such as for-profit corporations) with vested interests in study results; researchers may have financial interests in those entities; and regulatory oversight of research may be inadequate.[16] Nevertheless the authority that scientific studies convey has been very effective in marketing Mindfulness.

A particularly clear example appeared in August 2017, just as this book was going to press. That month, Public Broadcasting Service stations began airing a thirty-minute infomercial called *Mindfulness Goes Mainstream*.[17] A press release insisted four times in five paragraphs that scientific evidence has "proven" the mental and physical health benefits of mindfulness. "No longer limited to Eastern philosophers or California hippies," readers were assured, "mindfulness is now embraced by millions of ordinary people trying to survive in a totally stressed out world." More than "1,500 studies have now been published citing how meditation lowers stress, improves heart and lung functionality and dramatically enhances focus and performance," the document continued. The film itself insisted unequivocally that mindfulness reduces depression, anxiety, addictive behavior, and chronic pain and that it increases focus, empathy, compassion, and happiness.

While these are clearly good things, neither the marketing material nor the film mentions any of the methodological critiques of Mindfulness research, or the ambiguous results of some studies, or meta-analyses suggesting that measurable benefits from MBIs may be ambiguous or small. Also unmentioned are potentially harmful effects from meditation undertaken too intensively or without adequate guidance from experienced teachers. Mindfulness is simply "scientifically proven" to be beneficial in myriad ways. While claiming this authority, the program actually sidestepped the sort of peer-review and critique that are fundamental to the scientific method, as well as to careful scholarship in the humanities. It also made no reference to the ethical underpinnings of meditation in Buddhism and yoga and offered no analysis of the process by which these disciplines have became medicalized, commodified, and corporatized.

The sixty-minute PBS program included forty minutes of pseudo-documentary, punctuated by two ten-minute pledge breaks in which viewers were urged to become sustaining contributors to their local PBS affiliate stations. For $7 per month or an annual contribution of $84, viewers could own a copy of the film; for $10 per month or $120 per year, they would also receive a gift-pack of two DVDs and an audio CD that would teach them mindfulness techniques. I am a sustaining supporter of my local PBS station who believes meditation can be beneficial, but I found the whole program nauseating. Another reason for this was that the film is a perfect example of troubling racial and gender dynamics explored in this book, about which more will be said below.

Strategic Occidentalism and Orientalism

A third characteristic the Mindfulness movement shares with the religious traditions that inform it is a tendency toward both "strategic Occidentalism," that is, using Western cultural resources and methods to promote Asian religions, and "strategic Orientalism," using Asian religious systems to critique certain aspects of Western culture. As we saw, the use of Western scientific rhetoric to legitimize the religious disciplines of meditation and yoga is an example of strategic Occidentalism. So is the claim that Buddhism, shorn of all its magical, miraculous elements and reduced to a philosophy grounded in selected texts, is more compatible with Western science than Christianity. A third example of strategic Occidentalism is the efforts some Asian gurus have made to promote their religious claims with the support of European and American celebrities and rock stars. Transcendental Meditation is one such case.

During the nineteenth and early twentieth centuries, Sri Lankan, Japanese, and Chinese Buddhist reformers engaged in strategic Occidentalism to great effect. They learned Western philosophy and methods of textual analysis and deployed them to revitalize and reinterpret their religious traditions at home and to advance their own religious and political agendas abroad. Asian Buddhist scholars were inspired by Orientalist translations of their scriptures to explore their sacred literature and traditions afresh, and to recover "forms of knowledge which were atrophying and might otherwise have been lost."[18]

In Sri Lanka, Buddhist modernizers used Protestant methods to combat the Protestant missionary activity that accompanied British colonialism. For example, reformers adopted Protestant styles of preaching and religious education and used printing technology to revitalize Buddhist institutions and argue for the superiority of their own traditions over Christianity. In this project, they were aided by the white founders of the Theosophical Society: Henry Steel Olcott and Helena P. Blavatsky.[19] Theosophists and other sympathetic Orientalists also supported Hindu reformers in India who challenged British colonial rule and promoted Hindu nationalism.

During the Meiji Era in Japan, Buddhist institutions facing state persecution sent missionaries abroad to study Western philosophy and Orientalist scholarship. These missionaries then reinterpreted Buddhist philosophy through the lenses of German idealism and social Darwinism, and defended Buddhism as a modern, rational, ethical philosophy more compatible with Western science than was Christianity. They promoted their modernist reformulations at home, where the Japanese were eagerly appropriating Western technologies and fashions. They also promoted their ideas abroad, particularly at the 1893 World's Parliament of Religions. The modernist versions of Buddhism they presented appealed to Western audiences in part because they had been designed to do so. Judith Snodgrass has argued that underlying efforts to present Japanese

Zen as equal—or superior—to Christianity were the missionaries' desires to defend their religion against Western characterizations of Buddhism as nihilistic, superstitious, and backward, and politically, to secure the revision of unequal treaties between imperial Japan and Western countries.[20]

A more recent example of strategic Occidentalism is the Dalai Lama's dialogues with Western scientists on the neuroscience of meditation, conducted under the auspices of the Mind and Life Institute. These dialogues counter a Chinese government narrative that characterizes Tibetan Buddhist culture as feudal and backward, offered to justify intervention by the Chinese state.

At the World's Parliament, Vivekenanda and Dharmapāla (among others) also engaged in strategic Orientalism: they drew from their own Asian traditions and their knowledge of Christianity to assert the superiority of their religions over Christian monotheism. Vivekenanda argued that belief in an omnipotent God who allows human suffering is "unscientific" in comparison to the impersonal workings of karma, a deft use of both strategic Occidentalism and Orientalism. He critiqued the bigotry, individualism, and dogmatism he perceived in Western, missionary Christianity.[21] Dharmapāla, in a speech before the Parliament, proclaimed pointedly, "The crude conceptions of anthropomorphic deism are being relegated to the limbo of oblivion. Lip service of prayer is giving place to a life of altruism. Personal self-sacrifice is gaining the place of a vicarious sacrifice." According to Buddhist ethics, he said, "Prohibited employments include slave dealing, sale of weapons of warfare, sale of poisons, sale of intoxicants, sale of flesh—all deemed the lowest of professions." Dharmapāla, Vivekenanda, and other Asians used the platform provided by Protestants at the Columbian Exposition—which had been carefully designed by its white organizers to demonstrate the superiority of Protestant civilization— to critique Protestant doctrine, practice, and hypocrisy.

Likewise, contemporary missionaries for Mindfulness, particularly those who are sympathetic to Buddhism and Hinduism, practice both strategic Occidentalism and strategic Orientalism. They interpret, promote, and describe meditation in Western scientific terms, while simultaneously deploying "the East as a means of intellectual and cultural criticism."[22] J. J. Clarke observes:

Arguably, these orientalist strategies could be seen as appropriating Eastern cultural products for the benefit of a manifestly Western project, commodification of Eastern traditions for Western consumption. But at the same time it must be recalled that universalizing projects such as these were often subversive and counter-cultural within the Western context, designed to confront indigenous Western religious and philosophical assumptions and practices with a radical alternative, and in this sense they are expressive of ruptures within the West itself. And while projects such as universalism are effectively ways of subsuming Eastern systems of thought under the "intellectual authority" of Western categories and for purposes that flow from specifically Western aspirations, they are nevertheless premised on a belief that Eastern contributions to these projects have an inherent excellence that Western sources lack.[23]

Advocates of MBIs and New Thought have promoted meditation as an antidote to the stresses caused by Western civilization, and mental therapeutics as an antidote to the shortcomings of mainstream Western medicine and technologically driven culture.

Coziness with Consumer Capitalism

Like Individualist New Thought, the individualistic, lay-oriented, and therapeutic approach to meditation found in MBIs is particularly well suited to consumer capitalism. It can be easily commodified: taught in books, workshops, and classes. It does not require either monastic training or long-term formation in a religious congregation. It also squares very nicely with Krishnamurti's injunctions to reject institutional forms of religion and chart one's own path.[24] It is ideal for those who like to think of themselves as "spiritual but not religious": the target audience for *Mindful* magazine. In its most secularized and simplified versions, Jeff Wilson wryly observed, Mindfulness

> requires no gurus, no initiation, no foreign mantras, no years on a cushion, no silence, no devotion, no moral restraint, no belief, no physical flexibility, no wisdom, no patience, no submission, no money, no community, no costumes. In some cases, it doesn't even require meditation for more than a minute at a time. Yet . . . it promises everything: it can allegedly improve any conceivable activity and provide unlimited practical benefits. Perhaps it can even save the world.[25]

The online program *10 Percent Happier*, for example, developed by ABC News correspondent Dan Harris and Vipassana teacher Joseph Goldstein, offers "Clear, Simple Meditation. (No Robes. No Crystals.)" to a target audience of "fidgety skeptics," defined as people "interested in meditation but allergic to woo-woo." It provides video and audio lessons and a personal meditation coach, but "you don't have to sit in a funny position. (Unless you want to, of course.) You also don't have to: light incense, chant, or believe in anything in particular. There's nothing to join, no special outfits to wear." A subscription costs just under $30 for three months and $80 per year.[26] In the PBS infomercial *Mindfulness Goes Mainstream*, which features Harris, Chade Meng Tan says, "One breath a day is all I ask."[27]

Ron Purser and David Loy famously dubbed corporate and commercialized meditation training "McMindfulness," which is advertised as a means of personal self-fulfillment, a competitive edge, and "a reprieve from the trials and tribulations of cutthroat corporate life." As the singer-songwriter Jewel put it in *Mindfulness Goes Mainstream*, "It's not trying to solve world problems when you meditate; it's just a willingness to take a brain break." This sort of individualized and consumerist approach "may be effective for self-preservation and self-advancement," Loy and Purser note, "but is essentially impotent for mitigating the causes of collective and organizational distress."[28]

Advocates of McMindfulness, they say, "argue that transformational change starts with oneself: if one's mind can become more focused and peaceful, then social and organizational transformation will naturally follow." This is a claim frequently advanced by speakers at big Mindfulness conventions, like the Wisdom 2.0 business conferences or the annual Mindful Leadership Summit in the District of Columbia. The flaw in this claim, Purser and Loy argue, is that "the three unwholesome motivations that Buddhism highlights—greed, ill will, and delusion—are no longer confined to individual minds, but have become institutionalized into forces beyond personal control." I would argue that they are deeply entrenched in a globalized capitalist economy, institutionalized racism and sexism, the military-industrial complex, the prison-industrial complex, the healthcare industry, and government bureaucracies. They are reflected in unprecedented income inequality and the destruction of ecosystems worldwide. Purser and Loy continue:

> Up to now, the mindfulness movement has avoided any serious consideration of why stress is so pervasive in modern business

institutions. Instead, corporations have jumped on the mind-fulness bandwagon because it conveniently shifts the burden onto the individual employee: stress is framed as a personal problem, and mindfulness is offered as just the right medicine to help employees work more efficiently and calmly within toxic environments. Cloaked in an aura of care and humanity, mindfulness is refashioned into a safety valve, as a way to let off steam—a technique for coping with and adapting to the stresses and strains of corporate life.[29]

In *Mindfulness Goes Mainstream* the CEO of Aetna, a medical insurance company, credits mindfulness for helping him deal nonpharmaceutically with chronic pain; he says a twelve-week corporate wellness program involving three hundred employees, which included mindfulness and yoga, generated sixty-nine more minutes of productivity per month (he doesn't explain how this figure was derived) and a 7 percent drop in corporate healthcare expenses. I do not mean to suggest that these are not good things, but they do little to change the fact that millions of people lack access to basic medical care or that the American medical system is the most expensive in the world, despite health indicators that are frequently far worse than those of other developed countries (e.g., rates of heart disease, obesity, diabetes, cancer, infant mortality).

Jeremy Carrette and Richard King have sharply critiqued a psychologically oriented and consumerist approach to "spirituality." While it may claim to offer freedom from dogma and institutional constraints, they argue, it is in fact embedded in the assumptions, values, and power structures of neoliberalism and serves the interests of consumer capitalism. The rhetoric of individual "spirituality"

> established a form of thought-control by turning religious discourse into private and individualised constructions, which pacified the social, and potentially revolutionary, aspects of religion. Under the terms set by political liberalism, religion could exist in the modern secular state so long as it was pushed safely into the private sphere. One way to achieve this is by containing it within psychological registers of meaning that would thereby limit the possibilities for threat to ruling elites.[30]

Erasing its religious roots, rejecting forms of religious practice that require renunciation, and operating outside religious institutions, capitalist spirituality "offers personalized packages of meaning and social accommodation rather than recipes for social change and identification with others. In this sense, capitalist spirituality is the psychological sedative for a culture that is in the process of rejecting the values of community and social justice."[31] Carrette and King acknowledge that religious traditions "are not without their own dark histories of thought-control, oppression, and violence. Nevertheless, what they also offer are ways to overcome the pernicious consequences of individualism, self-interest, and greed throughout history."[32] At their best, religions can help practitioners to transcend such vices.

The late Marc Poirier, a lay teacher of Zen, saw the commodification of mindfulness and meditation as problematic for several reasons:

> It obscures the importance of at least three key aspects of traditional Buddhist training: (1) a sustained commitment to practice over time; (2) the usefulness of the community of practice in stabilizing and expanding individual practice; and (3) the importance of guidance from a learned and trusted teacher or elder with whom the student develops a long-term disciple relationship. These three elements are essential for those who wish to explore more deeply what mindfulness and meditation can offer as a way of life.[33]

Without commitment, community, and wise, ethical guidance, critics say, corporate "McMindfulness" is about as wholesome as most other fast food.

Divergences: What Got Lost

Having considered characteristics that Mind Cure and MBIs have in common, let us consider how they differ, and the implications of those differences. First, early New Thought, like the Emmanuel Movement, was largely *community*-oriented. In the early New Thought movement, white women and black men founded religious communities that helped people to cultivate character and develop spiritually. Many members of these communities also worked politically for social reforms, such as women's suffrage, changes to marriage and divorce laws, and antilynching legislation. Others worked for economic empowerment and self-sufficiency for all women and for black men. Changing unhelpful habits of mind was simply the first step to *liberation*—not just spiritually, but in political, legal, and economic terms. However, as mental therapeutics became medicalized, "positive thinking" became more commercialized, and the public sphere became increasingly secular, the religiously motivated social justice agendas of early New Thought communities fell by the wayside. Their ethical and political concerns were privatized and faded from view.

Freudian psychotherapy had a strongly atheist bias, and as mental therapeutics shifted from the Mind Curers to the Emmanuel Movement to the purview of mainstream doctors, it became ever more individualized and secularized. "Talk therapy" certainly can provide a confidential space for confession and reflection, but it is not rooted in any particular ethical or spiritual framework. This development was not inevitable, however. Other groups have managed to maintain relatively successful syntheses of psychological counseling and spiritual formation.

Alcoholics Anonymous, the Salvation Army, and Clinical Pastoral Education (CPE) have all blended various forms of psychological counseling (professional or peer) with religious community, ethical formation, and social support. These three institutions occupy a space between traditional churches and the medical establishment. CPE trains clergy candidates to understand themselves better psychologically and to provide more effective pastoral counseling in institutions that serve religiously diverse populations. Chaplains are trained in peer groups and generally are also accountable to the churches and denominations that ordain or otherwise authorize their ministries. AA and the Salvation Army reach out to the most isolated and alienated people in society: those who are poor, ill, homeless, and/or addicted. The Salvation Army, which represents the conservative, evangelical end of the Protestant spectrum, offers residential treatment for substance abuse, counseling, job training, transitional housing, and other supportive services. AA retains its Protestant flavor but makes room for the unchurched, the agnostic or atheist, the "spiritual but not religious," and those who identify with religions other than Christianity. Fellowship is central to the success of those who find recovery in these organizations. Neither is oriented toward social, economic, or political change, however.

In the spaces that such groups provide, people can form friendships and interpersonal networks; learn the value of community; mature psychologically, ethically, and spiritually; participate in democratic processes;

exercise responsible leadership; and perform acts of service. They practice introspection and are encouraged to become more sensitive and compassionate to others. They foster "faith instead of disbelief, community in place of alienation, ethical striving rather than self-indulgence."[34] These organizations have "convinced millions of spiritually and socially alienated Americans that, in their pursuit of well-being, they needed to turn to God and fellowship, and that to do this they had to become more honest and altruistic."[35] AA also helps people adapt to religious pluralism, as members encounter and must serve alongside those who orient toward religion differently from themselves. The Mindfulness movement seems too privatized to foster such benefits effectively.

Community

When a spiritual discipline like meditation is individualized, medicalized, instrumentalized, and commodified, the most fundamental loss is the benefit of long-term immersion in a community that transcends the bonds of kinship or tribe. Religious congregations, for all their flaws, can create social and civic bonds that make people and communities happier and healthier. They can motivate people to work for social change, as they did during both the Civil Rights movement and the Reagan Revolution. MBSR protocols, on the other hand, have students interact primarily with instructors, so relationships among classmates have little opportunity to form. In online or DVD-based courses, students can practice entirely alone. And in both kinds of courses, some participants will stop practicing after the course ends because meditation is difficult to maintain on one's own, especially when painful emotions or memories arise.

In Buddhist groups, practitioners take refuge in Three Jewels: the Buddha (i.e., a qualified teacher), the Dharma, and the Sangha (a community of practice). In the monastic traditions, the Sangha embodies

quite literally, a critique of mainstream social values and cultural norms. . . . It necessitated a radical change in the way one lived; one was required to opt out of family ties and worldly pursuits, and opt in to an alternative, communal, celibate, and highly regulated lifestyle. Modern teachers of mindfulness rarely make such demands of their students; the liberating, or if you will therapeutic, benefits apparently do not require dramatic changes in the way one lives. Rather than enjoining practitioners to renounce carnal and sensual pleasure, mindfulness is touted as a way to more fulfilling sensual experiences. Rather than enjoining practitioners to renounce mainstream American culture, mindfulness is seen as a way to better cope with it.[36]

Rigorous, monastic practices of "poverty, celibacy, homelessness, and lack of any personal attachments or possessions . . . is the expression of the core truths of impermanence, non-clinging, and interdependency. In none of these traditions was meditation separable either from an all-encompassing form of life or from a strict ethical set of precepts governing all aspects of conduct," write Barry Magid and Marc Poirier, both nonmonastic teachers of Zen. Even among laity, however, Buddhist moral precepts are fundamental.[37] In most forms of Buddhism, the most basic act of affiliation with the tradition is publicly to "take refuge" in the Three Jewels and vow to practice at least five basic precepts: not to kill, steal, lie, misuse sexuality, or use intoxicants.

Nowadays it is fashionable and common to proclaim oneself "spiritual but not religious"; according to surveys conducted by the Pew Forum on the American Religious Landscape, "nones" are the fastest growing group in American society. When I probe with college students what they mean by this, it turns out that many ascribe to the category "religion" everything they dislike—rules, structures, institutions, exclusiveness, judgmentalism— and ascribe to "spirituality" everything they like: wisdom, compassion, reverence, generosity, love, unsullied nature, and so on. Frequently, behind this categorization is negative experience with a highly dogmatic form of religiosity and limited exposure to alternatives. Because I have learned to cultivate much of my own "spiritual" life through specifically "religious" disciplines, I see the dichotomy as a false one. Religious communities certainly can promote toxic, hateful ideologies, and religious disciplines and rituals certainly can be done in rote, empty, ineffective ways. But such disciplines and rituals are not *inherently* ineffective, or they would not have lasted for centuries and millennia in the institutions that practice and preserve them.

Robert Sharf, a scholar of East Asian Buddhism, made cogent observations about problems that attend any individualistic, de-institutionalized approach to Buddhism:

I think this deep suspicion of religious institutions is understandable but also misguided. The organized, rule-bound and tradition-bound institution of the sangha provides a framework that, at least ideally, helps to efface egocentrism. The sangha literally embodies the Buddhist tradition; it transcends the self-concerns of any individual, especially the concerns that arise from placing our inner life at the center of the universe. So we must ask whether Buddhism, when practiced without the ties of community and tradition, instead of mitigating our tendency toward narcissism, actually feeds it.[38]

Sharf was careful to add:

I certainly don't think that personal experience, meditation, spirituality, and the like are unimportant or that they have no place in Buddhism. The Buddha, after all, attained enlightenment while meditating under the Bodhi tree. My concern is with how Buddhist modernism has isolated meditation from the context of the whole of Buddhist religious life. So much of what was once considered integral to the tradition has been abandoned in this rush to celebrate meditation or mindfulness or personal transformation or mystical experience as the *sine qua non* of Buddhism. . . . It's really not a question of right or wrong. It's a question of what gets lost.[39]

What gets lost, he explains, are the corporate dimensions of Buddhist formation—the texts, rituals, and traditions that have inspired and shaped Buddhist communities over two and a half millennia. Although advocates of MBSR insist that mindfulness is "a way of life and not a technique," this vehicle for promoting Mindfulness does not provide, and may not even succeed in encouraging, the kinds of long-term, community-based formation that might help people to internalize that way of life.

Poirier and Magid "can see the legitimate need for avoiding anything that appears to be proselytizing of a particular religious faith within corporate or educational settings. But it is also part of the secular, market-based pitch that mindfulness is a technique that can be separated from any long-term commitments, lifestyle changes, or ethical concerns."[40] Designating a practice as *religious* implies a long-term commitment: not just to the practice itself, but to the *community* of practice. Further, many of the values that Buddhist ethics promote are *social* values.

For the notion of sangha to be viable, we must have a group of practitioners who are committed to one another, not just to their own meditation practice. They must be united by something more substantial than the coincidence of meeting up at irregular intervals at a smorgasbord of workshops. The commitment is not merely a matter of peer support but of a shared ethical responsibility, based on the precepts.[41]

Poirier points out that it is possible to develop a sequence of instruction that begins with short modules and leads to longer periods of practice, and eventually to a relationship with an experienced meditation teacher and community. The secularized Shambhala Training developed by a Tibetan teacher, Chögyam Trungpa, did this: "The workshop model was used at the front end, but there was a door beyond it leading to a structure more supportive of sustained practice."[42] As Stephanie Muravchick has pointed out, the Emmanuel Movement, the Salvation Army, and Alcoholics Anonymous (and its offshoots) all managed to create forms of psychoreligious therapy and healing grounded in *communities* of practice.

Some MBSR teachers do offer regular meditation groups or classes to provide ongoing instruction and support. The Center for Mindfulness does this. In Baltimore, an MBSR teacher and psychotherapist, Trish Magyari, worked with colleagues to establish a weekly meditation group affiliated with the Insight Meditation Community of Washington, D.C., to provide ongoing support for MBSR graduates and others. It meets in a yoga studio.

Even people embedded in American Buddhist communities can have a myopic and ahistorical view of Buddhist history and traditions, however—especially if they emphasize meditation (or other practices such as chanting) to the exclusion of other forms of Buddhist practice, including devotional rituals and formal studies. Two examples will illustrate the point. A March 2008 article in a popular Buddhist magazine surveyed clinical research on meditation and noted that to make mindfulness broadly palatable, "researchers and clinicians have stripped away vipassana's South Asian *cultural and ritual baggage* and presented it as a simple way to walk through mental and emotional turmoil—much, perhaps, as the Buddha himself did 2,500 years ago [emphasis added]."[43] A more recent Mindfulness advocate, responding in *Mindful* magazine to critics who expressed concern that a secularized approach to meditation fosters a superficial, watered-down version of Buddhism, said this:

I think these critiques come from more fundamentalist Buddhists. I mean, if you want to see watered-down Buddhism, travel to the beautiful Zen temples of Korea, a country where Buddhism is still alive and well, and you'll see all the ladies in the temples working their malas, chatting about their kids, sometimes shucking peas; the temples are very much village and urban gathering places. How many people are deeply practicing?[44]

In my view, this remark reflects the same kind of cultural arrogance that led European Orientalists to claim in the nineteenth century that "real" Buddhism was the philosophical and ethical teachings to be found in Pali scriptures, and that devotional and ritual practices, as well as the social and communal life of temples, were "corruptions" of that "pure" tradition.

A version of Buddhism in which meditation is the "essence," purified of extraneous "cultural baggage" and universally applicable to all, may be closer to fundamentalism, in that it takes a highly selective reading of a complex and diverse religious tradition, particularly its textual tradition, and projects it backward in time in order to valorize an imagined "golden age" before "corruption" and "decline" set in—which, of course, modern Westerners must now recapture. It is a patronizing, colonial mentality. White, Euro-American converts to meditation-oriented Buddhism—and I am one—tend to say this sort of thing when we practice and talk mostly with one another rather than with other sorts of Buddhists. Asian American scholars of Buddhism such as Chenxing Han, Funie Hsu, the late blogger "Angry Asian Buddhist," the Dharma teacher Mushim Ikeda, African American Dharma teachers such as Zenju Earthlyn Manuel, angel Kyodo williams, Lama Rod Owens, and others have repeatedly pointed this out in American Buddhist media over the past decade or more.

It will take a long time—perhaps centuries—for the West to engage with the Buddhist tradition at a deeper level. Such an engagement will require that we see past the confines of our own historical and cultural situation and gain a greater appreciation of the depth and complexity of the Buddhist heritage. Certainly one impediment to that is the idea that the only thing that matters is meditation and that everything else is just excess baggage.[45]

And what of the "cultural baggage" that the white, meditation-focused, *convert* described above is carrying? It is a mark of unexamined white privilege to assume that others have "cultural baggage" but oneself does not.

Ethics

As we saw in chapter 5, mindfulness is only one element of a comprehensive path of spiritual cultivation called the Eightfold Path, said to lead to spiritual insight and liberation from suffering. Three elements of the Eightfold Path deal with moral conduct: right speech (not lying, engaging in harsh or divisive speech, gossiping, or participating in idle chatter), right conduct (not killing, stealing, intoxicating oneself, or misusing sexuality), and right livelihood (not making a living based on wrong speech or conduct, e.g., butchery, dealing weapons or intoxicants, prostitution or human trafficking). One of the factors aiding the spread of Buddhism along trade routes such as the Silk Road was that it provided a system of ethics not dependent upon one's social class (*varna*), tribe, or clan. Right Mindfulness, the seventh element of the Eightfold Path, has an ethical function: to help practitioners distinguish wholesome from unwholesome actions and states of mind. Ethical conduct is understood to be fundamental to meditative calm.

Early Buddhist scriptures such as "The Chapter of the Eights" in the *Sutta Nipata* and the *Sigālaka Sutta* in the *Dīgha Nikāya* are strongly ethical in character. "The Chapter of the Eights" is a series of aphorisms discouraging greed, sensuality, dogmatism, arrogance, contentiousness, violence, and so forth, and lauding the renunciate life of a wandering monk.[46] The *Sigālaka Sutta* contains "Advice to Lay People"; it discourages addiction, gambling, and keeping poor company, and encourages respect for parents and teachers and fair dealings with one's spouse, friends, employees, and servants. Generosity is the most fundamental Buddhist virtue. In most forms of Buddhism it is traditional for laity to adopt five moral precepts, and when people ordain as monks and nuns, they formally adopt at least ten and often hundreds of precepts governing every aspect of comportment and daily life.

But ethical training is not necessarily part of Mindfulness training. At a Day of Mindfulness retreat I attended in North Carolina as part of early research for this book, participants were asked simply to maintain silence and avoid eye contact with one another. In the Vipassanā retreats upon which the Day of Mindfulness is modeled, however, participants are normally asked to observe the five precepts for lay Buddhists during the event. In MBSR retreats, this is up to the leaders of the particular course.

Also absent from MBIs is an epistemological framework for meditative practice. Clearly, physical yoga, meditation, and lovingkindness visualizations can be helpful to people apart from Buddhist and Hindu doctrines. Yet these practices are grounded in assumptions about the nature of reality, humans' capacity to discern reality, and the ethical implications of such discernment. For example, one consequence of the Vedanta teaching that the divine manifests in all things is that people try, through various forms of yoga, to learn to see God everywhere, in everything and everyone. Buddhist liberation is predicated on the recognition that what we imagine to be the "self" lacks any independent, unchanging, enduring essence. The ethical consequence of this realization is that people must learn to overcome the grasping, aversion, and ignorance that arise from attachment to the putative "self."

Kabat-Zinn disputes the claim that MBIs ignore ethics in favor of a few decontextualized techniques:

> First, it is inevitably the personal responsibility of each person engaging in this work to attend with care and intentionality to how we are actually living our lives, both personally and professionally, in terms of ethical behavior. An awareness of one's conduct and the quality of one's relationships, inwardly and outwardly, in terms of their potential to cause harm, are intrinsic elements of the cultivation of mindfulness as I am describing it here.[47]

He also argues that ethics are built into the structure and setting of MBSR in various ways. These include the fundamental ethical imperatives to "do no harm," and for healthcare providers to place patients' needs before their own. Kabat-Zinn even compares the Hippocratic Oath to the Māhāyana Buddhist Bodhisattva Vow.[48] But the Hippocratic Oath refers to *physicians'* obligation not to harm people in their care because there is a power imbalance in the doctor-patient relationship and patients are considered vulnerable. The oath says nothing about how Mindfulness students should behave toward their corporate coworkers once they leave the classroom or meditation hall, or how mindful soldiers and police should regard the people in their gunsights.

Because Buddhism is, at its roots, a monastic, renunciant tradition, which has survived through the dedication of monastics and the patronage of aristocrats and monarchs for much of its history, it has not developed the same kinds of prophetic, social justice traditions that are central to the Abrahamic religions of Judaism, Christianity, and Islam. A number of contemporary Buddhist leaders—monastics, priests, and lay teachers—have been working to develop social ethics grounded in Buddhist teachings about compassion, which are in turn grounded in wisdom teachings about the impermanent, interdependently co-arising, self-less nature of reality. In a 2013 essay in the *Huffington Post* titled "Beyond McMindfulness," Purser and Loy assert that separating mindfulness from its spiritually transformative purposes, as well as from social ethics, "amounts to a Faustian bargain. Rather than applying mindfulness as a means to awaken individuals and organizations from the unwholesome roots of greed, ill will and delusion, it is usually being refashioned into a banal, therapeutic, self-help technique that can actually reinforce those roots."[49] Hozan Alan Senauke, an American Zen teacher and political activist, writes:

> In recent years Google, General Mills, Procter & Gamble, Monsanto, and other corporate giants hired mindfulness trainers to de-stress their employees. The development of mindfulness programs in corporate and military settings raises compelling ethical questions, including the problem of commodification. Corporate environments can be pressure cookers. The ability to practice meditation and mindfulness, even for the space of a few breaths, can immediately alter one's inner environment, which is part of the larger whole. In itself this is beneficial. But lacking a view of the precepts the question is not asked: what is the purpose of this corporation; what are we making?"[50]

Citing the *Vanijja Sutta*, Senauke quotes the Buddha's instructions to lay followers not to traffic in weapons, human beings, meat, intoxicants, or poisons.

Before and during World War II, he adds, leading Zen teachers and schools of Japanese Buddhism jumped on the bandwagon as Imperial Japan committed atrocities in Russia, China, Manchuria, and Korea during expansionist wars and military occupations. " 'Imperial Way Zen' melded the Buddhist principles of selflessness, discipline, and mindfulness with the aggressive goals of an expansionist, militarist state, concocting a witch's brew of violent nationalism."[51] We are seeing similar violence today in other cultures where Buddhism has been joined to nationalism: the persecution of Rohingya Muslims in Myanmar and of

Tamil Hindus in Sri Lanka, for example. In response to the moral failings of Japanese Buddhism, the scholars Hakamaya Noriaki and Matsumoto Shirō have promoted what they call "Critical Buddhism," arguing that these failings are a result of the "Buddha-nature doctrine," the innate-ist interpretation of enlightenment discussed in the previous chapter, because it fosters social, ethical, and political passivity. If all beings already possess the Buddha-nature, one can argue, there is no need for rigorous monastic and ethical practice. This innate-ist view of awakening underlies Kabat-Zinn's understanding of Mindfulness, even though he advocates rigorous practice.

No doubt Mindfulness can be helpful to stressed employees, to schoolchildren, and to military veterans with posttraumatic stress and physical, emotional, and moral injuries. But because it minimizes the need for rigorous ethical behavior and downplays Buddhist teachings about the interrelatedness of all phenomena, there is a risk that it can also mute critiques of dysfunctional organizational structures or flawed goals, such as short-term profits at any cost or soldiers who are better "armored" emotionally to withstand the horrors of war.

Senauke asks:

- If one is practicing mindfulness in a corporation, what are you making and selling, how are you treating your workers in a distant land, and at what cost are you extracting resources from the earth?
- If one is working in a prison, on either side of the bars, do you see the common humanity of prisoners, guards, and administrators?
- If one is bringing mindfulness programs to active-duty soldiers, what if they are taking part in wars that might be viewed as illegal and unwinnable, and what does it mean to take orders and directions from a political structure that is not accountable for the widespread violence of its own policies?
- And finally: Before we minister to corporations, prisons, and the military, perhaps we should consider that the members of our government and the policymakers on corporate boards and in the so-called justice system are the ones who most need instruction in right mindfulness.[52]

In Buddhist tradition, *Right* Mindfulness is our ability to distinguish what is wholesome from what is unwholesome in order to cultivate the former and renounce the latter.

Systemic Analysis of Suffering

Finally, an individualist approach to mental and physical well-being prevents a systemic analysis of suffering. While Kabat-Zinn has written about the social or systemic dimensions of suffering, MBIs are not designed to address them: they teach that the way to heal stress-related pain and illness is to focus on one's own present-moment experience. I certainly do not deny the value of this, but it does not help communities to understand and address structural problems that can affect psychological and physical health.

In fact, treating disease as an individual problem can actively impede analysis of these social factors. Kabat-Zinn acknowledges that "it may be profoundly unwise to focus solely on our own individual well-being and security, because our well-being and security are intimately interconnected with everything else in this ever-smaller world we inhabit."[53] He argues that meditation can be "an act of love, an inward gesture of benevolence and kindness toward ourselves and toward others, a gesture of the heart that recognizes our perfection even in our obvious imperfection, with all our shortcomings, our wounds, our attachments, our vexations, and our persistent habits of unawareness. It is a very brave gesture: to take one's seat for a time and drop in on the present moment without adornment."[54] I agree. But at some point, one must rise from the cushion, and deal directly with problems that have everything to do with individual and communal health and wellbeing: racism, sexism, homophobia, transphobia, poverty, and inadequate medical insurance.

Perhaps one reason MBIs do not include systemic analyses of illness and other forms of suffering is that many of the people involved have better access to medical care and are less directly afflicted by racism, and poverty. Mindfulness training costs several hundred dollars and is accessible only to people who can devote eight or more hours to it a week, for at least two months. Certification as an instructor costs thousands of dollars: at the Center for Mindfulness in Medicine, Healthcare and Society, MBSR teacher training and certification costs $10,300 to $10,840, plus the cost of supplemental retreats. Teacher training for the two-day "Search Inside Yourself" program developed at Google is $7,500.

An annual convention in the District of Columbia called the Mindful Leadership Summit gathers several hundred current and aspiring leaders who want to become "more conscious and effective" in their fields and to transform themselves, their organizations, their communities, and the world.[55] In 2017 registration fees for the two-day summit ranged from $499 for "early birds" to $899 (regular), plus $199 per night for lodging in the conference hotel, plus travel and meal expenses—not to mention optional "leadership intensives" on the days before and after the summit proper.[56] Tickets for the three-day Wisdom 2.0 conference in San Francisco ranged from $499 to $1,550. Wisdom 2.0 Intersect, a weekend "retreat for change makers" in Hawaii, cost $1,500 to $2,500, plus travel, lodging, and meals.

Let us consider such costs alongside the racial and gender composition of the conference presenters. Of fourteen listed on the event website as this manuscript went to press in mid-August 2017, ten were male, and ten appeared to be white. The white men included a professor of psychiatry at the UCLA School of Medicine, a senior lecturer at MIT Sloan School of Management, an executive coach, the CEO of an engineering firm that is a military contractor, the CEO of an accounting and wealth-management firm, the founder of a company that develops corporate training programs based on mindfulness, and the *New York Times* reporter who launched *10 Percent Happier*, the online meditation program for "fidgety skeptics allergic to woo-woo." The three men of color included a black retired minor league baseball player; the black president of a division of the aforementioned defense contractor; and a South Asian professor of marketing who cofounded the Conscious Capitalism movement.[57] The four women included a white retired corporate attorney who has built a second career in the Mindfulness industry; the white director of the Office of Work-Life at Harvard; and the cofounders of a consulting company that offers training in what it calls "sustainable abundance," one of whom appears to be white, the other black. Their three-course sequence begins with an online course delivered for a sliding scale of $150 to $500, is followed by two, two-day, in-person courses in Massachusetts, which cost from $300 to $995 each and which are occasionally offered as "destination courses" in the Bahamas.[58] The program aims to help people overcome a mindset of "scarcity," which the founders themselves would appear to be transcending through high-end consulting and training fees.

People who can afford conferences on "mindful leadership" and courses in "sustainable abundance" in the Bahamas, like those who can afford certification as Mindfulness coaches, are the very people most likely already to have access to good medical insurance, healthy food, clean water, safe neighborhoods, and stable housing.[59] *Unnatural Causes*, a seven-part documentary film exploring racial and socioeconomic disparities in health

and medical care, shows that one's zip code is the single greatest pre-
dictor of health and life expectancy. People in poor neighborhoods, who
cope daily with the chronic stress imposed by poverty, live shorter, less
healthy lives than people who live in affluent neighborhoods, the majority
of whom are white.[60]

"Worldwide, the most routine obstacle to human happiness is poverty,"
notes Barbara Ehrenreich in *Bright-Sided*, a characteristically scathing
analysis of American "positive thinking."[61] To illustrate the point, she cites
a 2009 *New York Times* survey of New York neighborhoods, which found
that "the happiest areas were also the most affluent and, not coincidentally, the most thickly supplied with cafés, civic associations, theaters, and
opportunities for social interaction." The least happy neighborhood was
"characterized by abandoned buildings, mounds of uncollected garbage,
and the highest unemployment rate in the city."[62] Poverty disproportion-
ately affects people of color, women, and children.

Racial and gender disparities among spokespersons for the
Mindfulness movement were particularly glaring in the PBS infomercial *Mindfulness Goes Mainstream*. Of eleven featured speakers, ten are
white and nine are male. Six of the eight white men interviewed hold
doctoral degrees: Jon Kabat-Zinn, PhD; Jack Kornfield, PhD, a founder of
the Vipassana or Insight Meditation movement in American Buddhism,
described as a "meditation thought leader" not a lay Buddhist teacher;
Richard Davidson, PhD, of the Center for Healthy Minds at the University
of Wisconsin–Madison, where he has been a major recipient of federal
grants for mindfulness research; Dan Siegel, MD, of the University of
California–Los Angeles School of Medicine, another major researcher in
the field; and Saki Santorelli, EdD, and Judson Brewer, MD, PhD, of the
University of Massachusetts Center for Mindfulness. The other men are
Mark Bertolini, chairman and CEO of the medical insurer Aetna; Dan
Harris, the ABC News correspondent who cofounded *10 Percent Happier*;
and the sole person of color, Chade Meng Tan, who developed Google's
"Search Inside Yourself" program and who emphasized the competitive
advantages and profitability of corporate Mindfulness training. The two
women, both white, are Eileen Fisher, a fashion designer and CEO of an
eponymous clothing company, and singer-songwriter Jewel, who credits
Mindfulness with helping her go from homelessness to stardom. Two
other white women led the PBS pledge breaks.

Surprisingly absent from the film was any mention of the Holistic Life
Foundation in Baltimore, which was cofounded by three men of color
to teach meditation and yoga to children in the city's poorest schools,

most of whom are black or brown. An earlier PBS program had focused briefly on HLF teachers and students: they got one minute and twenty seconds of airtime in a 2012 segment of *Religion & Ethics Newsweekly* lasting eight minutes and forty-two seconds total, also titled *Mindfulness Goes Mainstream*. The rest of the time was devoted to Congressman Tim Ryan and Jon Kabat-Zinn, both of whom are white. But even a time ratio of 6:1 was better than in the sixty-minute PBS infomercial five years later, in which the only people of color were occasional participants in Mindfulness courses, shown in the background. Women may outnumber men as students in Mindfulness classes and as front-line Mindfulness teachers, just as they outnumbered men among early Mind Curers. But once the Emmanuel Movement appeared, the principal spokespersons for Mind Cure became elite white men, and that dynamic has persisted throughout the Mindfulness movement. The visible spokespersons are overwhelmingly white, male, highly educated, and affluent. The stresses they endure, and the resources they have for coping with that stress, are fundamentally different than for the chronically poor.

Kabat-Zinn is a frequent headliner at events promoting Mindfulness, and while he is clearly benefiting from the industry he helped to create, it would be unfair to suggest that he is oblivious to systemic suffering. In *Coming to Our Senses*, he acknowledges "all those who are disenfranchised, disempowered, who appear to be hopelessly at the mercy of forces they have no direct say in or control over." But this sentence continues, "until, as in South Africa and in countless other places, they all of a sudden surprise the world and effect what seemed impossible the moment before, and without resorting to violence."[63] This seems a rather optimistic view of how the end of apartheid in South Africa came about. It did not occur "all of a sudden"; it was the result of many decades of concerted, collective, international, political and economic pressure, and the process was not nonviolent. Opponents of apartheid sometimes resorted to terrorist violence and rioting, and the apartheid regime engaged in brutally violent repression.

In another essay, Kabat-Zinn writes, "Of course, the eight-hour workday, child labor laws, gender equality, and desegregation were all won through popular grassroots movements that started small, and that doggedly badgered and perturbed the system, often at huge sacrifice of many anonymous individuals, until it responded and shifted."[64] This seems a more realistic assessment—although eight-hour workdays, gender equality, and desegregation have not been entirely won. His socioeconomic analysis seems limited and, if I may suggest, might be blinkered somewhat by unexamined racial, gendered, educational, and economic privilege.

Kabat-Zinn is politically liberal, extremely effective as a public speaker, and, I assume, sincere. I happen to share many of his political and ethical opinions. For example, I agree with the following:

> It requires great patience and forbearance to not turn away from the suffering of the world, yet not be overwhelmed by the enormity of it either, or destroyed by it. It requires great patience and forbearance not to think we can magically fix it all or get it all right just by throwing money at what we see as a problem, perhaps trying to buy influence or allegiance, or impose our own values on others. Clarity and peace do not come easily to us as individuals, even less so as a society. In one way, we need to work at continually cultivating those qualities of mind and attention that nurture clarity and peace, selflessness and kindness, even though, seen another way, they are part of us and accessible to us in their fullness even now, and actually, only now. At the same time, we need to recognize the impulses in ourselves toward self-righteousness, arrogance, aggression, cruelty, dominance, and indifference so as not to be caught by them and blindsided.[65]

Such an attitude has resonances with Protestant perfectionism and millennialism, and like Kabat-Zinn, I have been shaped by these aspects of American culture and history. As a (white, middle-class, highly educated, American, convert, meditation-oriented, modernist) Buddhist, I also agree, as I have said, that the specific practices and attitudes that MBSR promotes can be very helpful. Yet I am less optimistic about the ability of mindfulness *itself* to bring about social and political transformation.

Some would argue that mindfulness, and the insight it can produce, may equip people morally, that compassion inevitably flows from the recognition of impermanence and interdependence. This is certainly a strong theme in *Mindfulness Goes Mainstream*. But I am not convinced that this is true.[66] Compelling counterevidence includes repeated leadership scandals in American Buddhist communities, in which revered, supposedly enlightened—usually male—teachers are alleged to have preyed sexually on students, most of whom were female, and some of whom were ostracized for speaking out.[67] I believe instead that compassion and moral conduct must be actively *cultivated* in communities; that meditation is helpful but not sufficient for that purpose; and that people in positions of spiritual authority must be embedded in systems that hold them account-able to people other than those they teach and counsel.[68]

Just as we cannot learn to become less greedy, aversive, and igno-rant individuals without the help of others, we cannot correct systemic inequities solely through individual efforts because such problems are rooted in collective power dynamics: one group's domination of another—legally, economically, politically, culturally. Systemic inequities are maintained by the privilege a dominant group enjoys as a result of the history of domination, whether that dominance is based upon racial, gendered, economic, religious, or other social distinctions. Members of a dominant group enjoy privilege regardless of whether or not individual members of that group want to have it. And privilege works in such a way that those who have it are seldom required to notice that they have it and how it functions in daily life. It is simply the air one breathes, without realizing how other people are choking on the exhaust. The work of seeing it is endless, essential, and frequently uncomfortable, even quite painful.

A reluctance to confront painful truths is a deeply problematic feature of American culture, writes Ehrenreich. A penchant for positive thinking led people to ignore or minimize warning signs that could have helped to prevent the terrorist attacks of 9/11, the dot-com bust, massive flooding during Hurricane Katrina, protracted wars in Iraq and Afghanistan, and the financial collapse of 2008. "Sometimes," she says, "we need to heed our fears and negative thoughts, and at all times we need to be alert to the world outside ourselves, even when that includes absorbing bad news and entertaining the views of 'negative' people." We cannot solve economic, military, social, and infrastructure problems unless people think clearly and critically about them, with "vigilant realism." We face real threats and problems, which require action in the real world: "Build up the levees, get food to the hungry, find the cure, strengthen the 'first responders'!"[69] We certainly need respite from those efforts, which meditation and Mindfulness can help to provide, but then we have to get back to work.

Efforts to change structural, systemic inequalities must address such problems systemically, by changing institutionalized power relations. For that, we should take a lesson from the early Mind Cure movement: changing one's mind is good and important, but not sufficient by itself to overcome oppressive economic, political, legal, and social structures. To transform those, we need engaged religious communities; well-funded educational institutions; reasonable working conditions, wages, healthcare, and housing; and *collective* political action for the *common* good.

Notes on Methods and Theory

Although I have told this story of how we got from Mind Cure to Mindfulness in chronological order, tracing personal contacts and intellectual influences among the principal characters, it has been a challenging story to piece together and challenging to tell. One difficulty is that New Thought, Theosophy, and Spiritualism are "metaphysical religions," and unlike more hierarchically organized religious institutions, these tend to be diffuse networks of people and ideas, lacking well-developed denominational structures.

In her groundbreaking study of metaphysical religions in the United States, *A Republic of Mind and Spirit*, Catherine Albanese points to four characteristics that metaphysical movements have in common. These were described in chapter 5, but to reiterate briefly: first, they are preoccupied with the mind and its powers. "Mind" refers not just to the brain but also to consciousness and intuition. Second, they assume a correspondence between the material and spiritual realms—a feature that derives from Swedenborg's theology. This can mean that each individual is a microcosm reflecting macrocosmic qualities or that the spiritual realm resembles the material world. It can also mean that thoughts and intentions have discernible effects on the physical world. Third, metaphysical religions tend to speak in terms of flux, movement, and energies. Fourth, they understand salvation in terms of therapy and healing. Although metaphysical religions have received relatively little attention from scholars of religion in the Americas until recently, Albanese makes a compelling case that "metaphysics is a normal, recurring, and pervasive feature of the American spiritual landscape."[1]

The diffuse character of metaphysical religions makes them difficult for historians to study, however. One cannot go, for example, to a denominational headquarters to study its archives. This is probably one reason that scholars of American religious history have paid metaphysical religions relatively little attention and treated them as marginal. Although countless New Thought books are available, in its early days the movement spread primarily through magazines and other serial publications, and those that survive are scattered across a handful of libraries around the country.[2] This makes research time-consuming and expensive.

Another difficulty has been the way that disciplinary boundaries are typically drawn in the academy, which encourages scholars to specialize deeply in narrowly drawn fields. For example, specialists in "American religion" focus primarily on what happens within the geographic boundaries of the continental United States. This makes it harder for us to see global interactions that have shaped traditions in the U.S. In *Rethinking American History in a Global Age*, Thomas Bender points out that American scholars of American religion generally do not read the works of scholars of American religion based in other countries, and vice versa.[3] Academic focus on Asian religions in the West has only begun to gather steam over the past two or three decades.

Material relevant to this study is scattered across multiple academic disciplines. Swedenborg's religious thought has received little attention from American scholars of religion and is typically discussed in literature about Western esotericism, for example. Scholarly studies of Mesmer and his successors can be found in the histories of psychology of medicine. Studies of New Thought are found in the literature of American religious history. The roles of women and African Americans in New Thought might be discussed in the subfields of women's studies in religion, or African American religions, but tend not to be treated as integral to American religious history as a whole. Even Albanese, who recognizes the pervasiveness of metaphysical religion in the United States, treats African American variants as "subaltern." Research on modernist forms of Buddhism and Hinduism are found in the fields of Buddhist studies or Indian religions. Richard Seager, a historian of American religions who has written about Buddhism in the United States, observes, "Scholars of American religious history are at a disadvantage for at least two reasons when studying the Americanization of Buddhism. First, we rarely understand the Asian background of groups before they arrive in the United States. Second, we do not necessarily look beyond the limited horizon of our own culture to locate the American experience in the broad contours of globalization."[4] A number of scholars trained in both Asian religions and American religions have begun to change this, as has the Buddhism in the West unit of the American Academy of Religion.

One consequence of most Americanists' unfamiliarity with Asian Buddhist histories is that these scholars may not recognize just how anomalous the Mindfulness movement's approach to meditation really is. Devotional, supernatural, and merit-making practices, which have been the mainstay of most forms of Buddhism throughout most of Buddhist history, tend to get dismissed as "cultural baggage." However, scholars specializing in modernist Buddhism have shown that several widespread American assumptions about Buddhism—for example, that it is fundamentally about meditation, that it is compatible with modern science, or that its teachings are universal—are rooted in very specific historical and cultural circumstances, and in particular missionary strategies that deployed both strategic Orientalism and Occidentalism.

Not many scholars work across the boundaries of these various disciplines. Academic histories of New Thought do not explore its meditation practices. The literature on Mindfulness tends to appear either in scientific journals or popular books and magazines dealing with mind-body medicine. *A Republic of Mind and Spirit* is both panoramic and attentive to details, but because Albanese's attention is focused on American religious history, she does not discuss other histories related to those of the groups she covers. Her discussion of Mesmerism, for example, does not mention the medical hypnotists John Elliotson or James Esdaile, who repeatedly performed surgeries on hypnotized patients, or James Braid, who coined the term "hypnosis." This information is found in histories of psychology. In Albanese's discussion of New Thought, no mention is made of Sarah Farmer or Greenacre; much of the available information about them must be found in Bahá'í sources. Nor does Albanese mention Seichō-no-Ie, although it is perhaps the largest New Thought organization in the world; this movement is more likely to be familiar to scholars of modern Japanese religions. She does not incorporate extended discussion of contemporary mind-body medicine. While one certainly can argue that this is a topic outside the scope of religious studies, I have shown points of overlap and connection. In fact the Mindfulness movement has all the characteristics Albanese attributes to American metaphysical religion, despite its claim to be completely secular.

When specialists in Western religious traditions do discuss Asian religions, they may conflate categories in problematic ways. For example, Albanese describes several modern Buddhist and Hindu leaders as "Asian metaphysical teachers," without noting either the Western religious assumptions embedded in such a description or the Asian missionary strategies that have drawn upon and encouraged such assumptions.[5] Huston Smith, one of the writers on religion most popular with American audiences, exhibited this same tendency. Richard Payne, a specialist in Japanese Buddhism, offers the following critique: "To call . . . any Buddhist thinker a 'metaphysician' is to impose a category that is effectively absent from Buddhist thought, the closest Buddhist analogue to metaphysics being abhidharma, which is itself highly psychological in character, and which does not propound any notion of a transcendent absolute."[6] Just as problematic as applying Western concepts uncritically to Asian religions, Payne says, is the claim that particular religious ideas apply universally across different times and cultures: "Universalizing religious concepts and categories involves treating them as if they were unproblematically applicable to [other] religious traditions without regard to historical or social location—as context neutral. . . . Doing so . . . misleads the reader into thinking that they understand something, such as Buddhism, when they are in fact being led to something quite different."[7] As we have seen, both tendencies are clearly evident in the rhetoric of the contemporary Mindfulness movement.

The first book to address Mesmerism, New Thought, and meditation-as-medicine between two covers was published in 2008: *The Cure Within: A History of Mind-Body Medicine* by Anne Harrington, a thoughtful and respected historian of science who has made important contributions to scholarly discussions of the placebo response, among other topics, and who has been active in interdisciplinary conversations on mind-body healing. She describes six cultural narratives that people have employed during different eras over the past three centuries to talk about the mind's role in illness and healing. She treats as three separate topics "The Power of Suggestion" deriving from Mesmer's work, the "Positive Thinking" of Individualist New Thought, and medical interest in meditation ("Eastward Journeys"). Harrington says these reflect different narratives within the very broad category of mind-body healing.[8] Like other scholars, she assumes that meditation as a form of mind-body healing did not generate interest until the late twentieth century. Her account also tends to equate New Thought with Peale-esque "Positive Thinking," but for many white women and black men and women, community-oriented New Thought was also about providing social support and working for systemic change. Harrington's analysis generally privileges the perspective of orthodox medicine rather than, say, those of scholars or practitioners of unorthodox medical systems or members of minority religions.

The Cure Within does not address gendered differences in the history of mind-body medicine or the effects of gender or racial bias in medical research, particularly on the subject of "stress."[9] For example, while it notes that homophobia has been a factor in mortality rates for AIDS—a very important point—it does not discuss racism as a source of stress for minority groups, a contributor to bias in medical research, or a factor in some kinds of illness, such as heart disease, diabetes, and conditions correlated with poverty. Harrington's assertion that Chinese medicine first arrived in the United States in the wake of Richard Nixon's diplomatic efforts ignores its presence among Chinese immigrants since the mid-nineteenth century.[10]

Harrington recognizes Western Orientalism but not Asian "Occidentalism," although she provides one very clear example: the Dalai Lama's political reasons for supporting brain research on Buddhist monks. Immediately before the Tibetan leader gave Harvard medical researcher Herbert Benson permission to study meditating monks in 1979, Harrington quotes him as saying, "Our friends in the East [meaning the Chinese] might be impressed with a Western explanation of what we are doing." She underscores the point: "The Dalai Lama had not been allowed to be overtly political during this trip to the United States, but he was not going to turn down an opportunity to improve the image of Tibet and its religious culture in the West and China."[11]

The Cure Within treats New Thought as an example of one kind of narrative, "The Power of Positive Thinking," and MBSR as an example of a different kind of narrative, "Eastward Journeys." Harrington's core insight—that different narratives create different kinds of behavior and experience—is very helpful in making sense of the broad (and vague) category "mind-body medicine." But because this book treats "Positive Thinking" and "Eastward Journeys" as separate narratives, it does not reflect upon some of the parallels and continuities between them.

A Republic of Mind and Spirit and *The Cure Within* highlight different dimensions of mental healing, the former in terms of the history of religions, and the latter in terms of the history of medicine. Neither brings these disciplines fully into conversation. Nor do they incorporate perspectives from feminist studies, ethnic studies, Buddhist or Hindu studies, or postcolonial theory. John S. Haller Jr. offers a fine history of mind-body medicine in *Swedenborg, Mesmer, and the Mind/Body Connection*, which covers many of the same people I discuss. However, he pays almost no attention to women or to Asian people or religions, and none to African Americans. Haller's *The History of the New Thought Movement* discusses some women, but focuses most of its discussion on white men.[12] If one considers mental healing from the perspectives of both the history of religions and the history of science, and also draws upon insights from some of the other disciplines and discourses mentioned above, additional dimensions of mind-body healing become apparent.

MORE OR LESS HELPFUL METAPHORS

Describing this tangled web of histories, interactions, and overlapping networks and processes has been a challenge. Michel Foucault argued that in writing historical accounts, we must avoid simplistic, linear searches for origins. The historian must uncover the truth that what lies behind things is "not a timeless and essential secret, but the secret that they have no essence or that their essence was fabricated in a piecemeal fashion from alien forms." Historians attempting to trace the descent (*Herkunft*) of particular phenomena or ideas must seek "the subtle, singular, and subindividual marks that might possibly intersect in them to form a network that is difficult to unravel."[13]

Albanese has argued that contact, combination, and exchange are normal features of American religious life, and that metaphysical religions in particular must be understood in terms of "networks" rather than institutions or denominations. One needs "a historiography of connection, one noticing that contact is much of what there is to tell. . . . Religion in the United States, in general, needs to be noticed for its overlapping between and among cultural worlds."[14]

Jeff Wilson characterizes everything that happened before the 1970s as "roots," and MBSR as the "trunk."[15] Presumably the various forms of the broader Mindfulness movement are its "branches." Although this may seem to be an elegant botanical metaphor, Jacob Dorman points out that it breaks down when applied to complex cultural processes, such as the development of religious, medical, or religiomedical healing movements. The roots and branches of a tree are all clearly and directly connected, but the "disembodied nature of culture means that it can jump the synapses between generations, races, cultures, and continents, necessarily being reinvented and reimagined with every leap."[16]

A more helpful image for imagining the networks and processes this book describes is that of rhizomatic plants, as proposed by the philosophers Gilles Deleuze and Félix Guattari.[17] Dorman employs the image in his brilliant study of Black Hebrew Israelite movements:

> Rhizomatic cultural systems are lateral, nonhierarchical, and multiple. They are modeled on plants such as tubers, grass, or aspen trees, which share complex root systems. Any point of their underground rhizomes can be connected to any other point. Rhizomes form a subterranean latticework of connections. Instead of the root-tree metaphors which embed notions of causality and false genealogies, grass-like rhizomes endlessly branch and make connections.[18]

Any node (tuber or bulb) of a rhizomatic plant or system can produce additional, horizontal "runners," as well as "shoots" that may become visible aboveground. This is a better image for the sorts of networks I have tried to describe. In addition, Dorman suggests,

> rhizomatic plants also commonly propagate themselves on the wind, sending out plumes of pollen, spores, or seeds. Culture is similarly dematerialized and airborne, spread by itinerant preachers, by hucksters, by sailors and railroad workers, by advertising, by newspapers, pamphlets, and books, by traveling tented circuses, and by temporary tented revivals. Like seeds carried by little more than the wind, new cultural innovations often spread through means that are more ideational than material.[19]

One weakness of this metaphor is that it may seem to suggest the spread of a single species of plant, and in the case of both New Thought and the Mindfulness movement, interactions, borrowings, and transformations have occurred between different "species." New Thought and Theosophy can both be classified as "metaphysical religions" with common philosophical influences, but they also differ in important ways. Modernist forms of Buddhism, Hinduism, and Protestantism all share certain modernist assumptions, but in some respects, these forms of religious modernism also differ. Many psychologists, physicians, and scientists would sharply distinguish their fields from the category "religion" altogether.

We must attend as well to power relations, asking what sociopolitical, economic, and ideological interests are at stake in whatever historical encounters, problems, or events we are considering. We must ask questions about the appropriation—or misappropriation—of minority traditions by a dominant culture, and about ways that minority agents resist a dominant culture, sometimes by strategically adopting elements from it and adapting them to the minority group's own purposes.

Fluid metaphors may help to overcome some of these conceptual limitations. In *Crossing and Dwelling*, Thomas Tweed argues that religions can be understood as "confluences of organic-cultural flows."[20] The terms "confluences" and "flows" "signify that religions are not reified substances but complex processes," he says. "Each is a flowing together of currents—some enforced as 'orthodox' by institutions—traversing multiple fields, where other religions, other transverse currents also cross, thereby creating new spiritual streams."[21] Religions are not tightly bounded phenomena, Tweed emphasizes; they are "dynamic and relational."[22] They move, intermingle, and diverge. They are not like solid objects with fixed boundaries, not like nouns; they are more like verbs. Religions are permeable and ever-changing as they move across landscapes and cultures.

By calling religions *"organic-cultural* flows," Tweed indicates that they are both personal and social and are shaped by the biological constraints of the human organism, as well as by cultural conditions.[23] The same is true of other dimensions of human culture, including sciences and medical systems, which are socially and historically situated phenomena, as are the people who theorize about them.[24] We must not imagine these categories to be monolithic, but instead recognize the dynamics of contact, conflict, borrowing, synthesis, and exchange between sciences, religions, and cultures. Fluid metaphors create some interpretive problems, however. They may help us to conceptualize complex, nonlinear systems, but Tweed muses, "Will interpreters be washed away by trying to trace the transfluence of innumerable causal currents?"[25]

Tweed employs spatial and temporal metaphors as well, describing religions as "maps," "itineraries," "watches," and "compasses." Calling them "maps" can seem to suggest that the terrain they depict is static, however, or that they offer a universal perspective. As long as we remember that maps, like theories, are always *"sightings from sites . . .* positioned representations of a changing terrain by an itinerant cartographer,"[26] this metaphor is useful in that it points to what religions *do*. They *orient* practitioners "in the body, the home, the homeland, and the cosmos." They tell us who we are, where we came from, to whom we belong, and when we are in time and space. As "itineraries," religions are both plans for and descriptions of journeys. They offer an ultimate horizon: a sense of where we're headed, how we should get there, and why. As "watches" and "compasses," they help us cross into different phases of life (birth, student-hood, puberty, marriage, death), and they may involve literal crossings such as pilgrimage, exile, or conquest. "Religions . . . are partial, tentative, and continually redrawn sketches of where we are, where we've been, and where we're going."[27]

This historical account should be understood in a similar way. It is partial, in that I have chosen a somewhat arbitrary point of origin. I could trace the history of mind-body medicine much further back than I do here. I do not offer an ultimate horizon, although I suggest that observing the past and present from the various angles of view that I offer enables us to see how different trajectories can lead to different problems and benefits. It certainly highlights the need for interdisciplinary research, the imperative of including race and gender as categories of analysis, and the limitations of conceiving of "American" religious movements as confined to the geographic boundaries of the United States.

Notes

1. Murphy and Donovan, *The Physical and Psychological Effects of Meditation*, 153–277. Most of the references are articles in peer-reviewed academic and scientific journals; a few are books oriented toward more general audiences. Of the studies published before 1970, most were authored in the 1960s by Indian researchers studying physiological effects of yoga and by Japanese researchers studying effects of Zen meditation. A bibliography published more than a decade earlier by the American Theological Library Association included more than 2,200 entries, including 937 articles in journals and magazines; more than 1,000 books in English, German, French, Spanish, and Portuguese; 200 dissertations and theses; 32 motion pictures; 93 sound recordings; and 32 societies and associations. Jarrell, *International Meditation Bibliography*. A 1989 bibliography on studies of yoga and meditation lists 1,275 articles; 31 books, dissertations, and reports; and 292 conferences, symposia, and seminars. Monro et al., *Yoga Research Bibliography*.
2. Kabat-Zinn, "Some Reflections on the Origins of MBSR," 284; Wilson, *Mindful America*, 100, 50.
3. Association for Mindfulness in Education, "Mindful Education Map," http://www.mindfuleducation.org/mindful-education-map/, accessed June 27, 2016.
4. American Mindfulness Research Association, "Resources/Find a Program," https://goamra.org/resources/find-program/, accessed July 20, 2017.
5. The Center for Contemplative Mind in Society, "Contemplative Degree Programs and Concentrations," http://www.contemplativemind.org/resources/study, accessed July 20, 2017.
6. Search Inside Yourself Leadership Institute, "About," https://siyli.org/about, accessed July 20, 2017.
7. See Mindful Leadership, "Mindfulness at Work Summit," http://www.mindfulleader.org, accessed July 20, 2017.

8. Self-Compassion, "The Three Elements of Self-Compassion," http://self-compassion.org/the-three-elements-of-self-compassion-2/, accessed June 26, 2016.

9. Wilson, *Mindful America*.

10. Jon Kabat-Zinn, *Wherever You Go There You Are* (New York: Hyperion, 1994), 4; and Jon Kabat-Zinn, "Some Reflections on the Origins of MBSR, Skillful Means, and the Trouble with Maps," *Contemporary Buddhism* 12, no. 1 (May 2011): 291.

11. Kabat-Zinn, "Some Reflections on the Origins of MBSR," 282.

12. Ibid., 286.

13. Kabat-Zinn, "Indra's Net at Work," 227.

14. Kabat-Zinn, "Toward the Mainstreaming of American Dharma Practice," 481.

15. Caplan, *Mind Games*, 65, 87–88.

16. Ibid.; Gevitz, *Other Healers*; Whorton, *Nature Cures*.

17. "Mindful Awareness Research Center"; Bishop, "What Do We Really Know about Mindfulness-Based Stress Reduction?"; Davidson et al., "Alterations in Brain and Immune Function"; Kabat-Zinn and University of Massachusetts Medical Center/Worcester Stress Reduction Clinic, *Full Catastrophe Living*; Leuchter et al., "Changes in Brain Function"; Lutz et al., "Long-Term Meditators Self-Induce High-Amplitude Gamma Synchrony"; Murphy and Donovan.

18. National Institutes of Health, Research Portfolio Online Reporting Tools, Expenditures and Results, https://projectreporter.nih.gov/reporter.cfm, accessed August 11, 2017.

19. Benson-Henry Institute for Mind-Body Medicine, "Bringing the Best Self Care Techniques to Your Health Care Plan," http://www.bensonhenryinstitute.org/mission-history, accessed June 26, 2015.

20. Wilson, *Mindful America*, 32.

21. Boyce, "Two Sciences of Mind."

22. Wilson, *Mindful America*, 31.

23. Several Black Israelite communities bear this name. Dorman, *Chosen People*, 159, 66–69.

24. "Modernity" refers to the period from the European Enlightenment of the eighteenth century, through the Industrial Revolution, to the mid-twentieth century. Academics call the postindustrial era of globalization, multinational corporations, and consumer capitalism that we now occupy "postmodernity."

25. The classic analysis of Protestant modernism is Hutchison, *The Modernist Impulse in American Protestantism*. On Buddhist modernism, see McMahan, *The Making of Buddhist Modernism*.

26. International New Thought Alliance, "Declaration of Principles," https://newthoughtalliance.org, accessed July 21, 2018.

27. Jane Claypool, "New Thought—New Woman," https://janeclaypool.com/2013/03/25/new-thought-new-woman/, accessed June 12, 2016.

28. "American Rhetoric, Top 100 Speeches, Russell Conwell, 'Acres of Diamonds,'" n.p., http://www.americanrhetoric.com/speeches/rconwellacresofdiamonds. htm, accessed July 21, 2018.

29. Bowler, *Blessed*.

30. An admirable survey of the history and widespread influences of neo-Vedanta and yoga is already available, so I devote relatively little attention to that history and focus instead on understudied contacts and exchanges between New Thought and modernist Buddhists. See Goldberg, *American Veda*. This is an excellent survey of the profound impact that Hindu Vedanta has had on American culture. It is sweeping in scope, rich in detail, and enjoyable to read. Goldberg covers the careers of well-known gurus whose influence was wide-ranging, and many lesser-known figures with more localized constituencies. The major figures include Vivekananda, founder of the Vedanta Society, and other monks of the Ramakrishna Order; the iconoclastic Jiddu Krishnamurti (1895–1986), who rejected his role as "world teacher" of the Theosophical Society; Paramahansa Yogananda (1893–1952), who launched the Self-Realization Fellowship, authored the wildly popular *Autobiography of a Yogi* in 1946, and lectured widely; the silent Meher Baba (1894–1969), who toured the United States in the 1930s; Ramana Maharshi (1879–1950), one of the important influences on Jon Kabat-Zinn; Swami Muktananda (1908–1982), who brought Siddha Yoga to the West; Sri Aurobindo (1872–1950), who developed Integral Yoga® and promoted it with his spiritual collaborator "the Mother" (1878–1973) and his student Sri Chinmoy (1931–2007). Aurobindo was an important influence on Michael Murphy, cofounder of Esalen. Swami Satchidananda Saraswati, who had been influenced by Aurobindo and Maharshi, taught Integral Yoga® as well, and founded Yogaville in Virginia, which continues to churn out American yoga teachers. Goldberg also covers Maharishi Mahesh Yogi, who launched the Transcendental Meditation movement and the Maharishi University of Management; A.C. Bhaktivedanta Swami Prabhupada, founder of the International Society for Krishna Consciousness ("Hare Krishnas"); and the controversial Baghwan Shree Rajneesh, who amassed a fleet of Rolls Royces and encouraged sexual freedom at an ashram in Oregon. The ashram, Rajneeshpuram, collapsed amid revelations of assaults and attempted murders, weapons stockpiles, immigration and election frauds, wiretapping, and conspiracy.

CHAPTER 1

1. Fully half of Swedenborg's theological corpus is devoted to verse-by-verse exegeses of Genesis, Exodus, and Revelation.

2. In short, the feminine corresponds to love and will, the male to wisdom and understanding. Both are necessary to spiritual growth, and marriage is the best way to realize this ideal.

3. Woofenden and Rose, *Swedenborg Explorer's Guidebook*, 6–17.

4. In a review of Swedenborg's impact on the English-speaking world of the nineteenth century, Robert Kirven and David Eller point to Swedenborgian influences in antislavery efforts, English Romanticism, Transcendentalism, Spiritualism, Shakerism, utopian socialism, homeopathy, vegetarianism, and the New Thought movement. Kirven, "Swedenborg's Contributions to the History of Ideas"; Kirven and Eller, "Selected Examples of Swedenborg's Influence in Great Britain and the United States." A 1983 doctoral dissertation by Richard Silver, "The Spiritual Kingdom in America," focuses on Swedenborg's influence in four areas of American culture from 1850 to 1860: Spiritualism, medical theory, art, and antebellum efforts to promote public education. The Swedish seer also influenced several important early figures in American Buddhist history (Hickey, "Swedenborg").

5. Albanese, *A Republic of Mind and Spirit*, 30.

6. According to Jewish Kabbalah, the divine manifests through ten emanations or Sephiroth. Johann Kemper (1697–1796) was a Jewish convert to Christianity who lived in Uppsala and worked for the university while Swedenborg was enrolled there; Kemper also tutored students in Hebrew. Some scholars have suggested that Swedenborg studied with Kemper, who wrote a detailed commentary on the Zohar, a foundational Kabbalist text. Swedenborg's brother-in-law Eric Benzelius purchased a copy of Kemper's Zohar commentary for the university. See Schuchard, *Why Mrs Blake Cried*. In earlier work, the Swedenborg scholar Jane Williams-Hogan expresses doubt that Swedenborg had worked directly with Kemper but notes a few references to Kabbalah in Swedenborg's notebooks. Jane Williams-Hogan, "Swedenborg Studies 2002: On the Shoulders of Giants," *New Philosophy Online, Journal of the Swedenborg Scientific Association*, January–June 2002, http://swedenborg-philosophy.org/article/swedenborg-studies-2002-on-the-shoulders-of-giants/, accessed September 30, 2007 and July 21, 2018.

7. Larsen et al., *Emanuel Swedenborg*, 514.

8. I am indebted to the Rev. Dr. James Lawrence, dean of the Swedenborg House of Studies in Berkeley, California, for his careful reading of the foregoing summary and his suggestions for improving its accuracy. Surveys of Swedenborg's basic ideas may be found at Silver, 21–43; Dole, "Key Concepts in the Theology of Emanuel Swedenborg"; Dole and Kirven, *A Scientist Explores Spirit*.

9. Sidney Ahlstrom's classic *Religious History of the American People* devoted seven pages to Swedenborg and his influence. More recent surveys of American religious history have said much less; see, for example, Williams, *America's Religions*, 331, 333, 335. Some do not mention the seer at all. Leigh Schmidt discusses Swedenborg in *Restless Souls*.

10. Albanese, 142–45, citing evidence provided by the Mormon scholar D. Michael Quinn.

11. Harding, *Emerson's Library*. This bibliography lists sixteen scientific and theological works by Swedenborg on 263–64. Silver (87–115, especially nn1–10) notes
that Harding's list differs slightly from a list prepared by the Concord Historical
Society. Wilkinson was an English friend of Henry James Sr., who was also
Swedenborgian and carried a trunk of Swedenborg's writings with him when he
traveled. Henry James Sr.'s trunk is now held by the Swedenborg Archives at the
Swedenborg House of Studies, on the campus of the Pacific School of Religion
in Berkeley, California.

12. Emerson and Porte, "Representative Men," 666, 667.

13. Floyd, "Scientific Medicine." See also North, "Benjamin Rush, MD."

14. Whorton, 4–5.

15. Silver, 213–15.

16. Materra, "Women in Early New Thought," 38. Materra also cites Sheryl Burt
Ruzek, *The Women's Health Movement: Feminist Alternatives to Medical Control*
(New York: Praeger, 1978), and Ann Douglas Wood, "'The Fashionable
Diseases': Women's Complaints and Their Treatment in Nineteenth-Century
America," in *Women and Health in America*, edited by Judith Walzer Leavitt
(Madison: University of Wisconsin Press, 1984), 222–38.

17. Two very helpful surveys of nineteenth-century medical reform movements are
Whorton's *Nature Cures* and Gevitz's *Other Healers*.

18. For a comparison of Swedenborg, Davis, and Quimby, see Judah, *The History
and Philosophy of the Metaphysical Movements in America*, 149–54.

19. Silver, 225–26.

20. Claims about Mesmer's precise birthplace vary: Adam Crabtree says it was
near Radolfzell; Margaret Goldsmith says it was Iznang; and Frank Podmore
says the location is uncertain, but one account places it at Meersburg. All three
historians agree it was somewhere near Lake Constance in Swabia. Crabtree,
From Mesmer to Freud, 3; *Franz Anton Mesmer*, 42; Podmore, *From Mesmer to
Christian Science*, 1.

21. Crabtree, *Animal Magnetism, Early Hypnotism, and Psychical Research*, 1–2. See
also Goldsmith, 49–52.

22. Hell and Mesmer were not the first to employ magnets in healing. During the
European Renaissance, Paracelsus, a German-Swiss alchemist, physician, and
surgeon (a.k.a. Theophrastus Bombastus (Philippus Aureolus) von Hohenheim,
1493?–1541), applied magnets to his patients' bodies during medical treatment
and is widely regarded as the first European to have done so. See Podmore,
29–30; Albanese, 35–37. During the late seventeenth century, Van Helmont
(n.d.) and Robert Fludd (n.d.) were early systematizers of the theory that heavenly bodies affect earthly ones, and that earthly bodies can affect one another at
a distance by means of attractive and repulsive forces called magnetism. "The
attractive and repulsive action of the magnet corresponded to the alternation of

light and darkness, heat and cold, the flux and reflux of the tides, centrifugal and centripetal action, and the mystery of the sexes" (Podmore, 37).

23. Goldsmith, 118. Pages 117–21 include an English translation of Mesmer's twenty-seven propositions concerning animal magnetism. For scholarly citations of Mesmer's "Dissertation on the Discovery of Animal Magnetism" in the original French and in English translation, see Crabtree, *Animal Magnetism*, 4–5.

   Mesmer's posited "magnetic fluid" differed significantly from mineral magnetism as we understand it today. He believed magnetic fluid was the medium by which stars and planets affected humans.

24. Mesmer's method of inducing a therapeutic "crisis" or catharsis may have had roots in the healing work of a Swabian priest and exorcist named J. J. Gassner (n.d.), a contemporary of Mesmer's, who attributed illness to evil spirits (Podmore, 27). Mesmer differed significantly from Gassner, however, in that he did not posit any divine intervention. Mesmer became the best known and most influential early theorist of magnetic healing during the Enlightenment.

25. Bailly, *Rapport Des Commisaires Chárges Par Le Roi De L'examen Du Magnétisme Animal*. See also Crabtree, *Animal Magnetism*, 10–11. The following books also discuss the Paris commissions: Crabtree, *From Mesmer to Freud*; Goldsmith; Podmore; Fuller, *Mesmerism and the American Cure of Souls*; Wyckoff, *Franz Anton Mesmer*.

26. Fuller, *Mesmerism and the American Cure of Souls*, 7–8.

27. Ibid., 8.

28. Podmore.

29. Dods's ideas are summarized in Whorton, 112–15. They are laid out in detail in Dods, *The Philosophy of Electrical Psychology*.

30. Still and Palmer are discussed at length in Whorton and in Gevitz. The latter touches briefly on Davis. For a more extended scholarly discussion of Davis, see chapter 4 in Albanese; this book also draws its title from Davis's writing. Podmore discusses Davis on 220–33.

31. Crabtree, *From Mesmer to Freud*, 39. The characteristics of magnetic sleep are described on 40–47.

32. Gabay, *The Covert Enlightenment*, 48.

33. Ibid., 47–48.

34. Ibid., 37–41. See also Crabtree, *Animal Magnetism* and *From Mesmer to Freud*. Research on such paranormal phenomena was conducted at Duke from 1927 to the 1960s. It continues at the Rhine Research Center off-campus, near the Duke Medical Center.

35. Crabtree, *From Mesmer to Freud*, 184–89.

36. Judah, 52.

37. Einstein's theory of special relativity, published in 1905, showed that time does not proceed at the same rate for all observers; it varies according to one's position and relative velocity. This disproved the hypotheses that the universe is

in a steady state pervaded by ether and that time is uniform—though Einstein himself was uncomfortable at first with the idea of a dynamic universe. His theory of general relativity, published in 1915, showed that space-time is a four-dimensional "fabric" curved by the presence of massive bodies, and this curvature accounts for the force of gravitation. Subsequent developments in quantum mechanics, string theories, brane theory, and M-theory, which may unify the macrocosmic phenomena described by relativity and the microcosmic phenomena described by quantum mechanics, are fascinating but cannot be considered here. The theoretical physicist Stephen Hawking has written several introductions to these ideas, accessible to people without training in advanced mathematics or theoretical physics. Recent discoveries about the Higgs Boson, which appears to give matter mass, and Dark Energy, hypothesized to pervade all of space, are intriguing but beyond my ability to understand mathematically.

38. The best bibliography on the subject is Crabtree's *Animal Magnetism, Early Hypnosis, and Psychical Research*, a book-length annotated listing of 1,905 texts in English, French, German, and Italian. It focuses on medical and psychological works and explicitly excludes those dealing with *religious* movements interested in clairvoyance, such as Spiritualism and Theosophy.

39. Gauld, *A History of Hypnotism*.

40. Elliotson et al., *Numerous Cases of Surgical Operations without Pain in the Mesmeric State*; Esdaile and Kroger, *Hypnosis in Medicine and Surgery*. Elliotson, founder of a magazine dealing with Mesmerism called *The Zoist*, was an eminent physician until he began urging his colleagues to investigate Mesmerism. This advocacy irrevocably damaged his reputation among many of his medical colleagues.

41. Esdaile and Kroger, 148.

42. Satter, *Each Mind a Kingdom*, 50–51.

43. Crabtree, *From Mesmer to Freud*, 155–62. See also Braid and Waite, *Braid on Hypnotism*.

44. Janet employed the theory of dissociation to explain the phenomenon commonly called "multiple personality disorder," now called Dissociative Disorder. Crabtree and Gauld both discuss Janet's work. Ann Taves in *Fits, Trances, and Visions* initially argued that psychological dissociation might help to explain religious phenomena such as Mind Cure, ecstatic states during revivals, and spirit mediums. She has since proposed, in "Where (Fragmented) Selves Meet Cultures," that these phenomena may be better explained by research on hypnosis and suggestibility.

45. Gauld and Crabtree discuss these various streams or intellectual lineages in great detail.

46. This correspondence is included in appendix C to Bush's *Mesmer and Swedenborg*, 254–81.

47. Gabay, 17, 48. Podmore, 205–17, Crabtree, *From Mesmer to Freud*, 196–98, and Gauld, 141–44, also trace interest in both Mesmerism and Swedenborgianism

in Germany; Gauld notes in particular its influences on German "nature philosophy" and Romanticism, another link to American Transcendentalism.

48. Bush, *Mesmer and Swedenborg*, 161. Emphasis in original.

49. Ibid., 155–218. Albanese notes that Bush's enthusiasm for Davis later cooled, possibly because of opposition from Bush's colleagues in the New Church and allegations that Davis, who claimed not to read, had plagiarized Swedenborg and others (208–9).

50. Anderson, *Healing Hypotheses*, 120–21; Lawrence, "An Extraordinary Season in Prayer."

51. James, *The Varieties of Religious Experience*, 91, 93, 233.

52. Whitehead, *The Illusions of Christian Science*, 224.

53. Seale, *Phineas Parkhurst Quimby*, 19–29.

54. Poyen's account of his tour is *Progress of Animal Magnetism in New England*.

55. Collyer, *Lights and Shadows of American Life*. This forty-page, newsprint booklet describes Collyer's travels through and observations about life in New England. He describes visiting New York City; Boston, Lowell, Salem, and Newburyport, Massachusetts; Nashua, New Hampshire; Providence, Rhode Island; Philadelphia; Baltimore; Washington, DC; and Portland and Bangor, Maine.

56. Seale, *Phineas Parkhurst Quimby*, 103.

57. Ibid., 103–4.

58. Ibid., 31–52.

59. Ibid., 56.

60. Ibid., 53.

61. Quimby and Dresser, *The Quimby Manuscripts* (1961), 32.

62. Ibid., 150–51.

63. Seale, *Phineas Parkhurst Quimby*, 371.

64. Ibid., 155.

65. Quimby and Dresser, *The Quimby Manuscripts* (1961), 176.

66. Seale, *Phineas Parkhurst Quimby*, 264.

67. Quimby and Dresser, *The Quimby Manuscripts* (1961), 283.

CHAPTER 2

1. Braude, "Women's History *Is* American Religious History," 88.

2. Almond, *The British Discovery of Buddhism*; King, *Orientalism and Religion*; Long, *Significations*; Lopez, *Curators of the Buddha*; Masuzawa, *The Invention of World Religions*; Said, *Orientalism*.

3. Gottschalk, "Christian Science and Harmonialism," 160.

4. Among the best online sources of information about New Thought authors is an anonymously authored website, Cornerstone Books, a purveyor of New Thought

titles, and the New Thought Webring of which its site is a part. See http://corner-stone.wwwhubs.com/framepage.htm, accessed September 5, 2016.

5. In *The Varieties of Religious Experience* the psychologist William James called people whose religious conversions are preceded by anguished grappling with evil, suffering, and doubt the "twice born." The book is based on James's 1902 Gifford Lectures.

6. Satter, *Each Mind a Kingdom*, 58.

7. The elder Dressers published their claim in an 1884 circular and followed it up in 1887 with Julius's *The True History of Mental Science*. Annetta's book, *The Philosophy of P. P. Quimby with Selections from His Manuscripts and a Sketch of His Life*, was published in 1895, the same year the Mother Church of Christian Science was dedicated in Boston (Judah, 169).

8. "True Origin of Christian Science."

9. Twain, *Christian Science.*

10. Craig James Hazen asserts that Dresser edited Quimby's ideas to conform more closely with Dresser's own philosophical idealism (*The Village Enlightenment in America*, 145–47).

11. Judah, 182.

12. Parker, *Mind Cure in New England*, 48–56. Chapter 4 of Braden's *Spirits in Rebellion* also deals at length with Evans's books, as does chapter 4 of Larson, *New Thought*.

13. Evans, *Mental Medicine*, 210.

14. Stephen Gottschalk, a historian of Eddy's Christian Science church (and himself a Christian Scientist), argued that Evans developed his theories of mental healing earlier than Quimby. As evidence, he cites a secondhand 1888 report by the mind-curer A. J. Swartz saying "Quimby's methods were 'like those [Evans] had employed for some years'" (Gottschalk, "Christian Science and Harmonialism," 904, citing A. J. Swartz, "Editorial Reports," *Mental Science Magazine* [March 1888]). Certainly it is true that Evans was far more widely published and broadly influential than Quimby, particularly during the sixteen years between Quimby's death and the publication of Eddy's *Science and Health*. A single, secondhand report twelve years after Quimby's death is not completely convincing evidence, however. Gottschalk also points to a statement by Horatio Dresser "that Evans said what Quimby would have wished to say had he had the education and skill to do so"—an assertion that cannot be proved (Gottschalk, *The Emergence of Christian Science in American Religious Life*, 88, citing Horatio W. Dresser, *Health and the Inner Life* [New York and London: G. P. Putnam's Sons, 1906]).

15. Taves, *Fits, Trances, and Visions*, 223. She cites Evans, *The Mental Cure*, 252; Peel, *Mary Baker Eddy*, 163.

16. Materra, 136, 140.

17. Satter, *Each Mind a Kingdom*, 82.

18. Keller et al., *Encyclopedia of Women and Religion in North America*, 758.

19. Malinda Cramer described this in "Spiritual Experience," *Harmony Magazine* 7, no. 1 (October 1894). It is available online at http://divinescience.com/bio_malindaRecord.htm, accessed June 14, 2015.

20. "Divine Science: History," http://divinescience.com/ds_history.htm; "Malinda Cramer: Founder of Divine Science," http://malindacramer.wwwhubs.com; "The Early History of Divine Science," Divine Science Federation International, http://www.divinesciencefederation.org/our-teaching/founders/; "Casualties and Damage after the 1906 Earthquake," U.S. Geological Survey, http://earthquake.usgs.gov/regional/nca/1906/18april/casualties.php; all accessed June 14, 2015; "New Thought Authors: Malinda Elliott Cramer," http://www.newthoughtwisdom.com/malinda-cramer.html, accessed July 21, 2018.

21. "History," Unity, http://www.unity.org/about-us/history, accessed July 2, 2017.

22. "The Early History of Divine Science," Divine Science Federation International, http://www.divinesciencefederation.org/our-teaching/founders/ and "Organizational Members," Divine Science Federation International, http://www.divinesciencefederation.org/what-we-offer/ministries/, accessed June 14, 2015.

23. Martin, "The Life and Work of Sarah Jane Farmer," 2–3, 26. Hannah Farmer's humanitarian activities included prison reform efforts, assistance to soldiers, a campaign to save Boston's Old South Church from demolition, student scholarships, and a summer camp for poor children in Boston (6).

24. Martin, 9. Coffin's Asia travels are described in Griffis, *Charles Carleton Coffin*. See especially chapters 17–19.

25. Sanborn, "Green Acre."

26. Cameron, *Transcendentalists in Transition*.

27. Franklin Sanborn, letter dated June 2, 1913, published in *Springfield (MA) Republican*, June 4, 1913, reproduced in Cameron, 254–55; Franklin Sanborn, "Greenacre on the Piscataqua," *Springfield (MA) Republican*, June 30, 1913, reproduced in Cameron, 255–56; Martin, 220.

28. Martin, 83, 198–204; Cameron, 254–56.

29. Although a fire in 1905 destroyed Farmer's home and many Greenacre records, a few accounts of its early days survive. James Douglas Martin's 1967 master's thesis is the most detailed biography of Farmer and history of Greenacre available. It draws heavily on Farmer's correspondence and other materials held in Bahá'í archives. The journalist Franklin Sanborn, who became a close friend of Farmer's and a Greenacre regular, wrote more than a hundred newspaper and magazine articles about Greenacre activities; in 1980 Kenneth Walter Cameron compiled these, as well as prospectuses and programs from the conferences, in *Transcendentalists in Transition*. Another regular at Greenacre events produced a short history: Anna Josephine Ingersoll, *Greenacre on the Piscataqua*. An ardent

American Bahá'í wrote an unsystematic memoir of his Greenacre experiences from about 1906 through World War II: Charles Mason Remey, "Reminiscences of the Summer School Green-Acre." The Bahá'í Publishing Trust also produced a history of Greenacre in 1991, which it revised in 2005, to celebrate the centennial of the Portsmouth Treaty ending the Russo-Japanese War: Anne Gordon Perry et al., *Green Acre on the Piscataqua*.

30. Materra, especially 299–308.
31. Jane Claypool, "New Thought—New Woman," blog, https://janeclaypool.com/2013/03/25/new-thought-new-woman/, accessed June 12, 2016.
32. Sprague, "Christian Science and Social Reform."
33. Materra, 301–2.
34. Ibid., 301.
35. Christ Universal Temple ranks 1,241st in a list of 3,329 megachurches in the United States; the list of those reporting was last updated in 2010: Hartford Institute for Religion Research, "Database of Megachurches in the U.S.," sorted by size, http://hirr.hartsem.edu/cgi-bin/mega/db.pl?db=default&uid=default&view_records=1&ID=*&sb=3&so=descend, accessed July 3, 2017.
36. Murphy et al., *Encyclopedia of African American Religions*, 190–91. See also 793–94.
37. "Member Churches," UFBL, http://ufbl.org/ufbl-churches/#churches, accessed June 29, 2017. The network has shrunk a bit in recent years; on February 29, 2008, the Universal Foundation for Better Living (UFBL) website listed ten satellites and a total of thirteen study and discussion groups.
38. Christ Universal Temple for Better Living, "Our Founder," http://cutemple.org/?page_id=1163, accessed June 29, 2017.
39. Christ Universal Temple for Better Living, "Latest Sermon" http://www.cutemple.org, accessed June 29, 2017.
40. See also Frederick, *Between Sundays*. Reverend Ike (1935–2009) founded the United Church and Science of Living Institute in Manhattan. According to the 1993 *Encyclopedia of African American Religions*, more than five thousand people attended Ike's weekly services at that time, and in 1982 he claimed 7 million subscribers to his "Science of Living Study Guide." Ike has been quoted as saying "The lack of money is the root of all evil"; his church's website promotes "Thinkonomics" and asserts that cheerful giving to good causes, such as his ministry, will draw prosperity to the giver. Murphy et al., 247–48. See also his website, http://www.revike.org. The same encyclopedia lists another African American New Thought organization, the Antioch Association of Metaphysical Science, founded in 1932 by Dr. H. Lewis Johnson. Although it claimed five congregations in 1965, no further information about the group was available, and a Google search revealed no current presence on the World Wide Web. It is possible, but not currently verifiable, that Dr. Johnson (b. 1890) was female.
41. Materra, 258.

42. Ibid., 259.

43. Ibid., 331–32.

44. Dresser, *A History of the New Thought Movement*, 309.

45. Ibid., 359–61; see 309 for reference to women leaders.

46. Meyer, *The Positive Thinkers*, 46–47.

47. Harley, *Emma Curtis Hopkins*.

48. One chapter of Braden's *These Also Believe* treats the movement separately as a "cult" or minority religion, however, rather than as an expression of New Thought.

49. Albanese, 233–53.

50. Jill Watts estimates thirty thousand, based on subscriptions to the Peace Mission serial *The New Day* (*God, Harlem U.S.A.*, 142). *Time* magazine reported membership at fifty thousand, a figure that Robert Weisbrot found plausible after examining estimates ranging from a few thousand to 2 million and analyzing the methods used to derive the various figures (*Father Divine and the Struggle for Racial Equality*, 68–70).

51. Braden, *These Also Believe*, 12, 15.

52. Weisbrot, 70.

53. Ibid., 28, 33n53; Griffith, *Born Again Bodies*, 141–44, 148, 154; Braden, *These Also Believe*, 73–75.

54. Weisbrot, 11–13.

55. Watts, 65.

56. Satter, "Marcus Garvey, Father Divine and the Gender Politics of Race Difference and Race Neutrality," 54.

57. Braden, *These Also Believe*, 20.

58. Parker.

59. Weisbrot, 37–41.

60. Ibid., 37.

61. Mabee, *Promised Land*, 81.

62. Ibid., 67.

63. Satter, "Marcus Garvey, Father Divine," 65.

64. Murphy et al., 293–95.

65. Satter, "Marcus Garvey, Father Divine," 59.

66. Watts, 88–90.

67. Satter, "Marcus Garvey, Father Divine," 64.

68. Ibid., 53.

69. Weisbrot, 100, 102.

70. Burnham, *God Comes to America*, 40–41.

71. Satter, "Marcus Garvey, Father Divine," 60–63.

72. Griffith, *Born Again Bodies*, 140–55.

73. Curtis, *Islam in Black America*, 56–61. Curtis says that chapters 1–19 of Ali's text were copied directly from Dowling's book, and that chapters 20–44 were copied from *Infinite Wisdom*.

74. Sedgwick, *Against the Modern World*.

75. For more information on Moorish Science, see Baer and Singer, *African American Religion*, 120–24; Curtis, 45–62; Murphy et al., 31, 507; Turner, *Islam in the African-American Experience*, 71–108; Long and Wilkins, "The Uncommon Yogi."

76. Dorman, 159, 66–69. See also Chireau and Deutsch, *Black Zion*.

77. One film traces African American interest in Hindu philosophy, yoga, and meditation (Long and Wilkins). It includes references to the Theosophical Society; the African American religious movements inspired by Theosophy and New Thought; a study group founded in 1926 by Paramahansa Yogananda; leaders such as Howard and Sue Thurman and Martin Luther King Jr., who were inspired by Mohandas K. Gandhi; black disciples of Paramahansa Yogananda, Satchidananda, Satya Sai Baba, Chinmayananda, the Maharishi Mahesh Yogi, and Yogi Bhajan; and members of the contemporary Black Yoga Teachers Alliance. Among the celebrity yogis mentioned are film star Herb Jeffries, singer and actress Eartha Kitt, jazz saxophonist Sonny Rollins, activist Angela Davis, and Alice Coltrane, widow of John Coltrane, who founded an ashram in Santa Monica, California.

CHAPTER 3

1. Schmidt, *Restless Souls*, 146.

2. Schmidt is the only historian of American religious history I have found who devotes any sustained attention to meditation in New Thought (ibid., chapter 4, "Meditation for Americans," 143–79). One of the most extensive histories of the New Thought movement, Charles Braden's *Spirits in Rebellion*, spans more than 570 pages; its index lists only seven passing references to meditation. John Haller's 389-page history of the movement, *The History of New Thought*, mentions it four times. Catherine Albanese's *A Republic of Mind and Spirit*, a 628-page history of metaphysical religion in the United States, mentions meditation twice in relation to New Thought. The index to Judah's *The History and Philosophy of the Metaphysical Movements in America* does not include the term "meditation" at all.

3. Generally the term "Vedanta" (end of the Vedas) refers to philosophical speculation on the Vedas, found in the Upanishads. Here, however, the term refers more narrowly to the teachings and practices promoted among Americans by Vivekenanda and others in the Vedanta Society.

4. Haller, *The History of New Thought*, 114–15.

5. James, *The Varieties of Religious Experience*, 319.

6. Ibid., 105.

7. De Jong, *A Brief History of Buddhist Studies in Europe and America*, 27–47. For a chronological bibliography of translations of Buddhist texts and descriptions of Buddhist practices, Theravāda, Mahāyāna, and Vajrayāna, see Droit, *The Cult of Nothingness*, 191–259. See also Edmunds, "A Buddhist Bibliography."

8. Volumes 10, 11, and 13 of *Sacred Books of the East* (all published in 1881) include various Pali Suttas and Vinaya texts; volumes 17 (1882) and 20 (1885) contain additional Vinaya texts; volume 19 (1883) contains Aśvaghoṣa's biography of the Buddha from a Chinese translation; and volume 21 (1884) contains the Lotus Sutra. Later volumes, 35 (1890) and 36 (1894), contain the Questions of King Milinda. Volume 49 (1894) contains a collection of important Mahāyāna texts, including Pure Land sūtras, the Diamond Sutra, and two Perfection of Wisdom sūtras. See "Sacred Books of the East Index," Internet Sacred Text Archive, http://www.sacred-texts.com/sbe/index.htm, accessed July 6, 2017.

9. Tweed, *The American Encounter with Buddhism*, 29.

10. Jackson, "The New Thought Movement and the Nineteenth Century Discovery of Oriental Philosophy," 526.

11. Ibid.

12. Evans, *Esoteric Christianity and Mental Therapeutics*, 158.

13. Ibid., 14. Emphasis in original.

14. The Theosophical Society's three objectives: "1. To form the nucleus of a universal brotherhood of humanity, without distinction of race, creed, sex, caste or color. 2. The study of ancient and modern religions, philosophies, and sciences. 3. The investigation of the unexplained laws of nature and the psychical powers latent in man" (Goodrick-Clarke, ed. *Helena Blavatsky*, 11).

15. Sinnett, *The Rationale of Mesmerism*.

16. Prothero, *The White Buddhist*, 23–24, 107–10.

17. Ibid., 107–8.

18. Dharmapala, "Diary Leaves of the Late Ven. Anagarika Dharmapāla," *Maha Bodhi* 64, no. 3 (1956): 100, entry for March 14, 1897.

19. Blavatsky, *Isis Unveiled*, 216.

20. Besant, *Psychology*. The first article on hypnosis, titled in this collection "Hypnotism I," was originally published in the Theosophical journal *Lucifer* in October 1889; "Hypnotism II" was originally published in the *Universal Review* in February 1890. "Clairvoyance and Mental Healing" was a lecture delivered at Steinway Hall in Chicago (n.d.) and reported in a publication identified only as "The Progressive Thinker."

21. Besant, *Psychology*, 302.

22. Materra, 127n60.

23. The passage from Farmer, dated October 20, 1903, is included in a personal email communication to Wakoh Shannon Hickey from the Greenacre historian Anne Gordon Perry, on September 23, 2007. She sent several excerpts from Farmer's writings, from Perry's personal research files. The quotation is from

C. W. Leadbeater's *Invisible Helpers,* chapter 17, three paragraphs from the end of the book. The earliest edition of the book included in WorldCat was published in London in 1899. A 1915 American edition is available on the internet at http://www.anandgholap.net/Invisible_Helpers-CWL.htm, accessed January 5, 2008.

24. Cameron, 173–75, 89, 242; Martin, 240.

25. Sheldon, *Theosophy and New Thought,* 134. Sheldon's book discusses each movement separately and is critical of both.

26. Dresser,, 303–4.

27. Ibid., 303.

28. Schmidt, *Restless Souls,* 161; Payne, "Buddhism and the Powers of the Mind," 242.

29. Schmidt, *Restless Souls,* 160–62. See also Besant, *A Study in Consciousness,* 194, 213.

30. In Olcott, *A Buddhist Catechism,* answers to Questions 39 and 42 describe the Buddha's meditation under the Bodhi Tree; the answer to Question 63 lists the Eightfold Path, including Right Meditation; the answer to 102 specifies, "The entire system of Buddhism came to his [the Buddha's] mind during the Great Meditation"; the answer to 145 notes that attaining the meditative state(s) known as *jhana* leads to the recollection of past lives; and the answer to 150 asserts that seemingly miraculous (but actually natural) powers can be developed by practicing Dhyana, an alternate spelling of *jhana,* meaning meditative concentration. (No page numbers are given in this edition of the *Catechism.*)

31. Evans, *Esoteric Christianity and Mental Therapeutics,* 63.

32. The only edition of Olcott's *A Buddhist Catechism* available to me from Evans's time is a special edition to commemorate the opening of the Adyar Oriental Library (1886). The relevant passage is the answer to Question 50 (no page numbers given): "Q. What did he [Buddha] obtain that night? A. The knowledge of his previous births, of the causes of rebirth, and of the way to extinguish desires. Just before the break of the next day his mind was entirely opened, like the full-blown lotus flower; the light of supreme knowledge, or the Four Truths, poured in upon him; he had become Buddha—the Enlightened, the All-knowing."

33. Evans, *Esoteric Christianity and Mental Therapeutics,* 68.

34. Ibid., 158–59, quoting *Precepts of the Dhammapada,* v. 126. A search in WorldCat for the title *Precepts of the Dhammapada* returned only the following record, which dates from Evans's time: Gray, *The Dhammapada.* The quoted passage, on page 13, v. 126, differs slightly from Evans's version: "Some are born (in their mothers' womb); evil-doers are born in hell; the virtuous go to heaven; those free from worldly desires attain *Nibbân.*"

35. The other four constituents are physical form (*rūpa*); perception, or the mind's capacity to discern phenomena and their characteristics, through the five physical senses as well as ideas or concepts (*saṃjñā*); volitions or intentions (*saṃskāra*),

which shape patterns of behavior and character; and awareness (*vijñāna*), both conscious and subliminal (Keown, *Oxford Dictionary of Buddhism*).

36. Evans, *Esoteric Christianity and Mental Therapeutics*, 117.

37. Ibid., 116–17.

38. For further discussion of most of these Buddhist terms, see Keown. The seven factors of enlightenment and their scriptural sources may be found in Harvey, *An Introduction to Buddhism*, 65.

39. Evans, *Esoteric Christianity and Mental Therapeutics*, 103–4.

40. "Digital Dictionary of Buddhism: Sanskrit Terms Index," updated January 15, 2016, Dictionaries for the Study of Buddhist and East Asian Language and Thought, http://buddhism-dict.net/ddb/indexes/term-sa.html, accessed March 21, 2008. See also Keown, 8.

41. "Mental Therapeutics and Esoteric Christianity." The erroneous title of the book is in the original article.

42. Anderson, 306; Lawrence, 39n21.

43. Devin Zuber, a Swedenborg specialist, critiques Schuchard's scholarly methods and asserts, "None of the world's leading scholars on Swedenborg have accepted Schuchard's contentions that he was a lifelong closet Kabbalist, expert in sexual Yoga, secret spy for the Swedish government, and an active member of Masonic lodges" ("The Buddha of the North," 9–10n6). Zuber cites Talbot, "Schuchard's Swedenborg." Among the scholars who find possible Swedenborg-Tantra connections more persuasive are Kripal, *Esalen*, 139–41; Chetty, "Was Swedenborg a Yogi?"; Larsen, "Swedenborg and the Visionary Tradition"; Loy, "The Dharma of Emanuel Swedenborg," *Buddhist-Christian Studies*. Also "The Dharma of Emanuel Swedenborg," in *Swedenborg*.

44. Hallengren, "The Secret of Great Tartary," 37.

45. Emanuel Swedenborg, *The Book of the Apocalypse Revealed: Uncovering the Secrets That Were Foretold There and Have Lain Hidden until Now* (Lutherville, MD: Swedenborg Project, Swedenborg Digital Library, 2007), http://www.smallcanonsearch.com/read.php?book=ar&section=11, paragraph 11.3–4; Emanuel Swedenborg, *True Christian Religion: Containing the Whole Theology of the New Church Predicted by the Lord in Daniel 7:13–14 and Revelation 21:1–2* (1946; Lutherville, MD: Swedenborg Project, Swedenborg Digital Library, 2007), paragraphs 279.3, 4, http://www.smallcanonsearch.com/read.php?book=tcr&section=279. Both sites accessed July 21, 2018. From *True Christian Religion*: "[3] Of that ancient Word which existed in Asia before the Israelitish Word, I am permitted to state this new thing, namely, that it is still preserved there among the people who dwell in Great Tartary. In the spiritual world I have talked with spirits and angels from that country, who said that they have a Word, and have had it from ancient times; and that they conduct their Divine worship according to this Word, and that it consists solely of correspondences. They said, that in it also is the Book of Jasher, which is

mentioned in Joshua (10:12, 13), and in 2 Samuel (1:17, 18); and that they have also among them the books called the Wars of Jehovah and Enunciations, which are mentioned by Moses (Num. 21:14, 15, and 27–30); and when I read to them the words that Moses had quoted therefrom, they searched to see if they were there, and found them; from which it was evident to me that the ancient Word is still among that people. While talking with them they said that they worshiped Jehovah, some as an invisible God, and some as visible. [4] They also told me that they do not permit foreigners to come among them, except the Chinese, with whom they cultivate peaceful relations, because the Chinese Emperor is from their country; also that the population is so great that they do not believe that any region in the whole world is more populous, which is indeed credible from the wall so many miles in length which the Chinese formerly built as a protection against invasion from these people. I have further heard from the angels, that the first chapters of Genesis which treat of creation, of Adam and Eve, the garden of Eden, their sons and their posterity down to the flood, and of Noah and his sons, are also contained in that Word, and thus were transcribed from it by Moses. The angels and spirits from Great Tartary are seen in the southern quarter on its eastern side, and are separated from others by dwelling in a higher expanse, and by their not permitting anyone to come to them from the Christian world, or, if any ascend, by guarding them to prevent their return. Their possessing a different Word is the cause of this separation."

46. Schuchard, "Why Mrs. Blake Cried," 55–57. See also *Why Mrs Blake Cried*, 102–9, 116–20, 152–54. She argues that Swedenborg was involved in the Moravian congregation at London's Fetter Lane. Schuchard notes that Moravian missionaries gained a number of converts in Ceylon, another possible source of information about Buddhism.

47. See the following by Blavatsky: *Isis Unveiled*, online; *A Modern Panarion*; "A Collection of Notes and Appendices on an Article Entitled 'The Âryan-Arhat Esoteric Tenets on the Sevenfold Principle in Man,' by T. Subba Row"; and "Lamas and Druses."

48. Jackson, *Oriental Religions and American Thought*, 257–58.

49. Sinnett's *Esoteric Buddhism* draws heavily on Vedanta as well.

50. Evans, *Esoteric Christianity and Mental Therapeutics*, 95.

51. Ibid., 96–97.

52. Ibid., 154.

53. Ibid., 141.

54. See, for example, Jackson, *The Oriental Religions and American Thought* and *Vedanta for the West*; Ketelaar, "Strategic Occidentalism"; Seager, *The World's Parliament of Religions*; Seager and Council for a Parliament of the World's Religions, *The Dawn of Religious Pluralism*; Snodgrass, *Presenting Japanese Buddhism to the West*; and Ziolkowski, *A Museum of Faiths*. For primary source material on the Parliament, see Barrows, *The World's Parliament of Religions*; Hanson,

The World's Congress of Religions; and Houghton, *Neely's History of the Parliament of Religions and Religious Congresses at the World's Columbian Exposition.*

55. For example, the Theosophical congress was attended by "a very large congregation" that included "Catholics, Episcopalians, Lutherans, Congregationalists, and members of other denominations" (Houghton, 926). Vivekenanda gave the closing address to a large gathering at the Buddhist congress (963–65). In addition, a Swedenborgian congress lasted three days, a Universalist congress five days, and a Unitarian congress eight days (915, 919, 928).

56. Hanson, 1174; Houghton, 934.

57. The two accounts listed above have slight discrepancies in the names of two speakers: D. A. Eason (in Hanson) and B. A. Eastman (in Houghton), and A. M. Knott (in Hanson) and A. H. Knott (in Houghton), but these may simply be typographical errors. Four of the speakers are identifiably female; two are identified only by initials. See also Gottschalk, *The Emergence of Christian Science in American Religious Life*, 193–94.

58. Materra, 136–40; Satter, *Each Mind a Kingdom*, 127.

59. Materra, 213–14. Braden makes only a passing reference to this congress, stating that Charles and Myrtle Fillmore, founders of Unity, attended (*Spirits in Rebellion*, 239).

60. Williamson, *Transcendent in America*, 34.

61. Fields, *How the Swans Came to the Lake*, 168–70.

62. For Buddhism, see Jaffe, "Seeking Śakyamuni"; Ketelaar, *Of Heretics and Martyrs in Meiji Japan* and "Strategic Occidentalism"; Lopez, *Curators of the Buddha*; Sharf, "The Zen of Japanese Nationalism" and "Buddhist Modernism and the Rhetoric of Meditative Experience"; Snodgrass. Similar research on the Tibetan Buddhism that arrived in the United States after 1965 can be found in Lopez, *Prisoners of Shangri-La*. Thomas Tweed addressed similar themes in "American Occultism and Japanese Buddhism." For a wide-ranging discussion of Buddhist modernism, see McMahan, *The Making of Buddhist Modernism*. For Vedanta, see three works by Jackson: *The Oriental Religions and American Thought*; *Vedanta for the West*; "The New Thought Movement and the Nineteenth Century Discovery of Oriental Philosophy"; Goldberg; and Williamson.

63. Sharf, "Buddhist Modernism," 246–47.

64. Ketelaar, "Strategic Occidentalism," 42.

65. Sharf, "Buddhist Modernism."

66. Snodgrass.

67. Sharf, "Buddhist Modernism," 252.

68. See Reader and Tanabe, *Practically Religious*; Williams, *The Other Side of Zen*; Wilson, *Mindful America.*

69. Lopez, *The Scientific Buddha.*

70. Ibid., 34–35.

71. Prothero, *The White Buddhist*.

72. "Scientific Healing Affirmations," Self-Realization Fellowship, http://www.yogananda-srf.org/affirmations.aspx#.V3LNGlcopkg, accessed June 28, 2016.

73. For references at Greenacre to the New Thought leaders named in this paragraph and notes 75–82 below, see Cameron, 21, 42, 45–46, 54, 57, 61, 62, 67–68, 76, 78, 80, 82, 95, 168, 178, 181, 194–204, 221–22, 249, 257, 259.

74. It is possible that New Thought speakers appeared in other years but went unmentioned in Sanborn's accounts or were not easy to identify on Greenacre programs because they have less name recognition today. Thus I may have omitted them from my list (Martin, 240–42).

75. On Abby Morton Diaz, see Albanese, 324; Materra, 222–23, 234–35, 415–16, 532; Satter, *Each Mind a Kingdom*, 182, 192, 196–98, 200, 211.

76. On Ursula Gestefeld, see Braden, *Spirits in Rebellion*, especially 138–40; Dresser, 140–41, 196; Gottschalk, *The Emergence of Christian Science in American Religious Life*, 103–4, 109–10, 113, 117; Judah, 171–72, 239, 286; Satter, *Each Mind a Kingdom*, especially chapter 4. Also Materra, 420–22, 471.

77. On Fanny Harley, see Materra, 507, 535.

78. On Orison Swett Marden, see Braden, *Spirits in Rebellion*, 363–67, 373, 385, 469, 474, 478, 521; Dresser, 243, 273, 299; Materra, 429, 479–80; Meyer, 167–68, 246 (incorrectly identifies him as "Orestes S. Marden"); Satter, *Each Mind a Kingdom*, 6, 226.

79. On Charles Brodie Patterson, see Braden, *Spirits in Rebellion*, 11, 150, 153, 159, 179, 184, 185, 191, 209, 210, 324, 327, 330, 413; Dresser, 153–54, 185, 196, 262; Parker, 128, 129; Gottschalk, *Emergence of Christian Science*, 118–20, 122; Judah, 173–74; Materra, 432–33, 484; Meyer, 43, 73; Satter, *Each Mind a Kingdom*, 213–14, 243.

80. On Ralph Waldo Trine, see Albanese, 324, 394–98, 401, 407, 417, 424, 433, 439–40, 444; Braden, *Spirits in Rebellion*, 164, 167, 168, 184, 186, 351, 352, 405, 463, 469, 474, 478, 536; Dresser, 172, 178, 198, 273; Judah, 189, 192, 198; Materra, 440, 492; Meyer, 43, 73, 78–79, 111–13, 196–99; Parker, 7–10, 55–56, 58, 61, 70–79, 82, 90, 91, 93, 105, 113, 155; Satter, *Each Mind a Kingdom*, 6, 79, 181, 209, 226, 242, 243, 311n51.

81. On Helen Van-Anderson, see Albanese, 317, 323; Braden, *Spirits in Rebellion*, 153, 170, 179, 180, 184; Dresser, especially 174–76; Materra, 440–41, 493; Satter, *Each Mind a Kingdom*, chapter 4.

82. On Henry Wood, see Albanese, 417, 425; Braden, *Spirits in Rebellion*, 153, 154, 156, 161, 170, 181, 351, 377, 390, 405, 537; Dresser, 149, 151, 154, 157–58, 164–72, 178, 188, 194, 196, 274; Judah, 170, 179, 182, 189, 209; Materra, 445, 497; Meyer, 91, 109–10; Parker, 16, 28, 43–44, 55–56, 61–75, 81, 82, 85, 91, 93, 95, 101.

83. Dresser, 177.

84. Martin, 143. See also 50, 63, 134–35, 141–45. Although clearly disdainful of New Thought, Martin underscores Farmer's role.

85. Braden, *Spirits in Rebellion*, 173; Dresser, 196.
86. Franklin Sanborn, "From the Greenacre Schools: Unique University Extension," *Springfield Republican*, August 15, 1897, p. 7 col. 2, reproduced in Cameron, 222.
87. Ibid.
88. Ingersoll.
89. Remey.
90. Perry et al.
91. Letter from Sarah Farmer to Lewis Janes, date uncertain. Perry et al., 26, includes a lengthy excerpt from the letter, including the quoted material, and dates it 1898. Martin, 59, gives the date of the letter as April 14, 1896.
92. "We have groped our way in darkness, sometimes crying out with Siddartha—'I would not let one cry / Whom I could save! How can it be that Brahm / Would make a world, and keep it miserable, / Since, if all powerful, he leaves it so, / He is not good, and if not powerful / He is not God?'" (Farmer, "The Abundant Life," 30, 36). The source of the *Light of Asia* quotation is Arnold, *The Light of Asia*, 80. The source of the quotation from the Vedas is unknown.
93. Available accounts differ slightly in the years that each swami attended. Martin's thesis provides a list of speakers and the years they attended Greenacre, but it is much less complete than my list, compiled from Sanborn's eyewitness accounts, reproduced in Cameron. For the three men who taught at Greenacre in 1894–99, Swamis Vivekenanda, Saradananda, and Abhedananda, my list agrees with a list provided by the current Greenacre archivist, Roseanne Adams in email communication, September 11, 2007.
94. Cameron, 21, 22, 77, 88–89, 97–98, 104, 108, 181, 194, 195, 199, 224, 236, 243, 256.
95. Perry et al., 103, 105, 116. Also Martin, 36–37, 78–79. Nivedita (d. 1911) was born Margaret Noble in Ireland; it is not clear what year she visited Greenacre. A brief sketch of her work in the Ramakrishna Order can be found in Oldmeadow, *Journeys East*, 38–43. She became Vivekenanda's disciple during his 1895 tour of England and took the name Nivedita after her 1898 arrival in Calcutta, when she made vows as a novice in the Ramakrishna Order, so she probably did not attend Greenacre until after that year. More information is available in Foxe, *Long Journey Home*. See also Jackson, *Vedanta for the West*, 30.
96. Martin, 61n70, citing several letters from Sarah Farmer to Lewis Janes.
97. "Buddhism and Other Religions Taught at Greenacre." Nakamura is mentioned only in passing as the teacher of a class in Buddhism in 1895. Sanborn reported at some length on one of Nakamura's lectures that year, titled "What Is Japanism?," in which Buddhism is discussed. Franklin Sanborn, "The Greenacre Congress," *Boston Evening Transcript*, July 20, 1985, reproduced in Cameron, 30–33.
98. Cameron, 104, 123, 125–26, 128, 140, 163, 183, 240–41.
99. Ibid., 80.
100. Martin, 38.

101. Franklin Sanborn, "The Greenacre Congress," *Boston Evening Transcript*, August 21, 1895, reproduced in Cameron, 58–61.

102. Cameron, 32–33, 70, 106, 117, 125, 128, 188. For more on Johnston, see Martin, 210n87; the Theosophical sites *The Word*, http://www.sacred-texts.com/cla/pdm/pdm07.htm and Charles Johnston, "The Crest-Jewel of Wisdom and Other Writings of Sankaracharya," 1946/1999, http://www.theosociety.org/pasadena/crest/crest-hp.htm, both accessed January 1, 2008. He is listed there as author or translator of several texts; the latter site spells his surname "Johnson." The acronym MRAS stands for Member of the Royal Asiatic Society. Johnston gave a series of lectures at Greenacre titled "Records of Inspiration," including the Upanishads; the Popul Vuh; teachings of Buddhism, Confucius, and Laotzu; and Chaldean, Persian, Jewish, Islamic, Egyptian, Slavonic, Teutonic, and Celtic traditions. Cameron, 127–29.

103. Cameron, 123. See also Fields, 144.

104. Martin, 56, 66–67, 69, 70–71, 74, 211. Janes disagreed strongly with Farmer over the direction of the program; he wanted a more academic approach that included Bahá'í as one tradition among many rather than the unifying tradition into which all others could be subsumed. He ran an independent Monsalvat program in Eliot in 1901. Fillmore Moore ran a competing program that year, as well (70). Tweed, *The American Encounter with Buddhism*, 62, 87, identifies both as Buddhist sympathizers. He also discusses Canavarro at length.

105. Sr. Sanghamitta, a.k.a. Marie Canavarro, also studied Bahá'í and Vedanta (Tweed, *The American Encounter with Buddhism*, 58).

106. "Buddhism and Other Religions Taught at Greenacre."

107. See, for example, Vivekenanda, *The Complete Works*, 6:39, 50; 7:42.

108. Veysey, "Vedanta Monasteries." Also Vivekenanda, 7:247–48, 252–53, 266–67.

109. Martin, 49.

110. Ibid., 171.

111. Ibid., 156.

112. Franklin Sanborn, "The Greenacre Lectures," *Boston Evening Transcript*, July 26, 1897, reproduced in Cameron, 87–90.

113. Martin, 52.

114. Franklin Sanborn, "Vivekenanda at Greenacre," *Boston Evening Transcript*, July 7, 1894, reproduced in Cameron, 21.

115. Letter from Vivekenanda to "Joe Joe" of Wimbledon, England, dated October 7, 1896, in Vivekenanda, 7:473–75.

116. Franklin Sanborn, "The Greenacre Opening," *Boston Evening Transcript*, July 1, 1898, reproduced in Cameron, 107–9. "During the season of 1897 between one and two thousand would-be visitors were refused entertainment, so overtasked were the resources of Greenacre and the town of Eliot as a whole, and the indications are that the present season will be more successful than ever; for many new buildings have been erected in the town of Eliot for the

accommodation of those who would share the privilege of this delightful resort"
(107). Ingersoll wrote, "Thousands have come to Greenacre, and thousands
have been turned away for lack of accommodations" (19).

117. Martin, 47.

118. Richardson, "The Rise and Fall of the Parliament of Religions at Greenacre."

119. "Monsalvat School of Comparative Religion."

120. Martin, 154.

121. Perry et al., 34. See also a photo of Lewis Janes and Abhedananda in Ingersoll,
facing page 12.

122. This New Thought organization, founded in 1895, should not be confused with
the similarly named group that operated during the 1870s and was founded
by William James, Charles Peirce, Oliver Wendell Holmes Jr., and others. The
New Thought group led to the formation of the International New Thought
Alliance in 1914 (Dresser, *History of the New Thought Movement*, 179–83).

123. Ibid., 179.

124. See, for example, Dharmapala, "Diary Leaves of the Late Ven. Anagarika
Dharmapāla," *Maha Bodhi* 64, no. 6 (June 1956): 295–302, entries for April 3–
30, 1897, during which time he stayed primarily at Sarah Bull's Boston home
and spent time with Lewis Janes; 64, no. 7 (July 1956): 340–50, entries for May,
1897, which contain repeated references to Janes and additional stays with Bull;
64, no. 9 (September 1956): 428–31, entries for June 1897, referring to Janes
and Phelps; 64, no. 10 (October 1956): 463–65, entries for July 13 and 15, 1897,
referring to Phelps; and 65, no. 2 (February 1957): 45, entry for July 16, 1897,
referring to Bull, Janes, and Phelps. Dharmapāla's 1897 visit to Greenacre is
recorded in 65, no. 7 (July 1957): 293–97; 65, no. 9 (September 1957): 361–67;
65, no. 11 (November 1957): 433–37; and 65, no. 12 (December 1957): 474–80.
Collectively these diary entries span the month of August 1897.

125. Ibid., 65, no. 7 (July 1957): 297, entry for August 3, 1897; 65, no. 9 (August
1957): 362, entry for August 8.

126. Richardson, 135.

127. Dharmapala, "Diary Leaves of the Late Ven. Anagarika Dharmapāla," *Maha
Bodhi* 65, no. 12 (December 1957): 477, entry for August 26, 1897.

128. Richardson, 136–37.

129. Dharmapala, "Diary Leaves of the Late Ven. Anagarika Dharmapāla," *Maha
Bodhi* 65, no. 12 (December 1957): 477.

130. Bahiyyih Randal Winckler, "Sarah Jane Farmer 1847–1916," unpublished reference material in the Green Acre Archives, 5–6, quoted in Perry et al., 17. Perry
states that Winckler was the daughter of a man who played a major role in
developing Greenacre as a Bahá'í institution and that she collected the Farmer
papers preserved in the National Bahá'í Archives.

131. Dharmapala, "Diary Leaves of the Late Ven. Anagarika Dharmapāla,"
Maha Bodhi, 65, no. 9 (September 1957): 366. The relevant chapter of the

Visuddhimagga can be found in Buddhaghosa, *Visuddhimagga*, 259–85. It refers to the following scriptures: Saṁutta Nikāya v. 321; and the Vinaya, Suttavibhaṅga 1, 70. The Ānāpānasati Sutta, or "Discourse on the Mindfulness of Breathing," also can be found at Majjhima Nikāya 118. The Eight Precepts are to refrain from killing, theft, sexual misconduct, false speech, taking intoxicants, participating in entertainments and wearing ornaments or perfumes, eating after noon, and sleeping in a luxurious bed.

132. Dharmapala, "Diary Leaves of the Late Ven. Anagarika Dharmapāla," *Maha Bodhi* 65, no. 9 (September 1957): 366.

133. Ibid., 65, no. 3 (March 1957): 101, 103.

134. Ibid., 66, no. 2 (February 1958): 49, entry for July 23, 1897.

135. Ibid., 65, no. 11 (November 1957): 433.

136. "Buddhism and Other Religions Taught at Greenacre," *Boston Sunday Journal*, ibid.

137. She does not name the book, and the Greenacre archivist could not identify it. Perry et al., 18.

138. From Franklin Sanborn, "Our Weekly Boston Letter," *Springfield Republican*, July 28, 1906, reproduced in Cameron, 240–41.

139. Email to Wakoh Shannon Hickey from Brian Nagata, director of the Numata Center for Buddhist Translation and Research in Berkeley, California, March 20, 2008. Mr. Nagata cited his source as BCA Centennial History Project Committee, *Buddhist Churches of America*, 55.

140. The page, dated July 25, 1906, is reproduced in Perry et al, 133.

141. Jaffe, 89–90.

142. Cameron, 78–80.

143. Materra, 94; Dharmapala, "Diary Leaves of the Late Ven. Anagarika Dharmapāla," *Maha Bodhi* 64, no. 3 (March 1956): 102, entry for March 21, 1897.

144. Dharmapala, "Diary Leaves of the Late Ven. Anagarika Dharmapāla," *Maha Bodhi* 64, no. 3 (March 1956): 98, entry for March 3, 1897.

145. Ibid., 64, no. 3 (March 1956): 99, entry for March 9, 1897.

146. Ibid., 64, no. 2 (February 1956): 53, entry for February 15, 1897.

147. Ibid., 64, no. 9 (September 1956): 427, entry for June 17, 1897; Materra, 420–22.

148. Gottschalk, *The Emergence of Christian Science in American Religious Life*, 103.

149. Dharmapala, "Diary Leaves of the Late Ven. Anagarika Dharmapāla," *Maha Bodhi* 64, no. 6 (June 1956): 294–302, entries for April, 1897.

150. Jackson, "New Thought and Oriental Religions." In *Vedanta for the West*, 51, Jackson says Abhedenanda regularly reached audiences of five hundred or more (not entirely New Thought), and in two cases, audiences of one thousand and seven thousand. Schmidt, *Restless Souls*, discusses Paramananda on 165. Materra lists forty-three books by Atkinson (399, 457–60).

151. James Boyle O'Reilly, "PEACE; BE STILL! The Infinite always is silent; / It is only the Finite speaks; / Our words are the idle wave caps / On a deep that never

breaks. / We question with wand of science— / Explain decide and discuss; / But only in meditation / The mystery speaks to us." The original source of this poem is unknown, but it was included in *Metaphysical Magazine* 5 (January–May 1897): 230, http://books.google.com/books?id=amr9q5TfOi8C, accessed January 10, 2008.

152. Dresser, 178.

153. Franklin Sanborn, "From The Greenacre Schools: Unique University Extension," *Springfield Republican*, reproduced in Cameron, 222.

154. Franklin Sanborn, "The Season at Greenacre," *Boston Evening Transcript*, August 12, 1904, reproduced in Cameron, 168.

155. Dresser, 178, 179.

156. Braden, *Spirits in Rebellion*, 163.

157. Ibid., 171.

158. Schmidt, *Restless Souls*, 151–52.

159. Materra, 95, 114, 128n76. The publication citation is not dated.

160. Ibid., 154–59.

161. Ibid., 183.

162. Satter, *Each Mind a Kingdom*, 122–23, 132, 290n62.

163. McCollum, *Full Text of Class Lessons in Practical Psychology as They Are Personally Given to Her Classes*, 33, 39, 46, 55–56. This typewritten manuscript bears an inscription dated 1932, signed Harriett McCollum. It was a gift to the GTU library by J. Stillson Judah. McCollum also recommends a good diet, exercise, deep breaths, lots of water, enemas, daily baths, chewing food thoroughly as recommended by the "Great Masticator" Horace Fletcher, vitamins, plenty of milk, and sex only for procreation.

164. Trine, *In Tune with the Infinite*, 213.

165. Ibid., 214.

166. Braden, *Spirits in Rebellion*, 164–65.

167. Ibid., 353.

168. Holmes, *The Science of Mind*, 290. Visualization instructions are at 287–89.

169. Ibid., 48.

170. Ibid., 323.

171. Ibid., 318. Instructions for meditation can be found at 226–28.

172. Holmes, "Text Book of Practical Healing," 40.

173. Ibid., 47. Ernest Holmes discusses karma in *Science of Mind*, 67, 98, 118, 123, where he quotes Besant.

174. "Contact Points," Seicho-no-Ie International Headquarters, http://www.seicho-no-ie.org/eng/center/index.html, accessed July 8, 2017.

175. Davis, *Miracle Man of Japan*, 20, 145–46.

176. Ibid., 39, 41, 43.

177. Ibid, 39.

178. Ibid., 20.

179. Taniguchi, *Truth of Life*, 26.

180. Ibid., 39, 52–53.

181. Ibid., 220–21.

182. The text of the sūtra was previously available online at http://www.snitruth.org/
servo3.htm, accessed January 9, 2008, but the site has been discontinued. As
of this writing, it was available for purchase at Seicho-No-Ie New York, http://
www.sniny.com/store/c7/Books_English.html. Accessed July 24, 2017.

183. Taniguchi, *Truth of Life*, 89.

184. Detailed instructions for Shinsokan can be found at "A Brief Introduction to
Shinsokan," https://s3.amazonaws.com/media.cloversites.com/35/35524cdo-
9b31-4449-a3dd-eec3f8a61dbe/documents/A_Brief_Introduction_to_
Shinsokan.pdf Accessed July 24, 2017.

185. Taniguchi, *Recovery from All Diseases*.

186. Braden, *Spirits in Rebellion*, 496. He does not cite the source of this statistic.

187. Davis, *Miracle Man of Japan*, 99, 127–33. Websites for Seicho-no-Ie branches
in Japan and Brazil are in Japanese and Portuguese, respectively, so Davis's
book is the only published, extended survey of the group available in English.
A 1995 doctoral dissertation provides a more scholarly treatment, focusing on
Taniguchi's thought in Japan before and during World War II: Richard Edward
Negron, "The Department Store of Religions: Taniguchi Masaharu's Modernist
Spiritual Vision in Pre-War and Wartime Japan" (PhD diss., University of
California, Davis, 1995). Braden's *Spirits in Rebellion* devotes fewer than four
pages to Seicho-no-Ie (496–99).

188. Negron, 1, 239.

189. D'Andrade, *Charles Fillmore*.

190. "Silence," photocopy of twelve-page pamphlet from the Unity Archives, sent to
the author by archivist Eric Page, February 26, 2007, pp. 1, 11.

191. Charles Fillmore, "Notes and Comments," *Unity* 66, no. 1 (January 1927): 7.

192. "Lessons in Truth by H. Emilie Cady," https://www.truthunity.net/books/
emilie-cady-lessons-in-truth, accessed July 17, 2018.

193. *Modern Thought* 1, no. 1 (April 1889): 10.

194. *Modern Thought* 1, no. 3 (June 1889): 16.

195. *Modern Thought* 1, no. 5 (August 1889): 11.

196. *Modern Thought* 1, no. 10 (February 1890): 1.

197. Ibid., 14–15.

198. *Unity*, April 1, 1896, 14. In the January 1927 issue of the magazine, Fillmore
reaffirmed "the Buddhist or Theosophical idea of reincarnation of souls"
and reported a meeting with the formerly Theosophical "World Teacher"
Krishnamurti on pp. 3, 6.

199. In 2008, the *Daily Word* circulation figure included 647,909 regular and large-
print publications in English and Spanish; 153,010 visits to www.dailyword.
com; 430 mobile subscriptions; 90,000 subscriptions outside the United States;

20,000 free copies to hospitals and prisons; and 2,000 additional free copies. The "total reach" figure included 912,000 "pass-alongs"; that is, it assumed that nonsubscribers also read these publications. *Unity Magazine* had a circulation of 22,790 and a total reach of 55,790. The circulation figure includes free distribution of 240; the total reach includes 33,000 pass-alongs. Email from *Unity* circulation manager Michele Bartlett to Wakoh Shannon Hickey, April 21, 2008.

200. In 1963, in *Spirits in Rebellion*, Braden cited a *Wee Wisdom* circulation of 250,000. According to Unity archivist Eric E. Page, the figure was 174,000 in 1986, and 84,000 when it ceased publication in December 1991. Email from Eric Page to Shannon Hickey, April 15, 2008.

201. Braden, *Spirits in Rebellion*, 233–63; "About," Unity, http://www.unityonline. org/aboutunity/whoWeAre/faq.html, accessed July 24, 2017; de Chant, "Myrtle Fillmore and Her Daughters," 103.

202. See, for example, a promotion for *Woman's World* and *Messenger of Truth* in *Buddhist Ray* 1, no. 4 (April 1888): 32; and commentaries on articles about Buddhism published previously in *New Thought*, which appeared in *Buddhist Ray* 2, no. 4 (April 1889): 28; and 2, no. 5 (May 1889): 36.

203. *Buddhist Ray* 2, no. 2 (February 1889): 10.

204. Schmidt, *Restless Souls*, 170–71.

CHAPTER 4

1. Frankiel, *California's Spiritual Frontiers*; Braden, *Spirits in Rebellion*, 164–65. Trine's ideas about the "law of attraction"—that we draw positive or negative things to ourselves with our thoughts—have endured for more than a century. Rhonda Byrne's 2007 book, *The Secret*, which discusses the law of attraction, was likewise a smash hit, and as of July 2015 it was still Amazon.com's top seller in the "Mental and Spiritual Healing" category.

2. Satter, *Each Mind a Kingdom*, 80. The magazine article she cites is Paul Tyner, "The Metaphysical Movement," *American Monthly Review of Reviews* 25, no. 3 (March 1902): 312–13.

3. The organizations were Light, Love, Truth, (launched c. 1885, by Elizabeth Stuart); the Hopkins Christian Science Association (1886, by Emma Curtis Hopkins); Divine Science (1886, by Malinda Cramer and Nona Brooks); the Homes of Truth (1887, by Annie Rix Militz); the Unity School of Christianity (1890, by Myrtle and Charles Fillmore); Mental Science (c. 1895, by Helen Wilmans); and the Church and School of the New Civilization (1905, by Julia Seton Sears). Two national New Thought organizations ceased operating by 1919, when the first history of the New Thought movement was produced (Materra, 87–89).

4. Frankiel, 69, 152n19.

5. For a list of seminaries and schools, see "International New Thought Alliance," https://newthoughtalliance.org, accessed July 21, 2018. Scroll down for the list

of links. The member organization data comes from "Group Members," *New Thought* (Spring 2018), 18–22, https://newthoughtalliance.org/wp-content/uploads/2018/06/2018-Spring-New-Thought-mag.pdf, accessed July 21, 2018. Major New Thought denominations today include the Universal Foundation for Better Living, the Association of Unity Churches International, the Divine Science Federation International, the Centers for Spiritual Living (formerly the Church of Religious Science), and Seicho-no-Ie.

6. Materra, appendix 2, 396–455.

7. Ibid., 110, 359–60, 398–501. Of the 117 early New Thought journals, twenty-one continued after 1905, making a total of more than sixty in circulation through at least the first decade of the twentieth century. Most of these journals ceased publication by the 1920s; one continued to 1951, and at least one, *Unity*, is still in print. A bibliography of New Thought books produced in 1973 listed more than two thousand titles (Whaley, "The Collection and Preservation of the Materials of the New Thought Movement"). Satter, *Each Mind a Kingdom*, 80. Satter cites a magazine article estimating the number of New Thought adherents at one million in 1902: Paul Tyner, "The Metaphysical Movement," *American Monthly Review of Reviews* 25, no. 3 (March 1902): 312–13. According to Lola Williamson, Psychiana began as a New Thought denomination in 1928 and spread through mail-order lessons; another group, called the I AM Activity, spread during the 1930s, and at its peak in 1938 claimed a million members (31).

8. Satter, *Each Mind a Kingdom*, 226.

9. Carroll, Henry King. *The Religious Forces of the United States: Enumerated, Classified, and Described: Returns for 1900 and 1910 Compared with the Government Census of 1890: Condition and Characteristics of Christianity in the United States.* Rev. and brought down to 1910 ed. New York: Charles Scribner, 1912.

10. James, *The Varieties of Religious Experience*, 90–91.

11. Ibid., 91.

12. Worcester et al., *Religion and Medicine*, 51. Worcester calls mercury, strychnine, and arsenic "old standbys" in medical treatment.

13. The Spanish Flu pandemic of 1918 affected an estimated one-third of the global population and killed tens of millions worldwide, including hundreds of thousands of Americans. Orthodox medical methods were little help. Alternative therapies may have been less toxic, but faith in the mind's power to overcome the flu virus must have been sorely challenged by the mortality rate.

14. Caplan, 3–4.

15. Ibid., 4.

16. Ibid., 84–88.

17. Tweed, *The American Encounter with Buddhism*, 92–94.

18. Zinn, *A People's History of the United States*, chapter 11, "Robber Barons and Rebels."

19. Baker, "The Spiritual Unrest," 193–94.
20. Gifford, *The Emmanuel Movement*, 16–21. Incidentally, Worcester was related to several Swedenborgian ministers (10–12).
21. Worcester, *Life's Adventure*, 275.
22. Worcester et al., 14.
23. Ibid., 4.
24. Ibid., 10.
25. Ibid., 137.
26. Ibid., 10–11.
27. Ibid., 12.
28. Baker, "The Spiritual Unrest," 192.
29. Worcester et al., 382–83.
30. Baker, "The Spiritual Unrest," 203.
31. Worcester et al., 6.
32. Greene, "The Emmanuel Movement," 504, 509.
33. Caplan, 130; Greene, 518.
34. Worcester et al., 2.
35. Ibid., 111.
36. Ibid., 133.
37. Smith and Adelman, "In Sickness and in Wealth."
38. Worcester et al., 147–48.
39. Ibid., 4–5.
40. Ibid., 111–12.
41. Ibid., 134.
42. Ibid.
43. Ibid., 123.
44. Ibid., 134.
45. Ibid., 137. Invoking a stereotype, Worcester described Jews as an exception to this rule, "as they are both sober and nervous."
46. Ibid.
47. Ibid., 138.
48. Ibid., 139.
49. Ibid.
50. Ibid., 159.
51. Ibid., 158.
52. Worcester, *Life's Adventure*, 275.
53. Worcester et al., 140.
54. Ibid., 237.
55. Ibid., 241.
56. To offer just a few recent examples: Glaser, "The False Gospel of Alcoholics Anonymous"; Hari, *Chasing the Scream* and "The Likely Cause of Addiction Has Been Discovered, and It Is Not What You Think."

57. Worcester et al., 249.
58. Ibid., 66.
59. Ibid., 69.
60. Ibid., 67.
61. Ibid., 317–18.
62. Ibid., 152.
63. Ibid., 93.
64. Ibid., 106.
65. Ibid., 106–7.
66. Both Worcester and McComb indicate that they are familiar with both Buddhism and Vedanta, and that they admire the Buddha, but like most other European and American observers during the Victorian period, they regard Buddhism as fundamentally negating everything they regard as "religion": God, the soul, prayer, and immortality (ibid., 11). See also Tweed, *The American Encounter with Buddhism*. Although practices of renunciation are fundamental to Buddhist monasticism, particularly in the Theravāda tradition, much Māhāyana Buddhist philosophy tends to be more world-affirming.
67. Worcester et al., 94–95.
68. Ibid., 103.
69. Ibid., 103–4.
70. Ibid., 107.
71. Ibid., 219.
72. Ibid., 220.
73. Ibid., 222.
74. Ibid., 232.
75. Ibid., 233.
76. Ibid., 351.
77. Ibid., 54.
78. Ibid., 54.
79. Ibid., 55.
80. Ibid., 57.
81. Ibid., 152.
82. Baker, "The Spiritual Unrest," 202.
83. Worcester et al., 381.
84. Prothero, *American Jesus*, 56–79, 87–97.
85. Worcester et al., 272.
86. Ibid., 331.
87. Stokes, *Ministry after Freud*, 26; Kehl, "The History and Method of the Immanuel [sic] Movement and of Associated Groups," 9; Caplan, 125–31, 200n9, 203–204n90; and Guthrie, ed. *Reader's Guide to Periodic Literature*, 714.
88. See the following by Worcester: "The Emmanuel Church Tuberculosis Class"; "The Results of the Emmanuel Movement," (February 1909); 27; and "The Results of the Emmanuel Movement," (December 1908); 25.

89. Benson, "What the 'Emmanuel Movement' Means as Interpreted by Dr. Worcester." This article also says Worcester had received 2,200 letters of inquiry over a period of six weeks.

90. Baker, "The Spiritual Unrest"; Caplan, 123–24; Kehl, 13.

91. Cunningham, "The Emmanuel Movement," 56–57.

92. Baker, "The Spiritual Unrest," 192.

93. Ibid.

94. Greene, 507–8. He cites sensational stories in the *Boston Journal*, December 13, 1906; *Detroit News*, December 16, 1906; and *Chicago Examiner*, June 9, 1907; and Worcester's denial in *Boston Transcript*, December 13, 1906.

95. Kehl, 9.

96. Baker, "The Spiritual Unrest," 205. Emphasis in original.

97. Ibid.

98. Ibid.

99. Coincidentally, Worcester, Massachusetts, is also the city where current medical interest in mindfulness meditation began. See chapter 4.

100. Caplan, *Mind Games*, 150–51.

101. Ibid., 119.

102. Stokes, 37–63, 195 nn10 and 13, citing Boisen, *Out of the Depths: An Autobiographical Study of Mental Disorder and Religious Experience* (New York: Harper & Brothers, 1960), 38–39.

103. The preceding history comes from Stokes, chapter 3, and "The Biography of Anton Theophilus Boisen," an undated essay by Rev. Robert Leas, past history manager for the Association for Clinical Pastoral Education, which published the document.

104. "Profile: Helen Flanders Dunbar," Psychology's Feminist Voices," http://www.feministvoices.com/helen-flanders-dunbar/, n.d., accessed July 21, 2018. See also Stokes, 77–89.

105. Stokes, 111.

106. Ibid., 114.

107. These include the Religio-Psychiatric Clinic in Peale's church (1935–50); the American Foundation of Religion and Psychiatry (1951–71), which gave rise to the American Association of Pastoral Counselors in 1963; the Academy of Religion and Mental Health (1954–71); the Blanton Peale Graduate Institute (founded 1968); and the Institutes of Religion and Health (founded 1972). "Blanton-Peale Timeline," Blanton-Peale Institute and Counseling Center, http://www.blantonpeale.org/timeline.html, accessed May 25, 2015.

108. Ehrenreich, *Bright-Sided*, 92, 212n32. She quotes Peale's comment on the back cover of Fenwicke L. Holmes, *Ernest Holmes: His Life and Times*: "Only those who knew me as a boy can fully appreciate what Ernest Holmes did for me. Why, he made me a positive thinker!" The book is available online at Self-Improvement E-books, http://self-improvement-ebooks.com/books/ehhlat.php, accessed July 9, 2017.

109. Harrington, *The Cure Within*, 121.
110. Peale, *The Power of Positive Thinking*, 184.
111. Materra, 332.
112. Although Henry Beecher is widely regarded as the discoverer of the placebo response, he was not the first to notice it. His 1955 paper, "The Powerful Placebo," was extremely influential, however. In it, he provided a meta-analysis of fifteen clinical trials that had used placebo controls and argued that, on average, a third of patients demonstrated measurable responses to placebo treatment, although the placebo substances were supposed to be inert. Subsequent critiques of this study have pointed to various problems in Beecher's analysis, but the article was nevertheless a major impetus for the adoption of randomized controlled trials in pharmaceutical research. Beecher had argued that randomized trials would distribute "placebo responder" patients more evenly across treatment groups and thereby improve the reliability of study results. He said that if roughly equal numbers of placebo responders were assigned to the control group, which received a placebo, and to the treatment group, which actually received the drug being studied, then any significant improvement in the treatment group could be attributed to the drug.
113. Daniel Moerman, Anne Harrington, and others have written interesting studies of the roles that cultural meanings play in the ways that placebos have been understood over time and the kinds of responses that patients have to them. In *Meaning, Medicine, and the "Placebo Effect,"* Moerman notes, for example, that larger placebo pills tend to evoke a stronger response than smaller ones. Four pills evoke stronger responses than two; capsules evoke stronger responses than tablets; injections stronger responses than pills. Responses vary by culture, as well. Harrington states in "The Many Meanings of the Placebo Effect" that within orthodox medicine, placebos were once seen as unethical; today they are widely regarded as an essential control in clinical trials. Placebo responses have been regarded as a "medical humbug," as a medical mystery, and as powerful evidence for the benefits of mind-body medicine. See also Harrison, *The Placebo Effect*.
114. Iwamura, *Virtual Orientalism*. Chapter 2 is an insightful media analysis of Suzuki as the personification of Zen.
115. Harrington and Dunne, "When Mindfulness Is Therapy," 623.
116. Ibid., 624.
117. Barrett, *Zen Buddhism*, 3, citing Suzuki, *Essays in Zen Buddhism*, 11.
118. Harrington and Dunne, 623.
119. Ibid., 624.
120. Fromm and Suzuki, *Zen Buddhism and Psychoanalysis*. See also Dawn Lawson, "D. T. Suzuki," *American National Biography Online*, http://www.anb.org/articles/08/08-01898.html, accessed June 19, 2016; Fields, 206.
121. Williamson, 55–71. See also the website of the Self-Realization Fellowship: https://www.yogananda-srf.org.

122. Goldberg, 134.

123. Kabat-Zinn, "Some Reflections on the Origins of MBSR."

124. Williamson writes, "This may be because European Orientalists and missionaries in India, from the eighteenth to the early twentieth centuries imagined a pristine Golden Age, identified with the ancient scriptures of the *Vedas* and *Upanishads*. They contrasted this with a later perverse and degenerate age, which they believed began with the growth of Tantra in the Middle Ages. During the Hindu Renaissance (also referred to as the Bengal Renaissance) of the nineteenth and early twentieth centuries, Hindus accepted this viewpoint as their own and began to propagate it" (14).

125. Ibid., 23.

126. Williamson notes that Ram Mohun Roy, who founded the Brahmo Samaj (Divine Society) in India in 1828 and was a key developer of neo-Hinduism, was strongly influenced by Unitarianism, which emphasized rationality and downplayed ritual: he helped to establish a Unitarian church in India and corresponded with the American Unitarian ministers William Ellery Channing and Henry Ware (24).

127. Ibid., 15, 18–20. She examines three groups that she describes as Hindu-Inspired Meditation Movements, or HIMMs: the Self-Realization Fellowship, founded by Paramahansa Yogananda in 1920; Transcendental Meditation, founded by Maharishi Mahesh Yogi in 1961; and Siddha Yoga Dham Associates (SYDA), founded by Swami Muktananda in 1975.

128. Goldberg, 166; see 51–75 for an extended discussion of the Maharishi. Obituary: http://www.nytimes.com/2008/02/06/world/asia/06maharishi-1.html?_r=0, accessed July 5, 2016.

129. Koppel, "Maharishi Mahesh Yogi, Spiritual Leader, Dies." See also the Transcendental Meditation website: https://www.tm.org.

130. Benson and Proctor's *Beyond the Relaxation Response* claims that religious faith can enhance the physiological benefits of the relaxation response, and stresses that the specific content of one's faith does not matter.

131. Harrington and Dunne, 626.

132. In addition to Murphy and Donovan, the most thorough bibliography is Jarrell, 12. Regarding TM, see Kanellakos and Ferguson, *The Psychobiology of Transcendental Meditation*. A revised edition under the same title was published in 1982 and is listed by Maharishi International University, "Bibliography and Reprint Catalogue: Scientific Research on the Transcendental Meditation and TM-Siddhi Program, Revised May 1982" (Wright State University Library, 1982). See also Monro et al.

133. Maharishi International University, "Bibliography and Reprint Catalogue."

134. Mansky and Wallerstedt, "Complementary Medicine in Palliative Care and Cancer Symptom Management"; Seeman et al., "Religiosity/Spirituality and Health"; Kondwani and Lollis, "Is There a Role for Stress Management in Reducing Hypertension in African Americans?"; Frumkin et al., "Nonpharmacologic Control of Essential Hypertension in Man."

135. Krisanaprakornkit et al., "Meditation Therapy for Anxiety Disorders"; Canter and Ernst, "Insufficient Evidence to Conclude Whether or Not Transcendental Meditation Decreases Blood Pressure" and "The Cumulative Effects of Transcendental Meditation on Cognitive Function."
136. Murphy and Donovan. Murphy discusses his meditation practice and early influences in Badiner, "A Buddhist-Psychedelic History of Esalen Institute."
137. Kripal.
138. Ibid., 141.
139. Crabtree, *From Mesmer to Freud*, vii.
140. McMahan, *The Making of Buddhist Modernism*.

CHAPTER 5

1. Worcester and McComb, *The Christian Religion as a Healing Power*, 96.
2. Kabat-Zinn, "Some Reflections on the Origins of MBSR," 282.
3. Kabat-Zinn, *Coming to Our Senses*.
4. Kabat-Zinn, "Coming to Our Senses," author's field notes. Kabat-Zinn reiterated this assertion three times during the lecture.
5. Kabat-Zinn, "Toward the Mainstreaming of American Dharma Practice," 505.
6. Ibid., 489.
7. Kabat-Zinn, "Some Reflections on the Origins of MBSR," 285.
8. Ibid., 287.
9. Tweed, *Crossing and Dwelling*, 55.
10. "Mountains and Waters Sutra," 99.
11. Wilson, "The Religion of Mindfulness," 120.
12. Wilson, *Mindful America*.
13. Tweed, *Crossing and Dwelling*, 54.
14. Smart, *The World's Religions*, 11–22.
15. Albanese, 13–15.
16. Kabat-Zinn, "Toward the Mainstreaming of American Dharma Practice," 483.
17. See Keown, 194–95.
18. Kabat-Zinn and University of Massachusetts Medical Center/Worcester Stress Reduction Clinic, 168.
19. Ibid., 157.
20. Ibid., 242. Note that "thoughts, feelings, perceptions, and impulses" recall the Four Foundations of Mindfulness described in the Buddhist sūtra by that name. In that Buddhist text, however, the four are physical sensations, reactions to stimuli (positive, negative, or neutral), consciousness, and mental objects. The latter two terms refer to specific states of mind and related doctrines, known as the Three Poisons, the Five Hindrances, the Six Internal and External Sense Bases, the Seven Factors of Enlightenment, and the Four Noble Truths.
21. Kabat-Zinn, "Some Reflections on the Origins of MBSR," 300.

22. Braden, *Spirits in Rebellion*, 10.

23. Kabat-Zinn, *Coming to Our Senses*, 540. The series of essays is grouped under the heading "Healing the Body Politic," 499–580.

24. Kabat-Zinn, *Coming to Our Senses*, 483.

25. Ibid., 479.

26. Ibid., 515.

27. Ibid., 495.

28. Gethin, "On Some Definitions of Mindfulness," 268.

29. Williams and Kabat-Zinn, "Mindfulness."

30. Fronsdal and Erdstein, "Two Practices, One Path," 97–98. During intensive meditation practice in Burma, Fronsdal experienced a profound inner stillness, "a dimension of mind or of awareness that is unconstructed, with no movement or agitation in [it]. It is somewhat like remaining aware of a peaceful silence while simultaneously hearing the ring of a bell. The sense of the unconstructed became very important because it highlighted how everything else is constructed. Any understanding or sense of self is a construction of the mind—it has its role in life but it has no inherent existence. Any understanding of the world or even of Buddhist practice is a construct of the mind. Paradoxically, for practitioners, Buddhist teachings are constructs of mind that point beyond themselves" (102).

31. Gethin, 263.

32. Bodhi, "What Does Mindfulness Really Mean?," 25.

33. Ibid., 22.

34. Ibid., 26.

35. Ibid., 28. Note: In *The Questions of King Milinda*, the monk Nāgasena emphasizes the ethical dimensions of mindful in distinguishing wholesome from unwholesome mental states.

36. Gethin, 275.

37. Sharf, "Epilogue," 140–41.

38. See, for example, Arai, *Bringing Zen Home*; Reader and Tanabe, *Practically Religious*; Williams, *The Other Side of Zen*; and Wilson, *Mindful America*.

39. Other formulations include skillful means in preaching the dharma (*upāya-kauśalya*), vow, spiritual powers, and knowledge.

40. "Highlights from the Science and Clinical Applications of Meditation Conference: An Overview of the Investigating the Mind 2005 Meeting with the Dalai Lama," (Washington, D.C.: Mind and Life Institute, Mind and Life XIII, 2007), CD-ROM. These remarks occur at the end of the concluding presentation by Ralph Snyderman, M.D., of Duke University Medical Center.

41. Magid and Poirier, "The Three Shaky Pillars of Western Buddhism," 40.

42. Ibid., 41.

43. Ibid., 42.

44. Ibid., 44.

45. See Dunne, "Toward an Understanding of Non-Dual Mindfulness."

46. Sharf, "Sanbōkyōdan," 418.
47. A nice anthology of essays exploring this point is Wirth et al., *Engaging Dōgen's Zen*.
48. Magid and Poirier, 45.
49. Bodhi, 25.
50. Kabat-Zinn, "Some Reflections on the Origins of MBSR," 286–87.
51. The Kwan Um School of Zen website, http://www.kwanumzen.org/zen-centers/, accessed July 21, 2018.
52. Kabat-Zinn, "Some Reflections on the Origins of MBSR," 287.
53. Ibid., 289.
54. In the acknowledgments of *Full Catastrophe Living*, Kabat-Zinn thanks the following Vipassanā teachers: Larry Rosenberg, Christopher Titmuss, Christina Feldman, and Corrado Pensa.
55. Kabat-Zinn, "Some Reflections on the Origins of MBSR," 289.
56. Found in the Pali Canon at both Majjhima Nikāya 10 and Dīgha Nikāya 22.
57. Kabat-Zinn, "Toward the Mainstreaming of American Dharma Practice," references throughout the text. Also Kabat-Zinn, "Some Reflections on the Origins of MBSR," 285.
58. Kabat-Zinn, "Some Reflections on the Origins of MBSR," 285.
59. In the Council Process, a group sits in a circle and passes an object, called a "talking piece," among participants. Whoever holds the object has the floor and is allowed to speak uninterruptedly. When finished, the person relinquishes the object, and another picks it up and speaks. Participants are asked to give complete attention to each speaker, instead of formulating responses, and to speak spontaneously "from the heart" when holding the talking piece. This process is also said to be a tradition among Plains and Iroquois Federation tribes. Zimmerman and Coyle, *The Way of Council*, 4. Zimmerman and Coyle learned it at Ojai Foundation, a California retreat center founded on land originally purchased by the Theosophical Society leader Annie Besant in 1927. Joan Halifax was director of the Ojai Foundation from 1979 to 1990, when she moved to Santa Fe, New Mexico, and launched the Upaya Zen Center. During her tenure at Ojai, various Buddhist teachers led retreats and classes there. Ojai Foundation website, https://ojaifoundation.org/about-us/our-history/, accessed July 21, 2018. Halifax is a leader of the Zen Peacemaker Order, which employs the Council Process at its gatherings. Hickey, "Religious Leadership in American Zen." According to the Ojai Foundation website, the Council Process is also employed at Spirit Rock Meditation Center, a Vipassanā retreat facility in Woodacre, California.
60. Annie Besant had groomed J. Krishnamurti from childhood to lead the Theosophical Society. He broke with it in 1929; he lived (and died) at Ojai.
61. See, for example, "Insight Meditation on Choiceless Awareness," Insight Meditation, http://www.insightmeditation.org/insight-meditation-on-choiceless-awarene, accessed July 25, 2017.

62. Kabat-Zinn, "Some Reflections on the Origins of MBSR," 292.

63. Williams and Kabat-Zinn, "Mindfulness," 3.

64. Kabat-Zinn and University of Massachusetts Medical Center/Worcester Stress Reduction Clinic, *Full Catastrophe Living*, 12.

65. Kabat-Zinn, "Some Reflections on the Origins of MBSR," 283.

66. Ibid., 290.

67. Ibid., 298.

68. Ibid., 299.

69. Kabat-Zinn, "Toward the Mainstreaming of American Dharma Practice," 481.

70. Kabat-Zinn also universalizes the Buddhist community, or *sangha*: "I try to look at *sangha* nonlinearly and nondualistically, so the *sangha's* everybody, as far as I can see, and it's not just the Buddhists" (ibid., 526). A more traditional definition of *sangha* is either limited to the community of ordained Buddhist monks and nuns or to the "fourfold *sangha*" of Buddhist monks, nuns, laymen and laywomen. According to *The Oxford Dictionary of Buddhism*, a reputable reference work, "the minimal requirements for admission to the Saṃgha [variant spelling] are faith in the 'three jewels' (*triratna*) of the Buddha, the Dharma, and the Saṃgha (in this context meaning the arya-saṃgha [ordained monks and nuns]), usually demonstrated in the act of 'taking refuge'" (Keown, 20, 247, 310). Kabat-Zinn's universal definition is, again, a modern interpretation.

71. Murphy and Donovan, 2.

72. Payne, "How Not to Talk about the Pure Land," 150. See also Sharf, "Buddhist Modernism and the Rhetoric of Meditative Experience" and "Epilogue"; Cooper, "Losing Our Religion"; McMahan, *The Making of Buddhist Modernism*.

73. Sharf, "Epilogue," 142.

74. Sharf, "Buddhist Modernism and the Rhetoric of Meditative Experience," 258–59.

75. Sharf, "Epilogue," 150.

76. Ibid., 145.

77. Ibid.

78. Ibid., 146.

79. Ibid., 151.

80. Ibid., 147.

81. Sharf, "Sanbōkyōdan," 427–28. Note that I have replaced Sharf's spelling, Sanbōkyōdan, with the spelling used by the movement.

82. Haga and Kisala, "The New Age in Japan," 239.

83. Heuman, "A New Way Forward," 48.

84. Ibid., 49.

85. Ibid., 50.

86. Ibid., 102.

87. Ibid., 102–3.

CHAPTER 6

1. Jeff Brantley, Mindfulness-Based Stress Reduction, class at Duke University, author's field notes, April 18, 2007.

2. Kabat-Zinn stresses this point repeatedly in his writings and public statements. One recent example can be found at Kabat-Zinn, "Indra's Net at Work," 240. In the same document, however, he notes that Mindfulness practice improved athletic performances by the Chicago Bulls basketball team and the 1984 U.S. Olympic Men's Rowing Team (247–48).

3. Kabat-Zinn, "Some Reflections on the Origins of MBSR," 292.

4. Ibid., 293.

5. Ibid., 297.

6. As we have seen, Linehan's version of Zen is a very modern one. Linehan, *Cognitive-Behavioral Treatment of Borderline Personality Disorder*.

7. Gyatso, *Ethics for the New Millennium*.

8. Goleman, *Destructive Emotions*, 7.

9. Ibid., 7–11.

10. "A Map of the Human Brain," *The Week*, August 12, 2016, 21. Susan Scutti, "New Brain Map Identifies 97 Previously Unknown Regions," CNN.com, July 20, 2016, http://www.cnn.com/2016/07/20/health/new-brain-map/index.html, accessed August 14, 2016, citing Glasser et al., "A Multi-Modal Parcellation of Human Cerebral Cortex."

11. Dumit, "Producing Brain Images of Mind." My thanks to Barry Saunders of the University of North Carolina–Chapel Hill School of Medicine for bringing these issues to my attention. Mellon-Sawyer Seminar: Human Being, Human Diversity, and Human Welfare, a Cross-Disciplinary and Cross-Cultural Study in Culture, Science, and Medicine, at the Franklin Humanities Institute, Duke University, March 19, 2007.

12. Eklund et al., "Cluster Failure."

13. Rosenbaum, "Mindfulness Myths," 55–57.

14. Britton, "Mindful Binge Drinking and Blobology."

15. Poirier, "Mischief in the Marketplace for Mindfulness," 23.

16. For additional information about this research, see Harrington, *The Cure Within*, 230–42.

17. Britton.

18. Tang et al., "The Neuroscience of Mindfulness Meditation."

19. Purser and Loy, "Beyond McMindfulness."

20. Tang et al., 214.

21. Grossman and Van Dam, "Mindfulness, by Any Other Name," 221.

22. Rosenbaum, "Mindfulness Myths."

23. Britton.

24. Baer, "Measuring Mindfulness."

25. Rosenbaum, "Mindfulness Myths," 61.

26. Ibid., 63.
27. Ibid.
28. Ibid., 64.
29. Ibid., 66.
30. Ibid., 67.
31. Ibid., 68.
32. Kabat-Zinn, "Some Reflections on the Origins of MBSR," 281–82.
33. Ibid., 284.
34. Ibid.
35. Ibid., 296.
36. Tisdale, "The Buffet," 87–88.
37. Booth, "Mindfulness Therapy Comes at a High Price for Some."
38. Lindahl et al., "The Varieties of Contemplative Experience." This information appears on page 4 of the PDF version; the online version does not include page numbers. Additional page citations below also refer to the PDF version.
39. "The Varieties of Contemplative Experience: Project Overview," https://www.brown.edu/research/labs/britton/research/varieties-contemplative-experience, accessed July 14, 2017.
40. Ibid., 15.
41. Ibid., 21.
42. Ibid., 29.
43. Ibid., 26.
44. Ibid., 25.
45. Poirier, 26.
46. Brown, "Does Mindfulness Belong in Public Schools?"
47. Ibid., 64.
48. Considerable literature has developed on prayer and healing, and a number of clinical studies have explored it with varied results, but that subject is beyond the scope of this book. Here I focus on meditation and yoga. For more information on prayer and healing, see, for example, works by Daniel J. Benor, Larry Dossey, Harold Koenig, Keith Meador, Marilyn Schlitz, and Jeff Levin. For more on religion and medicine, see the work of Linda L. Barnes, Pierce Salguero, and other scholars associated with the Religions, Medicines, and Healing Unit of the American Academy of Religion.
49. Bodhi, 36.

CHAPTER 7

1. Thanks to Jeff Wilson for suggesting this term.
2. Perennialism is also a feature of Theosophy and of the late twentieth-century New Age religions that New Thought helped to birth.
3. Among the largest collections of New Thought materials are those of the New York Public Library, the Mary Baker Eddy Library in Boston, the Library of Congress, the Graduate Theological Union in Berkeley, and the University of

California (especially the Berkeley, Los Angeles, and Santa Barbara campuses). The extensive collection of materials assembled by Charles Braden and initially housed at the Bridwell Library of Southern Methodist University was donated to the International New Thought Alliance. Housed in Tempe, Arizona, the archives have no online catalogue and are staffed by a very part-time archivist. The Unity archive at Unity Village, near Kansas City, Missouri, also has a large collection of materials and a helpful archivist. Two bibliographies would be useful in this research. The most recent was compiled by Materra and included in several appendices to his PhD dissertation. The first is an annotated list of fifty-three New Thought serials that he consulted; appendix 2 is a sixty-page bibliography of New Thought books and journals published through 1905; appendix 3 is a forty-five-page bibliography of materials published from 1906 to 1918. Appendix 7 lists periodicals available at the New York Public Library, the Library of Congress, the Unity archives, and the University of California, Santa Barbara. Another, ninety-page bibliography containing approximately 2,000 titles is by Whaley. A copy is available in the reference section of the Graduate Theological Union library.

4. Stark and Bainbridge, *The Future of Religion*. See especially chapter 2.
5. Huxley, *The Perennial Philosophy*, vii.
6. Risher, "World View."
7. Schreiber, "The Surprising Science of Mindfulness," 10–11.
8. Shaffer, "14 Ways to Find More Zen."
9. Kabat-Zinn, *Coming to Our Senses*, 7.
10. Ibid., 131.
11. Eddy, *Science and Health with Key to the Scriptures*, 147.
12. Gottschalk, *The Emergence of Christian Science in American Religious Life*, 249–50.
13. Holmes, *Science of Mind*, 177–78.
14. Kabat-Zinn, "Toward the Mainstreaming of American Dharma Practice," 487–88.
15. Ibid., 515.
16. Such problems have been cited recently in meta-analyses of research on antidepressant drugs. See, for example, "Anti-Depressants' 'Little Effect': New Generation Anti-Depressants Have Little Clinical Benefit for Most Patients, Research Suggests," *BBC News Online*, February 26, 2008, http://news.bbc.co.uk/2/hi/health/7263494.stm. Critics charge that when these factors are considered, available evidence suggests that certain drugs may be only slightly more effective than placebos. In the case of research on meditation, corporate interests may not be a significant factor (meditation is a less profitable product than pharmaceuticals), but research designs and interpretation of results can still be problematic.
17. *PBS Presents: Mindfulness Goes Mainstream*, produced by Nicolas Stein, Anne Adams, and Laurie Donnelly (Public Broadcasting Service, released August 4, 2017), https://www.pbs.org/video/mindfulness-goes-mainstream-jjfwvu/, accessed November 3, 2018.

18. Clarke, *Oriental Enlightenment*, 207.

19. See Prothero, *The White Buddhist*.

20. Snodgrass; Droit.

21. Vivekenanda, "Hinduism as a Religion." He also remarked that "some of the very best" rishis who transmitted Vedic revelations were women, obscuring the strongly patriarchal norms of Vedic and Hindu tradition.

22. Ibid., 107.

23. Clarke, 207.

24. As noted earlier, Kabat-Zinn is an admirer of Krishnamurti, and the meditation practice of "Choiceless Awareness" that Krishnamurti advocated is taught in MBSR courses.

25. Wilson, *Mindful America*, 73.

26. The website of *10 Percent Happier* is http://www.10percenthappier.com; see also https://gifts.10percenthappier.com/collections/frontpage, both accessed August 15, 2017.

27. See *PBS Presents: Mindfulness Goes Mainstream*.

28. Ron Purser and David Loy, "Beyond McMindfulness," Huffington Post July 1, 2013, updated August 31, 2013. http://www.huffingtonpost.com/ron-purser/beyond-mcmindfulness_b_3519289.html, accessed November 3, 2018.

29. Ibid.

30. Carrette and King, *Selling Spirituality*, 66–67.

31. Ibid., 83. The sociologist Robert Bellah dubbed this approach to religion "Sheilaism," after the nurse who described her version of it during an interview for his book *Habits of the Heart*.

32. Carrette and King, 78.

33. Poirier, 14.

34. Muravchik, *American Protestantism in the Age of Psychology*, 14.

35. Ibid., 4.

36. Sharf, "Epilogue," 149.

37. Magid and Poirier, 48.

38. Cooper, "Losing Our Religion," 48.

39. Ibid., 47.

40. Magid and Poirier, 50.

41. Ibid., 51.

42. Poirier, 21.

43. Stroud, "Mindfulness of Mind," 112.

44. Trudy Goodman, in Blacker et al., "Forum: The Mindfulness Movement." Now Trudy Goodman Kornfield, she is the founder and executive director of InsightLA, which teaches Vipassanā meditation, MBSR, and Mindfulness-Based Compassion Training. The spouse of Vipassanā founder Jack Kornfield, she cofounded the Institute for Meditation and Psychotherapy in Cambridge, Massachusetts.

45. Cooper, "Losing Our Religion," 49.

46. Saddhatissa, "The Chapter of the Eights."

47. Kabat-Zinn, "Some Reflections on the Origins of MBSR," 294.
48. Ibid., 294–95.
49. Senauke, "One Body, Whole Life," 75.
50. Ibid.
51. Ibid.
52. Ibid., 78.
53. Kabat-Zinn, *Coming to Our Senses*, 14.
54. Ibid., 69–70.
55. According to the conference website, mindful leadership is "about recognizing that your leadership is in service to others. It's about creating the space in your life to cultivate self-awareness and compassion, and leading with authenticity in a way that inspires others. Doing this, we can transform our own lives, our organizations, our communities—and the world." "2017 Mindful Leadership Summit," Mindful Leader, http://www.mindfulleader.org/#home, accessed August 10, 2017.
56. Personal email to Wakoh Shannon Hickey from Jennifer Fiore, events and outreach coordinator for Mindful Leader, August 10, 2017; "Mindful Leadership Summit Venue & Hotel," http://www.mindfulleader.org/2017-venue-hotel/, accessed August 10, 2017.
57. The white cofounder of Conscious Capitalism is John Mackey, CEO of Whole Foods, where *Mindful* magazine can be purchased at checkout registers. Whole Foods was recently gobbled up by Amazon, reportedly netting Mackey $8 million. A pioneering purveyor of organic foods, he is noted for libertarian political and economic views; a relatively modest lifestyle, given his fortune; and opposition to organized labor and universal, publicly funded healthcare.
58. "Seven Stones Leadership: Course of Study" and "Destination Courses," https://www.sevenstonesleadership.com/programs-services/individuals/course-of-study/; https://www.sevenstonesleadership.com/programs-services/individuals/destination-courses/, both accessed August 10, 2017.
59. Even in the "Varieties of Contemplative Experience" study, described in chapter 6, among the sixty participants, 94 percent were white, and 67 percent held graduate degrees (Lindahl et al., 14).
60. Smith and Adelman, "In Sickness and in Wealth."
61. Ehrenreich conflates Christian Science, New Thought, and Peale-esque "positive thinking" in ways I do not.
62. Ehrenreich, 205–6.
63. Kabat-Zinn, *Coming to Our Senses*, 516.
64. Ibid., 549.
65. Ibid., 519.
66. This attitude—or perhaps faith—is also apparent in Varela et al., *The Embodied Mind*.
67. The list is long and troubling: Eido Tai Shimano, Joshu Sasaki, Chögyam Trungpa, Ösel Tendzin, Sakyong Mipham Rinpoche, Taizan Maezumi, Dainen

Katagiri, Richard Baker, Dennis Genpo Merzel, Jetsunma Akhön Lhamo, Noah Levine, and more.

68. Hickey, "Religious Leadership in American Zen"; Hickey, "Meditation Is Not Enough."

69. Ehrenreich, 206.

APPENDIX

1. Albanese, 16.

2. Early New Thought materials can be found in the Library of Congress, the New York Public Library, the Mary Baker Eddy Library in Boston, the Newberry Library in Chicago, the Graduate Theological Union Library in Berkeley, California, and two campuses of the University of California, at Santa Barbara and Berkeley. The archives of the International New Thought Alliance, in Scottsdale, Arizona, are still largely uncatalogued.

3. Bender, *Rethinking American History in a Global Age.*

4. Seager, *Encountering the Dharma*, xi.

5. Albanese, 506. Among the teachers so characterized are "Ramana Maharshi, Chögyam Trungpa, Tarthang Tulku, [Shunryu] Suzuki Roshi, and Jiddu Krishnamurti." On p. 483 she also characterizes American interpreters of Taoism as promoting a kind of East Asian Vedanta, another inappropriate conflation of categories.

6. Payne, "How Not to Talk about the Pure Land," 163.

7. Ibid., 155.

8. Harrington, *The Cure Within.*

9. Harrington persuasively critiques the concept of "stress" as "deeply unwieldy," in part because it "had come to stand in for virtually every class of human unease, distress, and malaise" (ibid., 253). However, one example of gender bias in medical research can be found in a 2000 study showing that women's responses to stress differ significantly from men's. While both women and men may have a *physiological* "fight or flight" reaction, which can be countered by the "relaxation response" that Herbert Benson discovered in his studies of Transcendental Meditation, *behaviorally* women typically respond to stress in a pattern the researchers called "tend and befriend." In other words, women engage in nurturing activities and affiliate with others in ways that promote safety and reduce risk, both for themselves and their children. This may be related to gender-related biochemical differences: fight-or-flight is associated with the production of androgens, and tend-and-befriend is associated with the production of estrogen and oxytocin. The study also noted that before 1995, only about 17 percent of participants in laboratory research were women. After reviewing two hundred studies related to stress conducted from 1985 to 2000, the researchers found that 66 percent of the 14,548 participants were male. Taylor et al., "Behavioral Responses to Stress in Females."

10. Harrington, *The Cure Within*, 124.

11. Ibid., 232.

12. Haller, *Swedenborg, Mesmer, and the Mind-Body Connection; The History of New Thought.*

13. Foucault, "Nietzsche, Genealogy, History."

14. Albanese, 515.

15. Wilson, *Mindful America*, 31.

16. Dorman, 5.

17. Deleuze and Guattari, *A Thousand Plateaus.*

18. Dorman, 6.

19. Ibid., 6–7.

20. Tweed's entire definition: "Religions are confluences of organic-cultural flows that intensify joy and confront suffering by drawing on human and suprahuman forces to make homes and cross boundaries." This definition is discussed further in chapter 5. Tweed's book examines his definition in detail (*Crossing and Dwelling*, 54).

21. Ibid., 59, 60.

22. Ibid., 57.

23. "As embodied beings produced by organic processes as much as by cultural practices, humans have certain neurological and physiological constraints on how they interact and how they transform their environment. However malleable human brains might be, they work in certain ways. Human eyes are positioned in the front of the body. And so on. Organic and cultural processes combine in complex ways" (ibid., 66).

24. In the anthology *Science and Religion around the World*, David N. Livingstone argues that when considering relationships, encounters, or conflicts between "science" and "religion," we do well to "pluralize, localize, hybridize, [and] politicize" our analysis. In other words, we must recognize that there are many sciences, which cannot all be lumped into a unitary category: they vary by time and place, ask different kinds of questions, employ different methods, and rest on different assumptions about the natural world. Thus we must *localize* the discussion, identifying the particular geographical and temporal contexts in which these terms are understood. Livingstone, "Which Science? Whose Religion?," 282.

25. Ibid., 172.

26. Tweed, *Crossing and Dwelling*, 13.

27. Ibid., 74.

Bibliography

SERIALS CONSULTED

American Historical Review
American Magazine
American Quarterly
The Atlantic
Buddhadharma
The Buddhist Ray
Daily Word
Harmony
Ladies' Home Journal
Lion's Roar
Maha Bodhi
Mindful
Modern Thought
The Nautilus
New Thought
Shambhala Sun
Tricycle
Unity
The Week

PRIMARY AND SECONDARY SOURCES

Adams, Fred Winslow. *Answer of the Emmanuel Movement: What Must I Do to Be Saved from Disease?* What Must I Do to Be Saved Series. Schenectady, NY: Capt. Webb Men's Club of the First Methodist Episcopal Church, 1908.

Ahlstrom, Sydney E. *A Religious History of the American People*. 2nd ed. New Haven, CT: Yale University Press, 2004.

Aiken, Bill, Al Rapaport, and Brian D. Hotchkiss. *Buddhism in America: The Official Record of the Landmark Conference on the Future of Buddhist Meditative Practices in the West, Boston, January 17–19, 1997*. Rutland, VT: Charles E. Tuttle, 1998.

Albanese, Catherine L. *A Republic of Mind and Spirit: A Cultural History of American Metaphysical Religion*. New Haven, CT: Yale University Press, 2007.

Allen, James. *As a Man Thinketh*. Family Inspirational Library. New York: Grosset & Dunlap, 1959.

Allen, Nicholas B., Richard Chambers, Wendy Knight, and Group Melbourne Academic Mindfulness Interest. "Mindfulness-Based Psychotherapies: A Review of Conceptual Foundations, Empirical Evidence and Practical Considerations." *Australian & New Zealand Journal of Psychiatry* 40, no. 4 (April 2006): 285–94.

Almond, Philip C. *The British Discovery of Buddhism*. Cambridge, UK: Cambridge University Press, 1988.

Anderson, C. Alan. *Healing Hypotheses: Horatio W. Dresser and the Philosophy of New Thought*. New York: Garland, 1993.

Arai, Paula Kane Robinson. *Bringing Zen Home: The Healing Heart of Japanese Women's Rituals*. Honolulu: University of Hawaiʻi Press, 2011.

Arnold, Sir Edwin. *The Light of Asia*. 1969. Reprint. Adyar, India: Theosophical Publishing House, 1997.

Austin, James H. *Zen and the Brain: Toward an Understanding of Meditation and Consciousness*. Cambridge: Massachusetts Institute of Technology Press, 1998.

Badiner, Allan Hunt. "A Buddhist-Psychedelic History of Esalen Institute: An Interview with Founder Michael Murphy and President George Leonard." In *Zig Zag Zen*, edited by Allan Hunt Badiner and Alex Grey, 77–83. San Francisco: Chronicle Books, 2002.

Baer, Hans A., and Merrill Singer. *African American Religion: Varieties of Protest and Accommodation*. 2nd ed. Knoxville: University of Tennessee Press, 2002.

Baer, Ruth A. "Measuring Mindfulness." *Contemporary Buddhism* 12, no. 1 (2011): 241–61.

———. "Mindfulness Training as a Clinical Intervention: A Conceptual and Empirical Review." *Clinical Psychology: Science and Practice* 10, no. 2 (2003): 125–43.

Bailly, Jean Sylvain, ed. *Rapport Des Commisaires Chárges Par Le Roi De L'examen Du Magnétisme Animal*. Paris: Imprimerie Royal, 1784.

Baker, Ray Stannard. *New Ideals in Healing*. New York: Stokes, 1909. Hathi Trust Digital Library. http://catalog.hathitrust.org/api/volumes/oclc/1678447.html.

———. "The Spiritual Unrest." *American Magazine* 67, no. 2 (December 1908): 192–205.

———. "The Spiritual Unrest: The New Mission of the Doctor." *American Magazine* (December 1909): 231–44.

Barrett, William, ed. *Zen Buddhism: Selected Writings of D. T. Suzuki*. Image edition. New York: Doubleday, 1956.

Barrows, John Henry. *The World's Parliament of Religions; an Illustrated and Popular Story of the World's First Parliament of Religions, Held in Chicago in Connection with the Columbian Exposition of 1893*. Chicago: Parliament Publishing Company, 1893.

Batchelor, Martine. "Meditation and Mindfulness." *Contemporary Buddhism* 12, no. 1 (2011): 157–64.

BCA Centennial History Project Committee, ed. *Buddhist Churches of America: A Legacy of the First 100 Years*. San Francisco: Buddhist Churches of America, 1998.

Bechert, Heinz. "Buddhist Revival in East and West." In *The World of Buddhism: Buddhist Monks and Nuns in Society and Culture*, edited by Richard F. Gombrich and Heinz Bechert, 273–85. New York: Thames and Hudson, 1991.

Beebe, Tom. *Who's Who in New Thought: Biographical Dictionary of New Thought—Personnel, Centers, Authors' Publications*. Lakemont, GA: CSA Press, 1977.

Beecher, H. K. "The Powerful Placebo." *Journal of the American Medical Association* 159, no. 17 (1955): 1602–6.

Bellah, Robert N. *Habits of the Heart: Individualism and Commitment in American Life*. Updated ed. Berkeley: University of California Press, 1996.

Bender, Thomas. *Rethinking American History in a Global Age*. Berkeley: University of California Press, 2002.

Benson, Allan L. "What the 'Emmanuel Movement' Means as Interpreted by Dr. Worcester: A Combination of Science and Religion in Treating Disease Its Basic Principle. Acts through Mental Suggestion and Aims to Aid and Supplement Physicians' Work." *New York Times*, November 22, 1908.

Benson, Herbert. *The Relaxation Response*. New York: Morrow, 1975.

Benson, Herbert, and William Proctor. *Beyond the Relaxation Response: How to Harness the Healing Power of Your Personal Beliefs*. New York: Berkley Books, 1985.

Besant, Annie. *Psychology: Essays and Addresses*. Vol. 1. Los Angeles: Theosophical Publishing House, American Branch, 1919.

Besant, Annie Wood. *A Study in Consciousness: A Contribution to the Science of Psychology*. 3d Adyar ed. Madras: Theosophical Publishing House, 1954.

Bishop, S. R. "What Do We Really Know about Mindfulness-Based Stress Reduction?" *Psychosomatic Medicine* 64 (2002): 71–83.

Blacker, Melissa Myozen, Barry Boyce, Diana Winston, Trudy Goodman, and Jenny Wilks. "Forum: The Mindfulness Movement. What Does It Mean for Buddhism?" *Buddhadharma, the Practitioner's Quarterly* (Spring 2015): 46–55.

Blavatsky, H. P. "A Collection of Notes and Appendices on an Article Entitled 'The Âryan-Arhat Esoteric Tenets on the Sevenfold Principle in Man,' by T. Subba Row, B.A., B.L." *The Theosophist* 3, no. 4 (1882). http://www.theosophy.org/Blavatsky/Articles/NotesOnSomeAryan-ArhatEsotericTenets.htm.

————. *Isis Unveiled: A Master-Key to the Mysteries of Ancient and Modern Science and Theology*. Vol. 1. 1877. Reprint. Los Angeles: Theosophy Co., 1975.

————. "Lamas and Druses." *The Theosophist* 2 (June 1881). Theosophy Library Online. http://www.theosophy.org/Blavatsky/Articles/LamasAndDruses.htm.

Blavatsky, Helena P. *Isis Unveiled: A Master-Key to the Mysteries of Ancient and Modern Science and Theology*. Los Angeles: Theosophy Co., 1977. Theosophy Library Online. http://www.theosophy.org/Blavatsky/Isis Unveiled/isis_unveiled1.htm.

————. *A Modern Panarion: A Collection of Fugitive Fragments*. Los Angeles: Theosophy Co., 1981. Theosophy Library Online. http://www.theosophy.org/Blavatsky/Modern Panarion/Panarion.htm.

Bodhi, Bhikkhu. "What Does Mindfulness Really Mean? A Canonical Perspective." *Contemporary Buddhism* 12, no. 1 (2011): 19–39.

Booth, Robert. "Mindfulness Therapy Comes at a High Price for Some, Say Experts." *The Guardian*, August 25, 2014.

Bowler, Kate. *Blessed: A History of the American Prosperity Gospel*. New York: Oxford University Press, 2013.

Boyce, Barry. "Two Sciences of Mind." *Lion's Roar*, September 1, 2005. http://www.lionsroar.com/two-sciences-of-mind/.

Braden, Charles S. *Spirits in Rebellion: The Rise and Development of New Thought*. Dallas, TX: Southern Methodist University Press, 1963.

————. *These Also Believe: A Study of Modern American Cults and Minority Religious Movements*. New York: Macmillan, 1949.

Braid, James, and Arthur Edward Waite. *Braid on Hypnotism: The Beginnings of Modern Hypnosis*. New York: Julian Press, 1960.

Braude, Ann. *Radical Spirits: Spiritualism and Women's Rights in Nineteenth Century America*. 2d ed. Bloomington: Indiana University Press, 2001.

————. "Women's History *Is* American Religious History." In *Retelling U.S. Religious History*, edited by Thomas A. Tweed, 87–107. Berkeley: University of California Press, 1997.

Britton, Willoughby B. "Mindful Binge Drinking and Blobology: The Promises and Perils of Contemplative Neuroscience." Presentation at 2012 Buddhist Geeks Conference. YouTube, September 20, 2012. https://www.youtube.com/watch?v=RlmqoQVm8nU.

Brooke, John Hedley, and Ronald L. Numbers, eds. *Science and Religion around the World*. New York: Oxford University Press, 2011.

Brown, Candy Gunther. "Does Mindfulness Belong in Public Schools? Two Views: No." *Tricycle, the Buddhist Review* (Spring 2016): 63–67.

————. *The Healing Gods: Complementary and Alternative Medicine in Christian America*. New York: Oxford University Press, 2013.

Buddhaghosa. *Visuddhimagga*. Translated by Bhikkhu Ñāṇamoli. Edited by B. P. S. Pariyatti. Seattle: Buddhist Publication Society, 1999.

"Buddhism and Other Religions Taught at Greenacre." *Boston Sunday Journal*, July 19, 1903.

Burnham, Kenneth E. *God Comes to America: Father Divine and the Peace Mission Movement*. Boston: Lambeth Press, 1979.

Bush, George. *Mesmer and Swedenborg; or, the Relation of the Developments of Mesmerism to the Doctrines and Disclosures of Swedenborg*. New York: John Allen, 1847.

Bush, Mirabai. "Mindfulness in Higher Education." *Contemporary Buddhism* 12, no. 1 (2011): 183–97.

Cameron, Kenneth Walter. *Transcendentalists in Transition: Popularization of Emerson, Thoreau, and the Concord School of Philosophy in the Greenacre Summer Conferences and the Monsalvat School (1894–1909). The Roles of Charles Malloy and Franklin Benjamin Sanborn before the Triumph of the Baha'i Movement in Eliot, Maine*. Hartford, CT: Transcendental Books, 1980.

Canter, Peter H., and Edzard Ernst. "The Cumulative Effects of Transcendental Meditation on Cognitive Function—A Systematic Review of Randomised Controlled Trials." *Wiener Klinische Wochenschrift* 115, nos. 21–22 (November 28, 2003): 758–66.

———. "Insufficient Evidence to Conclude Whether or Not Transcendental Meditation Decreases Blood Pressure: Results of a Systematic Review of Randomized Clinical Trials." *Journal of Hypertension* 22, no. 11 (November 2004): 2049–54.

Caplan, Eric. *Mind Games: American Culture and the Birth of Psychotherapy*. 1998. Berkeley: University of California Press, 2001.

Carrette, Jeremy, and Richard King. *Selling Spirituality: The Silent Takeover of Religion*. London: Routledge, 2004.

Chetty, D. Gopal. "Was Swedenborg a Yogi?" In *New Light upon Indian Philosophy, or Swedenborg and Saiva Siddhanta*, 125–46. London: J. M. Dent, 1923.

Chireau, Yvonne Patricia, and Nathaniel Deutsch. *Black Zion: African American Religious Encounters with Judaism*. Religion in America Series. New York: Oxford University Press, 2000.

Clarke, J. J. *Oriental Enlightenment: The Encounter between Asian and Western Thought*. London: Routledge, 1997.

Collyer, Robert H. *Lights and Shadows of American Life*. Boston: Redding, 1844.

Conwell, Russell Herman. "Acres of Diamonds." In *American Religions: A Documentary History*, edited by R. Marie Griffith, 301–9. New York: Oxford University Press, 2007.

Cooper, Andrew. "Losing Our Religion: An Interview with Robert Sharf." *Tricycle* (Summer 2007): 44–49.

Crabtree, Adam. *Animal Magnetism, Early Hypnotism, and Psychical Research, 1766–1925: An Annotated Bibliography*. Bibliographies in the History of Psychology and Psychiatry. White Plains, NY: Kraus International, 1988.

————. *From Mesmer to Freud: Magnetic Sleep and the Roots of Psychological Healing.* New Haven, CT: Yale University Press, 1993.

Cramer, M. E. *Basic Statements and Health Treatment of Truth: A System of Instruction in Divine Science Treatment for Class Training, and for Home and Private Use.* 5th ed. San Francisco: N.p., 1895.

Croce, Paul Jerome. *Science and Religion in the Era of William James.* Chapel Hill: University of North Carolina Press, 1995.

Cunningham, Raymond Joseph. "The Emmanuel Movement: A Variety of American Religious Experience." *American Quarterly* 14, no. 1 (Spring 1962): 48–63.

————. "The Impact of Christian Science on the American Churches 1890–1910." *American Historical Review* 72, no. 3 (April 1967): 885–905.

————. "Ministry of Healing: The Origins of the Psychotherapeutic Role of the American Churches." PhD dissertation. Johns Hopkins University, 1965.

Curtis, Edward E. *Islam in Black America: Identity, Liberation, and Difference in African-American Islamic Thought.* Albany: State University of New York Press, 2002.

D'Andrade, Hugh. *Charles Fillmore: Herald of the New Age.* New York: Harper & Row, 1974.

Dàsa, Philangi. *Swedenborg, the Buddhist, or the Higher Swedenborgianism: Its Secrets and Tibetan Origin.* 1887. Charleston, SC: Swedenborg Association, 2003.

Davidson, R. J., et al. "Alterations in Brain and Immune Function Produced by Mindfulness Meditation." *Psychosomatic Medicine,* no. 65 (2003): 564–70.

Davis, Roy Eugene. *Miracle Man of Japan: The Life and Work of Masaharu Taniguchi.* Lakemont, GA: CSA Press, 1970.

de Chant, Dell. "Myrtle Fillmore and Her Daughters: An Observation and Analysis of the Role of Women in Unity." In *Women's Leadership in Marginal Religions: Explorations outside the Mainstream,* edited by Catherine Wessinger, 102–24. Urbana: University of Illinois Press, 1993.

de Jong, J. W. *A Brief History of Buddhist Studies in Europe and America.* Tokyo: Kosei, 1997.

Deleuze, Gilles, and Félix Guattari. *A Thousand Plateaus: Capitalism and Schizophrenia.* Minneapolis: University of Minnesota Press, 1987.

Deleuze, J. P. F., and Thomas C. Hartshorn. *Practical Instruction in Animal Magnetism, or Mesmerism.* London: Cleave, 1843.

Dharmapala, Anagarika. "Diary Leaves of the Late Ven. Anagarika Dharmapāla." *Maha Bodhi* 64, nos. 2, 3, 6, 7, 9, 10 (February, March, June, July, September, October 1956); 65, nos. 2, 3, 7, 9, 11, 12 (February, March, July, September, November, December 1957); 66, no. 2 (February 1958).

————. "The World's Debt to Buddha." In *The World's Congress of Religions: The Addresses and Papers Delivered before the Parliament, and an Abstract of the Congresses Held in the Art Institute under the Auspices of the World's Columbian Exposition,* edited by J. W. Hanson, 377–87. Chicago: W. W. Houston, 1893.

Dods, John Bovee. *The Philosophy of Electrical Psychology, in a Course of Twelve Lectures*. Stereotype ed. New York: Fowlers & Wells, 1851.

Dole, George F. "Key Concepts in the Theology of Emanuel Swedenborg." In *Emanuel Swedenborg: A Continuing Vision*, edited by Robin Larsen et al., 507–9. New York: Swedenborg Foundation, 1988.

Dole, George F., and Robert H. Kirven. *A Scientist Explores Spirit: A Biography of Emanuel Swedenborg with Key Concepts of His Theology*. New York: Swedenborg Foundation, 1997.

Dorman, Jacob S. *Chosen People: The Rise of American Black Israelite Religions*. New York: Oxford University Press, 2013.

Dresser, Horatio W. *A History of the New Thought Movement*. New York: T. Y. Crowell, 1919.

Dresser, Horatio W., and History of Medicine Collections (Duke University). *A Physician to the Soul*. New York: Putnam, Knickerbocker Press, 1908.

Dreyfus, Georges. "Is Mindfulness Present-Centred and Non-Judgmental? A Discussion of the Cognitive Dimensions of Mindfulness." *Contemporary Buddhism* 12, no. 1 (2011): 41–54.

Droit, Roger-Pol. *The Cult of Nothingness: The Philosophers and the Buddha*. Translated by David Streight and Pamela Vohnson. Chapel Hill: University of North Carolina Press, 2003.

Dubiel, Richard Michael. *The Road to Fellowship: The Role of the Emmanuel Movement and the Jacoby Club in the Development of Alcoholics Anonymous*. Hindsfoot Foundation Series on the History of Alcoholism Treatment. New York: iUniverse, 2004.

Dubois, Paul. *The Psychic Treatment of Nervous Disorders*. Translated by Smith Ely Jelliffe and William A. White. 7th ed. New York: Funk & Wagnalls, 1909.

Duke Center for Integrative Medicine. *Class Workbook: Mindfulness-Based Stress Reduction Program*. Durham, NC: Duke Center for Integrative Medicine, 2004–6.

Dumit, Joseph. "Producing Brain Images of Mind." In *Picturing Personhood: Brain Scans and Biomedical Identity*, 53–105. Princeton, NJ: Princeton University Press, 2004.

Dunne, John. "Toward an Understanding of Non-Dual Mindfulness." *Contemporary Buddhism* 12, no. 1 (2011): 71–88.

Dwyer, Walter W. *Spiritual Healing in the United States and Great Britain*. New York: N.p., 1950.

Eddy, Mary Baker. *Science and Health with Key to the Scriptures*. Boston: Christian Science Board of Directors, 1994.

Edmunds, Albert J. "A Buddhist Bibliography, Based upon the Libraries of Philadelphia." *Journal of the Pali Text Society* (1902–3): 1–60.

———. "F. W. H. Meyers, Swedenborg, and Buddha." *Proceedings of the American Society for Psychical Research* 8 (1914): 253–85.

———. "Has Swedenborg's 'Lost Word' Been Found?" *Journal of the American Society for Psychical Research* 7, no. 5 (1913): 257–71.

Ehrenreich, Barbara. *Bright-Sided: How the Relentless Promotion of Positive Thinking Has Undermined America*. New York: Metropolitan Books, 2009.

Eklund, Anders, Thomas E. Nichols, and Hans Knutsson. "Cluster Failure: Why FMRI Inferences for Spatial-Extent Have Inflated False-Positive Rates." *Proceedings of the National Academy of Sciences of the United States of America* 113 (June 28, 2016): 7900–7905.

Elliotson, John, James Esdaile, Robert Macnish, and Daniel N. Robinson. *Numerous Cases of Surgical Operations without Pain in the Mesmeric State*. Significant Contributions to the History of Psychology, 1750–1920. Series a, Orientations vol. 10. Washington, DC: University Publications of America, 1977.

Emerson, Ralph Waldo, and Joel Porte. *Representative Men*. New York: Library of America, 1983.

Esdaile, James, and William S. Kroger. *Hypnosis in Medicine and Surgery*. New York: Julian Press, 1957.

Evans, Dylan. *Placebo: The Belief Effect*. London: HarperCollins, 2003.

Evans, W. F. *Esoteric Christianity and Mental Therapeutics*. Boston: H. H. Carter & Karrick, 1886.

———. *The Mental Cure, Illustrating the Influence of the Mind on the Body*. Boston: H. H. & T. W. Carter, 1869.

———. *Mental Medicine: A Theoretical and Practical Treatise on Medical Psychology*. Boston: Carter & Pettee, 1873.

Farmer, Sarah. "The Abundant Life." In *The Spirit of the New Thought: Essays and Addresses by Representative Authors and Leaders*, edited by Horatio W. Dresser, 29–36. New York: Thomas Y. Crowell, 1917.

Feldman, Christina, and Willem Kuyken. "Compassion in the Landscape of Suffering." *Contemporary Buddhism* 12, no. 1 (2011): 143–55.

Fennell, Melanie, and Zindel Segal. "Mindfulness-Based Cognitive Therapy: Culture Clash or Creative Fusion?" *Contemporary Buddhism* 12, no. 1 (2011): 125–42.

Fields, Rick. *How the Swans Came to the Lake: A Narrative History of Buddhism in America*. 3d ed. Boston: Shambhala, 1992.

Fillmore, Charles, and James Gaither. *The Essential Charles Fillmore: Collected Writings of a Missouri Mystic*. Unity Village, MO: Unity Books, 1999.

Floyd, Barbara. "Scientific Medicine." In *From Quackery to Bacteriology: The Emergence of Modern Medicine in 19th Century America*. University of Toledo Libraries. http://www.utoledo.edu/library/canaday/exhibits/quackery/quack2.html.

Foucault, Michel. "Nietzsche, Genealogy, History." In *The Foucault Reader*, edited by Paul Rabinow, 76–100. New York: Pantheon/Random House, 1984.

Foxe, Barbara. *Long Journey Home: A Biography of Margaret Noble (Nivedita)*. London: Rider, 1975.

Frankiel, Susan. *California's Spiritual Frontiers: Religious Alternatives in Anglo-Protestantism, 1850–1910.* Berkeley: University of California Press, 1988.

Frederick, Marla Faye. *Between Sundays: Black Women and Everyday Struggles of Faith.* Berkeley: University of California Press, 2003.

Fromm, Erich, and Daisetz Teitaro Suzuki. *Zen Buddhism and Psychoanalysis.* New York: Harper, 1960.

Fronsdal, Gil, and Max Erdstein. "Two Practices, One Path." In *What's Wrong with Mindfulness (and What Isn't): Zen Perspectives,* edited by Robert Meikyo Rosenbaum and Barry Magid, 93–107. Somerville, MA: Wisdom Publications, 2016.

Frumkin, K., R. J. Nathan, M. F. Prout, and M. C. Cohen. "Nonpharmacologic Control of Essential Hypertension in Man: A Critical Review of the Experimental Literature." *Psychosomatic Medicine* 40, no. 4 (June 1978): 294–320.

Fuller, Robert C. "The American Mesmerists, 1835–1900." PhD dissertation, University of Chicago, 1978.

———. *Mesmerism and the American Cure of Souls.* Philadelphia: University of Pennsylvania Press, 1982.

Gabay, Alfred J. *The Covert Enlightenment: Eighteenth Century Counterculture and Its Aftermath.* Swedenborg Studies. Vol. 17. West Chester, PA: Swedenborg Foundation, 2005.

Gauld, Alan. *A History of Hypnotism.* Cambridge, UK: Cambridge University Press, 1992.

Gaustad, Edwin S., and Leigh Eric Schmidt. *The Religious History of America: The Heart of the American Story from Colonial Times to Today.* San Francisco: Harper SanFrancisco, 2002.

Gestefeld, Ursula N. *The Breath of Life: A Series of Self-Treatments.* 1897. 3d ed. Pelham, NY: Gestefeld Publishing, 1901.

———. *The Builder and the Plan: A Textbook of the Science of Being.* Pelham, NY: Gestefeld Publishing, 1901.

———. *A Chicago Bible Class.* N.p.: N.p., 1892.

———. *How to Control Circumstances.* Pelham, NY: Gestefeld Publishing, 1901.

———. *How We Master Our Fate.* 2d ed. New York: Gestefeld Publishing, 1897.

———. *Jesuitism in Christian Science.* Chicago: Self-published, 1888.

———. *The Science of the Christ: An Advanced Statement of Christian Science with an Interpretation of Genesis.* Chicago: Self-published, 1889.

———. *Ursula N. Gestefeld's Statement of Christian Science, Comprised in Eighteen Lessons and Twelve Sections.* 2d ed. Chicago: Self-published, 1888.

Gethin, Rupert. "On Some Definitions of Mindfulness." *Contemporary Buddhism* 12, no. 1 (2011): 263–79.

Gevitz, Norman. *Other Healers: Unorthodox Medicine in America.* Baltimore: Johns Hopkins University Press, 1988.

Gifford, Sanford. *The Emmanuel Movement (Boston, 1904–1929): The Origins of Group Treatment and the Assault on Lay Psychotherapy.* Boston: Distributed by Harvard University Press for the Francis Countway Library of Medicine, 1997.

Glaser, Gabrielle. "The False Gospel of Alcoholics Anonymous." *The Atlantic,* 2015, 50–60.

Glasser, Matthew F., et al. "A Multi-Modal Parcellation of Human Cerebral Cortex." *Nature* 536 (August 11, 2016): 171–78.

Goldberg, Philip. *American Veda: From Emerson and the Beatles to Yoga and Meditation. How Indian Spirituality Changed the West.* New York: Harmony Books, 2010.

Goldsmith, Margaret L. *Franz Anton Mesmer: A History of Mesmerism.* Garden City, NY: Doubleday, Doran, 1934.

Goleman, Daniel. *Destructive Emotions: How Can We Overcome Them? A Scientific Dialogue with the Dalai Lama.* New York: Bantam Books, 2003.

———. *Healing Emotions: Conversations with the Dalai Lama on Mindfulness, Emotions, and Health.* Boston: Shambhala, 2003.

Gombrich, Richard Francis, and Gananath Obeyesekere. *Buddhism Transformed: Religious Change in Sri Lanka.* Princeton, NJ: Princeton University Press, 1988.

Gómez, Luis O. "Unspoken Paradigms: Meanderings through the Metaphors of a Field." *Journal of the International Association of Buddhist Studies* 18, no. 2 (1995): 183–230.

Goodrick-Clarke, Nicholas, ed. *Helena Blavatsky.* Western Esoteric Masters Series. Berkeley, CA: North Atlantic Books, 2004.

Gottschalk, Stephen. "Christian Science and Harmonialism." In *Encyclopedia of the American Religious Experience,* edited by Charles H. Lippy and Peter W. Williams, 901–16. New York: Charles Scribner's Sons, 1988.

———. *The Emergence of Christian Science in American Religious Life.* Berkeley: University of California Press, 1973.

Gray, James. *The Dhammapada, or Scriptural Texts: A Book of Buddhist Proverbs, Precepts, and Maxims.* Rangoon, Myanmar: American Mission Press, 1881.

Greene, John Gardner. "The Emmanuel Movement: 1906–1929." *New England Quarterly* 7, no. 3 (1934): 494–532.

Griffis, William Elliot. *Charles Carleton Coffin: War Correspondent, Traveller, Author, and Statesman.* Boston: Colonial Press, 1897. Project Gutenberg eBook #22238.

Griffith, R. Marie. "Body Salvation: New Thought, Father Divine, and the Feast of Material Pleasures." *Religion and American Culture: A Journal of Interpretation* 11, no. 2 (June 1, 2001): 119–53.

———. *Born Again Bodies: Flesh and Spirit in American Christianity.* California Studies in Food and Culture 12. Berkeley: University of California Press, 2004.

Grossman, Paul, and Nicholas T. Van Dam. "Mindfulness, by Any Other Name . . . : Trials and Tribulations of Sati in Western Psychology and Science." *Contemporary Buddhism* 12, no. 1 (2011): 219–39.

Grubin, David. "Healing from Within." In *Healing and the Mind with Bill Moyers*, vol. 3, edited by David Grubin. 87 min. Ambrose Video, 1993.

Guthrie, Anna Lorraine, ed. *Reader's Guide to Periodic Literature 1905–1909*. Vol. 2. Minneapolis, MN: H. W. Wilson, 1910.

Gyatso, Tenzin, 14th Dalai Lama. *Ethics for the New Millennium*. New York: Riverhead Books, 1999.

Haga, Manabu, and Robert J. Kisala. "The New Age in Japan." *Japanese Journal of Religious Studies* 22, nos. 3–4 (1995): 235–47.

Hallengren, Anders. "The Secret of Great Tartary." *Arcana* 1, no. 1 (1994): 35–54.

Haller, John S., Jr. *The History of New Thought: From Mind Cure to Positive Thinking and the Prosperity Gospel*. West Chester, PA: Swedenborg Foundation Press, 2012.

———. *Swedenborg, Mesmer, and the Mind-Body Connection*. West Chester, PA: Swedenborg Foundation Press, 2010.

Hanson, J. W. *The World's Congress of Religions, the Addresses and Papers Delivered before the Parliament, and an Abstract of the Congresses Held in the Art Institute, Chicago, Illinois, U.S.A., August 25 to October 15, 1893, under the Auspices of the World's Columbia Exposition*. Providence, RI: W. W. Thompson, 1894.

Harding, Walter Roy. *Emerson's Library*. Charlottesville: University Press of Virginia, 1967.

Hari, Johann. *Chasing the Scream: The First and Last Days of the War on Drugs*. New York: Bloomsbury, 2015.

———. "The Likely Cause of Addiction Has Been Discovered, and It Is Not What You Think." *Huffpost Politics*, updated January 25, 2016. http://www.huffingtonpost.com/johann-hari/the-real-cause-of-addicti_b_6506936.html.

Harley, Gail M. *Emma Curtis Hopkins: Forgotten Founder of New Thought*. New Religious Movements. Syracuse, NY: Syracuse University Press, 2002.

Harrell, David Edwin. *All Things Are Possible: The Healing and Charismatic Revivals in Modern America*. Bloomington: Indiana University Press, 1975.

Harrington, Anne. *The Cure Within: A History of Mind-Body Medicine*. New York: W. W. Norton, 2008.

———. "The Many Meanings of the Placebo Effect: Where They Came From, Why They Matter." *BioSocieties* 1 (2006): 181–93.

———. *Medicine, Mind, and the Double Brain: A Study in Nineteenth-Century Thought*. Princeton, NJ: Princeton University Press, 1987.

———. *The Placebo Effect: An Interdisciplinary Exploration*. Cambridge, MA: Harvard University Press, 1997.

Harrington, Anne, and John D. Dunne. "When Mindfulness Is Therapy: Ethical Qualms, Historical Perspectives." "The Emergence of Mindfulness in Basic and Clinical Psychological Science." Special issue of *American Psychologist* 70, no. 7 (October 2015): 621–31.

Harvey, Peter. *An Introduction to Buddhism: Teachings, History and Practices*. Cambridge, UK: Cambridge University Press, 1990.

Hazen, Craig James. *The Village Enlightenment in America: Popular Religion and Science in the Nineteenth Century.* Urbana: University of Illinois Press, 2000.

Heine, Steven, and Charles S. Prebish. *Buddhism in the Modern World: Adaptations of an Ancient Tradition.* New York: Oxford University Press, 2003.

Heuman, Linda. "A New Way Forward." *Tricycle* (Spring 2015): 47–51, 100–103.

Hickey, Shannon. "Religious Leadership in American Zen: A Comparative Study of Priesthood in Three Communities of American Converts to Sōtō Zen." MA thesis, Pacific School of Religion, 2001.

Hickey, Wakoh Shannon. "Meditation as Medicine: A Critique." *Crosscurrents* 60, no. 2 (Summer 2010): 168–84.

———. "Meditation Is Not Enough: Chaplaincy Training for Buddhists." In *Arts of Contemplative Care: Pioneering Voices in Buddhist Chaplaincy and Pastoral Work*, edited by L. Willa Miller and Cheryl Giles, 17–26. Boston: Wisdom Publications, 2012.

———. "Mind Cure, Meditation, and Medicine: Hidden Histories of Mental Healing in the United States." PhD dissertation, Duke University, 2008.

———. "Review: The Way of Tenderness: Awakening through Race, Sexuality, and Gender, by Zenju Earthlyn Manuel (Boston: Wisdom Publications, 2015)." *Buddhist-Christian Studies* 36 (2016): 237–41.

———. "Swedenborg: A Modern Buddha?" *Pacific World: Journal of the Institute of Buddhist Studies* 10 (Summer 2008): 101–29.

———. "Two Buddhisms, Three Buddhisms, and Racism." in *Buddhism beyond Borders: New Perspectives on Buddhism in the United States*, edited by Scott A. Mitchell and Natalie E. F. Quli, 35–56. New York: SUNY Press, 2015.

Hickey, Wakoh Shannon, and C. Denise Yarbrough. "Deepening the Heart of Wisdom: Buddhist and Christian Contemplative Dialogue and Practice." *Buddhist-Christian Studies* 33 (2013): 83–99.

Highlights from the Science and Clinical Applications of Meditation Conference: An Overview of the Investigating the Mind 2005 Meeting with the Dalai Lama. Washington, DC: Mind and Life Institute, 2007. CD-ROM.

Holmes, Ernest. *The Science of Mind: A Complete Course of Lessons in the Science of Mind and Spirit.* New York: R. M. McBride, 1926.

Holmes, Fenwicke L. "Text Book of Practical Healing: The 'Just How Course' in Healing the Mental Science Way." Berkeley, CA: Graduate Theological Union Library, 1943.

Hopkins, Emma Curtis. *Class Lessons, 1888.* Marina del Rey, CA: DeVorss, 1977.

Hoppes, Kimberly. "The Application of Mindfulness-Based Cognitive Interventions in the Treatment of Co-Occurring Addictive and Mood Disorders." *CNS Spectrums* 11 (November 2006): 829–51.

Houghton, Walter R. *Neely's History of the Parliament of Religions and Religious Congresses at the World's Columbian Exposition.* 4th ed. Chicago: F. T. Neely, 1894.

Hovenkamp, Herbert. *Science and Religion in America, 1800–1860*. Philadelphia: University of Pennsylvania Press, 1978.

Hrobjartsson, Asbjorn, and Peter C. Gotzsche. "Is the Placebo Powerless? An Analysis of Clinical Trials Comparing Placebo with No Treatment." *New England Journal of Medicine* 344, no. 21 (2001): 1594–602.

Hughes, Ron. "Phineas Parkhurst Quimby Resource Center." http://www.ppquimby.com/index.html.

Hutchison, William R. *The Modernist Impulse in American Protestantism*. Cambridge, MA: Harvard University Press, 1976.

Huxley, Aldous. *The Perennial Philosophy*. 1944. Reprint. New York: Harper Colophon, Harper and Row, 1970.

Ingersoll, Anna Josephine. *Greenacre on the Piscataqua*. New York: Alliance, 1900.

Iwamura, Jane Naomi. *Virtual Orientalism: Asian Religions and American Popular Culture*. New York: Oxford University Press, 2011.

Jackson, Carl T. "The New Thought Movement and the Nineteenth Century Discovery of Oriental Philosophy." *Journal of Popular Culture* 9, no. 3 (Winter 1975): 523–48.

———. *The Oriental Religions and American Thought: Nineteenth-Century Explorations*. Westport, CT: Greenwood Press, 1981.

———. *Vedanta for the West: The Ramakrishna Movement in the United States*. Bloomington: Indiana University Press, 1994. e-book.

Jaffe, Richard. "Seeking Śakyamuni: Travel and the Reconstruction of Japanese Buddhism." *Journal of Japanese Studies* 30, no. 1 (2004): 65–96.

James, William. *The Varieties of Religious Experience: A Study in Human Nature*. 1902. New York: Modern Library, 1997.

Jarrell, Howard R. *International Meditation Bibliography 1950–1982*. ATLA Bibliography Series, vol. 12. Metuchen, NJ: American Theological Library Association and Scarecrow Press, 1985.

Judah, J. Stillson. *The History and Philosophy of the Metaphysical Movements in America*. Philadelphia: Westminster Press, 1967.

Kabat-Zinn, Jon. "Coming to Our Senses." Lecture, Meymandi Hall, Progress Energy Center (Memorial Auditorium), Raleigh, NC. Sponsored by the Susan G. Komen Breast Cancer Foundation, NC Triangle Affiliate, September 28, 2006.

———. *Coming to Our Senses: Healing Ourselves and the World through Mindfulness*. New York: Hyperion, 2005.

———. "Indra's Net at Work: The Mainstreaming of Dharma Practice in Society." In *The Psychology of Awakening: Buddhism, Science, and Our Day to Day Lives*, edited by Gay Watson and Stephen Batchelor, 225–49. York Beach, ME: S. Weiser, 2000.

———. "Some Reflections on the Origins of MBSR, Skillful Means, and the Trouble with Maps." *Contemporary Buddhism* 12, no. 1 (May 2011): 281–306.

———. "Toward the Mainstreaming of American Dharma Practice." In *Buddhism in America: The Official Record of the Landmark Conference on the Future of Buddhist*

Meditative Practices in the West, Boston, January 17–19, 1997, edited by Al Rapaport and Brian D. Hotchkiss, 478–528. Rutland, VT: Charles E. Tuttle, 1998.

———. *Wherever You Go There You Are*. New York: Hyperion, 1994.

Kabat-Zinn, Jon, and University of Massachusetts Medical Center/Worcester Stress Reduction Clinic. *Full Catastrophe Living: Using the Wisdom of Your Body and Mind to Face Stress, Pain, and Illness*. New York: Delta, 1991.

Kaku, K. T., ed., and Y. Haruki, convener. *Meditation as Health Promotion: A Lifestyle Modification Approach*. Proceedings of the 6th Conference, July 20 and 21, 2000. Organized by the Transnational Network for the Study of Physical, Psychological & Spiritual Wellbeing. Golden Tulip Conference Hotel. Noordwijkerhout, The Netherlands: Eburon, 2000.

Kanellakos, Demetri P., and Phillip Ferguson. *The Psychobiology of Transcendental Meditation: An Annotated Bibliography*. Los Angeles: Maharishi International University, 1973.

Kapleau, Philip. *The Three Pillars of Zen: Teaching, Practice, and Enlightenment*. Revised and expanded ed. Garden City, NY: Anchor Press, 1980.

Kehl, George W. "The History and Method of the Immanuel [*sic*] Movement and of Associated Groups." MA thesis, Butler University, 1933.

Keller, Rosemary Skinner, Rosemary Radford Ruether, and Marie Cantlon, eds. *Encyclopedia of Women and Religion in North America*. Bloomington: Indiana University Press, 2006.

Keown, Damien. *Oxford Dictionary of Buddhism*. New York: Oxford University Press, 2004.

Kerr, Howard, and Charles L. Crow. *The Occult in America: New Historical Perspectives*. Urbana: University of Illinois Press, 1983.

Ketelaar, James Edward. *Of Heretics and Martyrs in Meiji Japan: Buddhism and Its Persecution*. Princeton, NJ: Princeton University Press, 1990.

———. "Strategic Occidentalism: Meiji Buddhists at the World's Parliament of Religions." *Buddhist-Christian Studies* 11 (1991): 37–56.

King, Richard. *Orientalism and Religion: Postcolonial Theory, India and "the Mystic East."* London: Routledge, 1999.

Kirven, Robert H. "Swedenborg's Contributions to the History of Ideas." In *Emanuel Swedenborg: A Continuing Vision*, 361–70. New York: Swedenborg Foundation, 1988.

Kirven, Robert H., and David B. Eller. "Selected Examples of Swedenborg's Influence in Great Britain and the United States." In *Emanuel Swedenborg: Essays for the New Century Edition on His Life, Work, and Impact*, edited by Stuart Shotwell, Jonathan S. Rose, and Mary Lou Bertucci, 195–242. The New Century Edition of the Works of Emanuel Swedenborg. West Chester, PA: Swedenborg Foundation, 2005.

Kleinman, Arthur. *Writing at the Margin: Discourse between Anthropology and Medicine*. Berkeley: University of California Press, 1995.

Kondwani, K. A., and C. M. Lollis. "Is There a Role for Stress Management in Reducing Hypertension in African Americans?" *Ethnicity & Disease* 11, no. 4 (2001): 788–92.

Koppel, Lily. "Maharishi Mahesh Yogi, Spiritual Leader, Dies." *New York Times,* February 6 2008.

Kripal, Jeffrey John. *Esalen: America and the Religion of No Religion.* Chicago: University of Chicago Press, 2007.

Kripal, Jeffrey John, and Glenn W. Shuck. *On the Edge of the Future: Esalen and the Evolution of American Culture.* Religion in North America. Bloomington: Indiana University Press, 2005.

Krisanaprakornkit, T., W. Krisanaprakornkit, N. Piyavhatkul, and M. Laopaiboon. "Meditation Therapy for Anxiety Disorders." *Cochrane Database of Systematic Reviews*, no. 1 (2006): CD004998.

Larsen, Robin, et al., eds. *Emanuel Swedenborg: A Continuing Vision.* New York: Swedenborg Foundation, 1988.

Larsen, Stephen. "Swedenborg and the Visionary Tradition." In *Emanuel Swedenborg: A Continuing Vision,* edited by Robin Larsen et al., 192–206. New York: Swedenborg Foundation, 1988.

Larson, Martin. *New Thought: A Modern Religious Approach.* New York: Philosophical Library, 1985.

Lawrence, James F. "An Extraordinary Season in Prayer: Warren Felt Evans' Journey into 'Scientific' Swedenborgian Spiritual Practice." *Studia Swedenborgiana* 12, no. 3 (2002): 31–68.

Leonard, William J. "The Pioneer Apostle of Mental Science: A Sketch of the Life and Work of the Reverend W. F. Evans, M.D." *Pamphlet* (July 1903): 1–8.

Leuchter, A. F., et al. "Changes in Brain Function of Depressed Subjects during Treatment with Placebo." *American Journal of Psychiatry* 160, no. 2 (2002): 387–88.

Lindahl, Jared R., Nathan E. Fisher, David J. Cooper, Rochelle K. Rosen, and Willoughby B. Britton. "The Varieties of Contemplative Experience: A Mixed-Methods Study of Meditation-Related Challenges in Western Buddhists." *PLoS ONE*, May 24, 2017. https://doi.org/10.1371/journal.pone.0176239.

Linehan, Marsha. *Cognitive-Behavioral Treatment of Borderline Personality Disorder.* Diagnosis and Treatment of Mental Disorders. New York: Guilford Press, 1993.

Livingstone, David N. "Which Science? Whose Religion?" In *Science and Religion around the World,* edited by John Hedley Brooke and Ronald L. Numbers, 278–96. Oxford: Oxford University Press, 2011.

Long, Charles H. *Significations: Signs, Symbols, and Images in the Interpretation of Religion.* Philadelphia: Fortress Press, 1986.

Long, Jana, and Lorenzo Wilkins. "The Uncommon Yogi: A History of Blacks and Yoga in the U.S." YouTube, August 29, 2016, https://www.youtube.com/watch?v=xQqSdB9PD38.

Lopez, Donald. *Buddhism and Science: A Guide for the Perplexed.* Buddhism and Modernity. Chicago: University of Chicago Press, 2008.

―――. *Critical Terms for the Study of Buddhism.* Buddhism and Modernity. Chicago: University of Chicago Press, 2005.

―――. *Curators of the Buddha: The Study of Buddhism under Colonialism.* Chicago: University of Chicago Press, 1995.

―――. *From Stone to Flesh: A Short History of the Buddha.* Buddhism and Modernity. Chicago: University of Chicago Press, 2013.

―――. *Prisoners of Shangri-La: Tibetan Buddhism and the West.* Chicago: Chicago University Press, 1998.

―――. *The Scientific Buddha: His Short and Happy Life.* Dwight Harrington Terry Foundation Lectures on Religion in the Light of Science and Philosophy. New Haven, CT: Yale University Press, 2012.

Loy, David. "The Dharma of Emanuel Swedenborg: A Buddhist Perspective." In *Swedenborg: Buddha of the North,* edited by Mary Lou Bertucci, 89–125. West Chester, PA: Swedenborg Foundation, 1996.

―――. "The Dharma of Emanuel Swedenborg: A Buddhist Perspective." *Buddhist-Christian Studies* 16 (1996): 11–35.

Lupton, Deborah. *Medicine as Culture: Illness, Disease and the Body in Western Societies.* 2d ed. London: Sage, 2003.

Lutz, A., L. L Greischar, N. B. Rawlings, M. Ricard, and R. J. Davidson. "Long-Term Meditators Self-Induce High-Amplitude Gamma Synchrony during Mental Practice." *Proceedings of the National Academy of Sciences* 101 (2004): 16369–73.

Mabee, Carleton. *Promised Land: Father Divine's Interracial Communities in Ulster County, New York.* Fleischmanns, NY: Purple Mountain Press, 2008.

MacDonald, Robert. Mind, Religion and Health, with an Appreciation of the Emmanuel Movement; How Its Principles Can Be Applied in Promoting Health and in the Enriching of Our Daily Life. London, Funk & Wagnalls, 1908. Internet Archive. http://hdl.loc.gov/loc.gdc/scd0001.00025987299.

Macomber, William. *History of the Emmanuel Movement from the Standpoint of a Patient.* Religion and Medicine. New York: Moffat, Yard, 1908.

Maex, Edel. "The Buddhist Roots of Mindfulness Training: A Practitioner's View." *Contemporary Buddhism* 12, no. 1 (2011): 165–75.

Magid, Barry, and Marc R. Poirier. "The Three Shaky Pillars of Western Buddhism: Deracination, Secularization, and Instrumentalization." In *What's Wrong with Mindfulness (and What Isn't): Zen Perspectives,* edited by Robert Meikyo Rosenbaum and Barry Magid, 39–52. Somerville, MA: Wisdom Publications, 2016.

Maharishi International University. "Bibliography and Reprint Catalogue: Scientific Research on the Transcendental Meditation and TM-Siddhi Program, Revised May 1982." Wright State University Library, 1982.

Mansky, Patrick J., and Dawn B. Wallerstedt. "Complementary Medicine in Palliative Care and Cancer Symptom Management." *Cancer Journal* 12, no. 5 (September–October 2006): 425–31.

Martin, James Douglas. "The Life and Work of Sarah Jane Farmer, 1847–1916." Master's thesis, University of Waterloo, 1967.

Maru, Sheela Hansraj. "The New Mission of the Doctor: Richard Cabot, the Emmanuel Movement, and the Development of the First American Medical Social Service Department." Honors thesis, A.B., Harvard University, 2002.

Masuzawa, Tomoko. *The Invention of World Religions, or, How European Universalism Was Preserved in the Language of Pluralism.* Chicago: University of Chicago Press, 2005.

Materra, Gary Ward. "Women in Early New Thought: Lives and Theology in Transition, from the Civil War to World War I." PhD dissertation, University of California, Santa Barbara, 1997.

May, Henry Farnham. *The Enlightenment in America.* New York: Oxford University Press, 1976.

McCarthy, Katherine. "Psychotherapy and Religion: The Emmanuel Movement." *Journal of Religion and Health* 23, no. 2 (Summer 1984): 92–105.

McCollum, Harriet Luella. *Full Text of Class Lessons in Practical Psychology as They Are Personally Given to Her Classes.* Berkeley, CA: Graduate Theological Union Library, n.d.

McMahan, David. L. *The Making of Buddhist Modernism.* Oxford: Oxford University Press, 2008.

———"Modernity and the Early Discourse of Scientific Buddhism." *Journal of the American Academy of Religion* 72, no. 4 (2004): 897–933.

McRae, John R. *Seeing through Zen: Encounter, Transformation, and Genealogy in Chinese Chan Buddhism.* Berkeley: University of California Press, 2003.

Melton, J. Gordon. *Encyclopedia of American Religions.* 6th ed. Detroit: Gale Research, 1999.

Memmott, Carol. "'Secret' to Happiness." *USA Today*, February 14, 2007.

"Mental Therapeutics and Esoteric Christianity." *The Theosophist* 9, no. 97 (October1887): 62–63.

Meyer, Donald B. *The Positive Thinkers: Popular Religious Psychology from Mary Baker Eddy to Norman Vincent Peale and Ronald Reagan.* Revised ed. Middletown, CT: Wesleyan University Press, Harper & Row, 1988.

Miller, Timothy, ed. *America's Alternative Religions.* Albany: SUNY Press, 1995.

"Mindful Awareness Research Center (MARC) at UCLA." UCLA Health. http://www.marc.ucla.edu/.

Moerman, Daniel E. *Meaning, Medicine, and the "Placebo Effect."* Cambridge Studies in Medical Anthropology 9. Cambridge, UK: Cambridge University Press, 2002.

Monro, Robin, A. K. Ghosh, and Daniel Kalish. *Yoga Research Bibliography: Scientific Studies on Yoga and Meditation.* Cambridge, UK: Yoga Biomedical Trust, 1989.

"Monsalvat School of Comparative Religion." *Outlook*, July 8, 1899, 583–84.

Moore, R. Laurence. *Religious Outsiders and the Making of Americans*. New York: Oxford University Press, 1986.

Moore, Robert Laurence. *In Search of White Crows: Spiritualism, Parapsychology, and American Culture*. New York: Oxford University Press, 1977.

"Mountains and Waters Sutra: Sansui-Kyō." Translated by Andrew Kotler and Kazuaki Tanhashi. In *Moon in a Dewdrop: Writings of Zen Master Dōgen*, edited by Kazuaki Tanhashi, 97–107. San Francisco: North Point Press, 1985.

Moyers, Bill. "Healing from Within." In *Healing and the Mind*. Vol. 3. New York: Ambrose Video and Public Affairs Television, 1993.

Mumford, James Gregory. *Some End-Results of Surgery*. Religion and Medicine. New York: Moffat, Yard, 1908.

Muravchik, Stephanie. *American Protestantism in the Age of Psychology*. Cambridge, UK: Cambridge University Press, 2011.

Murphy, Larry, J. Gordon Melton, and Gary L. Ward. *Encyclopedia of African American Religions*. New York: Garland, 1993.

Murphy, Michael, and Steven Donovan. *The Physical and Psychological Effects of Meditation: A Review of Contemporary Research with a Comprehensive Bibliography 1931–1996*. Edited by Eugene Taylor. 2d ed. Sausalito, CA: Institute of Noetic Sciences, 1999.

Needleman, Jacob. *The New Religions*. Garden City, NY: Doubleday, 1970.

Needleman, Jacob, and Frithjof Schuon. *The Sword of Gnosis: Metaphysics, Cosmology, Tradition, Symbolism*. Baltimore, MD: Penguin Books, 1974.

North, Robert L. "Benjamin Rush, MD: Assassin or Beloved Healer?" *Baylor University Medical Center Proceedings* 13, no. 1 (January 2000): 45–49.

Olcott, Henry Steel. *A Buddhist Catechism, according to the Sinhalese Canon*. Special edition to Commemorate the Opening of the Adyar Oriental Library. Madras: Scottish Press, 1886.

Oldmeadow, Harry. *Journeys East: 20th Century Western Encounters with Eastern Religious Traditions*. Bloomington, IN: World Wisdom, 2004.

Olendzki, Andrew. "The Construction of Mindfulness." *Contemporary Buddhism* 12, no. 1 (2011): 55–70.

Ott, Mary Jane. "Mindfulness Meditation: A Path of Transformation and Healing." *Journal of Psychosocial Nursing & Mental Health Services* 42, no. 7 (July 2004): 22–29.

Ott, Mary Jane, Rebecca L. Norris, and Susan M. Bauer-Wu. "Mindfulness Meditation for Oncology Patients: A Discussion and Critical Review." *Integrative Cancer Therapies* 5, no. 2 (June 2006): 98–108.

Ozanne, Rachel Lauren. "The Healing Subconscious Refocusing the Historiography of Psychology and Religion through the Emmanuel Movement." MA thesis, University of Texas, Austin. http://repositories.lib.utexas.edu/bitstream/handle/2152/ETD-UT-2009-12-545/OZANNE-MASTERS-REPORT.pdf.

Pallis, Marco. *Peaks and Lamas*. London: Cassell, 1940.

Parker, Gail Thain. *Mind Cure in New England: From the Civil War to World War I.* Hanover, NH: University Press of New England, 1973.

Parker, James N., and Philip M. Parker, eds. *Meditation: A Medical Dictionary, Bibliography, and Annotated Research Guide to Internet Resources.* San Diego, CA: ICON Health, 2003.

Payne, Richard K. "Buddhism and the Powers of the Mind." In *Buddhism in the Modern World*, edited by David L. McMahan, 234–55. Abingdon, UK: Routledge, 2012.

———. "How Not to Talk about the Pure Land: A Critique of Huston Smith's (Mis-)Representations." In *Path of No Path: Contemporary Studies in Pure Land Buddhism Honoring Roger Corless*, edited by Richard K. Payne, 147–72. Berkeley, CA: Numata Center for Buddhist Translation and Research, 2009.

———. "Traditionalist Representations of Buddhism." *Pacific World: Journal of the Institute of Buddhist Studies*, 3d series, no. 10 (2008): 177–223.

Peale, Norman Vincent. *The Inspirational Writings of Norman Vincent Peale.* New York: Inspirational Press, 1991.

———. *The Power of Positive Thinking.* New York: Prentice-Hall, 1952.

Peale, Norman Vincent, and Smiley Blanton. *The Art of Real Happiness.* New York: Prentice-Hall, 1987.

Peel, Robert. *Mary Baker Eddy: The Years of Discovery.* New York: Holt, 1966.

Perry, Anne Gordon, et al. *Green Acre on the Piscataqua.* 2d ed. Wilmette, IL: Baha'i Publishing Trust, 2005.

Phillips, Jeane. *Mary Baker Eddy's Early Writings Compared with the Quimby Manuscripts.* Pasadena, CA: Toujours, 1931.

Podmore, Frank. *From Mesmer to Christian Science: A Short History of Mental Healing.* New Hyde Park, NY: University Books, 1963.

Poirier, Marc R. "Mischief in the Marketplace for Mindfulness." In *What's Wrong with Mindfulness (and What Isn't): Zen Perspectives*, edited by Robert Meikyo Rosenbaum and Barry Magid, 13–27. Somerville, MA: Wisdom Publications, 2016.

Powell, Lyman P. *The Art of Natural Sleep, with Definite Directions for the Wholesome Cure of Sleeplessness, Illustrated by Cases Treated in Northampton and Elsewhere.* New York: G. P. Putnam's Sons, 1908.

———. *The Emmanuel Movement in a New England Town: A Systematic Account of Experiments and Reflections Designed to Determine the Proper Relationship between the Minister and the Doctor in the Light of Modern Needs.* New York: G. P. Putnam's Sons, 1909.

Powell, Robert Charles. "Healing and Wholeness: Helen Flanders Dunbar (1902–59) and an Extra-Medical Origin of the American Psychosomatic Movement, 1902–36." PhD diss., Duke University, 1974.

Poyen, Charles. *Progress of Animal Magnetism in New England.* Hypnosis and Altered States of Consciousness. New York: Da Capo Press, 1982.

Proctor, James D. *Science, Religion, and the Human Experience.* Oxford: Oxford University Press, 2005.

Prothero, Stephen R. *American Jesus: How the Son of God Became a National Icon.* New York: Farrar, Straus and Giroux, 2003.

———. *The White Buddhist: The Asian Odyssey of Henry Steel Olcott.* Religion in North America. Bloomington: Indiana University Press, 1996.

Proulx, Kathryn. "Integrating Mindfulness-Based Stress Reduction." *Holistic Nursing Practice* 17, no. 4 (July–August 2003): 201–8.

Purser, Ron, and David Loy. "Beyond McMindfulness." *Huffington Post,* updated August 31, 2013. http://www.huffingtonpost.com/ron-purser/beyond-mcmindfulness_b_3519289.html.

Queen, Christopher S., and Sallie B. King. *Engaged Buddhism: Buddhist Liberation Movements in Asia.* Albany: State University of New York Press, 1996.

Quimby, P. P., and Horatio W. Dresser. *The Quimby Manuscripts.* New York: Julian Press, 1961.

———. *The Quimby Manuscripts: Showing the Discovery of Spiritual Healing and the Origin of Christian Science.* 2d ed. New York: Thomas Y. Crowell, 1921.

Reader, Ian, and George Joji Tanabe. *Practically Religious: Worldly Benefits and the Common Religion of Japan.* Honolulu: University of Hawaiʻi Press, 1998.

Remey, Charles Mason. "Reminiscences of the Summer School Green-Acre, Eliot, Maine; of Seasons There, of Happenings There, and of Some of the People Who Went There and the Things They Did. In Two Volumes." In *Remey Family Records,* vol. 1, 1–77; vol. 2, 78–152. 1949. Revised ed. Boston: Harvard University Library, 1955.

Richards, Robert J. *The Romantic Conception of Life: Science and Philosophy in the Age of Goethe.* Science and Its Conceptual Foundations. Chicago: University of Chicago Press, 2002.

Richardson, Robert. "The Rise and Fall of the Parliament of Religions at Greenacre." *Open Court: A Quarterly Magazine Devoted to the Science of Religion* 45, no. 3 (March 1931): 129–66.

Risher, Brittany. "World View." In *The Power of Mindfulness,* edited by Alyssa Shafer, 23–25. New York: Centennial Media, 2017.

Rose, Anne C. *Transcendentalism as a Social Movement, 1830–1850.* New Haven, CT: Yale University Press, 1981.

Rosenbaum, Robert Meikyo. "'I' Doesn't Mind." In *What's Wrong with Mindfulness (and What Isn't): Zen Perspectives,* edited by Robert Meikyo Rosenbaum and Barry Magid, 29–38. Somerville, MA: Wisdom Publications, 2016.

———. "Mindfulness Myths: Fantasies and Facts." In *What's Wrong with Mindfulness (and What Isn't): Zen Perspectives,* edited by Robert Meikyo Rosenbaum and Barry Magid, 53–68. Somerville, MA: Wisdom Publications, 2016.

Rosenbaum, Robert Meikyo, and Barry Magid. "Introduction: Universal Mindfulness—Be Careful What You Wish For." In *What's Wrong with Mindfulness (and What Isn't): Zen Perspectives,* edited by Robert Meikyo Rosenbaum and Barry Magid, 1–10. Somerville, MA: Wisdom Publications, 2016.

————, eds. *What's Wrong with Mindfulness (and What Isn't): Zen Perspectives*. Somerville, MA: Wisdom Publications, 2016.

Saddhatissa, H. "The Chapter of the Eights." In *The Sutta-Nipāta*, 91–113. Richmond, Surrey, UK: Curzon, 1994.

Said, Edward. *Orientalism*. New York: Pantheon Books, 1978.

Salzberg, Sharon. "Mindfulness and Lovingkindness." *Contemporary Buddhism* 12, no. 1 (May 2011): 177–82.

Samuel, Geoffrey. "Between Buddhism and Science, between Mind and Body." *Religions* 5, no. 3 (2014): 560–79.

Sanborn, Franklin. "Green Acre." *New England Magazine* 34 (August 1906): 741–42.

Santorelli, Saki. "Does Mindfulness Belong in Public Schools? Two Views: Yes." *Tricycle, the Buddhist Review* (Spring 2016): 63–67.

————. "'Enjoy Your Death': Leadership Lessons Forged in the Crucible of Organizational Death and Rebirth Infused with Mindfulness and Mastery." *Contemporary Buddhism* 12, no. 1 (2011): 199–217.

————. *Heal Thyself: Lessons on Mindfulness in Medicine*. New York: Three Rivers Press, 2000.

Satter, Beryl. *Each Mind a Kingdom: American Women, Sexual Purity, and the New Thought Movement, 1875–1920*. Berkeley: University of California Press, 1999.

————. "Marcus Garvey, Father Divine and the Gender Politics of Race Difference and Race Neutrality." *American Quarterly* 48, no. 1 (1996): 43–76.

Sawada, Janine Anderson. *Practical Pursuits: Religion, Politics, and Personal Cultivation in Nineteenth-Century Japan*. Honolulu: University of Hawai'i Press, 2004.

Schmidt, Leigh Eric. *Restless Souls: The Making of American Spirituality*. San Francisco: HarperSanFrancisco, 2005.

Schmidt, Stefan. "Mindfulness and Healing Intention: Concepts, Practice, and Research Evaluation." *Journal of Alternative & Complementary Medicine* 10, suppl. 1 (2004): S7–S14.

Schopen, Gregory. *Bones, Stones, and Buddhist Monks: Collected Papers on the Archaeology, Epigraphy, and Texts of Monastic Buddhism in India*. Studies in the Buddhist Traditions. Honolulu: University of Hawai'i Press, 1997.

Schreiber, Katherine. "The Surprising Science of Mindfulness." In *The Power of Mindfulness*, edited by Alyssa Shafer, 8–11. New York: Centennial Media, 2017.

Schuchard, Marsha Keith. "Why Mrs. Blake Cried: Blake, Swedenborg, and the Sexual Basis of Spiritual Vision." *Esoterica* 2 (2000): 45–93.

————. *Why Mrs Blake Cried: William Blake and the Sexual Basis of Spiritual Vision*. London: Century, 2006.

Schwarz, Amelia Grant, and Elwood Worcester. *A Letter of Hope*. New York: Moffat, Yard, 1908.

Seager, Richard Hughes. *Buddhism in America*. Columbia Contemporary American Religion Series. New York: Columbia University Press, 1999.

———. *Encountering the Dharma: Daisaku Ikeda, Soka Gakkai, and the Globalization of Buddhist Humanism*. Berkeley: University of California Press, 2006.

———. *The World's Parliament of Religions: The East/West Encounter, Chicago, 1893*. Religion in North America. Bloomington: Indiana University Press, 1995.

Seager, Richard Hughes, and Council for a Parliament of the World's Religions. *The Dawn of Religious Pluralism: Voices from the World's Parliament of Religions, 1893*. La Salle, IL: Open Court Press, 1993.

Seale, Ervin, ed. *Phineas Parkhurst Quimby: The Complete Writings*. 3 vols. Marina del Rey, CA: DeVorss, 1988.

Sedgwick, Mark J. *Against the Modern World: Traditionalism and the Secret Intellectual History of the Twentieth Century*. New York: Oxford University Press, 2004.

Seeman, Teresa E., Linda Fagan Dubin, and Melvin Seeman. "Religiosity/Spirituality and Health. A Critical Review of the Evidence for Biological Pathways." *American Psychologist* 58, no. 1 (January 2003): 53–63.

Senauke, Hozan Alan. "One Body, Whole Life: Mindfulness and Zen." In *What's Wrong with Mindfulness (and What Isn't): Zen Perspectives*, edited by Robert Meikyo Rosenbaum and Barry Magid, 69–79. Somerville, MA: Wisdom Publications, 2016.

Shaffer, Alyssa. "14 Ways to Find More Zen." In *The Power of Mindfulness*, edited by Alyssa Shafer, 60–61. New York: Centennial Media, 2017.

Sharf, Robert H. "Buddhist Modernism and the Rhetoric of Meditative Experience." *Numen* 42 (1995): 228–83.

———. "Epilogue: Is Mindfulness Buddhist? (and Why It Matters)." In *What's Wrong with Mindfulness (and What Isn't): Zen Perspectives*, edited by Robert Meikyo Rosenbaum and Barry Magid, 139–51. Somerville, MA: Wisdom Publications, 2016.

———. "Sanbōkyōdan: Zen and the Way of the New Religions." *Japanese Journal of Religious Studies* 22, nos. 3–4 (1995): 417–57.

———. "The Zen of Japanese Nationalism." In *Curators of the Buddha: The Study of Buddhism under Colonialism*, edited by Donald S. Lopez Jr., 107–60. Chicago: University of Chicago Press, 1995.

Shearer, Gary W. *The Emmanuel Movement: A Guide to Sources in the Heritage Room, Pacific Union College Library*. Photocopy of typescript, 1993.

Sheldon, Henry C. *Theosophy and New Thought*. New York: Abingdon Press, 1916.

Shor, Ronald E., and Martin Theodore Orne. *The Nature of Hypnosis; Selected Basic Readings*. New York: Holt, 1965.

Silver, Richard Kenneth. "The Spiritual Kingdom in America: The Influence of Emanuel Swedenborg on American Society and Culture: 1815–1860." PhD dissertation, Stanford University, 1983.

Sinkler, Wharton. *Psychotherapy and the Emmanuel Movement*. Cleveland, OH. Reprinted from The Cleveland Medical Journal, July 1909.

Sinnett, A. P. *Esoteric Buddhism*. 1893. London: Theosophical Publishing House, 1972.

———. *The Rationale of Mesmerism*. London: K. Paul, Trench, Trübner, 1892.

Smart, Ninian. *The World's Religions*. Cambridge, UK: Cambridge University Press, 1989.

Smith, Llewellyn M., and Larry Adelman. "In Sickness and in Wealth." In *Unnatural Causes . . . Is Inequality Making Us Sick?*, edited by Chuck Scott, Andrea Williams, William A. Anderson, and Bernice Schneider. 56 min. California Newsreel, 2008.

Snodgrass, Judith. *Presenting Japanese Buddhism to the West: Orientalism, Occidentalism, and the Columbian Exposition*. Chapel Hill: University of North Carolina Press, 2003.

Speca, M., L. E. Carlson, E. Goodey, and M. Angen. "A Randomized, Wait-List Controlled Clinical Trial: The Effect of a Mindfulness-Based Stress Reduction Program on Mood and Symptoms of Stress in Cancer Outpatients." *Psychosomatic Medicine* 62 (2000): 613–22.

Sprague, Frank H. "Christian Science and Social Reform." *Christian Science Sentinel*, December 22, 1906. https://sentinel.christianscience.com/shared/view/1fatqwb7ss8.

Stark, Rodney. "How New Religions Succeed: A Theoretical Model." In *The Future of New Religious Movements*, edited by David G. Bromley, Phillip E. Hammond, and New Ecumenical Research Association, 11–29. Macon, GA: Mercer University Press, 1987.

Stark, Rodney, and William Sims Bainbridge. *The Future of Religion: Secularization, Revival and Cult Formation*. Berkeley: University of California Press, 1985.

Starr, Paul. *The Social Transformation of American Medicine*. New York: Basic Books, 1982.

Sternberg, Esther. *The Balance Within: The Science Connecting Health and Emotions*. New York: W. H. Freeman, 2000.

Stokes, Allison. *Ministry after Freud*. New York: Pilgrim Press, 1985.

Stroud, Michael. "Mindfulness of Mind." *Shambhala Sun*, March 2008, 47, 112–13.

Suzuki, D. T. *Swedenborg: Buddha of the North*. Translated by Andrew Bernstein. Swedenborg Studies. Edited by Mary Lou Bertucci. West Chester, PA: Swedenborg Foundation, 1996.

Suzuki, Daisetz Teitaro. *Essays in Zen Buddhism, First Series: His Complete Works*. London: Published for the Buddhist Society by Rider, 1949.

Swank, Scott Trego. "The Unfettered Conscience: A Study of Sectarianism, Spiritualism, and Social Reform in the New Jerusalem Church, 1840–1870." PhD dissertation, Department of History, University of Pennsylvania, 1970.

Swedenborg, Emanuel. *The Book of the Apocalypse Revealed: Uncovering the Secrets That Were Foretold There and Have Lain Hidden until Now*. Lutherville, MD: Swedenborg Project, Swedenborg Digital Library, 2007. http://www.swedenborgdigitallibrary.org.

———. *True Christian Religion: Containing the Whole Theology of the New Church Predicted by the Lord in Daniel 7:13–14 and Revelation 21:1–2* (1946; Lutherville,

MD: Swedenborg Project, Swedenborg Digital Library, 2007. http://www.swedenborgdigitallibrary.org.

Talbot, Brian. "Schuchard's Swedenborg." *New Philosophy* 110 (August 2007): 165–218.

Tang, Y. Y., B. K. Holzel, and M. I. Posner. "The Neuroscience of Mindfulness Meditation." *Nature Reviews Neuroscience* 16, no. 4 (April 2015): 213–25.

Taniguchi, Masaharu. *Recovery from All Diseases: Seicho-No-Ie's Method of Psychoanalysis.* Tokyo: Seicho-no-Ie Divine Publication Dept., 1963.

———. *Truth of Life.* Vol. 1. Tokyo: Seicho-no-Ie Foundation Divine Publication Dept., 1961.

Taves, Ann. *Fits, Trances, and Visions: Experiencing Religion and Explaining Experience from Wesley to James.* Princeton, NJ: Princeton University Press, 1999.

———. "Where (Fragmented) Selves Meet Cultures: Theorizing Spirit Possession." *Culture and Religion* 7, no. 2 (2006): 123–38.

Taylor, Eugene. "The Appearance of Swedenborg in the History of American Psychology." In *Swedenborg and His Influence,* edited by Erland G. Brock, 155–76. Bryn Athyn, PA: Academy of the New Church, 1988.

Taylor, Shelly E., Laura Cousino Klein, Brian P. Lewis, Tara L. Grunewald, Regan A. R. Gurung, and John A. Updegraff. "Behavioral Responses to Stress in Females: Tend-and-Befriend, Not Fight-or-Flight." *Psychological Review* 107, no. 3 (2000): 411–29.

Teahan, John F. "Warren Felt Evans and Mental Healing: Romantic Idealism and Practical Mysticism in Nineteenth-Century America." *Church History* 48, no. March (1979): 63–80.

Teasdale, John D., and Michael Chaskalson. "How Does Mindfulness Transform Suffering? I: The Nature and Origins of Dukkha." *Contemporary Buddhism* 12, no. 1 (2011): 89–102.

Timmons, Beverly, and Joe Kamiya. "The Psychology and Physiology of Meditation and Related Phenomena: A Bibliography." *Journal of Transpersonal Psychology* 2, no. 1 (1970): 41–59.

Tisdale, Sallie Jiko. "The Buffet: Adventures in the New Age." In *What's Wrong with Mindfulness (and What Isn't): Zen Perspectives,* edited by Robert Meikyo Rosenbaum and Barry Magid, 81–92. Somerville, MA: Wisdom Publications, 2016.

Trine, Ralph Waldo. *In Tune with the Infinite; or, Fullness of Peace, Power, and Plenty.* New York: Dodge, 1897.

———. *What All the World's a-Seeking: Or, the Vital Law of True Life, True Greatness, Power, and Happiness.* New York: T. Y. Crowell, 1899.

"True Origin of Christian Science." *New York Times,* July 10, 1904.

Turner, Richard Brent. *Islam in the African-American Experience.* 2d ed. Bloomington: Indiana University Press, 2003.

Twain, Mark. *Christian Science.* Buffalo, NY: Prometheus Books, 1986.

Tweed, Thomas A. *The American Encounter with Buddhism, 1844–1912: Victorian Culture and the Limits of Dissent.* Religion in North America. Bloomington: Indiana University Press, 1992.

———. "American Occultism and Japanese Buddhism: Albert J. Edmunds, D. T. Suzuki, and Translocative History." *Japanese Journal of Religious Studies* 32, no. 2 (2005): 294–81.

———. *Crossing and Dwelling: A Theory of Religion*. Cambridge, MA: Harvard University Press, 2006.

———, ed. *Retelling U.S. Religious History*. Berkeley: University of California Press, 1997.

Van Dusen, Wilson. *The Country of Spirit: Selected Writings*. San Francisco: J. Appleseed, 1992.

———. "The Same Supreme Doctrine in Swedenborg, Hinduism, and Buddhism." *Studia Swedenborgiana* 13, no. 2 (December 2003): 45–75.

Varela, Francisco J., Evan Thompson, and Eleanor Rosch. *The Embodied Mind: Cognitive Science and Human Experience*. Cambridge, MA: MIT Press, 1991.

Veysey, Laurence. "Vedanta Monasteries." In *The Communal Experience: Anarchist and Mystical Communities in Twentieth Century America*, 207–78. Chicago: University of Chicago Press, 1973.

Vivekenanda. *The Complete Works of Swami Vivekenanda*. 4th ed. Advaita Ashrama, Calcutta: Sri Gouranga Press, 1964.

———. "Hinduism as a Religion." In *The World's Congress of Religions: The Addresses and Papers Delivered before the Parliament, and an Abstract of the Congresses Held in the Art Institute under the Auspices of the World's Columbian Exposition*, edited by J. W. Hanson, 366–76. Chicago: W. W. Houston, 1893.

Waite, Arthur Edward. *The Occult Sciences: A Compendium of Transcendental Doctrine and Experiment, Embracing an Account of Magical Practices; of Secret Sciences in Connection with Magic; of the Professors of Magical Arts; and of Modern Spiritualism, Mesmerism and Theosophy*. London: K. Paul, Trench, Trubner, 1891.

Wallace, B. Alan. *Contemplative Science: Where Buddhism and Neuroscience Converge*. Columbia Series in Science and Religion. New York: Columbia University Press, 2007.

Walsh, Arlene M. Sanchez. "Warren F. Evans, Emanuel Swedenborg, and the Creation of New Thought." *Studia Swedenborgiana* 10, no. 3 (September 1997): 13–35.

Warman, Edward Barrett. *How to Live 100 Years—and Then Some, with a Supplement: The Emmanuel Church Movement*. American Sports Publishing, 1911. http://books.google.com/books?id=qtovAQAAMAAJ.

Washington, Peter. *Madame Blavatsky's Baboon: A History of the Mystics, Mediums, and Misfits Who Brought Spiritualism to America*. New York: Schocken Books, 1995.

Watson, Samuel Newell. *Psycho-Therapy and the Emmanuel Movement: A Lecture Delivered in St. Paul's Church, Akron, Ohio*. Akron, OH: Privately printed, 1909.

Watts, Jill. *God, Harlem U.S.A.: The Father Divine Story*. Berkeley: University of California Press, 1992.

Weisbrot, Robert. *Father Divine and the Struggle for Racial Equality*. Urbana: University of Illinois Press, 1983.

Whaley, Harold Barton. "The Collection and Preservation of the Materials of the New Thought Movement, to Which Is Appended a Bibliography of New Thought Literature from 1875 to the Present." MA thesis, University of Missouri, Columbia, 1973.

Whitehead, John. *The Illusions of Christian Science: Its Philosophy Rationally Examined, with an Appendix on Swedenborg and the Mental Healers.* Boston: The Garden Press, 1907.

Whorton, James C. *Nature Cures: The History of Alternative Medicine in America.* Oxford: Oxford University Press, 2002.

Williams, Duncan Ryūken. *The Other Side of Zen: A Social History of Sōtōzen. Buddhism in Tokugawa Japan.* Princeton, NJ: Princeton University Press, 2005.

Williams, J. Mark G., and Jon Kabat-Zinn. "Mindfulness: Diverse Perspectives on Its Meaning, Origins, and Multiple Applications at the Intersection of Science and Dharma." *Contemporary Buddhism* 12, no. 1 (2011): 1–18.

Williams, Peter W. *America's Religions: From Their Origins to the Twenty-First Century.* Urbana: University of Illinois Press, 2002.

Williamson, Lola. *Transcendent in America.* New York: New York University Press, 2010.

Wilson, Jeff. *Mindful America: The Mutual Transformation of Buddhist Meditation and American Culture.* Oxford: Oxford University Press, 2014.

———. "The Religion of Mindfulness." *Tricycle: The Buddhist Review* 25, no. 3 (Fall 2016): 91–92, 120.

Wilson, John Frederick. *Religion and the American Nation: Historiography and History.* George H. Shriver Lecture Series in Religion in American History, No. 1. Athens: University of Georgia Press, 2003.

Winterhalter, Robert. "New Thought and Vedanta." *Journal of Religion and Psychical Research* 16, no. 1 (January 1993): 14–20.

Wirth, Jason M., Brian Schroeder, and Bret W. Davis. *Engaging Dōgen's Zen: The Philosophy of Practice as Awakening.* Somerville, MA: Wisdom Publications, 2016.

Woofenden, William Ross, and Jonathan S. Rose. *Swedenborg Explorer's Guidebook: A Research Manual for Inquiring New Readers, Seekers of Spiritual Ideas, and Writers of Swedenborgian Treatises.* Swedenborg Studies. Revised 2d ed. West Chester, PA: Swedenborg Foundation, 2008.

Worcester, Elwood. "The Emmanuel Church Tuberculosis Class." *Ladies' Home Journal* 28 (March 1909): 17–18.

———. *Life's Adventure, the Story of a Varied Career.* New York: C. Scribner's Sons, 1932.

———. *Making Life Better: An Application of Religion and Psychology to Human Problems.* New York: C. Scribner's Sons, 1933.

———. *Religion and Life.* New York: Harper & Brothers, 1914.

———. "The Results of the Emmanuel Movement." *Ladies' Home Journal* 25 (November 1908): 7–8.

———. "The Results of the Emmanuel Movement." *Ladies' Home Journal* 26 (December 1908): 9–10.

———. "The Results of the Emmanuel Movement." *Ladies' Home Journal* 27 (January 1909): 17–18.

———. "The Results of the Emmanuel Movement." *Ladies' Home Journal* 28 (February 1909): 15–16.

Worcester, Elwood, and Samuel McComb. *Body, Mind and Spirit.* Boston: Marshall Jones, 1931.

———. *The Christian Religion as a Healing Power: A Defense and Exposition of the Emmanuel Movement.* New York: Moffat, Yard, 1909.

Worcester, Elwood, Samuel McComb, and Isador H. Coriat. *Religion and Medicine: The Moral Control of Nervous Disorders.* New York: Moffat, Yard, 1908.

Wright, Edward James. "Blessing or Blasphemy? Cooperative Healing and Medical Hegemony in the Emmanuel Movement, 1906–1911." PhD dissertation. Harvard University, 1984.

Wrobel, Arthur. *Pseudo-Science and Society in Nineteenth-Century America.* Lexington: University Press of Kentucky, 1987.

Wuthnow, Robert, and Wendy Cadge. "Buddhists and Buddhism in the United States: The Scope of Influence." *Journal for the Scientific Study of Religion* 43, no. 4 (2004): 363–80.

Wyckoff, James. *Franz Anton Mesmer: Between God and Devil.* Englewood Cliffs, NJ: Prentice-Hall, 1975.

Zimmerman, Jack, and Virginia Coyle. *The Way of Council.* Las Vegas, NV: Bramble Books, 1996.

Zinn, Howard. *A People's History of the United States: 1492–Present.* New ed. Harper Perennial Modern Classics. New York: HarperCollins, 2005.

Ziolkowski, Eric Jozef. *A Museum of Faiths: Histories and Legacies of the 1893 World's Parliament of Religions.* Classics in Religious Studies, No. 9. Atlanta, GA: Scholars Press, 1993.

Zuber, Devin. "The Buddha of the North: Swedenborg and Transpacific Zen." "Religion and Literature." Special issue of *Religion and the Arts*, no. 14 (2010): 1–33.

Zweig, Stefan, Eden Paul, and Cedar Paul. *Mental Healers: Franz Anton Mesmer, Mary Baker Eddy, Sigmund Freud.* Garden City, NY: Garden City Publishing, 1934.

Index

Note: Figures are indicated by an italic *f* following the page number; note numbers are shown with "n."